LEWD FOOD

LEWD

FOOD

The Complete Guide to
Aphrodisiac Edibles

ROBERT HENDRICKSON

Including
A Handy Index To Libido-Loosening Gourmet Foods
Bawdy Love Games From Stove To Mattress
The Sex Maniac's Quick Weight Loss Lust Diet
A Seven Course Cordon Bleu Aphrodisiac Dinner
And A Cornucopia Of Passion-Producing Prandial Delights And
Love Potions Prescribed Throughout History For The Naked Diner

Chilton Book Company
Radnor, Pennsylvania

LEWD
FOOD

LIBRARY OF CONGRESS CATALOGING IN PUBLICATION DATA

Hendrickson, Robert, 1933-
Lewd food; the complete guide to aphrodisiac edibles

1. Food.   2. Aphrodisiacs.   I. Title.
TX357.H46 1974   641.3   74-17328
ISBN 0-8019-5766-4

For Marilyn,
radiantly pregnant
as a result of our researches.
I love you more than yesterday,
less than tomorrow.

PREFACE

While sitting here shivering (pegged lobsters to the right and my love to the left of me) writing these lines in the nude and striking still another blow for the gonzo school of scholarship, I've come to the conclusion that your host may soon be banned from dining rooms in Boston, Brussels, Hamburg, and even Times Square. But, if our guests enjoy, no matter. I have no apologies and but one admonition to make—*don't eat any of the more exotic dishes such as sole or palm of people mentioned in these pages unless they come specifically recommended.* Anyway, don't say the warning wasn't italicized—there're some pretty sour souls around.

Heartfelt thanks are due here to the many people (some of whom *prefer* the anonymity space limitations demand) who supplied me with their secret love potions, as well as to my editor, Benton Arnovitz, and Crissie Lossing at Chilton (neither of whom, I hasten to add, provided any recipes at all). I only wish there were room to individually thank everyone concerned.

ix

It's good to be able to report that of all categories of books since time unremembered, love manuals and foodbooks have been among the most remarkably unsexist. The famed *Perfumed Garden*, for instance, regards women not as a tool but as man's equal, and the *Ananga Ranga* (the Code of Cupid) holds that a woman's sexual capacity is ten times stronger than a man's—a figure that falls only a devil's foot short of modern scientific findings, by the way. I've tried to follow in this true Rabelaisian tradition. As for the hundreds of palate-tempting posh aphrodisiac foods served up here, some of which have given men the gout and made women pregnant just contemplating them, I'd be the first to admit that they are *primarily* psychological in effect, the stories about the foods as important as the foods themselves. There's something more to it, but even that's admitting quite a lot. As Anatole Broyard wrote in reviewing a recent D'Annunzio biography (D'Annunzio even used strychnine as an aphrodisiac) *the first and foremost erogeneous zone is in the mind.* Let's just leave it there for the nonce and eat our way toward the *pièce de résistance.*

Far Rockaway, N.Y.
1974

BILL OF FARE

xiii

COURSE ONE

Shall We Eat In The Nude:
The Twin Breasts Of Love

"The sole love potion I ever used was kissing and embracing, by which alone I made men rave like beasts and compelled them to worship me like an idol."

—Lucretia, Sixth century, B.C.

Few would argue with the Roman courtesan's prescription for dynamic love quoted above, but the bare fact remains that throughout history certain foods and wines have constituted what the French call the twin breasts of love, highly valued amatory aids to make the quest for sex more pleasureable and heighten the sexual act itself. In the course of serving up and definitively evaluating these aphrodisiac viands from an historical and scientific standpoint, as far as this last is possible, it can be said at the outset that they all work—or worked for someone, sometime— if only because thinking made it so. Ovid best expressed this theme in *The Art Of Love* when he wrote that love "will not come to you gliding through the yielding air; the fair one that suits must be sought..." Or to

1

quote the French chef Grimod de la Reynière, who used to say that there were but two essentials for a lovenest—stove and mattress—"aphrodisiac foods are not only useful but desireable...there are many occasions where a lover would be far below best form if the culinary art did come to the aid of nature."

Reynière's art has come to the aid of nature in some rather strange ways, a number of which are barely culinary. Lovers have harnessed the same homeopathic magic, the law of similarity (like produces like) that Sir James Fraser described in *The Golden Bough:* teams of naked women and men alternately plowing and copulating in the fields at night to assure an abundant harvest; barren women resolutely making love under apple or pear trees laden with fruit. In the Middle Ages, to cite another ploy, it was common for a damsel desiring a man to lie stark naked with a small oven strapped to her buttocks in order to bake a bread or spice cake that she'd later share with her prospective lover. Bishop Burchard of Worms found one version of this practice so prevalent and appalling that he took great pains to warn his charges against it, providing explicit instructions and perhaps releasing his inhibitions in the process.

> Have you done what certain women are in the habit of doing? [the bishop admonished]. They prostrate themselves face downwards, rump upward and uncovered, and have a loaf of bread kneaded upon their nude nates; when it has been baked, they invite their husbands to come and eat it; this they do in order to inflame their men with a greater love for them.

More likely that would inflame the kneaded and the kneadee, not the needy husband, but even today there may still be a few Levittown ladies crouching nude nates against the electronic range where the devil's food cake is rising, hoping the cake doesn't fall with all that pounding or burn from excessive heat. Such extremes, however, bolster Lord Chesterfield's cynical argument about sexual congress: "The pleasure is momentary, the position is ridiculous, and the expense is damnable." There are certainly far better recipes, not always less outré but generally much more reliable. Some were served at naked dinner parties in the past. Casanova's contemporary the Duc de Richelieu, for instance, *un homme a femmes* and *un homme de cuisine*, often gave nude banquets during which all present—mistresses, titled ladies, and society beauties included—dined naked from oysters to marzipan. The Cardinal's nephew was emulated by, among others, the intrepid Field Marshall Soubise, justly "more famous for his dinners than his battles," who went him one better by inviting only women to his crowded *petit maison*. This bold old warrior could certainly have been no true male chauvinist either, judging by the number of ladies who vied for his invitations.

Naked dinners were not, as is generally believed, confined to that licentious era before the French Revolution, when two actors(?) had the temerity to present nonsimulated coition as a stage play before a packed house in the Palais Royal Theatre, when naked suppers held in the brothel of Mme. Dervieux became especially celebrated among the crème de la crème of society and restaurants often doubled as brothels where nude dancers of both sexes pirouetted around the tables as an aid to the diner's digestion. Wine glasses mounted on stems shaped like penises, sets of bowls decorated with representations of sexual intercourse—such were the props for similar dinners throughout history, tableware which graces only museum cases today. "At Roman orgies in the past cakes and sweetmeats were fashioned into the shapes of male testicles and penises, female breasts and so on, and eaten most avidly by unclad diners," observes one historian. "Drinking cups, whole sets of ware for the banqueting table were also designed in erotic shapes and forms, so that those participating...were never able to forget for an instant the enormous interest in eroticism and sexual effect." Exciting sexual desire was the sole thought in mind of the Egyptian cook, too, or so it would seem judging by the many erotic stimulants concocted for Egyptian tables. As for the Greeks, they sometimes used naked cupbearers to pour wine at their feasts, and it was the custom among the Tyrrhenians that maidservants wait upon the men nude. Athenaeus further notes that flute players appeared at private Greek festivals naked or in provocative Coan garments which strengthened the sexual effect of nakedness ("to do homage not only to Bacchus, but also to the god of love"), and unclad Thessalian dancers as well as nude female acrobats ("who with sharp swords did dangerous tricks") frequently performed at feasts and weddings of the time.

History has known such orgiastic and often horrible naked celebrations as the Saturnalia of the Romans and the Lupercalia of Caligula, Nero, Messalina and others, not to mention the nude outdoor banquets of the Etruscans, or the festivities held at Deer Park under Louis XV. At Roman orgies, for instance, guests were provided with slaves to hold their genitals steady while they relieved themselves and to tickle their palates with peacock feathers so that they could regurgitate and proceed to the next course of flaming flamingo tongues or the like. Nero, in fact, threw his orgies at the Circus Maximus, inviting all the prostitutes in Rome, but during the Renaissance, Cesare Borgia held a party that made the Emperor look provincial.

Fifty prostitutes...were present [wrote one eyewitness]. After the meal they danced with the servants and the others who were present. At first they wore their dresses, then they stripped themselves completely naked. The meal over, the lighted candles which were on the table were set out on the floor, and chestnuts were thrown down for the naked courtesans to pick up, crawling on their hands and knees between the candlesticks ...Finally a collection of silk cloaks, of hose, of broaches, and of other things were displayed, and these were promised to those who had connection with the greatest number of prostitutes. This took place in public. The spectators, who acted as judges, gave the prizes to those who were adjudged to be the victors.

Orgies haven't usually been so public, but here in America, to give but one example, our hornier heritage includes the Universal Church of the Brethren founded in Nebraska by that strange immigrant Imre Lopaczy, whose practice it was to preach in the nude to his all-nude female congregation—that is, until Sunday July 16, 1903, when old Imre was dragged leafless from the pulpit and lynched by irate farmers with unclad wives, daughters, mothers and grandmothers among his flock. Preacher Lopaczy's Sunday School picnics must have been interesting, yet they couldn't have compared to dinner at London's blue-blooded Hellfire Club, whose naked masked members (clubmembers) often formed some weird familial entanglements while at table. Licentious London was also famous for the "Tableaux Vivants" built in 1862 by "Mad William" Windham, "King of London's Streetwalkers." This tableaux featured nude men and women on a hand-cranked revolving stage that customers could choose from as it passed over their plates. Neither will the cookery soon forget confirmed male chauvinists like Casanova (Women, he said, were his cuisine), who often dined in the buff, or the poet-warrior Gabriele D'Annunzio, who not only carried condums into battle in Napoleon's own snuffbox ("A good soldier is prepared for any eventuality," said he), but often rode to the hounds in the raw with a comely companion at his side and once nonchalantly strolled nude into the dining room of his hotel before sitting down to peel his peppery white truffles. The celebrated English courtesan Cora Pearl was hardly less dramatic. Cora often took public champagne baths, and occasionally, at her more lavish banquets, her footmen would carry in an enormous silver dish, lift off the cover with a flourish and there she'd be curled up naked on the platter.

America has had native nude diners in abundance, including Herbert Barnum Seely, nephew of the great showman, who gave a private party at Louis Sherry's in 1896 that was thereafter called "The Awful Seely Dinner" because famed belly dancer Little Egypt did her things on the table clad only in black stockings and high heels. Then there was millionaire Ned McLean, who, lacking Greek statues, hired prostitutes to pose nude on pedestals at his garden parties. Nor can we ignore that ball

given by ill-fated architect Stanford White at the twilight of La Belle
Epoque where the diners yanked a long ribbon attached to a pie to pull
out a gorgeous showgirl wearing just a red satin arm band; she traipsed
down the long table and fell into Jim Brady's lap, feeding him his dessert
while eleven other lovelies, without armbands, entered to nurse the remaining guests.

By all accounts, Brady could probably have satisfied all twelve voluptuaries, at least judging by the immense quantities of furnace-firing
foods be consumed. "Diamond Jim," whose post-mortem revealled a
stomach six times the size of a normal person, used to eat as a "typical
dinner": two or three dozen oysters, six or so large crabs, two bowls of
turtle soup, seven or eight lobsters, two portions of turtle meat, a huge
sirloin steak, assorted vegetables, a bulging platter of pastries, and a two-
pound box of candy—all washed down with several gallons of orange
juice (he abjured alcohol). His breakfasts, brunches, lunches and midnight snacks were just as immense, and the women accompanying him
ate almost as much. It was, in fact, at the still thriving Luchow's in New
York that Brady proposed to Lillian Russell. Diamond Jim supposedly
plunked an open valise containing a million dollars on the table, carefully spread out a napkin on the floor, knelt down and promised the
actress, "This is all yours if you'll marry me." Miss Russell simply shook
her head and calmly ordered more Beluga caviar.

In our time, needless to say, an almost totally nude environment is
available—no longer is nudity the "upper-class characteristic" cited by
Kinsey. From the pages of men's and women's magazines to public beaches
and restaurants all signs point to a kind of coming of age for even the
public naked aphrodisiac dinner. At a popular club in Hawaii called
the Dunes even waiters serve lunch in the buff—no cover charge, but
reservations must be made two months in advance. Nudity or semi nudity has, however, posed a few minor problems at love feasts, particularly for prodigious male chefs preparing live lobsters (more about which
in Course Six) and well-endowed women eating soup. One irate French
gourmand has in fact complained of the "many resort restaurants now
catering to semi nude lady customers, their bare bosoms protruding into
their spaghetti sauce." Yet on the French isle of Levant there's been little
objection to and much gapejawed admiration of the one-piece Bikini-
type triangle called the "regulation minimum" that's the only requirement in cafes and must take full credit for such unusual pasta dishes.
Paris is less liberal, but topless sunbathing can be enjoyed at the grand
swimming pools along the Seine, right in the heart of the city, and there
remain restaurants like Laperouse on the banks of the Seine which contain *salons particuliers*—private rooms whose doors have no knobs and

whose locks have but one key entrusted to a *maitre d'* sworn to absolute discretion. In these "secret rooms" upstairs the love of good food and love are combined for as long as one or the other lasts. Or a couple can have their supper served supine at the fabulous L'Hotel in Paris. Especially recommended is Room 36, where the boudoir of Mistinguett, one of the 1920s most fabled *femmes fatales*, has been recreated in all its erotic splendor. Similar love nests are available throughout the world, at a price, but the only real requirement for an aphrodisiac dinner is about seven feet of space somewhere, someone to cook for and maybe a neck to nosh on. An invitation as simple as Saroyan's "Come Onna My House" is sufficient—"I'm a gonna giva you fish and pear and I love your hair—" Champagne and knishes...A loaf of bread, a jug of wine and thou...Just the bare ingredients are paradise enow.

Throughout history it's been known, as De Sade tells us, that "good plentiful food makes one efficient for physical love." All the great romantic poets have used foods as sexual metaphors, the author of the *Song of Solomon* alone offering numerous examples. Such foods are working metaphors, too. "A well-fed stomach plus an unclad body breeds lust in a man," says an old Chinese proverb. The French novelist Balzac observed that "Men became passionately attached to women who cosset them with delicate tidbits," and American author Thomas Wolfe assures us that "There is no spectacle on earth more appealing than that of a beautiful woman in the act of cooking dinner for someone she loves." One contemporary sexologist adds that "The mouth should only be opened by most women to be kissed and by most men to meet this need—or to eat. What happiness for a couple to do both at the same hour!"

Though instant virility cannot be assured in this or any other compendium of connubial concupiscence, there's no denying, in the words of Dr. Hans Balzi, that "after a perfect meal we are more susceptible to the ecstacy of love than at any other time," or to quote De Sade again, that "a plenteous meal produces voluptuous sensations." Not long ago a *Newsweek* survey revealed that people the world over are seeking the ingredients for such love meals more diligently than ever, noting that the brewing of ginseng (see Course Eighteen) "is approaching fad proportions among such show-business notables as Mae West, Cary Grant, Glenn Ford, Shelley Winters, Clint Walker, Peter Lupus, and George Maharis." At any rate, we're all learning that we're generally a lot hornier than we thought, even those of us who'd get a "G" rating at a naked dinner or who might be seeking income tax depletion allowances on our bodies. It seems that if you're between eighteen and twenty-five these days, according to Dr. Paul Cameron of the University of Louisville, thoughts of sex cross your mind every ten minutes. His survey of 3146 persons further revealed that the middle-aged think of sex every thirty-five minutes, and people over sixty-five once an hour. What a field day Rabelais or Boccaccio would have had with the strange fruits of this mixed human blessing, if only those dealing solely with sex and food. Consider, for example, the case of that city official (not Mayor Beame) that New York civil service probers found dining nude in his office during working hours—with the door unlocked, no less...Or the reveler who has brought suit against a Las Vegas nightclub for $403,700 because a naked go-go dancer fell off her platform, bounced off his head and landed in his shrimp cocktail...Or even that fellow writer who researched the film *De Sade* in Hamburg's notorious red-light district, this sensuous scribe submitting a cheat sheet that included such items as "a farewell dinner for 21 masochists and 21 sadists, $550...a party for 69 prostitutes $430...and a rest cure in Garmisch-Partenkirchen, $1850. ..." (No wonder writers and editors have the highest divorce rate in the country.)

We won't have to bill our publisher that much, but the search for the supreme aphrodisiac has taken our undercover agents thousands of miles over thousands of years of eroticism, and if they haven't found them all, they've had a ball or two trying. Not to mention intimate interviews with history's legendary lovers past and present, from Casanova, La Pompadour, DuBarry, and D'Annunzio (the same who used strychnine as an aphrodisiac) to such relative unknowns in the field as Attila the Hun, who is alleged to have died "the sweet death" after feasting with and while swyving with a luscious blonde (and it's good to know that even Attila was capable of making "love not war" in "the glorious battle abed"). In any case, our gourmand lovers have passed on their favorite recipes, recreated their secret love games and confided their most reliable love potions, including a low-calorie love-feast and a compleat aphrodisiac dinner, though some of their favorites will no doubt send you groaning for your Alka-Seltzer rather than your mate—the vilest of the beasts can be the belly, warns an old Greek proverb. More importantly, all the most fabled posh love foods will be singled out at length (truffles, oysters, caviar, et al.) and considerable space devoted to both their fascinating natural histories and their reputations as gourmet aphrodisiac foods, for good conversation, preferably well-spiced, is the main course of every well-planned love feast. Casanova has written that an accomplished lover should become a specialist in enjoyment, he or she must be expert in the little-known and seemingly irrelevant. As the anthropologist Hans Hasse observes, "the real enemy of human happiness is not *unhappiness* but satiation and the familiarity that breeds contempt." The answer is obviously to change all houseworn habits. There's a little-told story about France's Louis XV which illustrates this well. The king, often incognito, received numerous women in his villa the *Parc aux Cerfs* when in his advancing years, many of them arriving and departing in quick succession—so many that his doctor warned Louis to beware of his health. "But you told me I could make love as much I wanted to, so long as I used no aphrodisiacs!" the king insisted. "Ah! Sire!" said his physician, "change is the greatest aphrodisiac of all.

No one can vouchsafe that aphrodisiac foods will provide that change or charge necessary to rejuvenate the aged or ailing among us, but by the beard of St. Foutin, we can testify that old Louis and many like him lived and loved long on a diet of love foods.* Such fare did especially well for Cardinal Richelieu, particularly his bon-bons of ambergris. "The old mummy," as they called him at Versailles, carried on until his years numbered ninety-six, his fourth wife presenting him with a son when he was eighty-five. Up until this last marriage the cardinal even employed an old shrew solely to find girls for him and make all the necessary arrangements, these including crawling into the room of one of his married mistresses via a plank thrown over the street from the opposite house. Then we have France's great glutton Louis XIV, who, when he was seventy and his mistress Madame Maintenon seventy-five, compelled the lovely lady to ask her confessor if she really had to make love to him twice a day—the answer was yes, no matter how tired she felt. Or consider the seventeenth century French Courtesan Ninon de Lenclos, who seduced one gentlemen (de Sévigné) when she was thirty-four, his son when she was sixty and his grandson when she was seventy-six! But then nobody can equal England's Lord Hertford, connoisseur of fine wines and women, for sheer enthusiasm—at age seventy-four and half-paralyzed he had himself carried into his favorite brothels each evening by his footmen, his eyes at least always big-as-his-over-sized-dinner-plates.

Maybe it's just that a man is as old as he feels and a woman as old as she's felt, but it's a matter of record that most of the world's great lovers were great eaters. A case in point is the French actress Mademoiselle

---

*St. Foutin de Varailles, one of a number of phallic saints, was especially worshipped in Provence, where the people made votive offerings to him of "waxen models of the pudenda of both sexes," these often "strewn in great numbers over the floor of the chapel." St. Foutin was believed to make barren women fruitful, stimulate flagging husbands and cure a variety of sexual maladies. The enormous phallus representing the saint was in one town scraped by barren women, who mixed the particles in water and swallowed them in the hope of becoming fruitful. In another town, wine was poured over the phallus, this collected and allowed to sour into what was called "the holy vinegar"—which old women applied "to a most extraordinary purpose," of which there is no record.

Dubois, who often dined with Marshall Soubise at his naked supper parties. Mlle. Dubois left posterity an accounting of her conquests over a
twenty-year period. They totaled 16,527, or about 3 a day, surely a mark
deserving inclusion in *The Guinness Book of World Records*, at least until
someone better comes along.

If "her greed for gold was equal to her greed for pleasure," Mlle.
Dubois must have been a rich woman, *certainment*, and she doubtless ate
well. Dubois does have some stiff competition, though, in her contention
for the title of the world's busiest lover. Sex lore claims that the Roman
ladies Julia and Messalina, as well as Cleopatra, Queen of the Nile, gluttonous eaters all, each demanded and received more than one hundred
men in one night (Messalina, in fact, handling twenty-five men at a time
one evening). "Sober mathematical analysis raises some doubts, however," one skeptical observer charges, since the ladies would have required eight and a half hour nights, allowing only a mere five minutes
per joust. The *official* record holder would appear to be that anonymous
(though undoubtedly fish-fortified) man cited by Dr. Kinsey who aver-
aged 33.1 matings per week, or more than four times a day, over a period
of thirty years, apparently without harm to his health, for a grand total of
51,636. Only the Boston Strangler approaches that mark, though there
are some unofficial challengers. Novelist Frank Harris, for one (he relished "heavy meals and light ladies"), had Lloyd's of London insure the
card file of 2000 women he claimed he'd seduced in his lifetime for
$150,000, and our Italian poet D'Annunzio bragged that more than one
thousand husbands hated him. Then there is Shiek Abu Ben al Hashari,
who was slain in 1912 at the age of 117 during a palace coup led by his
son Raschid, aged 94 and 35th in a line of some 400 male offspring. If his
age and exploits haven't been exaggerated, the venerable Abu, assassi-
nated while breakfasting in bed with his sixteen-year-old bride (one of
forty-nine "active" wives and concubines), must have put even Don Juan
to shame. The real Don Juan (Spanish nobleman Don Juan Tenorio) had
but 2594 mistresses. Abu wouldn't have been much of a match, however,
for the Arabian shiek who deflowered 160 maidens in a fortnight with
the aid of Madame DuBarry's aphrodisiac ambergris bon-bons. Or even
for King Ibn-Saud of Saudi Arabia, who, according to Leonard Mosley's
recently published *Power Play*, "from the age of 11, until a few weeks
before his death in 1953 at the age of 72, had sexual relations with a
different woman every night, save during battles and while the pilgrim-
age to Mecca was in progress,"—perhaps 20,000 playmates. Yet the real
champion is probably ensconced safely somewhere in exurbia at the moment, enjoying his or her potent T.V. snacks and chuckling inwardly

about these so-called "records." Probably monogamous, too, and (if male) steeped in the advice of the *Kama Sutra:* "If you must wed, then marry one wife only—one alone is enough to satisfy two armies."

In search of prandial delights to help naked diners love so long and lustily our agents have toured the temples of ancient India, scouted the base of Parnassus in the Golden Age of Greece, traveled everywhere from Far Rockaway (where nothing's happening) to Rome (where everything's happened). Everywhere it has been the same. Priscianus Theodorus, a fourth century doctor, prescribed that all his patients with sexual troubles eat aphrodisiac meals, be surrounded by naked companions and be supplied suggestive books to read that would stimulate lust. Good sex and good food have always been inseparable, kissing itself, anthropologists surmise, probably stemming from mouth to mouth feeding. In modern times, one study conducted at the State University of New York State Medical Center reveals that women who enjoy food most are better able to enjoy sex. Sexual responsiveness in women was "positively and significantly correlated with their general positive attitude toward food and eating." Indeed, a study by two Chicago clinical psychologists, Drs. William Shipman and Ronald A. Schwartz, has found that "heavy women prefer to have sex more often than nonobese women," overweight wives preferring sex 11.9 times a month while those of average weight like sex 8.6 times a month. This study goes far to shatter the myth that given a choice zaftig women prefer the platter to the pillow. For that matter, it has long been known that the sensuous internal surface of the sex organs correspond to the taste buds of the mouth. Krause's end-bulbs, as they are called, are extremely sensitive to stimulation and are located mainly in the penis, clitoris and lips. Further support of this correspondence comes from a British psychiatrist who found that the divorce rate is up to 84% higher in countries where wives count calories, due in great part of sexual difficulties brought on by anxiety and anger. Along the same lines, a University of Minnesota experiment made the rather obvious finding that a semistarvation diet will eventually lead to sexual indifference.

Obsessive dieters of both sexes are too often reminiscent of those women in the Middle Ages who dined in private, subsisting mainly on broths because it was believed that the movement of the jaws deformed the contours of their faces and "distracted from the ethereal appearance of their beauty." Better to remember that the average sex act burns up 200 or more calories and that quite an invigorating meal can be made with low-calorie love foods. We're told that the "well-rounded look" is definitely very big today, anyway (see Course Twenty-One), so at least once in a while consign to the flames those diets where one "gets an education/in undernourishment and dehydration," eat something good for the gluteus maximus. Consume our bill of fare wisely and there's a chance "the very ceilings of the room will be pierced and the foundations of the house will get big with child." After all, this feast of love requires just flowers, soft music, good raunchy conversation, foods like symbolic oysters and asparagus stalks...and, of course, the proper frame of mind and a guest of honor. Perhaps today no diplomat in any sphere would risk a naked soiree, but the prospects for individual couples—the mini-orgy, so to speak—are still excellent if the proper foods are served; though, as Heliodorous said: "Great deeds need great preparations." Nudity or the clever suggestion of same does help (one Harvard psychiatrist has in fact reported that sexual relations generally improve when married couples become full-fledged nudists), but the feast itself is more important. "Make love, not haste," advises a noted clinical psychologist who specializes in sex therapy. "Some people spend $2000 for therapy," she observes, "but only five minutes in bed. Intimacy is very important. You should take time together, relax, don't rush things." And take time to make your La Grand Bouffe worthwhile. Never let it be said of the most modest love feast that "If the soup had been as warm as the wine; if the wine had been as cold as the turkey; and if the turkey had been blessed with a breast like the hostess, it would have been a memorable meal."

We'll serve up only restorative foods in these pages, love dishes so palate-tempting, it might be said, that at every course of this naked dinner "between two riches one must choose." Unlike certain cantharides, i.e., Spanish fly, and drugs like Quāālude, this vast banquet will cause no physical harm (*that* you'll have to do yourself). For we've eschewed drugs and "magic formulas" such as the snake oil that great millionaire-lover Jim Fisk made and peddled in his youth: "Dr. Henley's Male Elixir—Positively Guaranteed to Refresh, Stimulate and Strengthen You In The Performance of Marital Duties." Similar concoctions abound today, as they have since time unremembered. Yerba maté tea ($10.25 for five ounces), for example, has been barnumized as the "secret" of Antonion ("Little Knife") Velásquez, who could "satisfy four or five lusty Indian women in a single ferocious love bout," and the blessing of Don Diego Guitera, "who sired his 27th son at the age of 78." Yet Dr. Sidney R. Weinberg, chief of the urology division and clinical professor at the State University of New York writes that: "In response to your query concerning any aphrodisiac quality that can be ascribed to maté, I can state unequivocally, based on a chemical analysis of the tea that you forwarded to me, that maté is no more an aphrodisiac than an ordinary cup of coffee." Ditto for "European Love Drops No. 5," ($7 a bottle), which its makers claimed would endow all men with "bridegroom strength" and "prolonged power," but which New York's Bureau of Consumer Frauds and Protection analyzed and found to contain vitamins available at most drugstores for about 80¢.

Such preparations are either rip-offs or downright dangerous. It's true, for instance, that anesthetics like chloroform, ether, ethyl-chloride and nitrous oxide ("laughing gas") can induce vivid erotic dreams. More than one woman, on regaining consciousness, has accused her docile doctor or dentist of rape. Electric excitation is also common, and in 1970 workers piping a new kind of gas into homes in Harrogate, England, noted that it increased sexual desire. Then there are new drugs like L-DOPA, PCPA and amyl nitrite ampules ("poppers"), developed for the treatment of various ailments. But used as aphrodisiacs these all have unfavorable side effects too numerous to list, especially in incompetent hands. In the past even corrosive chemicals like borax have been recommended by "authorities." Indeed, the Roman gourmet Lucullus and poet Lucretius are said to have died when poisoned by such "aphrodisiacs," and Ovid warned against them in his *Remedia Amoris* over 2000 years ago. "Philters which bring pallor to the complexion are profitless for young women," he wrote. "They disturb the balance of the mind—and illuminate the fires of furious madness...."

The wise sinner waiting for dinner, female or male, married or single, will always give wide berth to such "magic elixirs." On the other hand, there's no doubt that a delicious erotic meal nourishes the passions, that "you are what you eat if you're not half-hearted about it." Love should be a pleasure, not a duty and these Pantagruelian meals prove this beyond a doubt, the best aphrodisiac foods invariably being the most tasty gourmet foods. Our entrees all come well recommended: one gourmet has even averred that they'll make you wish you had taste buds clear down to your stomach, but then he was given to all sorts of excesses. Nevertheless, the major ingredients of these erotic dinners have received the imprimatur of such diverse authorities as the infamous De Sade and the eminent Dutch gynecologist Van de Velde, author of *Ideal Marriage*, to name but two pioneering aphrodisiac sexperts.

The word aphrodisiac itself comes from the name of Aphrodite, the Greek goddess of love and beauty, who sprang beauteous from the foam *(aphros)* of the sea that gathered around the severed penis of her father Uranus after his son Cronos dethroned and mutilated him. The Cytherean, as she is also called, is probably a goddess of oriental origin; she bears a strong resemblance to the Asian Astarte. The Romans identified her with Venus. "Goddess born of the blue foam," mother of Eros and Priapus, Aphrodite had as lovers in various legends not only Adonis but Dionysus, Anchises and Paris. She became worshipped in two separate forms: as Aphrodite Urania, "the goddess of higher, purer love," and Aphrodite Pandemos, "the goddess of sensual lust"—a distinction which, significantly, wasn't made until later more repressed times. Fathered by Dionysus or Bacchus, god of wine and revelry, Aphrodite's son Priapus is identified with phallic worship, and the Cestus, her legendary girdle, is said to have endowed all its wearers with irresistible powers of love.

Through the ages literally thousands of foods have been thought to be blessed by or worthy of Aphrodite. Erotolabia—words like nuts, cherry, tart, dish, et al., used alternatively to express gastronomical or sexual meanings—illustrates this well. The language of love is rich with gastronomical metaphors and allusions such as chick, piece, tomato, cheesecake, beefcake, dumpling, tidbit, delicious morsel, feast your eyes upon her, etc. Often these stimulating foods resembled, tasted or smelled like the male or female genitalia, as Bobbie Burns well knew when he sang in his *Merry Muses:*

> *Coynte it was the porridge pot*
> *And penis was the ladle;*
> *Buttocks were the serving men*
> *That waited at the table.*

The prairie or mountain oysters served in Gay Nineties restaurants such as San Francisco's Poodle Dog and the Maison Dorée, equipped with bedroom suites for the dessert after dessert, offer another good example. (These breaded bull testicles did and do do some good, by the way, containing a certain amount of the male sex hormone.) Of course, many love foods certainly don't stand up or make anyone stand up or lay down from a strictly chemical standpoint. Almost all authorities agree, though, that "when nutritional deficiencies have been overcome, improved health and vigor will be reflected in greater virility and normal libido." In fact, some experiments on animals other than humans have found that restriction of vitamins B_{12} and E, proteins or caloric intake, for that matter, definitely limits sexual performance.

Those love foods that do work well fall mainly into two or a combination of two classifications. First come the biochemical aphrodisiacs, which have a direct effect on sexual activity. There are a number of such foods. Two of the best are asparagus, with its asparagine and aspartic acid—chemicals that act as diuretics—and fish, which contains sufficient amounts of phosphorous to have a limited but direct reaction on the genitourinary tract. The second and more important group of aphrodisiacs is psychophysiological in nature. These foods, by no means less effective, owe their prowess partly to the doctrine of signatures, man's ancient belief in the therapeutic efficacy of resemblances. According to this notion, the gods left a mark on every plant to show the use for which it had been created. Thus, any heart-shaped leaf would be just the thing for an ailing aorta. Especially effective for a happy love life were vegetables and other foods bearing visual and tactile resemblances to sexual objects. Their legendary reputations still often precede them wherever they go, well-known examples being the parsnip, which was regarded as an "incentive to venery" by American colonists, or the carrot or the cucumber or melon. Yet many foods, like truffles, belong to both these groups. Asparagus, so blatantly resembling the male sex organ, acts as both a biochemical and psychophysiological aphrodisiac. So do oysters—though these must be eaten in larger quantities to have a direct effect. Then there are substances like the controversial vitamin E, the "sexuality vitamin" found in many foods. In 1922, Drs. Katherine Bishop and Herbert Evans discovered d-alpha tocopherol, the chemical name for vitamin E. Their experiments on rats lead to the theory that vitamin E makes men better lovers and gives women a stronger sex drive. Among doctors today vitamin E has its fanatic supporters and detractors, but there's no doubt that vitamins and minerals in general are important in any virility diet. Vitamin D, for example, is said to increase sexual drive, while vitamin A supplies nourishment to the mucous membranes lubricating the sexual organs, and vitamin B_1 plays an important role in the sexual functionings of the pituitary gland.

For a long-term restorative diet or any organic problem, one should of course consult a physician, but the bill of fare offered here can do no damage and will certainly bring much joy if not many miracles; that is, if one avoids the really exotic examples that must be mentioned in a complete work of this kind. These perhaps unnecessary entrees including as we'll see: pubic hairs burned on a shovel and baked in bread; the "Bloody Marys" lovers drank of each other's blood; baked sparrow; bowels of bluejay; eye of wolf; ground emeralds and pearls; apples soaked in the sweat of one's lover's armpits; dove, duck and hummingbird hearts swallowed raw; and even the genitals certain savage Indians stooped so low as to slash off and eat before assuming conqueror's rights to the helpless women of an enemy tribe.

Such unappealing concoctions, which would never get by the F.D.A. anyway, at least show to what length both sexes will go for sex, yet love foods generally work on the principle of pleasure rather than pain. And those who refrain from such pleasures, who button up against the sun, become like Shaw's Englishman, not any more moral, merely more uncomfortable. For our part, we hope that this feast of love foods will tantalize and revive, both tititate and titillate, that our armamentarium of aphrodisiacs (nowhere have more been examined) will heighten the mystery, the romance and excitement of the chase. It's well known that one appetite can't be satisfied without satisfying the other, that "The mouth is used not only for eating, and a good meal puts you in the mood." We obviously shouldn't fast when ravenous or gorge ourselves when sated, yet art does heighten the pleasures of love, especially when combining sex with another natural function—eating, or better yet—dining well.

As Casanova wrote, man doubles his existence when he has the talent of multiplying his pleasures. Or to quote Aesop's fable *The Belly and the Members:* "They found that even the Belly, in its dull quiet way, was doing necessary work for the Body, and that all must work together or the Body will go to pieces." In any case, at these gates are all manner of pleasant foods, and there's nothing to lose but a few foolish inhibitions. *Bon appetit!* And may Rabelais' St. Foutin, "the fornicator's friend," be with each diner through every course. May this feast of fascinating full-bodied foods "heat the blood, quicken the senses, strengthen the muscles, and thereby rouse up, provoke, excite and enable the vigorous accomplishment of amorous dalliance."

COURSE TWO

Seaducers,
Or Angling For Aphrodisiacs:
Featuring Exotic Aquatics
From Shark-Fin Soup To Fugu

In Venice why so many wantons abound?
The reason sure is easy to be found:
Because, as learned sages all agree,
Fair Venus' birthplace was the salt, salt sea.
                    —Anonymous

Judging by their effect on *Homo sapiens*, it's hard to believe that fish are a cold-blooded species. No wonder diners at Very's in France during the Restoration were served naked girls on fish planks artfully surrounded by seafood, or that Casanova preferred fish to meat, as he tells us in his memoirs. In truth, Shakespeare's tawny-finned creatures are the ultimate aphrodisiac food, an indisputable fact recounted in legend, confirmed by psychologists and scientists, and vouched for by amorous anglers from Alaska to Acapulco.

We are told that wise old Aristotle was an "epicure of fish," the sage Omar Haleby highly recommends seafood as a stimulant, and the Greek

16

poet Asclepiades strongly advocated a meal consisting of "three large fish, ten smaller ones and twenty-four shrimp" for anyone planning an evening with a willing woman. "Male fish with the cream complete" is touted in the *Arabian Nights* and history records that Aztec runners were sent down to the sea a thousand miles away to bring back live ones in buckets of seawater for their emperor and his concubines. It was not only for physical and olfactory resemblances that the ancient Hebrews used the same word, *nun,* for the vagina as they did for fish. All seafood is indeed a food emblematic of sexual virtues, like the proverbial wine of Burgundy in that it is a man's dish most enjoyed by women after their men have eaten it—or vice versa, for that matter.

Ponder, for example, that proverbial fish story about the Sultan Saladin recounted by the renowned French gastronome Brillat-Savarin and others before him. Saladin, it seems, wanted to test the willpower of his holy men. To ascertain just how ascetic these ascetics would act under pressure, he invited two fasting dervishes to his palace and for a period of time fed them only the most succulent dishes. Soon all traces of their fasting vanished and they began putting on weight. At that point Saladin "gave them as companions a couple of ravishingly beautiful" harem girls, "but in spite of skillful provocation, the holy pair emerged unblemished from the trial." Saladin thought all was going well until someone went out and caught fish for the holy men: "The sultan kept them longer in his palace and, to celebrate their victory over the flesh, furnished them for several weeks with equally lavish fare, but this time he concentrated exclusively on fish. Once again he submitted them to the same combination of youth and beauty, but on this occasion nature triumphed and the overjoyed cenobites surprisingly succumbed..."

So that his point won't be lost about the love food par excellence, Brillat-Savarin also recounts the tale of a reunion of tottering old friars who were fed a delectable three-foot-long eel by a certain Madame Briguet. "In short," the chef noted, the conversation around the dinner table "settled on the most popular of mortal sins and remained there." Similarly, the second century author Appuleius, who penned the classic *Metamorphoses Of the Golden Ass,* having married a rich widow, was accused by her father of using love potions in order to gain her affections, a case paralleling that of Shakespeare's Othello. These love potions were said to be composed chiefly of shellfish, lobsters, sea hedgehogs, spiced oysters and cuttlefish, and the reason advanced for believing that Appuleius used fish for his nefarious purpose was "that they must necessarily have great efficacy in exciting women to venery, inasmuch as Venus [or Aphrodite] herself was born of the sea."

Brillat-Savarin advises that "analytic gastronomy" has unanimously observed how fish "acts strongly on the genetic sense, and awakes in both sexes the instincts of reproduction." He attributes this to several factors, including "various manners of preparing fish, of which the condiments are obviously irritating," and a "more active cause, which is the presence of phosphorus," observing that a fish diet "gave to certain religious orders a reputation like that of Hercules." By the same token, Rabelais extols the fecund fish as the food of harlots, citing Strabo and Pliny, who wrote that the waters of the Nile were "so prolific that Egyptian women brought forth their brats four at a time." Then there is the tale of that dedicated French chef Vatel, who committed suicide when the fish he ordered to stimulate the jaded appetites of the king didn't arrive on time; or the story of the insatiable emperor Domitian, who once convoked the entire Roman senate solely to determine in what kind of kettle he should cook a monstrous turbot presented to him; or the tale of the Sicilian ruler Dionysius, who consumed an overabundance of fish at the feast where he died of overeating, overdrinking and overloving.

But by no means need fish lovers rely on fish stories, as entertaining as they may be. That fish is the best of potent love foods is attested to by numerous medical authorities, who cite its high phosphorous and iodine content, phosphorous being a chemical agent that effects a direct reaction upon males and females alike. "Fish really have the property of bringing the spermatic secretion into activity," Dr. Jacobus X wrote in *The Genital Laws.* "They are rich in phosphorous and usually eaten with a large amount of salt, which adds to their action." In his book, *The Virility Diet,* Dr. George Belham qualifies this, observing that although fat fish such as herring can build up general health and virility over a period of time, any "immediate stimulating potential" depends "more on association of ideas, and the way fish lends itself to the skillful use of herbs in the course of preparation." On the other hand, both Drs. Albert Ellis and Van de Velde recommend seafood highly and Dr. Arnold Lorand mentions that fish act on the bladder and have an excitant effect. Fish and its byproducts are also quite high in vitamins A and D, especially cod-liver oil, which may be why so many bad little boys and girls forced to take it in days gone by became even worse in years to come.

History confirms this medical testimony. Wise men like Erasmus, who had such an aversion to seafood that the smell of it threw him into a fever, were few. The Annamites, a notably sensual people, counted fish as their favorite dish. Many ancient cults forbid their celibate priests seafood and the philosopher Epistomens went so far as to say that Lent was the most lecherous time of the year due to the increased consumption of fish. "No food is eaten that can prompt mankind to lascivious acts more than at that time," Rabelais adds, and he goes on to cite the herring and other seafoods eaten at Lent with great erotic results. Centuries before this, the Roman gourmet Apicius specifically recommended tuna, red mullet, sea bream and squid as love foods in his *De rerum conquinaria*; the Greek sorceress Medea used the skin of an eel as one of the ingredients of a rejuvenation tonic; and during the Middle Ages the small "stones," or otoliths, in the inner ears of perch were commonly added to love potions. Fish was long a favorite food of lovers in the French *cabinets particuliers*, the luxurious dining room boudoir suites featured by many nineteenth century Parisian restaurants, was often the *pièce de résistance* at those naked dinner parties French royalty held before the Revolution. Or just follow the example of Casanova, who usually ate fifty oysters for breakfast, sometimes sharing them with a companion in his bathtub built for two, or Madame Pompadour, the greatest of French mistresses, whose real name (Poisson) itself literally means fish and who often vouched for seafood as a *prelude d'amour*.

There are a number of reasons why fish have historically been considered a powerful aphrodisiac. One obvious one is that they lay large numbers of eggs. A second is the well-known Greek myth that Aphrodite was born from the foam of the sea that gathered around the genitals of Kronos' father after he killed and castrated him—implying that anything coming from the sea would be an aphrodisiac. Finally, there is the matter of seafood's high phosphorous content. The ancients knew this last well, one old story claiming that a chemist's drake, after drinking water from a vessel containing phosphorus, "ceased not gallanting his females" till he died of exhaustion.

John Davenport, in his pioneering *Aphrodisiacs and Anti-Aphrodisiacs*, reports that Leroy and Battatz, two highly-regarded French physicians of the eighteenth century, "tried the effects of phosphorus upon themselves, with similar results" as that fabled drake, though they luckily lived to tell the tale. Now to "gallant" until dropping dead of exhaustion and/or enjoyment would entail a prodigious amount of phosphorus—too many fish, by far—but all such folklore aside, it is still fair to say that of the many groups of so-called erotic foods, seafood is the one whose reputation is based *most* on fact. "We have observed," vowed Dr. Nicholas Venette in his *Tableau de l'Amour Conjugal*, "that those who live almost entirely on shellfish and fish ... are more ardent in love than all others."

Americans eat only an average of twelve pounds of fish a year per person. This is quite low when compared to say sixty-five pounds for the Japanese and a far cry from the seventeenth century when Francis Higginson wrote that "The abundance of Sea Fish [here] are almost beyond believing, and sure I would scarce have believed it except I had seene it with mine own Eyes." But like amorous people everywhere amorous Americans have always eaten more than their fair share. The impetus is more than psychological, too. Man probably evolved as a riparian creature, which goes far in explaining our physiological requirements for the iodine and salts supplied by seafood ranging from flounder to exotic dishes like fugu and bird's nest soup.

Bird's nest soup must strictly be regarded as a seafood rather than a game or meat aphrodisiac. This most recherché of exotic gourmet foods is much valued as a love potion, one variety made from swallow nests of the genus *Collichia*, whose nests are glutinous half-cups composed of the spawn of fish and seaweed bound together by the birds' cementlike saliva. The swiftlings whose nests are used for this soup, and for various dishes made with chicken and pigeons, are mainly found on the island of Borneo, where literally millions live in great systems of limestone caves, their nests of solidified saliva attached to the rock walls like terraces. To collect these nests is almost as daring as eating the soup. Bats mingle with the swifts over the raised hair of the collectors. Far below are rich deposits of guano, in places head high. Climbing jerry-built systems of poles and planks, many a poor wight has been killed, injured or polluted trying to please the palate of a Sinesian gourmet.

One reason for their reputation as an aphrodisiac is that *Collichia* are believed to be the only nonhuman birds that coit on the wing, but a more potent bird's nest soup is made from nests of the erroneously named sea swallow *(Salangane)*. The *Salanganes* build their nests only on high cliffs along the Annam coast in Java and off a few other Malayan islands. When the birds start nesting, just before the mating season, their swollen saliva glands produce a thick white liquid composed principally of nitrogenous matter that is insoluble in water. This they dribble out, lengths of sticky saliva stacked one atop the other, until a font-shaped crust, like a "fluffy white wax," is formed against a cliffside. The sticky substance holding the saliva together is also believed to come from seaweed and spawn of fish that the birds eat—both rich in phosphorous and having a powerful aphrodisiac effect. Before being packed in tins, the collected nests are washed in hot water and rubbed with ground nut oil to help remove feathers and dirt that might have accumulated inside. They must be soaked for two hours in cold water before they swell and become transparent for use in bird's nest soup. When the soup cooks, the nests fall to pieces, giving the brew its characteristic viscid texture.

Unfortunately, *Consomme au Nids d'hirondelles*, as the French call bird's nest soup, is very expensive even for the small cup quantities usually served; that is, when one's lucky enough to find the genuine article. This isn't often, for the nests usually sold are synthetic imitations made from agar-agar jelly, a seaweed product. Instead of buying the ½-ounce nests at $4 or so an ounce, a good substitute would be crayfish soup, which is similar in taste and effect. If the genuine nests can be obtained, the soups made with them are usually based on a clear but spicy chicken or beef broth, but they can even be added to a traditional fish soup. Crayfish and bird's nest soup may also be purchased at reliable Chinese restaurants. For instance, The Gold Full Restaurant on Canal Street in Manhattan's Chinatown claims to sell the real McCoy for about $3 a portion.

Shark-fin soup—or *yerchee*, as it's properly called—is also recommended by the Chinese as an aphrodisiac potion.* Shark itself, long a love food, was cooked by the Greeks after being stuffed with half-ripe mulberries, and the Chinese had a recipe for shark fins that took four days to prepare. This involved soaking the fins for three days, then boiling them five hours, taking care to change the water every fifteen minutes, and cooking them again in a complicated chicken broth. Anyone wanting to make homemade shark-fin soup according to a somewhat less complex oriental sex recipe may simply "catch your shark and boil its fins in water over a period of several days, boiling for one hour per day until the meat is pure white and peels off at a touch. Eat and await love's call."

Shark is really as good a dish as any fish found in the ocean—at least this is true of certain species, like the dreaded Mako. In fact, Mako is often served disguised as "swordfish" in swank restaurants and is included (its name disguised) in many common fish products imported from other countries. Anyone who does catch a shark, however, should be sure it's not exposed to the sun too long, as the meat spoils easily. As for serving shark steak, simply peel the skin off the tasty boneless fish, broil with butter and serve. At least you'll be trying something different in bed.

Other unusual fish aphrodisiacs include the Japanese *fugu* which few Americans have even heard of, much less eaten. *Fugu*, commonly known as the puffer fish, is so unusual that one can die from it—it hosts a deadly poison if prepared the wrong way. Ex-Kamikaze pilots, possibly pining for the good old days, first made a game of this gamefish by trusting all to an inexperienced chef and probably shouting *Banzai!* rather than *Kampai!* as they dug in. But the puffer fish has been a traditional Japanese gourmet love food for centuries and an estimated 300 people a year still die from the poison in its ovaries and liver. An ounce of this deadly tetrodoxin is theoretically able to kill 56,000 diners! Only a trained, licensed *fugu* chef (who must take a rigid government examination which

---

*As few have the opportunity or inclination to angle for sharks, we again suggest an authentic Chinese restaurant—such as the Temple Garden in New York's Chinatown, where the soup is available for about $2 a bowl.

only thirty percent of all candidates succeed in passing) is permitted by law to prepare the puffer fish. Thus the cost of a *fugu* dinner, consisting of raw, thinly sliced *fugu shashimi* and *fugu* vegetable stew, runs as high as $25, some species selling for about $5 an ounce. Yet the Japanese continue to consume their national love dish at the rate of about 7000 tons a year. Since amateur chefs persist in preparing the fish, and there is no known antidote for its poison, this amounts to a kind of aphrodisiac Russian roulette. One well-known love poem relates how *"Last night he and I ate fugu./ Today I help carry his coffin."* The puffer fish, so called because it inflates itself into the shape of a small balloon when caught, is so dangerous that it's forbidden to Japanese emperors. Most risky of all is the fabled love potion made from the fish, this consisting of a milky-white teaspoonful of *fugu* testes mixed with hot saki. If the amorous overly eager cook fails to slice away the deadly parts, this sex cocktail invariably drops from the drinker's paralyzed fingers after the first sip, death often coming within minutes. One home remedy calls for immediately burying the poisoned victim neck-deep in the ground, but he or she usually winds up horizontal in a permanent hole.

Passion-provoking Pompano, a relatively little-known American fish which Mark Twain averred was "as delicious as the less conventional forms of sin," offers none of the dangers of *fugu* and all of its advantages. Available today on the West Coast and in New Orleans, it deserves wider acceptance among Americans. The same cannot be said of the common starfish and seahorses still eaten in some remote places as aphrodisiacs, or the Chinese *Nuoc-Man*, a sauce made from an extract of highly decayed fish. Most diners could also do without such legendary love foods as the sea slug, "which doth swell and enlarge when touched," and the *cornuta* or *gurnard* mentioned by Pliny, the "phallic" horns of which he claimed were often a foot and half in length.

On the other hand, the phallic-armed octopus can be a delectable dish, and though it tastes like chewing gum to some (improperly prepared), the creature has been held in great repute by lovers everywhere. Plautus mentions octopus in one of his comedies, having an old man purchase an ample supply at the market for purposes of rejuvenation. The Japanese still credit the legendary sea beast with a certain mysterious potency and catch great quantities of the delicacy in a deceptively clever way—they simply lower a lidless pot to the ocean floor, and the octopus crawls inside this dark refuge and remains there until it's hauled to the surface. In the Polynesian kingdom of Tonga, natives catch the creature by using a lure fashioned into the shape of a rat, which the octopus attaches itself to. The Tonjans, it seems, believe that the rat is the octopus's worst enemy, their legend having it that an octopus once gave a drowning rat a ride to shore, whereupon the ungrateful rat alighted and called out: "O octopus, feel of your head; see what I have left there!" Could be, though, that the octopus goes for the lure because it resembles a crab, its favorite food.

The French enjoy octopus in *Poulpe Provencale,* and a traditional Greek recipe calls for cutting up the tentacles and middle (eyes and mouth removed), cooking it in oil and chopped onions, and then adding wine and the whole of its ink bag to give the dish its characteristic strong flavor and black color. Octopus flesh must always be tenderized. This is accomplished by beating the dead creature with a stick or bashing the resilient animal against the rocks, as Greek fishermen traditionally do to prove their strength and virility. Today octopus is available canned or frozen, and film critic Rex Reed writes that he's visited a restaurant in Hollywood where they serve octopus tentacles on skewers.

Even dried seaweed can be bought in supermarkets these days. Seaweed was the first substance to be ground into powder for the monosodium glutamate now used in so many products, its magical effect as a seasoning first noticed by the residents of coastal areas, who made sensuous stews from it. The Japanese actually cultivate about twenty species of seaweed, consuming some 5000 dry tons a year in pressed cellophane-like sheets, salads, soups, and assorted side dishes. They especially favor ribbonlike *wakame* dried seaweed, which is said to taste as good as garden-fresh spinach. As a matter of fact, all of us probably eat a large quantity of seaweed every day without knowing it. Many of the some 750 species, ranging from those treelike in growth to the fabled grass of the Sargasso Sea, are used in foods as a binder and thickener. These include fully half of all ice creams, chocolate milk, soda fountain syrups, jelly candies, marshmallows, candy bases, cheese spreads, jams, soups, sauces, gravies, salad dressings, and various pies and cakes—not to mention toothpaste, cosmetics, and certain medications.

Many sea fruits, as the French call seaweed and related seafoods, are still highly valued by the erotically inclined. Herbaceous eryngoes like the sea holly, for instance, are so potent that the Roman poet Juvenal advised failing lovers to "For fat eryngoes and fat oysters call," the puritanical *Ladies Dictionary* (1649) later warning that: "Eryngoes are not good to be taken,/ and Lust provoking meats must be forsaken." Rabelais tells an amusing story about sea holly. "Suppose a herd of goats to be rushing off at top speed," he writes. "You need but place a sprig of *erynguim* or sea holly in the mouth of the hindmost and the whole herd will come to a stop. Need I add that *erynguim* is a powerful aphrodisiac?"

Eating fish raw is probably the best way to take in its potent vitamins, and modern man is the only animal who generally prefers to cook it. A rare exception, universally, is seafood such as living clams and oysters, but fish, too, are still devoured alive in some places today. In Japanese *sushi* bars, diners enjoy raw fish like *maguro* (tuna), jellyfish cut into strips like spaghetti, and a kind of shrimp *(ebi)* that is eaten while still wriggling. Raw fish is finding some popularity in America today—there is even a cookbook devoted to its preparation. Sensuous *sashimi* (raw fish), for example, is easily made with about one-quarter pound each of cleaned and boned fresh red snappers, tuna, and striped bass. Just slice the chilled fish into paper-thin pieces, then mix together one-quarter of a cup of soy sauce, one teaspoon of horseradish, and one-quarter of a cup of lemon juice for dipping the fish at table.

No one has reported any interest in *live* fish here, though something might be said for it. Just fifteen years ago, for example, the Chinese tested an old folk recipe for birth control that had a number of women swallow twenty-four live tadpoles, which was supposed to produce sterility for five years. But the tadpoles did perhaps just about the opposite—more than half the women became pregnant within *one* year. This may be a testimonial of sorts for the raw seaducers like fish eyes and fish gills that are eaten in certain ports, or for those little sardines that South Sea fishermen customarily pluck from their nets, thrust into their mouths and devour bones and all after decorously biting off and spitting out the heads. Yet we can't find it in us to recommend them.

It is harder still to find anything appealing to say about the Roman's favorite garum love sauce, which was made from the putrified innards of fish. These were blended with fish blood and gills in an open tub, salted heavily and then exposed to the sun where they were stirred occasionally until the whole mass fermented, and then herbs were added. At the banquets of the vulgar Roman merchant Trimalchio, statuettes of four satyrs in the corners of the room poured vile-smelling garum sauce over fish molded to appear almost alive, to make it seem as if they were swimming in a jelly sea. But then one esteemed modern-day chef cites a recipe for sturgeon heads, and the natives of Iceland still devour hunks of shark meat as a substitute caviar, after the shark has rotted in barrels for two or three years. No panegyric can be written on *titmuck*, either. This Eskimo delicacy ripens in a hole filled with dirt and grass until the salmon used for it decay. As for the reproductive organs of jellyfish, scorpion fish, and pickled beaver tails, most people would forsake these, too. Should anyone seek even more exotic and/or disgusting aquatic turn-ons, however, we should mention salted crocodile semen, the orange-colored roe of prickly sea urchins that the Japanese and French consider an aphrodisiac either raw or pickled, swan's pizzle, the immense elongated muscle of the four-foot tridoca clam, the tails of blowfish—these taste like chicken and are often served in America as "sea squab"—or the ambergris so

many writers have recommended. All of these have been or are still valued as promoters of lust, but most of them seem better and safer talked
about than swallowed.

Of all the exotic aquatics historically prescribed, ambergris and whale
meat itself enjoy the best reputations. Ambergris—a valuable ingredient
in perfume manufacture—is a waxy secretion from the intestine of sick
whales that has long been fashionable for use in love potions. Old reliable Dr. Venette heartily recommended the substance, and as mentioned, the French Cardinal Richelieu regularly ate *chocolate des affliges*,
ambergris lozenges that French sailors brought home from the Far East,
attributing great aphrodisiac properties to them. The English used ambergris as an ingredient ("amber-greece") in several alcoholic beverages,
such as Sack Posset and honey mead, or metheglin, even going so far as
to add it to oatmeal pap as a flavoring. According to James Boswell, just
three grains of the substance made an Englishman noticeably stronger,
wiser, more cheerful and full of "venereal desires." Dr. Johnson's biogra-
pher added that as a medicine ambergris could "restore an effete old
man to juvenility."

The French called their ambergris pastilles by such enticing names as
"The Powder of Joy" and "The Tablets of Love"; Madame DuBarry used
them frequently to stimulate the flagging sexual appetites of Louis XV.
Used widely throughout Europe—even today when it can be obtained—
ambergris in its many forms ranks with the most popular aphrodisiacs of
all time. Even Brillat-Savarin, the final authority in so many matters gastronomic, said that whenever he felt "the burden of age" he took "as
much powdered ambergris as will lie on a shilling with a cup of coffee
...and it has always done me a great deal of good."

As for whale meat itself, this was so celebrated that in the Middle
Ages all whales taken in the sea were reserved for royalty only, whale
stew considered a great stimulant in England up until after the time of
Henry VIII and his wives. French kings, however, ate only the tongue
leaving the rest of the whale to the commoners. They either roasted the
tongue and served it in a highly spiced sauce or else salted and cooked it
in a court bouillon to which onions were added. In another age, though
Melville doesn't mention it, it is said that American whaling men's pores
were so permeated with the uniquely pungent smell of whale flesh and
blubber that the Hawaiian wahines found the Yankees walking aphrodisiacs. At any rate, whale meat is still avidly sought by lovers around
the world. The Eskimos find *mutuk*, the raw outer skin of the creature, to
be most pleasing to their wives, and the resulting odors are perhaps the
reason they rub noses instead of lips. We find that whale meat tastes
something like steak, though a little on the tough side, but others have

expressed a lower opinion of it. "I can't say anything bad about whale meat [says one gastronome], but neither do I feel I can say much that is good. Take a piece of lean beef and boil it in water in which a stale mackeral has been washed, mix this broth with some sort of piquant sauce and you'll have a dish similar to the one served to me under the name of *Escalope of whale à la Valois*." Anyone interested might be surprised to know that whale and smoked whalemeat steak is available today at several American sea-food restaurants, where state conservation laws don't outlaw its use. In Boston, in fact, one restaurant has been offering a free meal of the dish to anyone who can prove that his name is Jonah.

Unlike whale, the fabled paradisical skink is served nowhere at all today. This little crocodilelike lizard, variously called schink and scinus and native to Africa, was recommended for producing erection of the penis by one Roman writer. Mentioned in the *Arabian Nights* as a "seed-thickener," it was praised by Pliny as an aphrodisiac and used by the Persians for a potent potion in which it was combined with amber, opium, saffron, and ground pearls! The skink's snout, feet, and genitals were all employed in the cookery, but the area around the genitals was most valued. "With regard to the little crocodile, which we scarcely know in France" Dr. Venette assured his readers, "it is sufficient to say that the flesh around its loins, made into a powder, and partaken in sweet wine...works miracles in exciting a man to love."

We could go on with more miraculous stories of the strange *alieus* or fish meals of the lascivious Roman emperor Heliogalabus, who once entered Rome in a chariot drawn by naked women...spin tales about the emperor Geta, who had all sorts of odd aphrodisiac fish served up to him in alphabetical order...delve into the mystique of symbolic headless fish served at wedding breakfasts in Prussia...or suggest those stimulating electric eels that South American natives catch by herding their horses into the water—the eels attack the horses, discharge their electrical power, and can then be collected by hand.... Many might even come to enjoy such fare, for as Napoleon said when exiled on Elba, "A man's palate can, in time, become accustomed to anything"—especially for a purpose as grand as love. But few will want to do much more than discuss such provender. Before serving up a salamagundi of less fulsome amorous aquatics, we might conclude here with the words of William James: "Few of us are adventurous in the matter of food," the philosopher wrote; "in fact, most of us think there is something disgusting in a bill of fare to which we are unused."

So it goes. But then the quite commonplace seaducers to follow can be adventurous enough for the most daring seducer, if approached with the proper *espirit de hard core*....

COURSE THREE

Less Exotic Aquatics:
From Flounder To Bagels,
Lox And Cream Cheese

Old impotent Alden from Walden
Ate salmon to heat him to scaldin'
'Twas just the ticket
To stiffen his wicket
This salmon of amorous Alden.
   —Anonymous

Brillat-Savarin, the most glorified of gourmands, contended that fish contains "the most combustible elements in nature," and argued that a plain fish diet was the "most heating" of all. It is true that any ordinary fish can work unchaste wonders if given a chance and served in the proper manner. Hostesses at a love feast might prepare themselves à la Cleopatra, for example, the nymph of the Nile often wetting her sheer clothes with water so that they clung to her bountiful curves. Fortunately, most aphrodisiac seaducers are more prosaic than the dangerous *fugu*, or the octopus stewed in its own ink still on menus in parts of

27

Spain. So highly regarded is simple *Filet de sole*, for instance, that Madame Pompadour often served it to Louis XV during their intimate *petit soupers*. Her grand version was made by stuffing the rolled filets with a forcemeat of truffles and mushrooms and cooking them in champagne. Such filets can easily be made from that ubiquitous flat fish, the flounder, a word which the ancient Letts used as a synonym for the female procreative organ.

Common game fish, especially salmon, tuna, and trout, have also been touted as aphrodisiacs—which should be good news for America's 60 million sports fishermen. The braver and gamer the fish, the greater the virility it has been said to transfer to the eager diner. Scientists call this ancient belief the doctrine of signatures and its psychological implications can't be ignored by the wise aphrodisiac angler. As noted, shark meat and octopus meat have been treasured by many peoples as amatory aids, as has the flesh from numerous dangerous species. Among game fish, however, salmon is likely the most famous aphrodisiac food, perhaps because the anadromous fish goes through so much to spawn.

The salmon of amorous Alden is a tasty dish any way it's prepared. The Scotch often eat their salmon rolled with caviar, a recipe discovery of Roman emperor Hadrian, but one nineteenth century American cookbook, appropriately entitled *How To Keep A Husband*, cites a plain recipe called *salmon en papilotte*, the fish simply fried in butter with a little salt and a little more pepper. American Indians in the Northwest ate the year's first salmon with great pomp and ceremony, believing that by so doing its brothers and sisters would come rushing into the rivers to renew them. This "red red gold" fish lives to spawn, always instinctively making its way upstream (even ascending high fish ladders over dams) just to reproduce but one time, lose all interest in living, and die happily in the waters of its birth. Salmon have been found in Canada over a thousand miles from the sea. Scotch salmon is generally considered to be best and has been celebrated for centuries. Smoking salmon was first developed as an art in mid-eighteenth century Russia, and many Jewish families there found it to their liking and helped popularize it throughout the world, especially in the form of lox (the word itself from the Yiddish *laks* or the German *lachs* for salmon). This last is a truly delectable treat, as anyone knows who has knoshed on bagels, cream cheese, and lox or breakfasted on lox and scrambled eggs. New York aficiandos swear that the best salmon is not smoked abroad but right at home in Brooklyn, where two or three firms are still in the business. Just as sublime a dish is the Scandanavian Gravad Lax, smoked salmon cured with dill, salt, sugar, and pepper. Irish smoked salmon, which is leaner and drier than the Scotch, is also excellent. For a real treat Nova Scotia smoked salmon can be ordered direct from John Willy Krauch, Tangier, Halifax County, Nova Scotia, Canada. Mr. Krauch and his son ship orders all over the world from their little fishing village at a cost of $5.55 a pound, including postage, which is a bargain considering that the price of smoked salmon has risen to from $8 to $12 a pound in the United States.

"Of all God's creatures, the salmon is the cleanest," advises an old Welsh saying, yet pollution has been taking its toll of this superbly aphrodisiac fish—although the situation seems to be improving somewhat with the introduction of aquaculture. Salmon is scarce these days, but will probably never again be as rare as it was in the Paris of 1803, when Prince Talleyrand one-upped all Europe's royalty at a state dinner. The third course of Talleyrand's banquet that night called for a magnificent specimen of the fish, to which his salmon-starved guests looked forward with great relish. At the appropriate moment, the statesman's butler entered bearing a long silver tray on which lay an immense salmon. The guests' cries of enthusiasm were followed by groans when the coveted dish slipped from the butler's hands and splattered on the floor. All eyes turned upon him, Talleyrand simply said matter-of-factly, "Have them bring in another one," and a salmon even larger than the first was served according to plan.

A tuna salad, using fresh tuna, is probably the next best game fish choice. Tuna was particularly noted by Apicius for its powers; it has been served at such historic feasts as the coronation of Henry V and specifically recommended by several contemporary sexologists. Aristophanes gives us advice hard to follow when he tells us to "despise not the entrails of tunny" for greater virility, although raw tuna does taste something like beef. Carp is also a highly rated love fish, especially in such classic recipes as *Carpe en Matelote.* So is the ubiquitous cod: *"Spicy oyster sauce gives zest to cod,/ A fish when fresh to feast a god!"* Rabelais devotes ten full pages to praising the cod—he uses the word, however, as a euphemism for what's under the codpiece. Cod's head and oyster sauce was indeed a favorite among the Romans, who ate more fish than meat, and one might say that America was built in great part on codfish, which, along with bass, was on the first Thanksgiving feast bill of fare. George Cabot, founder of the great Boston family that spoke only to God, began by skippering a codfishing boat. Boston's Faneuil Hall, which Daniel Webster called "the cradle of liberty," was given to the city by codfish merchant Peter Faneuil. Boiled cod eyes and tongues, cod tripe, and even the air or swim bladders of cod were highly prized by Boston epicures, there being one old recipe called "Cod Tongues and Sounds [bladders]."

Cod roe has an especially excellent reputation for inducing virility, as does the turbot roe and flesh favored by the French novelist Dumas père and his mistress Mademoiselle Mars. The same can be said of Scotland's famed finnan haddie (smoked haddock) and halibut, which is justly famous in the recipe *Halibut à la Martin* garnished with shrimps and Normandy sauce. Trout, too, and sturgeon have their staunch defenders, and as for the common mackeral, anyone who hasn't tasted tiny tinker mackeral—babies weighing from half a pound to a pound each—doesn't know how tempting fish can be. Grimod de la Reynière said of the mackeral that "it has this in common with good women—it is loved by all the world." His definition of "good" is open to debate.

In ancient times, the mullet and lamprey were likely more highly regarded than any other fish seaducers. Thought to possess exceptional properties and praised by the poet Martial, the liver of the red mullet had such sex appeal that one large fish is said to have sold for 8000 sesterces at a Roman auction. Boutargue, a paste prepared from the dried and mashed grey mullet, was quite popular as an hors d'oeuvre in the sensuous salons of eighteenth-century France. Believed to increase the output of seminal fluid, the lamprey so pleased Julius Caesar that he served over 6000 of them at one triumphal supper. The Roman Vedius Pollio fattened his lampreys with human blood by ordering any servant who committed an offense to be thrown into his fishpond, which was nothing but a pit of snakes. "Surely he deserved a thousand deaths," Seneca observes, "whether he had his slaves thrown to the lampreys he was going to eat, or kept the lampreys for no other purpose but to feed them in this way." Seneca later relates how the emperor Augustus intervened on one lamprey-feeding occasion, drawing a moral of sorts from the tale: "Augustus was dining with Vedius Pollio. One of the host's slaves had broken a crystal dish and Vedius ordered him put to death in an extraordinary way—by being fed to the giant lampreys which he kept in his fishpond. Are we to believe that it was gluttony which dictated this order, not cruelty? The boy tore himself away and fell at the Emperor's feet to ask him this only—that he should die by some other death, and not to be fed to the fish. The cruelty of this unusual order moved the Emperor to indignation, and he ordered that the slave should be freed, that all the crystal dishes be smashed in his presence, and the fish-pond be filled up."

Lamprey's do seem to have a bloody history. Both England's Henry I and King John died from an overindulgence in this eellike fish, as did Charles V of Spain, but then, as someone has observed, there is nothing one can't die of if taken in excess—even abstinence. On the brighter side, a more moderate Queen Elizabeth I called lampreys "one of my passions," and Queen Victoria of all people had a twenty-pound lamprey pie garnished with truffles served at her Jubilee celebration. Giant lamprey or eel pie isn't often served today, but it seems just the dish for an orgy. The best way to rid the Great Lakes of its current plague of lampreys, as New York *Times* food and wine expert John Hess points out, might be to serve them in such triumphs of the French cuisine as *Lamproie à la bordelaise*.

The eel so prized by Brillat-Savarin (see Course Two) must always have been a phallic symbol; in fact, Ambrose Pare, the father of modern surgery, mentions a man who fainted dead away every time he saw an eel (perhaps an extreme case of penis envy). Roman epicureans favored all varieties of eel for their phallic associations, and the child-emperor Heliogalabus kept a large fishing fleet solely to catch eels for their roe, which he had made into a caviar. It is said that a Corinthean by the name of Nereuse made the conger eel "a dish fit for the gods," but the tastiest congers, claimed the Romans, were those fattened in tubs on the meat of the unfortunate Christian slaves who lost their battles in the Coliseum. Well-known in ancient and medieval times, eels have often served as provocative metaphors for sex. The ancient Letts, famed for their love songs, called the male sex organs "an eel's head and two small onions" and the vagina an "eel's pot" or "eel's river."

Today the English relish their eel or "green pies," seasoned with Worcestershire sauce, as well as jellied eel—smaller hunks of eel in green aspic sprinkled with chili vinegar. A noted modern French recipe for them is *Anguilles aux Champignons* (eels with mushrooms). All are potent combinations, but none compares with the exotic "Ye Collar Eele recipe" from the *Lucayos Cook Book* (1660), which is erotic even in its preparation, calling for both lovers to "take yor eeles and rub them with salt till all the skinne be quite taken off." Perhaps the only phallic dish to quite compare with this visually would be a platter of mixed eels, geoduck clams and frog's legs—all to follow on our menu.

Frog's legs might still be considered an exotic stimulant to many Americans—although we consume more of them every year. But Frenchmen, so often praised as great lovers, have for centuries justly praised this prandial delight as an aphrodisiac. The French really do enjoy their *cuisses de grenouilles*, though the "frogs" or "frog-eaters" of history do not subsist perpetually on such fare, as some tourists believe. France, in fact, must now import frogs from Hungary and snails from Czechoslovakia mainly to satisfy the appetites of foreign visitors. Unseasoned, frog's legs taste no better than chicken legs, but when garlic and other ingredients are added they assume an exquisite flavor all their own. Only the back legs of the unfortunate creatures are edible, everything else chopped off and discarded once they are caught. We import most of our frog's legs frozen from Japan these days, the traditional Louisiana catch declining more each year and the Japanese exporting some 900 tons annually.

Fresh frog's legs are much tastier than frozen ones, and to obtain these you'll almost certainly have to go out frog hunting with your mate. This old sport and new love-game (first reported here) consists of lying nude in the reeds equipped with a red flag and a special frog gun capable of shooting a small harpoon with a long length of string attached (although a net can be used instead if your reflexes are quick enough). One lover waves the red flag and the frog, theoretically, is supposed to be doomed by his own curiousity, popping out of the bullrushes to scrutinize the puzzling cloth while the other lover zaps or nets him. You might also use a flashlight to stun frogs at night, catching them with a net or bare hands—which is a more conventional method. Should any be caught either way, the frogs must be dismembered quickly, their back legs threaded on a skewer and soaked in cold water for several days until they swell, grow whiter, and are ready for your favorite French culinary recipe. Anyway, sensuous frog hunting lovers can follow other recipes in the reeds while waiting for their prey to appear, possibly leaving both hands free by attaching that red flag to his or her left foot.

Neither Europeans nor Americans can choose from any native specimens as large as the *seven pound* African species *Conraua goliath*, but we make do with the smaller frogs available. Some interesting recipes have resulted. In *The Accomplished Cook*, Robert May mentions frog pie as a favorite "animated Dish" of Elizabethan times: "When lifting first the lid off one pye, out skip some frogs, which make the ladies to skip and shriek...causing much delight and pleasure to the whole company." An American favorite is *Frog's legs à la poulette*, made from the big bullfrogs and pig frogs of the southern marshes. This dish won fame in San Francisco during the Gay Nineties, when those homey local restaurants with beds allowed their customers to choose from among live frogs for the dish. The connection between the frog and other four letter words can also be seen in the following bit of southern American folklore: "Place a live frog in an anthill and leave until the ants have cleaned the bones; then take the heart-shaped bone and the hook-shaped bone; keep the first yourself but hook the second in the clothing of a loved one." Love "will not fail to come to you"—if the A.S.P.C.A. doesn't get there first.

Seven hundred million Frenchmen can't be wrong about snails, either, and 700 million Frenchmen consume far more snails than they do frogs, devouring about three million pounds of escargot from March to October each year. Snails have traditionally been popular as banquet and love food. Petronius specifically mentioned snails' heads in a sauce as an aphrodisiac, and his fellow Romans particularly relished a breed specially fattened on milk until they became too plump to crawl back into their hardshell homes. In about 49 B.C., a Roman gourmet named Fulvius Hilpinus actually had enclosures constructed in his garden for the breeding and feeding of the creeping creatures, going so far as to keep separate species in separate pens. "There might be seen there," one early writer notes, drawing his information from Pliny, "the white snails of Reate, the grey and great snails of Illyricum, the fruitful snails of Africa, and the Solitan snails, most famous and excellent of all.... None of these were allowed to feed upon the shrubs and plants, but were given a kind of pap, made of sweet wine, honey and flour, by which they were greatly sought after and sold for eighty quadrants a quart." This was probably the first recorded snail farm in history, but monks and nuns in the Middle Ages, valuing snails for their lean meat, often raised them in the same kind of "parks" or snaileries.

According to all evidence, snails were among the commonest of neolithic foods. The first known admonition against them came when Moses forbid his people to use snails as meat. The Romans enjoyed snails grilled or sauteed in oil (Aristotle invented a special pointed snail spoon to pick them from their shells), and Caesar counted among his favorite dishes the little grey snail cooked in a ham sauce. Valued by the ancient Chinese and others as an aphrodisiac (especially their necks), snails seem to have become a food with snob appeal by medieval times. A 1394 cookbook relates that they were "eaten with spice and for rich people," although Rabelais says that they were fare game for the common man, too. France's Henri II liked his snails removed from their shells and cooked on a spit like meat. Louis XIV's sister-in-law made snails *au courant* at the French court, but when Diderot condemned them as a food fit only for peasants in his great encyclopedia, they went out of fashion for a time—at least until Talleyrand served a delectable dish of them to the Russian Czar at a state banquet. Across the channel in England they had fallen into a state of disrepute, though there had been a time when Spenser could loftily sing their praises in his *The Faerie Queene:*

> With our sharp weapons we shall thee fray
> And take the castill that thou lyest in;
> We shal thee flay out of thy foule skin,
> And in a dish, with onyons and peper,
> We shall thee dresse with strong vynegars.

Snails have not only been prized as a love food. The Romans long ago served them at the end of their sumptuous meals to help revive guests with hangovers, the eating of snails was once believed to relieve women in labor, and snail mucus has also been used to cure nose bleeds, soothe burns, and in a nineteenth-century beauty treatment to remove spots from the skin. Snails are easy enough to catch—the proverbial snail pace is only about one mile in three weeks—but care should be taken to gather only edible species. The nonedible species of Europe is fairly easy to identify, being a contrary creature with all its organs on the left and its shell winding counterclockwise. All snails can be fatally poisonous. Since they love to eat deadly nightshade, henbane, and wartwort, they must be starved for two weeks or so after capture to clear their digestive systems and then fattened on a special diet. They are finally cooked by plunging them into boiling water, removed from their shells with an instrument similar to a crochet hook, and washed thoroughly. Served either *enpots,* or forced back into sterilized shells (not usually their own, incidentally) they are considered a delicacy all over the world today. The garden snails of France, the vineyard *Karicollen* of Belgium, and the sea periwinkle of Scotland are among many favorite species. Even Englishmen and Americans are to some extent overcoming their national prejudices against the snail, at least those who have tasted dishes as provocative as snails with escargot butter—composed of butter, garlic, shallots, salt, pepper, parsley and perhaps a little crushed almonds, shredded coconut or even a dash of pernod. As an appetizer, French gourmets generally agree that snails should be accompanied with a white wine; a red wine is preferred if they are to be the main course. They are usually eaten by holding the shell in place with a special snail clamp, withdrawing the tasty meat with a two-pronged snail fork and dipping the snail in a garlicky butter sauce.

Among the most aristocratic of aphrodisiac seafoods is the turtle, and the turtle is the only food we know that is "hung for our sins to come." The extended head and neck of the turtle resembles the upright male member, which is possibly the reason why Venus has been depicted with her foot resting on a turtle's back in ancient sculpture, the creature supposedly sacred to her. One writer tells us that in Polynesia the turtle's flesh is taboo and reserved for tribal chiefs. "This is a protective measure," he notes. "The chieftans are jealous of their privileges, particularly if these enable them to excell. This delicate point would not have escaped Boccaccio's attention."

Turtles can weigh as much as 600 pounds, measuring up to four feet in length and three in width. The gelatinous substance directly beneath the shell comprises the creature's carapace and contains its most valuable erotic elements. To prepare turtle live in the kitchen presents a problem as the wily beast invariably hides in its shell and cannot be made into a potent soup till it pops its head out. When this last inevitably happens, the turtle is lassoed and hung up until it exposes its neck. The creature's strength and willpower may delay this for as long as three days. Finally, its sheer weight alone forces it to surrender exhausted; the leathery neck is thrust out, and the chef cuts its throat. Then a veritable arsenal of tools is needed—saws, hammers, chisels, pliers and more—to get at the meat inside. Further, turtle meat has to be cooked for some seven hours before the soup is ready to be served. Little time is left for love, which is good enough reason to buy your turtle soup canned. The purist may, however, hunt down the diamondback (a terrapin or land turtle) or other species here in the United States and consult a cookbook for the appropriate recipe, or even use imported dried turtle meat, which has to soak about three hours before softening. While tougher than beef, turtle meat has more protein, less fat and about half the calories. An outfit called Mari-culture, Ltd., in the British West Indies, is finally raising the threatened green turtle commercially (their frozen, tenderized turtle steaks are now carried by the Maryland Gourmet Market, 414 Amsterdam Ave., New York City, costing about $3.50 a pound). Up until this year turtle steaks had not been available anywhere. The steaks only take twenty-five minutes to prepare and are delicious.

A Chinese authority on aphrodisiacs confides that in Shanghai bistros steamed turtle soup and stir-fried fish entrails are often shared by lovers. "When a host urges his guest to help herself to these dishes," he observes, "a rougish twinkle in his eyes can often be spotted." Turtle meat itself occupies an honored shelf in the aphrodisiac larder, and though the terrapin is not usually considered as delectable as the sea turtle, it has been said that terrapin "was never intended for vulgar palates" and makes an excellent love soup.

Bouillabaisse, a Provencial concoction made of sea fish and shellfish, has a great reputation worldwide and is probably the most renowned of potent seafood soups. In Greece it is called *psaro*, in Italy it is *zuppa de pesce*, and in Belgium it's *Ghentsche waterzoaie*. Wrote Charles Monselet of bouillabaisse: *"And chilly beauties, not a few/ Will do whate'er you wish,/ Partaking, tête-à-tête with you,/ Of this perfidious dish."* Raymond Oliver, in his excellent chapter on the soup in his *Gastronomy of France*, tells the legend of the spurned lover who invented *rouille*, the hot pimento sauce that makes bouillabaisse so passionate a potage. This poor sailor sat on the Martigues quay sadly watching his beloved sail off with a rich Greek shipowner (they've always been around) when she added humiliation to heartbreak by tossing him the liver of a *racasse* or scorpion fish that the ship's cook had been cleaning on deck. "There, that's for you!" she cried scornfully. But the sailor treasured even these scraps from her lovely hands, and crushing the liver with garlic and oil, he cooked it with pimento and—marvellous to relate—from that moment on he found *all* girls pretty. "The reason that bouillabaisse has a world reputation is because it is aphrodisiac," Oliver concludes. "As *rouille* increases its erotic properties a hundredfold, the girl was forgotten on the spot. Once more, a fairy tale with a happy ending."

Oliver believes that bouillabaisse came originally from Martigues in France, but scores of places claim its invention, Marseille being most often accorded the honor. The soup can be traced back to the ancient Phoenicians, however, in the form of a recipe left behind by Pythagoras. Bouillabaisse simply means "boil low," or in English cookery "to simmer." Purists insist that at least fifteen varieties of fish must be included in a true bouillabaïsse, yet many cooks use considerably less to make this flavorful melange of seafood and vegetables simmered in an herb broth. In Marseilles, most renowned for the concoction today, the seafood· is removed from the broth and kept warm, and the broth is then served as a first course with the rust-colored peppery sauce called *rouille*, a tablespoon of which is stirred in. The soup is topped with slices of crusty fresh-baked bread or toast sprinkled with Gruyère, Parmesan or Romano cheese. The seafood itself is later served on warm plates. Some of the aquatics considered essential for bouillabaisse (although there's argument on this) include *racasse*, angler fish, chapon, conger eel, crabs, crawfish, red mullet, sea perch and whiting—all valued in the love cookery and so all the more powerful when blended together. For the soup's disputed history we defer to the many dissertations on that subject, being mainly concerned here with its reputation as a stimulant. That it has long been so enjoyed in America is noted in English novelist William Makepeace Thackeray's *Roundabout Papers*, which describes how at a "comfortable tavern on Pontchartrain," the gourmet-author "had a bouillabaisse than which a better was never eaten at Marseilles." One last gastronomic word on the soup, though. In France, as with snails, frog legs and onion soup, poorly prepared bouillabaisse has become something of a cliché aphrodisiac dish strictly for tourists. Care should be taken as to where it is eaten, both here and abroad.

Aphrodisiac shellfish such as clams, mussels and crabs are similar enough to be treated in the separate, following chapters on oysters and lobster, but a word should be said here about a few especially potent species. The geoduck clam *(Panope generosa)* of the U.S. Pacific Coast and elsewhere is particularly worthy. Pronounced "gooeyduck" by their diggers and "gweduc" by *Webster's*, this enormous intertidal clam indolently suns itself on warm days, its huge neck so "grotesquely" extending from the sand, we're told, "that ladies of an earlier day stayed at a discreet distance when their men went hunting them...the sight of the reclining geoduck, it was hinted, not being quite nice." The geoduck is difficult to catch. As soon as the huge clam senses danger, it begins digging furiously into the sand and you have to dig all the faster; two men are usually required to beat the clam at its game. *(Geoduck,* in fact, means "dig deep" in Nisqualli.) Those same ladies who feign disinterest must skin the geoduck and chop the big siphon in pieces for a chowder, also cutting the body into steaks which are breaded and fried till golden brown. The geoduck, of course, has numerous smaller sensuous relatives—not only the common suggestive steamer—similarly stimulating in appearance.

But the geoduck look-alike type is only one of many aphrodisiac shellfish. All smaller bivalves, of course, have flesh resembling the testicles and have been reputed to make lovers as happy as two clams at high tide. Especially the common hardshell clam *Venus mercenaria,* which takes its suggestive praenomen possibly because Venus has often been depicted standing nude in a large seashell, e.g., Botticelli's famed "The Birth of Venus," sometimes jocularly called "Venus on the Half Shell." Then, too, the *mons veneris* has in slang been called a "bearded clam." Bawdy tales from the annals of aphrodisia could also be told about mollusks like bearded mussels, which the French and Italians prize and cultivate; California's increasingly rare Pismo clam; tender bay and even ocean scallops (the coral roe of which is highly valued in Europe); the enormous horse clam (often mistaken for the geoduck); and the firm white "foot" of the giant abalone sea snail (steaks from this delicacy fetch over $4 a pound today). Some ancient mollusk recipes are far from appealing, though, even to the most desperate among us. One Chinese concoction calls for pounding "the shell of a male Venus's comb to a very fine powder," and adding "some urine." After letting this stand for three days, we must next "put it out at noon to dry in the sun." Then we dip the result in "donkey-water" (whatever that is) and allow it to steep three more days. After another drying in the noonday sun, the preparation must finally be sprinkled lightly with "the dew of flower blossoms," which will somehow "disperse the odor of the urine." The oriental cook does assure us, however, that if one "drinks from the solution at the time of copulation...one will be endowed with extraordinary potency."

America's favorite seafood, judging by sales alone, and a legendary aphrodisiac, shrimp is more to the sane lover's liking. Apicius is said to have traveled all the way to Africa, a considerable journey in those days, just to compare the local shrimp with those of Rome, where they were used as a provocative to drinking and lovemaking. Shrimp cooked in champagne, shrimp gumbo and shrimp Jambalaya all have well-earned reputations, and that knowledgeable French mistress Madame DuBarry prepared her shrimp in a sauterne sauce. As noted, the Japanese like their *ebi* alive and wriggling. They particularly relish a squirming delicacy called *ebi odori,* which is made by shelling, gutting and splitting a shrimp down the middle—the creature's nerves are still functioning when it is pressed into a small ball of rice that doesn't stop energetically wriggling until it's popped into the mouth. In America, however, we use only the tail and abdomen of the ten-legged crustacean in our shrimp cocktails and such, usually removing its feelers, eyes and all the rest of it. Sometimes shrimp are called prawns; the Italians call them *scampi;* and in French they are *crevettes.* Americans annually consume about a pound and a half of shrimp per person on an average, far more than of crab, its nearest seafood rival, and we have reached the point where we must import shrimp to supplement our domestic catch.

Casanova's frequent traveling companion, Agnolo Torredano, featured shrimp in his potent though quite ordinary seafood paella, which he claimed in later years was the "food of life that makes it possible for this cold, old body to still enjoy the heat of passion." Torredano must have known that of which he spoke, too—it is said that many of his amatory feats were stolen by Casanova for his memoirs. Old Agnolo finally died in Seville in 1799 at the age of ninety-two—"while in the embrace of his teenaged mistress." But the best aphrodisiac fish story about shrimp is recorded in the diaries of a shipmate of British explorer Captain James Cook. On his third voyage, in 1778, Cook visited a Pacific island kingdom whose strong, raven-haired King Lapetamaka II, remarkably in his eighties, claimed that it was his duty to deflower every native maiden, that, indeed, he had never been with the same woman twice and was still performing his appointed task eight to ten times a day, every day! He attributed his powers to a special diet featuring the following shrimp dish that really whet his appetite.

• KING LAPETAMAKA'S LUSTY SHRIMP •

2 pounds large unshelled shrimp	½ cup vinegar
1 small finely chopped pineapple	6 cloves
1 cup chicken broth	6 allspice
juice of large lemon	2 tablespoons salt
juice of one fresh pineapple	3 tablespoons molasses
1 scallion	2 tablespoons cornstarch
1 cup sugar	1 tablespoon ginger

Rapidly boil four quarts water, adding shrimp, scallion, allspice, salt, cloves, lemon juice and cooking for about ten minutes. Remove shrimp, shelling and cleaning them. In a saucepan, simmer the chicken broth, molasses, ginger, vinegar and sugar. Separately blend the cornstarch and pineapple juice, adding into the pan and stirring the sauce frequently over a medium heat until it thickens. Finally, add chopped pineapple and shrimp, heat for five minutes and serve.

A few words need be said here about the preparation and serving of all aphrodisiac seafood. First, any shellfish should be fresh and taken from unpolluted, unpoisoned waters. There are several ways to determine freshness. A clam that doesn't snap shut when tapped is dead and inedible, and the same holds true for mussels that do not close after running cold water over their shells for a few minutes. As concerns fish, fresh fish has no strong "fishy" odor, its gills aren't covered with slime, its flesh is firm and its eyes are bright and its skin shiny. Defrosted or slacked fish that unscrupulous dealers sometimes sell as fresh will look exactly the opposite—dull, broken and inelastic. Cook fresh fish only long enough to bring out the flavor, for it is naturally tender and overcooking only toughens the flesh in addition to violating any lover's sense of smell. Filleted fish has been effective since the ancient Agres of Rhodes first invented it, but try to cook fish whole for the best results. This seals in the precious life-giving juices and generally makes any species cook faster and taste better. As a love food, fish should not be drenched with lemon, which is regarded as an anaphrodisiac by many authorities. Better to serve it with a hot tartar sauce or use plain parsley, an herb lauded by Seneca, mentioned in the *Satyricon* and praised by Rabelais—parsley which "grows for the wicked but not for the just."

Since we're still awaiting the report of a researcher who hasn't come back—for one reason or another—since being assigned to test barracuda, piranha and other species, it would be premature to name the *ne plus ultra* of all aphrodisiac fish. But below are listed the forty or so common aquatics that experts have most recommended over the years.* Recipes for all can be found in any complete seafood cookbook. Unlike certain drugs, none of these seaducers, not even the caviar, great-clawed lobster or topless oysters still to be served in these pages, will make eighty-year-olds act like twenty-year-olds, but all will be far less dangerous, much more delicious and play downright dirty tricks on most, giving everyone concerned better fish to fry. "Fish dinners will make a man spring like a flea," Thomas Jordan wrote, and we might all heed the words of Rabelais who said, "I'll swallow any fish.... It's a sad end to be buried with a tall erection wondering all about life...." As Ovid advised in his *Art of Love*, with double or triple meaning: "Chance is powerful everywhere; let your hook be always hanging ready. In waters where you least think it, there will be a fish."

*These are alphabetically: anchovies, barbel, boullabaisse, carp, caviar, clams, cockles, cod, cod-liver oil, cod roe, crab, crayfish, cuttlefish, eels, fish soups, frogs' legs, haddock, halibut, herring, herring roe, kipper, lobster, mackeral, mullet, mussels, octopus, perch, pike, plaice, salmon, scallops, sea bream, shrimp, snails, sturgeon, squid, tripe, trout, tuna, turbot, turtle and whiting.

COURSE FOUR

Eat Oysters, Love Longer:
The Symbolic Topless Oyster

> *Then love was the pearl of the oyster*
> *And Venus rose red from the wine.*
> —Swinburne

Just as fish and shellfish have long ranked as the most efficacious group of love foods, oysters have been heralded as the most effective of all seaducers. "In marvellous fashion, oysters are a stimulant," proclaimed one anonymous early author, "hence shameless and lascivious women eat them in order to be more apt for the amatory act." Oysters, which can change their sex whenever it suits their reproductive purpose, have become almost synonymous with aphrodisiac—and for both genders. A woman "who deep midnight on oysters sups," according to Roman poet Juvenal, was by every definition a wanton woman. "My three passions," thundered Theodore, King of Corsica, "are love, military glory and the oyster!" The bivalves were lustful Louis XIV's favorite food (he made them the height of fashion, never eating less than 100 at a time); the French author Mirabeau once dined on 360 oysters; Balzac once downed 100 at his publisher's expense, "just for starters"; gargantuan Diamond Jim Brady demanded at least five dozen oysters at Delmonico's before he'd ever consider dinner or any post-prandial exercise; and Casanova himself pronounced the sensuous shellfish "a spur to the spirit and to love."

Among modern-day sexologists even Dr. David Reuben, who doesn't exactly wax eloquent about aphrodisiacs in his *Everything You Always Wanted To Know About Sex*, gives oysters some credit as a sexual stimulant. "In man's eternal quest for bigger and better (and more frequent) orgasms," he writes, "hundreds of foods and food combinations have been tried. Some of them depend on a physical resemblance to the sexual object. For example, oysters...resemble the testicles...The theory, apparently, is 'like breeds like'...." Dr. Reuben doesn't counsel us, as Juvenal did, that when "lewdly dancing at a midnight ball," we should "for hot eryngoes and fat oysters call." But several medical men do specifically recommend the bivalves. One highly respected chief of a genitourinary clinic in New York advises his impotent patients to "include plenty of oysters, raw and fried" in their diets. Medical writers have in fact prescribed phosphorous compounds on their lists of *materia aphrodisia* for centuries, even recommending the drinking of seawater because of its phosphorous content—and every oyster guzzles some 160 quarts of seawater a day. Better to enjoy one's phosphorous in something as delicious as an oyster, as Casanova did, than to take it dangerously neat or drink it from an increasingly polluted sea.

Casanova, we know, generally ate fifty oysters in the raw for breakfast, sometimes while navigating the waters of his intimate little bathtub built for two, and he once observed that eating "so delicate a morsel must be a sin in itself." But the most fabled of lovers found still better uses for the most fabled of aquatic love foods. Casanova followed the advice of the Oyster Institute of America centuries before that estimable organization coined its slogan "Eat Oysters, Love Longer." Out of his bathtub, he even played several delectable oyster love games, which he recommends to his "Voluptuous readers" and which are presented here for consideration by our voluptuous readers.

"We amused ourselves in eating oysters after the voluptuous fashion of lovers," Casanova writes in describing the first of his oyster "games of tongue," games he played with two attractive young ladies named Armelline and Emilie. "We then sucked the oysters in, one by one, after placing them on the other's lips. Voluptuous readers, try it and tell me whether it is not the nectar of the gods!" But more delectable still was the logical extension of this game, a devious version Casanova played with the desirable duo on another occasion. With obvious relish, the ingenious lover let an oyster slip from its shell while placing it between Emilie's lips. The oyster "fell on her ample bosom" and he claimed the right of salvaging it with his lips. Emilie had to unlace her bodice to let him do so, having such a good time that Armelline was more than willing to join in the festivities. Casanova quickly let another oyster slip, unlacing Armelline's corset "in such a way as to make it fall still lower." Needless to say, his ploy worked well, for we soon find him affixing his lips "to one of the blossoms of her breasts."

Doubtless Casanova delved farther down, diving deeper in his oyster games than those "alabaster spheres with blossoms" of the once chaste Armelline and Emilie. Like the poet Lord Byron, who called oysters "amatory food," the fare of his Don Juan, like Dr. Jacobus X, author of the *Genital Laws,* and so many others after him, the Crown Prince of Priapus had learned early that oysters shared tongue to tongue invariably lead to the ultimate *piece de resistance.* More important, Casanova's liaisons taught him that "A man [or woman] in love is provided with a kind of instinct, which tells him that the surest way to success is to provide the beloved object with pleasures that are new to her."

Oysters as a love food may still be something new for a few Ms.'s or Mr.'s, but they are far from novel in the history of lovemaking. The origin of the bivalve's reputation as an aphrodisiac is lost in antiquity. No doubt France's Marshal Turgot, who served under Napoleon, found courage for various charges in the 100 oversize mollusks he habitually ate for breakfast, and before him many of Rabelais' Rabelaisan tales were surely inspired by his favorite highly potent dish of oysters served with truffle-flavored sausages. The oyster's ability, however, is more psychophysiological than internal. Biochemically oysters can't be said to be a dynamite aphrodisiac, despite the phosphorus they contain, but in a psychophysiological sense they are all that folklore makes them. As one psychologist points out, the explanations of their aphrodisiac powers are best sought in the visual and tactile similarities that exist between oysters, "especially on the half shell," and the *pudenda muliebria.* (British slang bears him out on this point. Eric Partridge's *Dictionary of Slang and Unconventional English* gives one definition of "oyster" as "the female pudenda," and this is the case in a number of languages.) Oysters, many psychologists observe, arouse our libidinal thoughts like erotic pictures. More specifically, men are stimulated by the bivalve's mucous consistency, oysters on the half shell looking—to some—like a woman's shaved genitals. The same applies to the female of the species, to whom oysters resemble the testicles. It should also be noted that oysters are among the easiest foods to digest, which is one reason why they were among the dishes served lovers in the French *cabinets particuliers* and why Oysters Poulette was so popular in San Francisco's Poodle Dog and Maison Dorée, two early American restaurants similarly noted as much for their dining-bedrooms as for their cuisine. Theories that the oyster arouses in us the sense of our primordial past, however, are without foundation in fact, as is the belief that oyster meat is a high source of energy. The average raw oyster is 76–89% water and contains only seven calories, a boon to weight watchers but a bust for bedroom athletes hell-bent on breaking endurance records.

Australia's Joe Garcia is the recognized world champion oyster eater, having once swallowed 480 in 60 minutes. Mr. Garcia's world record may be a myth—judging by some gluttonous oyster eaters past and present—but then the solitary, silent oyster has always been much misunderstood by mankind. Despite his/her great powers (more about that double gender later), of all creatures on God's good earth the mollusk certainly has the least talent for self-aggrandizement. Its lips are literally sealed tight a majority of the time, and as a result myths and half-truths abound about the bivalve. For one example, history reveals far stauncher oyster-eating champions than Mr. Garcia. Like that Gilbert and Sullivan character, these oyster lovers "had often eaten oysters but never had enough." We are told that the infamous Roman emperor Vitellus "could with beastly voracity exemplify the gluttony which prevailed in the time of the Caesars by eating a round *thousand* of oysters at a sitting; and he increased the heinousness of the offense by availing himself of the abominable fashion then in vogue of tickling the palate with a peacock feather in order to make room for more indulgence." Even wise old Seneca, our chronicler goes on to add, "who praised poverty but could not live comfortably on millions of money, ate a few hundred oysters daily and then blamed the delicious mollusk for his indigestion." But then Seneca could excuse himself on the grounds that he believed oysters to be a brain food and ate them to sharpen his intellect, just as the Roman orator Cicero claimed he ate them to nourish his renowned eloquence. "Oyster dear to the gourmet," Seneca could rhapsodize, "beneficient Oyster, exciting rather than sating, all stomachs digest you, all stomachs bless you!" Quite a tribute from a philosopher to a mere food, though not when one considers that Tarterine oysters were among the most treasured repasts of Rome; all Roman orgies began with light foods like eggs and oysters.

The Romans, though, were no match for Irish or English lovers when it came to devouring oysters. In the 1850s an irrepressible Irish gastrolator named Dando earned a worldwide reputation as a passionate "professional oyster eater" without peer. Dando's ancestors were said to include a

Mayor of Colchester, who "married a mermaid and would sometimes eat half his own weight of oysters in a day." This would seem difficult, to say the least, as a dozen average-sized oysters, by Brillat-Savarin's estimate, weigh only a mere four ounces. A man of 150 pounds would have to swallow about 7200 to eat his weight in the bivalves—but possibly the Mayor's mermaid-wife counted the shell weight in the grand total. Anyway, great-grandson Dando would swagger from oyster house to oyster house lustily demonstrating his prowess and when he died of indigestion, his grave was appropriately encircled with oyster shells.

Among the French, who have always gone all out for love, amorous King Henry IV devoured an undisclosed number of oysters to get his historically famous stomachache, and Montaigne mentions a sensuous doctor who often "ate 30–40 dozen with impunity." Brillat-Savarin cites still another champion, an old but raunchy gentleman named Laporte, who complained that "he never had had a good bellyfull" of oysters. Resolving to "procure his satisfaction" the good gourmand supplied Laporte with thirty-two dozen, which Laporte finished in about an hour. Savarin further observes that many Frenchmen of his time "did not stop until they had swallowed a gross [144]" of oysters weighing a total of about three pounds, but Thackeray eulogizes the probable all-time historical oyster-eating champion, an Irish rival of Dando's who apparently put all stomachs to shame. "The day before he finally took to his bed, from which he never rose," the English novelist writes, "he devoured for a small wager a couple of hundred of full-sized Malahides, six score to the hundred, in nineteen minutes and thirty-five seconds, with ease...." That would come to over 725 oysters an hour, which appears to be the real world record for any oyster lover to beat.

England, land of the oyster-eating champions, has been justly praised for the lovemaking bivalves from the earliest days. British oysters from the River Colne, sent home packed in snow, were renowned in ancient Rome (where their shells are still occasionally found in the ruins) and lauded by Martial, Juvenàl and other Roman poets. "After all there is some good in the poor Britons," wrote the Roman historian Sallust—"they can produce an oyster." The origins of the famed Colchester Oyster Feast are lost in time and one medieval poet went so far as to suggest that English oysters altered the course of history:

> The Olde luxuryous Romans vaunte did make,
> Of lustful oisters tooke in Lucrine's lake;
> Your Essex better hath, and suche perchance
> As tempted Caesar first to pass from France.

Shakespeare, among other English writers, alludes to the aphrodisiac quality of oysters, and that they were a favorite of Queen Elizabeth's is evidenced by a letter from Sir Francis Walsingham to the "Bayliffes of Colchester" asking them to "lett me not fayle of oysters"—which he desperately needed for an imminent visit of the "Virgin Queen." Oysters, when low in price, were thought by the English to be the only possible hors d'oeurve, "in themselves a simple service of exquisite quality, brought to table with the attendant graces of mild and delicate vinegar or lemon-juice, brown bread, and a glass of light Chablis...the half dozen natives occupying the hollow shells and bathed in their own liquor."

Oysters were certainly quite cheap in seventeenth and eighteenth-century London, the "oyster tubs in rows" seen along the streets prompting one commentator to note that "poverty and oysters seem to go together"—an opinion no shopper would venture today. Dr. Johnson, never a rich man, regularly bought oysters for his cat Hodge and later, Mad William Windham, prince of London's pimps, economized by serving plump sweet oysters to his girls at the end of a hard shift. Writer Thomas Mouffet best summed up the English attitude about their native oysters, alluding to their aphrodisiac qualities. "Oisters do justly deserve a full treatice," he declared, "being so common and withall so wholesome a meat. They differ in colour, substance and bigness, but the best are thick, little and round-sheld, not slippery nor flaggy...but short, firm and thick of flesh, rising up round like a woman's breast, being in a manner all belly and no fins...Galen saith that they are heavy of digestion and engender phelgm; but had he tryed the goodness of our Oisters, which Pliny maketh the second best of the world, no doubt he would have given Oisters a better censure." That the English could go to even greater extremes over their homegrown bivalves is shown in Hogarth's caricature "The Election Entertainment," which depicts an old rake, gorged with oysters, dying with one dangling off his fork while a barber is trying to save him by bleeding.

In America, the amorous oyster dates back to prehistoric times. A fish-weir discovered in the heart of Boston in 1940 shows a huge oyster bed that the Indians had used 2500 to 3500 years ago, and another ancient heap in Maine is estimated to contain seven million bushels of shells. The small mangrove oysters of the Virginia colony, as well as the bountiful bivalves of Chesapeake Bay, were enjoyed by the settlers in 1607 and eastern oysters baked in their shells were served at the first Thanksgiving Day feast celebrated by the Pilgrims in Massachusetts. Oysters played an important part in the colonial diet, no doubt doing their bit to help populate the vast wilderness. They were plentiful, so plentiful that

Benjamin Franklin once ordered a bucketful of oysters for his *horse*—though Big Ben, as the knowledgeable Parisian ladies called him, used the mollusks as a ploy, getting a choice seat at the fire when everyone in the crowded tavern rushed outside to look at his amazing oyster-eating animal. We read of mouth-watering American "Chesapeake oyster roasts, "where the bivalves were roasted in hot ashes till their shells popped open, and bills of fare like that of New York's Astor House in 1838, which featured such dishes as "boiled cod fish and oysters," "oyster pie" and "turkey and oysters." So popular did oysters grow that they became almost a national mania. Americans consumed giant Lynnhavens, Chincoteaques, Blue Points, Cape Cods, Cotuits and many others by the dozens. Oyster eateries in New York offered all anyone could eat for only 6¢—a bad bargain, however, if the owner slipped a few tainted specimens into your order, which was a not uncommon practice.

The national oyster appetite in the United States surged westward with the wagon trains and years before the advent of the railways, oyster express wagon rushed the treasured bivalves from Baltimore to Pittsburgh, where they were packed in wet straw and shipped down river to oyster parlors in Cincinnati and farther inland. It's hard to find any prominent early American who didn't appreciate the oyster, from the Lincolns, who gave humble oyster roasts in Springfield, to the fabulous $100 to $5000 a plate Manhattan dinner parties of the 1890s, when a dozen six to eight-inch Lynnhavens mired in cocktail sauce might be served to each guest as an appetizer. On the West Coast, the tiny Olympias of Washington *(Ostrea edulis)* and imported East Coast oysters were consumed, and eventually, the huge Japanese or King Oyster *(Ostrea gigas)* came into cultivation. The Hangtown Fry, one of our most famous national oyster dishes, also comes out of the wild and wooly west. One story has it that a man about to be executed for rape in the mining center of Hangtown (afterwards named Placerville to appease its reformed citizenry) requested a last meal of "fried oysters with scrambled eggs on top and bacon on the side," this dish soon becoming the oysters rolled in cracker crumbs, soaked in beaten eggs and carefully browned that we enjoy today. More likely, though, the dish was named for one "Nick Hangtown," the *nom de cuisine* of a Hangtown cook who introduced the Hangtown Fry to San Francisco.

At no period in history were oysters not deservedly a gourmand's and lover's delight. Although there is no mention of the bivalves in the Bible, the Chinese have eaten and cultivated them for several millennia. "The palm and pleasure of the table," Pliny called oysters, and among many other learned Romans, Petronius claimed that they were a peerless aphrodisiac. Apicuis invented a method to keep oysters fresh, "as if from the sea," by storing them in jars treated with pitch and vinegar, and in 95 B.C. the Roman Sergius Orata founded the first recorded oyster farm in history, establishing his beds in Lake Lucrinus in Southern Italy. The Romans appear to have esteemed oysters *à la any way:* raw, roasted, stewed and in exotic sauces like "cod's head and oyster sauce." While neither the Egyptians nor Assyrians seem to have whet their libidos on them, the mollusks were a staple of the Greek diet. This led to the coining of the word ostracism, which comes directly from *ostrakon,* the Greek word for oyster shell. Ordinarily, voting in Athens was done by a simple show of hands. A vote of banishment, however, had to be written, as did any vote as serious as sending a man into exile for crimes against the democratic state. Because of the scarcity of paper or papyrus, the banishment ballot was generally written on common broken pieces of tile called *ostrakon,* this name having been first applied to the shell of the oyster, which the tile somewhat resembled. The Athenians soon bestowed the name *ostrakismos* upon the act of banishment itself, which gave us our word for to banish socially—to ostracize, or "oyster shell." Greek oysters also figure somewhere in what is probably the longest word in all literature, 184 letters in the Roman alphabet transliteration, a word coined by Aristophanes to describe a buffet meal including every food on the Greek bill of fare. For the record, with apologies to the proofreader, it is *lepadotemachoselachogaleokranioleipsanodrimhypotrimmatosilphiokarabomelitokatakec hymenokichlepikossyphophattoperisteralektyronoptokephalliokingklopepeiolagoiosiraiobaphetraganopterygon.*

The French may not have made such complicated constructions from their word for oyster—though *le huitre* is a slang synonym for the female pudendum—but they have probably put the bivalves to better use than any other people, long employing them as an aphrodisiac in a variety of ways. Wrote the irreverant Rabelais: "A monk in his cloister/ Is not worth an oyster;/ But just let him roister/ Outside—he's worth thirty!" And by no means is this the earthy French author's only mention of the sensuous shellfish. "...she would ransack me by labial extirpation,—much as you would gulp an oyster...." his Panurge says of one early Linda Lovelace. "Hello, oyster darling," he has a comely wench say to her lover in another place, and goes on to explain that an oyster "is an edible mollusc that sinks gladly into its bivalve shell to scatter seamen's pearls." Panurge asks suggestively still another time: "Shall we go and dig for cockle-oysters? Shall we open up some clammy shells?" Finally, we have Rabelais' bawdy poem with inimitable oyster and eel imagery:

> *Drink! I know I shall be wed.*
> *How my wife will love her bed!*

The pot snaps shut, the stout eel wriggles,
Lord! What juicy framblefriggles!
Marriage? Marriage is my oyster!
Harder, deeper, lower, moister.
Toss them down and drain them dry.
Hail the hymeneal urge
Of the perfect groom, Panurge!
Hail to marital relations!
Hail to joyous copulation!

Rabelais wasn't the only Frenchman to praise the prized bivalve. Louis XI feasted his professors at the Sorbonne on oysters at least once every year "lest their scholarship should become deficient," and no less a scholar than Voltaire went on record testifying that spiced oysters were renowned in France for their contributions to fecundity. The oyster in France has, in truth, always been the supreme ally of what Brillat-Savarin called the *sens génésique*—the sixth sense famed for drawing the sexes together that is dependent on all other senses for its power, especially mature or learned taste buds.

Of all French oysters, which like most European varieties belong to the *Ostrea* group, as opposed to the oviparous *Crassostrea* group dominant in America and elsewhere, the legendary Marennes are probably the most famous. It seems that during the eight-month seige of La Rochelle in 1573 the Catholics used whole oysters to bombard the Huguenots when they ran short of conventional ammunition. But some of their amatory missiles fell in the salt marshes, and when La Rochelle's inhabitants retrieved the oysters after the war ended, they found that they were colored a bright green. After much deliberation, the Marennes were eaten and found to be delicious, and they have been appreciated for centuries since. Their green color was later found to be caused by the vivid green sea algae or diatoms upon which the variety feeds. Other celebrated French varieties are *Claires*; *St. Vaast-la-Houges*, bred in cages in the English channel; Mont St. Michel's *Cancales*; and Brittany's esteemed *Belons*, these last often costing the discriminating diner $8 a dozen at Belon on the coast and up to $40 a dozen in swank Parisian restaurants.

Oddly enough, shipwrecked oysters are responsible for what is the world's largest "oyster farm" at Arcachon on the Bay of Biscay in France. A consignment of long curved-shelled Portuguese oysters that went down with a cargo boat at the mouth of the Gironde founded a colony so vast that the French at first thought it inexhaustible. When they finally realized the colony was in danger of extinction, precautions were taken, and in 1750, the oysters became protected by law. Their gathering was not allowed for four years and annually after that prohibited during the months from May to October. Nowadays oysters cultivated at Arcachon and Loqmariaques are considered a delicacy throughout the world. Most prefer them the way the French do—"like a pretty girl, at her best with the fewest possible clothes and the less make-up the better."

Though the French did much to improve *le huitre*, their law specifying no oyster harvesting between May and October reinforced the well-publicized old rumor that all oysters eaten in the breeding season can be injurious to health. Surely this is the most common of many canards about the magnificent mollusk. We are told that oysters are safe to eat only during months containing an "R." So prevalent is this myth that it has been commemorated in the poem "The Man Who Dared" by Stoddard King: "Let's sing a song of glory to Themistocles O'Shea,/ Who ate a dozen oysters on the second day of May." The U.S. Bureau of Commercial Fisheries has been trying to dispel this old wive's tale for years, but the rumor still finds its way into print, in one guise or another, and the real reasons for its long life is never given. Many of the origins of the hoary story have been lost in time. It is first mentioned in literature in William Butler's *Dyet's Dry Dinner* (1599), where Butler wrote: "It is unreasonable and unwholesome in all months that have an R in their name to eat an oyster." The "R" myth does derive partly from those days when poor refrigeration resulted in spoilage during "those melancholy hot months that are spelled without an 'R,'" as still another writer put it, but more important is the fact that the flat European oyster *(Ostrea edulis)*, only one of the more than 100 oyster species, is definitely *not* desirable for human food during the "non-R" months. *Ostrea edulis* is unique in that its young are retained by the mother until tiny shells are developed and the presence of these gritty shells while it's spawning makes the European oyster undesirable in the summer. This even prompted the ancients to believe that because of its spawning the oyster was more "venerious" in summertime—all the better for our purposes, but unfortunately untrue. Anyway, such is not the case with American oysters *(Crassostrea virginica*, Atlantic coast, and *Ostrea lurida*, Pacific coast), which do not incubate their young but disperse them in the water where they are fertilized outside the organism.

American oysters can be eaten safely by the "venerious" at any time of the year. Although no mollusk is at its best during the torrid summer months, this is no reason for oyster markets to practically shut down from May to September. In point of fact, American oysters reach the peak of perfection in May and June, months without an "R" between them, when they are fatter and taste better because they are beginning to store glycogen and animal starch in preparation for summer spawning. During summer and early autumn, oyster flavor declines. Due to the expenditure of the glycogen, the meat becomes skimpier and the nectar watery, yet the traditional oyster harvest time is still in the fall because the demand is seasonal, and the prices are highest at this time. If the oyster harvest time were changed to late spring, oyster lovers would not only enjoy meatier, tastier mollusks, but the entire oyster industry would reap important economic benefits. "Oyster mortalities usually are heaviest in summer," advises the U.S. Bureau of Commercial Fisheries, "and losses of 25 to 50 per cent are not uncommon. Thus, an earlier harvest could result in obtaining more bushels of oysters in a given area. Further, because oysters are fatter in the spring, there would be a much greater yield of meat in each bushel harvested. The tradition of the fall harvest is unlikely to change, however, until enough consumers become aware that the "R-month" rule is a myth and start asking for oysters in the spring months." Oyster lovers can take heart in the repeal last year of New York State's antiquated 1912 law that prohibited the sale of oysters from May 15th through August 31st. "It's hard to change people's habits when they've been told for the last 100 years they can't eat oysters in the summer," says the head of a large New York seafood company, but if other states follow suit the repeal may well push oysters ahead of the shrimp cocktail as America's favorite appetizer.

To dispel still another ancient galley tale—it is possible that you'll find a pearl of sorts in your oyster one day, but contrary to popular belief, edible oysters have no *true* pearls, and you'd be better off giving your love the oyster meat rather than the pearl, anyway. True pearl oysters are either of the genus *Pinctada*, resident in tropical waters, or the freshwater genus *Quadrala*, some of whose "river pearls" are found here in America. Pearls are produced by the mantle of the American ocean oyster, as well as by our clams and scallops, but they are usually valueless, misshapen and lacking luster. Natural pearls are formed when the cyst of a parasite, a broken shell or a piece of sand accidentally becomes embedded in an oyster's flesh and causes the creature to "cry." The oyster's mantle then sheds thousands of lime crystal "tears," or nacre, but it will deposit no more than one layer a day over the irritant, and it takes at least 1000 days for a pearl to form. The largest specimen in the world is the Hope Pearl, which is four and a half inches round and weighs three ounces, and King Phillip of Spain once owned a huge 250 carat beauty. But those stories about lovers finding marble-sized natural pearls in their oysters seem all the more incredulous when you consider the fact that only 20% of all oysters that grow eight-millimeter pearls live long enough to produce them and that in ten to eleven-millimeter sizes only 1% survive—this being the case with carefully farmed cultured pearls. Of natural pearls found in the sea near Ceylon, India, China, Japan and northwestern Australia, only one out of a thousand oysters brought up contains a pearl, and not one in a thousand of these is really a perfect specimen. In one recorded instance a week's catch of 35,000 pearl oysters yielded just twenty-one pearls, of which but three were suitable for commercial use.

The natural round calcareous concretions occasionally found in American oysters are usually embedded in the mantle or just under the surface of the meat, though they are sometimes "blisters" attached to the inside shell surface. There's no harm in looking, and the game makes the oyster a still more romantic food, but finding a true pearl in your American or European oyster is about as likely as finding a pearl in a hailstorm. (About two in a million, according to Chris Bastis of New York's Seafood of the Aegean restaurant, who will match your pearl with another from a jewelry store if you come across one lodged inside any of his oysters.) The devious diner might instead regale his/her love with stories about the fabulous pearls of history. Legend has it, for instance, that Cleopatra once gave a sumptuous banquet for Mark Antony and when her lover expressed astonishment at the costly meal, she promptly removed an immense pearl earring, dropping it in a cup of vinegar, letting it dissolve and telling him, "My draft to Antony [the cost of this banquet] shall far exceed it." Vinegar won't dissolve a pearl, however, and anything strong enough to do so wouldn't have been so conveniently at hand on Cleopatra's table. Unless the wileful woman planted it there—in which case it is just as possible that she used a fake pearl. Perhaps it might be safer still to offer the following pearls of wisdom to a companion while enjoying oysters. There is Robert Herrick's: *"Some ask'd how pearls did grow, and where?/ Then spoke I to my girl,/ To part her lips, and showed them there/ The quarelets of pearl."* Or Robert Cameron Roger's: *"The hours I spend with thee, dear heart,/ Are as a string of pearls to me."* Or even Dryden's prosaic, though utilitarian: "He who would search for pearls must dive below."

In any event, pearls and romantic man's quest for them has been among the least of the amorous oyster's problems. In a world he/she never made, the bisexual bivalve (his/her three-chambered heart courageously pumping royal blue blood) strives to thrive among us near-cannibals and other predators, yet the odds are all against the unfortunate creature, who has been cultivated, savored, swallowed live and maliciously maligned since time immemorial without being allowed the consolation of a single whimper of protest. All the oyster can do is "silently cry its real tears" in its solitude. Hector Bolitho proposes in his *The Magnificent Oyster* that the mollusks are so tender because they "rest day and night, never work or exercise, and loaf in bed waiting for their meals to come to them." However, this is merely a half-truth, looking at it from the oyster's point of view.

It's true that every oyster has what some would regard as the good fortune to be both male and female. The mollusk does regularly change its sex, and can be "a man today, a woman tomorrow," experiencing the best and worst of two worlds. As the limerick by Berton Braley goes, *"According to experts, the oyster/ In its shell—or crustacean cloister—/ May frequently be/ Either he or a she/ Or both, if it should be its choice ter."* The oyster begins its life as a male and when one or two years old becomes a young woman. This sex reversal is common, and the female European oyster often sheds its ova into the mantle cavity and becomes fully equipped as a male once more while still carrying its own embryos—truly a pregnant father. The American oyster, on the other hand, exhibits what is called alternative sexuality. Adults usually function seasonally as separate sexes. The young are predominantly male and after the first spawning season, the number of individuals of each sex becomes almost equal. About 10% of all adult American oysters change their sex annually during their winter resting periods—the percentage of sex reversals considerably higher among adult females than among males. The oysters spawn as soon as the water temperature is high enough. After October they enter an indifferent stage during which the sexes are almost indistinguishable, and then the process of sex reversal begins, if it occurs at all. The fecundity of *Crassostrea virginica* is obviously still another reason for its reputation as an aphrodisiac food. The average-sized female releases as many as 70 million eggs in a single spawning, while her aggressive boyfriends extrude over a *billion* sperm cells each. Furthermore, recent experiments have shown that American oysters are just as fruitful in their old age (the oldest live about forty years, growing to a maximum of fourteen inches long) as they are prolific in their youth. These experiments also disprove the ancient myth that females predominate among the oldest and largest oysters, the truth being that the sexes of these far from senile senior citizens are about evenly divided.

Yet its bisexuality, fecundity and sexual longevity are among the few consolations the oyster might derive from life. He/she can't even find any solace in the oft-repeated fish story that man is losing his taste for the inspiring love food. Just the opposite is true. In the early eighteenth century, John Gay could write that: *"The man had sure a palate covered o'er/ With brass or steel, that on some rocky shore/ First broke the oozy oyster's coat/ And risked the living morsel down his throat."* And some years later Jonathan Swift ventured that "He was a bold man that first ate an oyster," having one of his characters in *Polite Conversations* (1731) condemn oysters as "a cruel meat, because we eat them alive; an uncharitable meat, for we leave nothing to the poor; and...an ungodly meat, because we never say grace." Nevertheless, that legendary first bold man to eat an oyster has spawned millions more of oyster lovers, the major problem today not being man's preferences, but, until recently, declining production. Actually, a Gallup Poll late this year found that the oyster's appeal is ever-widening among contemporary men and women.

Why, then, have so many fewer oysters been harvested in modern times? The answer lies in the beneficient bivalve's bitter struggle for survival in a world he/she never made. Piscatorial prevariacators would have us believe that the hermaphroditic oyster leads a blissful existence submerged in the shallows: basking in the sun, matter-of-factly taking in water containing the algae and protozoans he/she eats and pumping it out at a rate as high as ten gallons an hour, quietly spawning and fertilizing his/her millions of eggs—but this is no more than an illogical extension of Bolitho's fable. The oyster hardly "mopeth idle in his shell" heaving Byronic "subterraqueous sighs." To the contrary, he quite literally trembles for his life—we can see this when we squirt a drop of lemon juice on our oyster and he twitches muscularly before our eyes. In the first place, though he can live and hide as deep as 4300 feet below the sea, the mollusk has no means whatsoever of attacking any natural enemy, including man who actually eats him/her alive. The oyster is one of the few organisms naturally equipped to be a pacifist. To begin with, many of the female's eggs aren't fertilized by male oyster sperm after they're discharged into the water. Again, vast numbers of both sexes are eaten by fish during the period when they swim free in the water. Then, millions of the pinhead-sized spat fail to find an object to which they can attach themselves on the ocean floor and die trying to adhere to sand and mud.

But it is not until the oyster finds an object to hold onto, that his troubles first begin. After they have settled to the ocean floor oysters are incapable of movement. No single Faulknerian sentence could contain the miseries they suffer thereafter, but the following attempt must be made, if only to pay tribute to the mollusk's majestic endurance. There is no logic, no rhyme or reason to the oyster's miserable chaotic life: storms and hurricanes bury him/her alive in sand; the avian oyster-catcher invariably swoops down at low tide for a fresh shore dinner; scores of diseases decimate the oyster's ranks each year; dying algae smother the creatures; drills (*Urosalpinx cinerea*) bore into their shells and scrape out oyster meat with ever-ready radula; the conch pushes open their shells, inserts its nose and greedily sups; starfish pull the bivalves apart with their feet, grotesquely sticking their whole stomachs out of their mouths and into the oyster shells to digest some soft meat; crabs grasp the mollusks between their claws and crack their shells piece by piece; "dive bomber" gulls open oysters by dropping them on rocks and roadways;

worms sneak inside the oyster's shell, take up residence, and nonchalantly eat their host; drum fish and skates crush the bivalves in their
teeth; oysters are blanketed and buried alive by shrimp, sponges and
barnacles; those oyster-in-laws, the mussels, defecate on and smother
their cousins; the horny *Crepidula fornicata*, or slipper limpet, multiplies
as fast as its Latin name suggests, spreading over and suffocating whole
beds of oysters; and jingle shells attach themselves to old oyster shells,
taking squatters rights on the very "wombs" young oyster spats need to
grow upon. Never again think that *we* have problems. For more indignities than are known to man, woman or masochist are heaped upon the
oyster, and against his predators, the secretive self-contained, solitary
sensualist has but one meagre defense. He/she can keep his/her mouth
shut. Having no means of attacking other animals, the oyster must rely
almost exclusively on the many tentacles protecting his mantle. These
warn him of chemical changes in the water, strain the water to keep
coarse particles from entering and, being sensitive to light, are able to
detect approaching enemies whose shadows darken the water. Once
warned, a large abductor muscle closes the shell, and the oyster can stay
closed for weeks at a time. Because the bivalve normally keeps its shell
open twenty-two out of twenty-four hours under favorable conditions,
his tentacles are important, but at best they are a poor defense against
the well-armed world around him.

Only poets have it as bad as oysters in this world, and at least poets
can write poems about their plight. There is, in fact, just one case on
record of oysters fighting back: three mice, it is said, were once beheaded
when they tried to partake of an oyster dinner and were long exhibited
with their bivalve guillotines in Ashburton's New Inn in London. Sometimes, though, the oyster *can* prolong his life by performing, not unlike a
trained dog or seal or poet. At least so goes an old story about a bivalve
due to be served at a restaurant in London's Drury Lane over a century
ago. One night in 1840 the restaurant's proprietor heard the sound of a
whistle coming from the basement below. He soon found the culprit to
be not a burglar but an oyster inside a large oyster barrel. The bivalve
had a small hole in its upper shell, and the water that was forced through
this aperture when it breathed causing the eery whistle. This "whistling
oyster" was promptly put on display and admired by Thackeray and
Dickens, among numerous celebrities, one of whom, a chauvinistic visiting American, claiming that it whistled "Yankee Doodle." Unfortunately, however, the vast majority of oysters aren't so talented and can't
learn to whistle or do anything besides appeal to the palate and stimulate
love among mankind. Which may be a blessing in disguise, or at least
make for a longer life, a respite from the oyster's merciless place in the

scheme of things. In truth, were it not for the selfish efforts of us amorous humans in cultivating him, the magnificent mollusk's other natural enemies might well render him extinct.

Of course this doesn't excuse our near-cannibalism. And the oyster eaters among us *are* near-cannibals, because we swallow the aristocratic mollusk while his/her three-chambered heart is still pumping its pale blue blood and while he/she can see and hear what we're doing—the bivalves, at any rate, being able to react to light and sound. "Oysters are more beautiful than any religion.... There's nothing in Christianity or Buddhism that quite matches the unselfishness of an oyster," said "Saki" (H.H. Munro), but like the Walrus and the Carpenter in *Through The Looking Glass*, lovers weep for the mollusk and deeply sympathize and eat up every one around. "There is something a trifle barbarous...in eating such a pretty little animal raw," mourned Voltaire, and make no mistake about it, we're not just omophagists, eaters of raw flesh, but cannibals of a kind when it comes to oysters. The English novelist Thackeray put it bluntly when he observed that swallowing one was like eating a baby alive, and a contemporary oyster farmer claims that he never eats his produce because "it's like devouring your friends."

The oyster isn't human, but he certainly is alive when he's lying there raw and helpless on the half shell. Not only do we eat him alive, heart and all, but we put him to death cruelly—in our stomachs, where he is slowly dissolved by our gastric juices. The creature is actually betrayed by the catch mechanism in the abductor muscle that serves him so well in the water. Because he can stay hermetically sealed for weeks at a time *C. virginica* can remain alive and in good condition for about four months, if kept at a temperature a few degrees above freezing. His ability to survive thus dooms the deaf, blind beast to a far more horrible death than exposure. Man's jaded appetites do have a place in the grand plan of things, however. It is probably just as well for everyone but oysters that the quadrillions of bivalves born each year have as many natural enemies as they do. The average American oyster produces about 16 to 80 million young a year. Thus, at the lesser rate, if all members of each generation lived long enough to reproduce, the great-great grandchildren, or fifth generation, of a single pair, would form a mass eight times the size of the earth!

Humankind has played a part in oyster population control since before we made our much-debated move from monkeydom (if that we ever did). But it took Yankee ingenuity to perfect the science of oyster farming and today the United States leads the world in oyster production. As a result, oyster prices have come down, though far from down enough. No longer does a plate of oysters command $20, as it did during California gold-rush days, yet oysters are not really inexpensive anywhere. Only on Kauau Island off New Zealand do the mollusks grow on trees. There they literally cluster like apples on the Poleutukawa, the lower branches of which dip into the sea, and it is said that amorously inclined monkeys open them by wedging stones between their jaws when "they yawn at night."

No place else but on Kauau are oysters the "poor man's food" that could be eaten in prodigious quantities by the likes of American author and early oyster-pirate Jack London—who vowed that he'd love 1000 women before he died. But it may well be America's destiny to save the mistreated mollusk, or at least to assure that there are always enough oysters around for amorous humans as well as monkeys to eat. Nationwide, oyster farming employs many thousands, constituting a $26,000,000 industry last year with Eastern or Atlantic oysters representing about 80% of U.S. production. No longer is there "a whole generation of people here who don't care about the oyster or its problems," as the Oyster Institute of America lamented to the *Wall Street Journal* several years ago. Man is now fast conquering overfishing and pollution, is in fact on the verge of an aquacultural revolution. One New York "oyster farm" has succeeded in cutting the oyster's natural mortality rate of 99.99% to virtually zero. The nationwide oyster catch went up last year by a whopping three million pounds, and the bivalve has become so popular on New York's Long Island, for one place, that thousands of visitors turn out annually for the oyster festival at Greenpoint each October 21st, many arriving aboard Long Island Railroad excursion trains. Visitors slurp down tens of thousands of oysters before the day is done, perhaps urged on by the ubiquitous buttons passed out to young and old alike reading: "Love Longer! Eat Long Island oysters." Another festival aficionados hate to miss is Chesapeake Appreciation Day (November 7th) at Annapolis, Maryland, where thousands come to eat oysters and watch the skipjack races off Sandy Point. The oyster-laden old boats—there are only forty-one left—run with ferocity and daring for the "buy boats" to get the best price for the day's haul. No powered fishing craft are allowed on Chesapeake Bay and these big shallow-draft "skipjacks," equipped with hand-hoisted dredges and up to sixty feet from bow to stern, are the last commercial ships under sail in America, working as they do among the last of our public oyster beds—many of which have been polluted beyond salvation.

Fortunately, despite the pollution of so many of our public oyster beds, most American oysters are now raised on well-protected seacoast "farms." Polluted oysters no longer present much of a threat to the naked diner. The oyster eater needn't really worry anymore about winding up in winding sheets rather than between his or her paramour's satin ones with stirrups. In fact, purification methods have recently made it possible to reclaim oysters from highly polluted areas. Experiments have even been made cultivating oysters in New York's foul East River, and they have been reared in treated sewage at Woods Hole, Massachusetts. Depuration, not generally accepted in the United States, has been practiced elsewhere for many years. In most cases this is accomplished by placing the oysters in tanks through which large quantities of pure water are passed. In a short time the bivalves are clean and safe to eat. Clean waters are so important because the most common health hazard in oysters, and all shellfish, is infectious hepatitis, whose virus is carried in human feces, a waste commonly pumped into our bays and rivers. Oysters can also store radioactivity in concentrations 1000 times as great as the waters they reside in, according to one government study. But the strictly enforced U.S. Public Health Service regulations are quite stringent as regards shellfish. These require, for example, that the water from which oysters are finally harvested be as pure as drinking water. Gone are the days when oystermen threw their catch in muddy holes on the way to market to keep it fresh. Any bad oyster can be linked through a tagging system to the oyster farmer who harvested it, and as soon as this happens his certification is lost and he can no longer do business. It would be difficult indeed these days to die "of a bad oyster," as we're told the inscription reads on the grave of a C. Pearl Swallow in Paris Hill, Maine— yet diners fearing hepatitis or typhoid still avoid oysters like the plague or else drown their bivalves in vinegar and ruin their delicate flavor.

Some diners also disdain oysters because they're frankly difficult to open. No modern machine has yet solved the problem of opening an oyster once you're ready to fete your loved one, although there is a U.S. patented device said to open the recalcitrant bivalve by driving a wedge-shaped piece of metal between the shells. There have been reports of one eccentric Casanova using an electric drill in desperation, but the old time-tested hand method can be quick enough for the most impatient voluptuary if properly employed. First, glove your weakest hand to prevent cuts. Then take a small hammer or pair of pliers and chip off a piece of the rounded shell or bill (as close as possible to the shell hinge where the growth rings start radiating), making a hole large enough to insert the tip of your oyster knife. Finally, just twist the knife backward and forward around the flat top shell until the stubborn beast is exhausted and gives up. Opened correctly, the tender morsel will be lying atop his/ her lower shell sensuously bathing in briny nectar. Shucking an oyster, incidentally, is called "doing it" in the trade. It's all akin to seducing someone cold on the outside, but whose passions run deep—that is, well worth the trouble.

To illustrate just how strong a willpower the obstinate oyster has before it succumbs to seduction, we might add that its springlike abductor muscle, which holds the shell shut, has such prodigious strength that it takes a continuous pull equal to twenty-three pounds to fatigue an adult American oyster in an hour. And it takes at least seventeen days to do so with a mere 2.2 pound pulling force. There is, however, a new trick designed for anyone who prefers devoting most of the evening to making an opening for love rather than grueling hand-to-hand combat opening bivalves. It's called "carbonated shucking," and was developed by Dr. H.F. Prytherch of the U.S. Fish and Wildlife Service. Dr. Prytherch got tired of prying and simply devised a method that consists of dipping the oysters in carbonated water which makes them relax and let go of their shells. Ordinary seltzer will do.

Once the oyster is dispossessed of his castle and vulnerable, he/she is ready for a variety of delicious love dishes, raw or cooked. But for a long time few gourmet sexperts would eat any cooked oyster, and some traditionalists still insist that cooking an oyster is a desecration comparable to baking a watermelon. The bivalve's delicate flavor, they contend, is authentic only when it's on the half shell, the sooner out of the water the better, and they prefer natural oysters to the blander cultivated kind—despite the former's iodine taste. Oysters, these cognoscenti say, most specifically, should be accompanied only by salt-buttered, thin-sliced, fine-grained brown bread and a light ale, and flavored with nothing more than a few quarters of lemon juice, neither horseradish sauce nor tabasco being within nose-range. Oyster stews, fried oysters and even baked Oysters Rockefeller are disdained by purists as nothing short of sacrilege. To do more than just "slurp 'em down raw," according to one English authority, would be "the thin wedge of the edge of heresy."

Actually, all such restrictions are nonsense. A dry white wine like a Meursault, Chablis or Champagne, or even plain stout, as well as pale ale, complements oysters perfectly at any love feast, and some authorities claim, incidentally, that the oysters will help save us from getting drunk on whatever we drink, the zinc that the mollusks contain counteracting alcohol. As for cooked oysters, "oyster peacemakers" (French bread scooped out in the center, buttered, and filled with fried oysters) did much more than pacify their wives when philandering Creole husbands brought them home and can hold their own with any oyster on the half shell. Moreover, our Caviar and Oyster Orgasmic recipe from the Near East (oysters with crushed caviar topping, seasoned with pepper, salt and cayenne and served on toast triangles) is second to no prandial delight. Angels on Horseback is another good bet (shelled oysters wrapped and broiled with bacon until the bacon turns crisp). So is creamy oyster stew deliciously effective, and Oysters Rockefeller (thus called because when first tasted at Antoinnes they were said to be "fit for a Rockefeller") shows that pure amatory ambrosia can be created from spinach, bacon and other common foodstuffs. Less well known but just as potent is *Oysters Kirkpatrick,* honoring James C. Kirkpatrick, manager of San Francisco's famed Palace Hotel in the late nineteenth century. The Palace, born during the Gold Rush, offers the following easy original recipe for the delectable dish: "Open oysters on deep shell, and put in the oven for about three or four minutes until oysters shrink. Pour off liquor, then add small strip of bacon and cover with catsup and place in a very hot oven for about five or six minutes (according to oven) until glazed to a nice golden brown."

One new "aphrodisiac" on the market, an oyster pill, claims that it "preserves 96% of the vital elements found in fresh, raw oysters harvested just before spawning." The oyster's enviable sexual performance, says an ad for the oyster pill, has been attributed to the full load of trace minerals oysters absorb from the sea. "The precise role of these trace minerals in the life (and love) process is not fully known," we're told. "However, it has been established that certain of them act as catalysts. Catalysts, everyone knows, activate or energize other bodies. (A single match ignites a huge fire!)." Whatever the truth behind such ads—"Ever try it on the bottom of the ocean in the sand? Oysters do it all the time— and enjoy it!"—it would seem more sensible to drink seawater than to take an oyster pill, and far wiser to eat any of the fabled dishes made from the mollusk. A joyous table worthy of Rabelais would be one caparisoned with dishes like Oysters Diable; the fabled Hangtown Fry; grilled, smoked or pickled oysters; Cold Oysters Venice; Oysters Tetrazzini; Oysters Meuière; Oysters Marèchale; Oysters Casino; Oysters Remick; Oysters Mornay; Oysters Provencale; Oysters Bienville; and Oysters Poulette, that stimulating recipe perfected by the storied Maison Dorée in San Francisco. All dishes, these, that inspire those regions in man and woman "midway between the two big toes." Instructions for their preparation can be found in any complete seafood cookbook, along with recipes for many other fabulous oyster creations. Actually, the only advantages raw oysters have to offer as a love food is their blatant appearance and the fact that raw bivalves (or pills made from them) contain fewer calories. Little of their nutritive value—vitamins, phosphorous salts, chalk, iron, zinc, copper, manganese and iodine—is lost in the cooking. As for the best way to eat them raw, most oyster fanciers prefer their bivalves served in the deeper shell and the uninhibited French disdain forks, holding the oyster in hand and sensuously slurping liquid and all from its natural container.

The famous amatory oyster species of old are becoming increasingly difficult to obtain. There are plenty of bluepoints and Capecods around, but contrary to popular belief these names have nothing to do with geography or quality. "Bluepoint" refers to any oyster about three and a half inches in diameter, "Capecod" to a large oyster. Gone are the times when the diner could order Oyster Bays, Narragansetts and a score more excellent choices, but many old favorites are still obtainable. Of the Eastern oyster these include the Chincoteague from Maryland, Gardiners Island oysters from Long Island, and the Canadian Malpeques. The latter two are sometimes hard to come by, especially the Malpeques (taken from beds in Malpeque Bay, Prince Edward Island, Canada), which are strictly regulated because they carry a disease to which they have become immune at home but which can infect other oysters if they are transplanted elsewhere.

An excellent and especially effective Pacific Coast oyster, similar to the flat European mollusk, is the tiny Olympia (*Ostrea lurdia*), which is occasionally shipped East from Washington shucked and packed in ice. Another popular Pacific species is the fabled King oyster (*Ostrea edulis*) introduced from Japan. These last are usually eaten "Western style." Bought packed in their own juices in twelve-ounce containers, they are simmered for five minutes in boiling water before being used for a stew or casserole. "Kings" are also tasty raw, especially those with a dark narrow frill under the lip edge. Then there are the one-foot diameter Australian oysters, once served at a famous Hollywood party as "The Oyster of Hercules Which You With Sword Will Carve"; the Loch Ryan; the Ostend, Cornish, Whitestable and Zeeland; plus all those famous species already mentioned. All in all, 100 to 360 kinds are to be found around the world (depending on whose estimate you accept), the best European variety probably being that "green oyster" we've cited that is found off the western coast of France. European oysters generally have a coppery taste compared to what Americans believe is the sweet, nutlike taste of the American variety. British Captain Frederick Marryat, however, in a classic example of one-upmanship, wrote that: "[U.S.] Oysters are very plentiful, very large, and, to an English palate, rather insipid. As the Americans assert that the English and French oysters taste of copper, and that they cannot eat them, I presume they do; and that's the reason why we do not like American oysters, copper being better than no flavor at all."

European oysters, Bluepoints and Capecods can be obtained from firms in many cities, and for those willing to pay the air freight costs for love, the Olympia Oyster Company in Shelton, Washington will take orders for the tiny (1400 to a gallon) Olympias. As for Canadian Malpeques, they may be had, between September and January, from Iron Gate Products of New York, in large cans of 250, or at posh restaurants like "21." Sometimes available, too, are the tiny oyster crabs found inside the mollusk, these a favorite of New York's Governor Nelson Rockefeller. But the oyster lover need not concern himself with exotic and expensive varieties. They can often be ordered at restaurants like New York's posh Plaza Oyster Bar (where the garbage is picked up by a Mercedes Benz truck, no less), or at our favorite, the famed Grand Central Station Oyster Bar, where the creamy oyster stew, brewed before your eyes, and other dishes are still made from time-tested century-old recipes. So do well-stocked shops in fish markets carry the hard-to-find varieties, but the difference in flavor between any Eastern oyster is no more than a difference of personal taste in any event. Your oyster supreme may well be found among numerous local varieties served at oyster bars and eateries from New York to New Orleans, from the Atlantic to the Pacific.* However, follow the advice of Dr. Humphrey T. Virility and always make sure that an honored guest doesn't devour too many of any kind. He or she may say, "Ah, I loved you, darling, but now I love oysters better," and just keep on sending out for more.

Someone has observed that if the Mayo Clinic officially declared the oyster to be an efficacious aphrodisiac, the announcement would cause no more than a yawn, so vaunted is the bivalve's reputation to regenerate sexual desire. Clams, the poor man's oyster, share in their glory, and far more little necks, slightly larger cherry stones, phalliclike steamers and quahog chowder clams are consumed each year. We've even come across one recipe called "bearded clam" (which is also slang for the female sex organ), this merely being raw clams arranged in a bed of curly parsley. However, no clam can compare to the oyster as a seaducer, be your choice raw or, even more suggestively, a creamed dish. Only a James Bond could afford to disdain the bivalves, as 007 did in *You Only Live Twice*, when he told a comely damsel, "Well, I don't need these!"

In any case, from both a medical and psychological standpoint, no food save truffles has been held in greater regard by mighty lovers than the mighty symbolic oyster, some even saying that your manhood or womanhood hasn't been reached until you've reached your oysterhood. One writer relates that "a waitress in Minneapolis once stared in astonishment when my female companion ordered oysters as an appetizer

*These would include Boston's Jimmy's Harborside; the Chesapeake House in Baltimore; Bookbinder's in Philadelphia; New Orleans's Royal Sonesta Oyster Bar; Chicago's famed Cape Cod Room at the Drake Hotel; and Brooklyn's Gage and Tollner's.

...she said she had never heard a woman order oysters before." So well grounded is the oyster legend in the world of aphrodisia! "The first oyster eaten alive, and on the shell is a kind of gastronomic loss of virginity," another observer tells us, and he is absolutely right. No orgy is worthy of the name without a few platters of oysters and they are the quintessential food with which to begin a love feast, the perfect prelude to the courses following—that is, if they don't inspire both parties to proceed directly to the *piece de résistance.*

COURSE FIVE

Harlot's Eggs, Or Caviar,
The Roe-Mantic Gems Of The Ocean

"Don't let this get around, but caviar is said to be a great aphrodisiac. It
has all the 47 vitamins known to man."

—Earl Wilson

A millionaire gourmet tells the story of the evening he indulged in some
stimulating caviar at Stockholm's plush Savoy Hotel. At the time he was
only an apprentice millionaire gourmet. He had no way of knowing that
the potent, prolific sturgeon, which produces the fashionable fortifying
fish eggs in erotic profusion, might be going the way of the passenger
pigeon, the buffalo, and the bald eagle, that what many have called mankind's most civilized food may well be sacrificed for "civilization" (as
those out to pave planet earth define the word). In fact, our gourmet was
unaware of most of the many popular misconceptions about caviar. At
any rate, when he finished his first delectable portion and the captain
silver-spooned some more choice Beluga on his plate, he was so pleased

that he tipped the man extravagantly. No sooner had he finished this helping than the captain heaped a third serving on his plate, which called for another generous tip. This went on until the sated gourmet had the bill toted up. The caviar box was weighed and the budding gastronome was glad to be a millionaire, for he was charged for each provocative portion and presented with a bill which even he found "incredible," and which disproves the old dictum that if you have to worry about the price of caviar, you shouldn't order it.

The moral of this story, in the millionaire's words, is that "caviar is not...passed around like mashed potatoes." For caviar, like truffles and *pâté de foie gras*, is more than a mere delicacy; caviar is a symbol of elegance, the quintessential fare of czars and czarinnas, queens and courtiers, kings and concubines. The choicest pearls of the Caspian—and these sturgeon eggs are the only caviar worthy of the name, bearing no relation to the salmon eggs which make red caviar—cost up to $100 for a "Russian pound" of 14 ounces today, and the supply is definitely limited. Indeed, the Colony, a posh New York restaurant, threatened to stop serving caviar not long ago because it was so scarce one helping would cost $20, and Romanoff Caviar, the chief American importer, has had to ration the fashionable fish eggs this year, for the United States has been allocated 140,000 pounds less Iranian caviar than the year before. Neither does the situation seem likely to change, even with the recent Russian announcement that they will market a synthetic product. This pseudocaviar has already been produced by the Soviet Union Laboratory of Physics, and Moscow plans a modern factory to capture the world market—more than 100 capitalist firms are already bidding for rights to the ersatz combination of albumin, polysaccharides, organic products and carbohydrates, but it's safe to predict that the commissars' artificial fish eggs won't please the palates of many fastidious gourmet lovers.

Caviar has been regarded as a love food with few peers precisely because it is so elusive, expensive and delicious. No delicacy save truffles would be more appreciated by anyone's paramour at today's prices, but much medical opinion also vouches for the vaunted food's aphrodisiac powers. In cases of complete and partial impotence, Dr. William J. Robinson, who at one time headed Bronx Hospital's Department of Genito-Urinary Diseases, advised that his patients eat heartily especially of caviar among the foods he recommended as constituting a beneficial diet. Scheuer, for another, wrote in his *Alphabet of Sex* that "Many observers ascribe a beneficial influence to the eating of fish, oysters...and caviar ..." Finally, Dr. Arnold Lorand probably best summed up the feelings of most sexologists on the subject of the fish eggs and love foods in general. "Other articles of diet," he observed, "particularly eggs and caviar, are supposed to exert a stimulating action upon sexual activity. It is customary to say, *vox populi, vox Dei,* and as far as foods (such as caviar) are concerned I would be inclined to consider that in the case of such empiric beliefs, which have been handed down to us from time immemorial, even medical science—which has frequently profited by such statements—should not pass them by without notice..."

Caviar has always been rare and expensive, and lovers have never failed to pay for the privilege of eating it. Last year consumers throughout the world paid some $4 million for about 300,000 pounds. In America, according to U.S. Department of Commerce figures, our portion of the caviar check was $1,217,116 for slightly over 106,000 pounds. Even in these days of shortages and outrageous prices, New York's "21" served more caviar than the year before and the Colony never did carry out its threatened boycott. So it has been throughout history. The lovers of caviar have always been "more general than Shakespeare knew," a fact that is borne out both by the statistics and by establishments like the Caviateria in New York, where dozens of varieties can be ordered.

The word caviar itself is in fact common to most European languages, although, strangely enough, it is not used by the Russians, who call the delicacy *ikra.* Caviar probably derives from the Italian *caviala,* or possibly the Turkish *khavyah* meaning salted sturgeon eggs. Alexander the Great enjoyed the Elysian food and the ancient Greeks served it, along with oysters and roasted grasshoppers, as "provocatives to drinking" in their version of the modern cocktail party. As mentioned, the Roman emperor Heliogabalus, the same who made his entry into Rome in a chariot drawn by naked women, and spent at least $10,000 each for his daily dinners, kept an entire fishing fleet just to catch eels for their caviar. The Roman orator Cicero couldn't afford such expenditures for the fish eggs, but he did declare that no man not a stoic could be indifferent to the merits of the "royal" sturgeon and its roe. The Romans actually used relays of slaves to run the sturgeon live in tubs all the way from the Caspian to their capital, and in the Middle Ages *Acipenser* was designated a royal fish which had to be turned over to the royal kitchen in many countries. That it was always among the *ne plus ultra* for epicures can be seen from a tale recounted in Dumas pere's *Dictionnaire de Cuisine.* An almost identical yarn has been told about Talleyrand and salmon (and turbot has also been so honored), but then all good things have a way of claiming the best stories for themselves. Anyway, let Dumas tell the complete tale in his own inimitable manner:

> One day the Grand Chancellor, Cambacérès, received, on the eve of a great banquet, two enormous sturgeons. One weighed 162 lbs., the other

187. The *mâitre d'hôtel* felt he ought to consult His Highness about this remarkable happening, for if both were to be served together the one would be prejudicial to the other, and if only one were served the other was lost; one could not possibly serve fish of the same kind two days running to the guests of His Highness. Cambacérès closeted himself with the *mâitre d'hôtel*, who emerged beaming a quarter of an hour later.

In fact they had hit upon a plan which would enable both fish, if not to be served, at least to be shown, and to sacrifice the first in honour of the second; to sacrifice it, moreover, in such a way as to redound to the credit of His Highness's table.

This is what Monseigneur and his *mâitre d'hôtel* had concocted between them. The sturgeon was to be served as a remove, after the soup. The less enormous of the two fish was placed upon a bed of foliage and flowers; its entry was announced by the sound of flute and violin. The flutist, in complete chef's garb, followed by two violinists similarly dressed, preceded the sturgeon, which made its appearance accompanied by four footmen carrying torches and two assistant cooks, knife in girdle, with a steward marching ahead, carrying his halberd.

The sturgeon, reposing on a ladder some eight to ten feet long, was borne upon the shoulders of two cooks. The procession entered to the sound of the violins and flute, and amid the cries of admiration, the guests, forgetting for a moment the respect due to their host, got up on their chairs to look at the monster.

But just as the circuit of the table was accomplished and the fish was about to be taken out and cut up to the applause of all the company, one of the bearers stumbled and fell on one knee, whilst the fish slipped off the ladder and fell on to the floor.

A long wail of despair proceeded from every heart, or rather stomach, and there was a momentary confusion, during which all tendered their advice. But the voice of Cambacérès dominated the tumult as with a simplicity worthy of an ancient Roman he cried: "Serve the other one!" And at that moment there was seen to enter a second procession, similar to the first, save that this time where were two flutes, four violins and four footmen. Applause succeeded the cries of anguish, and the first fish, which weighed 25 lbs. less than the other, was carried away.

The sturgeon and its even more precious roe had been eulogized as an epicurean love food by the Persians centuries before Dumas or even Cambacérès. Caviar itself was introduced to the West by Alexander the Great, who learned about the fecund fish and how to prepare caviar from his encounter with Darius. The fish eggs are mentioned by the irrepressible Rabalais in his *Pantagruel* in several places, and in Renaissance times, Italians invariably served caviar during the first part of their two-part meals—the *Credenza* or buffet—just as the English were to use it as an hors d'oeuvre and the Russians do today. *Boutargue*, a cheaper caviar made from the roe of grey mullet drained and mashed, was served in lascivious French salons when sturgeon eggs were unavailable, but the

French, as Brillat-Savarin indicates, always preferred the real thing as an aphrodisiac, adopting such Russian recipes as "smoked eels caviare" along with other dishes of foreign origins only out of necessity.

Aristology, the art of dining, has in more-modern times seen the eminently pleasurable sturgeon eggs become one of the staples of the great ocean-going luxury liners, including the *S.S. United States*, which once took a late but indispensable caviar order by helicopter and often dished out as much as 100 pounds a crossing—$10,000 at today's prices. About the only derogatory remark one can find anywhere about the savory sensuous dish is the old Italian proverb "Who eats caviar eats flies, dung and salt," although one anonymous writer declared the consumption of "caviare" to be a cause of the great plague in 1665. The slang expression "caviar" did, however, once refer to the "obnoxious matter" that was "blacked out" of foreign periodicals by the Russian Press Censor in Czarist days.

Medically, caviar's reputation as a potent aphrodisiac mainly derives from the fact that it contains phosphorous and many vitamins, and is extremely nutritious (30% protein and 16% fat). Besides those great lovers already cited, the fish eggs were also favored by Madame Pompadour, Madame DuBarry, Casanova and the infamous Rasputin. Many sexologists give elaborate recipes using caviar as a restorative (one such, called "Harlot's Eggs," consists of mixing tablespoons of pimento, anchovy paste, chopped chives and a dash of lemon juice with one-half cup of caviar for use as an hors d'oeuvre). The modern-day master chef Raymond Oliver believes that the royal roe is particularly effective for men. "In a lover's luncheon," he says, "the lion's share of the caviar should go to the man, despite the woman's inclination toward the delicate dish." This dilemma might only be resolved by ordering three portions for a party of two, but another way out would be to whip up some delicious *Petites Croutes de Caviar*. First cut out eight round pieces of bread about one inch in diameter and one-half inch thick, scooping out the centers enough to hold one teaspoon of caviar each. Mix three ounces of whole grain or pressed caviar with one teaspoon of chopped shallots, the juice of half a lemon and a pinch of cayenne. Then fry the croutes in hot butter until light brown in color, draining well on a paper towel. When cold fill each crisp croute with a teaspoon of the prepared caviar and garnish with sprigs of parsley.

It is little known that not even a century ago America actually shipped caviar to Europe for processing from California, New York, and New Jersey (100,000–150,000 pounds per year was taken from the lower Delaware at the turn of the century), or that some inexpensive caviar is still made in Amagansett, Long Island. Captain John Smith wrote that "We had more Sturgeon than could be devoured by Dog and Man," and several hundred years later, in 1897, 1.2 million pounds of "Albany beef," as the tasty sturgeon used to be called, was caught in New York and New Jersey. But pollution and overfishing have taken their toll. Both the white sturgeon *(Acipenser transmontanus)* and the short-nosed sturgeon *(A. brevirostrum)* are now classified by the U.S. Department of the Interior as endangered (their "survival and reproduction are in immediate jeopardy"), while the great sea sturgeon *(A. oxyrhynchus)* is classified as rare ("may be endangered if its environment worsens"). As for the primitive lake sturgeon weighing up to 300 pounds and exceeding 8 feet in length, it is already practically extinct. Some fishermen report that the Hudson still abounds with sturgeon despite its pollution—a 7½ footer whose roe weighed 50 pounds was taken in 1968—but the yearly catch at last count was a paltry 25,000 pounds.

Caviar was once so cheap here that caviar sandwiches were free in saloons with a nickel glass of beer, and sturgeons so plentiful that children on the waterfront streets of New York used their resilient snouts as rubber balls. But now we must look elsewhere for the food of royal lovers. We do *not* look to the Soviet Union. Few people are aware that 96% of imported caviar today comes not from Russia but from Iran, where the best sturgeon for caviar are caught. Last year we imported only about 4,300 pounds from Canada, as compared to Iran's 96,000 pound total. In fact, invitations to the Iranian ambassador's parties are now the most coveted in Washington, featuring as they do large silver Revere bowls of caviar in the center of each supper table, while it's said that the Russians serve one caviar canape and ten security men for each guest.

What we know as "quality caviar" today is not made from just any fish eggs but from the roe of particularly tasty species of sturgeon. (Two and one half pounds of roe are needed to make a pound of the appetizer of 2500 pounds, yield some three million eggs a year at maturity and live 200 to 300 years. Isinglass, traditionally used for making wines and jellies, as well as in repairing glass and pottery, is also made from the sturgeon. Some twenty species are known in European, Asiatic and North American rivers, most of these, though not the American variety, being "anadromous"—spending a great part of the year in the sea, ascending freshwater rivers in the spring to deposit their spawn, and rarely returning to salt water again. Most are in great abundance in southern Russia, where as many as 10,000 of the sluggish bottom-fish have been caught at a single fishing station during the upstream migration. Until 1953, Russia had a virtual monopoly on the caviar trade, Persian caviar, even in Iran itself, marketed under a Russian label and controlled by the Soviet food trust *Prodintorg.* But since the oil-rich Iranians have gone into business for themselves, operating out of their Caspian seaport Pahlevi, the Russians, who still eat more caviar than anyone else, have lost control of the world market.

The best and most potent caviar is made from select sturgeon species such as the small Sevruga, the medium-sized Ostrea, and the large Beluga, from which up to 130 pounds of roe, $13,000 worth, has been taken from one fish. Beluga, which is most highly regarded today, has large, sometimes buckshot-sized grains and is usually a dark steel-gray, while the others are smaller and vary from golden-brown to black in color. Caviar color really depends on how close sturgeon are to spawning—the closer they are, the grayer their eggs—and has nothing to do with flavor, adding only to eye-appeal. Probably the most famous caviar of all is the selected golden sterlet's eggs (they come, one *bon vivant* says, from sterlets "with a particularly happy frame of mind") once enjoyed by the Russian czars. Unfortunately, few of us will ever taste this smooth, velvety green gold delicacy made from the eggs of the small sterlet of the *Acipenser ruthenus* species, although it may still be served in the Kremlin and author Truman Capote has boasted that he was recently presented a jar by a Mideastern Shah. But then Capote likes all excellent caviars. In fact, the only way he can "bear to eat a potato" is baked and then heaped with mounds of "the freshest, the grayest, the biggest Beluga."

The esteemed and fabulously wealthy travel guide writer Temple Fielding is one incurable caviar addict who has eaten golden caviar in abundance. John McPhee describes the writer's addiction in a profile of Fielding in the *New Yorker* in which Fielding explains that only one in ten thousand pots of caviar is golden, "a beautiful berry—gorgeous burnished gold with gray overtones." As for black caviar, Fielding says he eats *that* for his midnight snacks, digging "perhaps fifty or seventy-five grams from the pot with an all mother-of-pearl caviar knife."

Centuries ago, whole villages of lusty swashbuckling Cossacks, household effects and all, swarmed to the river banks of Russia for a fortnight in spring (the spring catch is far better, for cold water renders all fish roe more compact) to net the sturgeon and sell them to rich caviar connoisseurs and dealers. Cannons were fired to frighten the fish and harpooners finished them off. Today, less colorful means are used to catch the sturgeon. Often the fish are "farmed," that is, they are caught during the breeding season as they return to the rivers and kept submerged in large floating cages the size of barges until their eggs become more palatable, the roe right after breeding being too greasy for consumption. Usually, the sturgeon are netted and clubbed unconscious. The ovarian sac containing the roe is removed, and the ovaries are then beaten and strained several times through a fine-threaded sieve to clear them of membranes, fibers and fatty matter. The eggs are next salted in varying degrees by a *nastavnic* or master taster, some of whom make the rather dubious claim that they can tell where a batch comes from simply by sampling a small mouthful. The relatively inexpensive pressed caviar preferred by many connoisseurs is made at this point by pouring the cleaned caviar into linen bags in which it hangs and drains. This destroys the shape of the eggs and makes the product quite salty. Other even coarser saltier caviar becomes the *Pajusnava* that is a staple article of food in Russia and Eastern Europe, while the loosely granulated and less salty *malossol* product becomes the caviar or *ikra* of legend. Most people think that *malossol* is a quality name, like Beluga, but it is not. One can have Beluga *malossol*, Sevruga *malossol*, etc.—in Russia alone there are eighty different varieties of black caviar. Roe prepared for consumption in the United States, however, is always a bit saltier, our laws requiring that it must be preserved in 3–4% salt and not the borax or boric acid permissible in Europe. Caviar made with borax is sweeter in taste and is sometimes smuggled into the United States, but it can only be served here legally at foreign embassies or on ships outside the three-mile limit.

Our children's children may be the last generation of lovers to eat caviar, according to some experts—at least no one will be eating it for breakfast, as Jacqueline Susann is reported to do. Fewer each year are the 4-pound tins of *malossol* and the 100-pound barrels of pressed caviar that importers receive. In Europe, as well as America, the sturgeon, which produces the most "civilized food," may indeed be going the way of so many other species sacrificed for "progress," a depressing situation for both the ecologist and the discerning diner. The majority of sturgeon used in preparing select caviar come from the Iranian side of the Caspian sea, where the waters are deeper and sweeter, but the Caspian becomes shallower and more saline every year due to Russian industrial pollution of the Volga. The water level has dropped between fifteen and twenty feet in the last thirty years because so much of the Volga's water has been used for industrial purposes, depriving the sturgeon of the fresh water they need to lay their eggs and limiting their mobility. In time their natural spawning grounds could become far too salty for their taste. The Russians and Iranians are building hatcheries to replace the vanishing sturgeon and there is talk of diverting freshwater Arctic rivers into the Caspian, as well as of linking it with the Black Sea, but these projects, if they do succeed, will take many years to replenish the sturgeon population. Even the fingerling sturgeon now being "hatchered" will require twenty-five years before they reach caviar-producing size. Still, the Russians have taken a no-nonsense approach to cleaning up the Volga, appropriating some one billion rubles for that purpose in 1973. Heavy fines are also levied for poaching, and one Volga dredge captain got an unreal five-year jail sentence for the offense recently.

Another reason for the great caviar shortage is that more people are developing a taste for the fish eggs and a relative worldwide economic prosperity allows them to indulge themselves. Germany, for example, is today Europe's leading sturgeon caviar importer, and bids briskly against Russia for Iran's supply. Here in the United States we now import some fifty tons annually, not to mention another 325,000 pounds of cheap dollar a pound nonsturgeon fish roe. The leading American importer is the Romanoff Caviar Company, founded in 1835 and absorbed in 1970 by the Houston, Texas fine foods conglomerate, Riviana Industries. Romanoff established offices in America in 1859 when Ferdinand Hansen, son of one of the founders, came here to buy caviar made from the sturgeon once abundant in the rivers along the Atlantic and Pacific for his Hamburg-based company. By the turn of the century, however, pollution had taken its toll and sturgeon had become almost extinct both here and in Europe, so Hansen signed an agreement with Russia's Romanov Imperial family to import caviar from the Volga River, establishing a fishing station in Astrakhan where the Volga empties into the Caspian. Today, neither Romanoff nor its New York competitors, Iron Gate Products, Vita, Purepak and M. Chernoff, feel that the caviar industry is in any immediate danger. Guenther F. Hansen-Sturm, chairman of the board of Romanoff and often called "the Caviar King," says that "The sturgeon may disappear, but not in this generation or the next." This might prove wishful thinking, but while the waters from the Caspian to Astrakhan, center for the Russian caviar fishing, evaporate and become mud flats, the caviar industry thrives and Romanoff, which last year imported 65% of the U.S. allocation from Iran, has no fears for the future. Especially of that Russian synthetic product, which they claim "doesn't look or taste like caviar at all." Romanoff, in fact, recently filled an incredible 768-pound order for the *S.S. France's* gourmet cooking cruise, and their "black diamonds" still sell briskly at posh New York restaurants like Quo Vadis, La Caravelle and La Grenouille for $24 a serving (2 teaspoons).

Quality caviar has traditionally been shipped refrigerated to America in great wooden barrels containing eighteen hand-sewn cloth sacks on racks inside, the sacks containing, in turn, three 4¼-lb. tins of sturgeon eggs. The cans are all vacuum-sealed with rubber bands and are sometimes numbered so that more caviar from the same sturgeon can be ordered. All caviar eggs should be firm, smooth and shiny; they should not have settled in the container and should not have a sour smell. It is important that the eggs be kept at a temperature of from 28 to 32°F; caviar below that temperature will freeze and become soup upon thawing, whereas, except for much-inferior pasteurized brands, caviar stored on a shelf at room temperature loses much of its taste, becoming waxy and chewy. The same holds true in good restaurants, where the tins are stored in cracked ice at a temperature of exactly 32°F. Once a can is opened in a restaurant, it must be watched even more carefully, for caviar spoils quickly and while caviar poisoning may be the ultimate in modes of dying, all such modes are final.

The best times to order caviar in a restaurant, cognoscenti claim, are May, June, October and November, although Romanoff, as would be expected, says that all times are equally good. It can be enjoyed in many ways. Capote's hot baked potato filled with cold caviar is delicious, as is caviar rolled in smoked salmon. Aristotle Onassis is said to prefer pressed caviar such as that served at The Russian Tea Room in New York, while Christian Dior liked to cook an egg over his caviar and devour it cold as an hors d'oeuvre. Others prefer their caviar with sour cream, sweet butter and blinis (small, thin pancakes made of buckwheat, white flour, sugar, salt and yeast). Yet many gourmets insist that blinis, chopped onion or egg, sour cream and cream cheese merely serve to stretch your caviar supply or to disguise an inferior grade. Nobody seems to eat caviar the way Dagwood Bumstead does—along with swiss cheese, salami, peanut butter, jelly, pickles, mayonnaise, mustard, ketchup, peppers, sardines, artichoke hearts, liverwurst, sliced sausage, ham, lettuce and tomatoes on his famous Dagwood Sandwiches—no matter how much those midnight snacks fortify him for Blondie. Ideally, expensive caviar should only be eaten spooned directly from its frosty tin or spread on sweet-buttered very thin toast and flavored with a dash of pepper or a squeeze of lemon. It should be accompanied only by chilled Vodka, aquavit or the most elegant Champagne, which goes well with everything. Vodka is especially favored, but only the mildest brands—certainly not the potent Polish White Spirit Vodka, which at 160 proof is the world's strongest commercially sold drink. When in times gone by the Czar had his Volga Beluga shipped to Moscow by *troika*, the fish were packed in wet hay and kept asleep with Vodka.

Many, perhaps even most, restaurants serve caviar with a silver spoon, but about the only advantage silver has here is its elegance. Temple Fielding and all the experts advise that spoons made of wood, bone, horn, tortoise, and mother-of-pearl are traditional throughout the world. "Caviar should be eaten from a natural substance," says Gerald Stein, the president of Iron Gate Products. "It's not only the fact that silver tarnishes, but you shouldn't taste metal when eating caviar." A silver-*handled* wooden spoon, available from Iron Gate, should serve your needs, though. If you can afford the caviar, you can afford the $10.

Anyone who really wants to be elegant might order from jeweler Harry Winston's a copy of the golden caviar ball they designed for our millionaire epicure Maurice Dreicer—the same who dined at the Savoy. Whenever Dreicer orders caviar, he plunges his golden ball into the tin, and times its descent with a stop watch, knowing that the quicker it goes through, the less salty and more tasty the fish eggs. But the serving of caviar in any quality restaurant is an elegant ritual with or without a golden ball, akin to the elaborate preparation of shish kebab or flaming desserts such as crêpes suzette. At banquets the eggs are often served in the shape of swans, bears and other animals and they have even been suggestively mounded in the midriffs of reclining ice nudes. Always there is the ceremony, however—ceremony easily emulated in the love nest. Perhaps after opening a tin, your waiter will brandish a small silver-handled spoon with which he'll expertly heap a hen egg-sized mound of fish eggs on your plate, heaping a second portion at its side with still another silver-handled spoon, perhaps using a whole tray of silver before serving your party, and all the while working with motions as practiced and graceful as those of any ballet performer. But even if he isn't a Nureyev, you can be sure he'll endeavor to be elegant throughout dinner (in part because he is enchanted by the caviar ritual itself; in part because he knows that his 15 to 20% tip will come off a very large check indeed).

In any case, caviar is always better served nearer the bedroom. In there, it's said, Dostoevski's wife regaled him with fish eggs and more after he finished each chapter of *Crime And Punishment*, which luckily didn't become entitled *Virtue And Reward* as a result. Anyone who can afford the precious eggs may wish, like Philoxenes, for "a neck like a crane, that the delicious morsels might be long in going down." As for their results upon getting there, well it's been reported that one voluptuous young woman meant to be taken literally when she promised, "You pay for the caviar and the rest of the evening will be on me." And if the real roe can't be afforded, there's a way out, too—for as Epicurus said, "the company makes the feast." If only nonsturgeon caviar can be managed as a prelude to the lobster and truffles to follow, even red salmon caviar or Icelandic lumpfish caviar at 63 cents an ounce, just serve it with a sauce of panache, carefully including a soupcon of exaggeration. Casanova had the same problem one time and he handled it in just about the same way, turning to his partner and saying: "Although we have not dined, come! Love and happiness will be our food!"

COURSE SIX

The Amorous Oddball Lobster

O have ye heard of monger Meg,
And how she loved the weaver, O
She let me see her red-haired coynte,
And sold it for a lobster, O...
  —Robert Burns, *Merry Muses*

He begins all sexual encounters with an awkward dance in time to a music of sorts; his mate guards with her life the eggs that he fertilizes, but as soon as their children hatch, both parents will eagerly eat them if hungry enough. He's an odd character all right. He's been called both cannibal and scavenger, a many-limbed miniature sea monster, a creature from inner space who is near blind despite his ten thousand tiny eyes or facets, who can cast off an endangered arm or leg and grow another at will. His marvellous mixed-up anatomy includes a nervous system centered in his belly and a minute brain both above and below his throat; he "hears" with his legs, "tastes" with his toes and has teeth in

74

his stomach. He is literally made inside out and upside down, his shell-bones enclosing his succulent flesh as if it were marrow, and, what's more, his family has been living thus without complaint for some 100 million years. Yet this second cousin of the spider, this vulture of the sea, is now close to becoming America's favorite food for love. Oysters, choice Beluga caviar, black and white truffles and *pâté de foie gras* are certainly his rivals, it's true, not to mention exotic foods like ortolan thighs and bird's nest soup, but he alone among them makes a main course in himself; and furthermore, he constitutes almost no carbohydrates and only eighty-eight calories for a three-quarter pound serving. No hymns have been written to *Homarus americanus,* the American lobster, no one has penned a panegyric on this princely dish, but the crotchety crustacean has to be crowned King of the Clawed Lovefish.

Much has been written in amatory treatises on the tempting lobster and his phalliclike claws, perhaps Brillat-Savarin alone among great cooks and erotologists neglecting to do *Homarus* homage. The long-clawed lobster has certainly lengthened and heightened the pleasures of Eros through the centuries. Casanova, Gabrielle D'Annunzio and all the proverbial Lotharios of life and literature have favored him. Lobster took its proper place in the famous paella recipe of Agnolo Torredana, Casanova's traveling companion, who appears to have been more macho than the maestro, at least judging by the fact that he died in the arms of his nineteen-year-old mistress while still a most vigorous ninety-two. Ribald Rabelais praises *Homarus* in several places: his Master Gaster reveling in it; the divers of his Queen Quintessence "setting nets to catch the wind and bagging great lobsters"; and Gargantua's friend Gymnastes advising that lobster be cooked "red as a cardinal's hat" for the best possible results.

It has been recorded that The King of London's Streetwalkers, "Mad" William Windham, regaled his girls with huge lobsters as well as plump oysters, and spiced crawfish (small lobsters without claws) were zaftig Lillian Russell's choice as a prelude to many a night of love. Similarly, the common crab, another lobster relative, figures in Crab Louis (the tender meat of Dungeness crabs lavished with hot chili sauce and whipped cream mayonnaise), which ranks among the most vaunted of aphrodisiac foods. When dining at his favorite New Orleans restaurant the greatest of tenors and exemplary lover Enrico Caruso would reorder this tasty dish, invented by a San Francisco chef, until there wasn't any left in the kitchen. Yet neither of these concoctions compares with lobster plain, or the many lobster dishes sensuous gourmets have invented over the years. What could work more wonders than combinations like Chinese Garlic Lobster, the Lobster With Whiskey mentioned by chef Raymond Oliver or a creamy Lobster Bisque made with a cup of cream and half a cup of wine and other hearty ingredients? The medical experts all seem to agree. Alan Hull Watson gives a recipe for a fortifying lobster omelette in his restorative regimen; Dr. George Belham commends the crustacean in his *Virility Diet*; and both Drs. Lorand and Scheuer cite *Homarus* as a highly beneficial food for sexual vigor.

Strangely enough, our thrifty Puritan ancestors, who had a lobster phobia that lasted until the nineteenth century (not to mention myriad sexual hang-ups), actually threw the redoubtable lobster away, or used him for fertilizer or bait. Perhaps this transpired because he so much resembled a "bug," which New England lobstermen still call *Homarus* to this day, the word "lobster" itself actually being a melding of two foreign words: the Latin *locasta*, meaning locust, and the Anglo-Saxon *loppe*, which means spider. Like all shellfish and insects, lobsters are really invertebrate anthropods, but at any rate, the entomological and etymological comparisons didn't help early American appetites. So plentiful were lobsters in colonial days that they sold for "a penny each" regardless of size, more lobster consumed at the first Thanksgiving than turkey. Plymouth youngsters waded out to catch them by hand and there is one early account of windrows of lobsters more than a foot high cast up by the sea after a hard storm. Governor Bradford of the Plymouth Plantation so disdained the dish that he could complain shamefacedly in 1622 that the only food colonists "could present their friends with was a lobster." But since about 1800, when *Homarus* was first fished commercially, the lobster, like the oyster before him, has gradually made the transformation from food for the poor to fare for the affluent. For various reasons, the fonder man has become of him, the scarcer *Homarus* has become. In 1880, for example, Maine lobstermen were paid 1.9 cents a pound for their catch; today, they receive about $2.50 a pound. The total catch itself declined tremendously from the late nineteenth century until about twenty years ago, when conservation measures and better fishing techniques began to improve the situation. Even so, the outlook is bleak indeed for lobster lovers as far as price is concerned. "With a growing population and rising incomes," says the U.S. Bureau of Commercial Fisheries, "lobsters will stay in the luxury food class for some time to come." In fact, many restaurateurs are already claiming that they lose money on every lobster they serve and some have even discontinued serving it because of its high price.

Man so values *Homarus* that we have no doubt become the mature lobster's greatest natural enemy, far more menacing to him than any denizen of the deep. Perhaps Art Buchwald is right and there should be a Society for the Prevention of Cruelty to Lobsters, but certainly, *Homarus*, as he changes to a bright delicious red while steaming in the pot, is one of the few animals who looks like he is asking to be eaten. That lobsters have been enjoyed by lovers since prehistoric times is proved by shell heaps and kitchen middens at least 10,000 years old. *Homarus* was considered a delicacy by the Mayans, and Soliman the Magnificent served him with pride to visiting royalty. References in literature to the kingly crustacean are legion. "James Stephens, along with broiled live lobster, is one of the reasons I shall never commit suicide," John Dos Passos confided in a letter to a friend. "And like a lobster boiled, the morn./ From black to red began to turn," wrote Samuel Butler in *Hudibras.* "Ah! who has seen the mailed lobster rise,/ Clap his broad wings, and soaring claim the skies?" sang John Hookam Frere in the *Progress of Man.* " 'Tis the voice of the lobster; I heard him declare,/ You have baked me too brown, I must sugar my hair,' " Lewis Carroll wrote in *Alice In Wonderland.* Francis Higginson observed in his *New England's Plantation* (1630) that there was such an abundance of lobsters in America that "For my own part I was soon cloyed with them, they were so great and fat and luscious."

Tonight, thanks to streamlined handling methods and transportation, lobsters will grace close to 25,000 dinner tables in the United States from the seacoast to deep inland. This is not counting those served off the premises, where a lobster revolution (despite the crustacean's high price) has been taking place over the last ten years which has resulted in *Homarus* challenging steak as man's favorite restaurant food from Bangor to Bangkok. People are becoming less inhibited about their eating habits, few seem picky about picking *Homarus* apart with their fingers anymore, this perhaps reflecting the premium price paid for him, and lobsters of all sizes are enjoyed by the most fastidious of diners ensconced behind plastic bibs. The grades available include chicken lobsters (¾ to 1 lb.), quarters (1½ lbs.), large (1½ to 2½ lbs.) and jumbos (over 2½ lbs.). Neither does the figure cited include servings of spiny lobster, the colorful yellow to purplish beauty from which mere lobster tails are obtained; or crayfish, a freshwater lobster that the French call *Ecrevisse;* or crawfish, that small European lobster with no claws. The spiny lobster, a different species, is the *langosta* or *langouste* featured in many posh restaurants— what you're served is just the severed tail of a spiny lobster, despite all the high-flown phrases. *Homarus,* to the contrary, is a true lobster, belonging to an exclusive club that counts just two other close relatives among its members: *Nephrops norvegicus,* the Norwegian lobster (variously called "scampi," "lady lobster," and "prawn" or *"Crevette* Rose"), this a bright orange specimen with white markings; and the smaller brighter blue lobster of Europe *(Homarus vulgaris).* The largest and best of the "prawns" is the Dublin Bay Prawn (which the French call *langoustini* and the Italians *scampi).* To sound a cautionary note, the prawn is poisonous to those allergic to shellfish if the black filaments in its back aren't removed before eating.

Besides a distinct difference in taste, true lobsters differ from the spiny lobsters used for lobster tails by having the large well-developed claws so often described in erotic culinary literature, and lacking a profusion of spines on their bodies. Spiny lobsters come from warm waters, mainly in South Africa, Honduras and Brazil, and cannot compare as a delicacy to the cold-water breed. Sometimes dubbed the Maine or North Atlantic lobster, *Homarus americanus,* is esteemed as the sweetest of the true cold-water varieties. Rarely, certain pigments may be lacking, producing different-colored individuals, but our *Homarus* is generally a bluish green mottled with black; before being cooked, that is. He is found in his natural state only on the eastern coast of North America, within a 1300-mile range which has as its most northern point Labrador and its most southern the coast of North Carolina. In this area *Homarus* is born, matures and is trapped by lobstermen; very rarely does he migrate more than a few miles from his birthplace.

Even before *Homarus* has to contend with *Homo sapien*'s taste buds, he must elude the predators of the deep. Over 99% of all lobsters die a few weeks after being born, but luckily the female lobster produces thousands of eggs. This prolific lady mates every two years. During the summer season her resistance weakens and her shell turns soft. She then releases a sex pheromone, a chemical messenger that subdues aggression and triggers amorous behavior in the male. After what seems to us an awkward, fifteen-minute courtship dance, a mating ritual that consists of the aggressive female briefly caressing the male with her antennae and both partners clicking their claws like castinets, the female rolls over on her back and the hard-shelled male quickly ejaculates his sperm into a sac that lies between his mate's fourth and fifth pair of legs, showing what one marine biologist has called "remarkable gentleness to the vulnerable female" during the eight-second long sexual act. The long-lived sperm is held in this pouch for at least nine months, until the following spring when the female actually spawns. To perform the spawning act, which takes about four hours, she lies on her back, flexing her abdomen into a pocket from which greenish black eggs are discharged in a steady flow from the genital openings, passing over the sperm sac on the way. At this time the sperm cells leave the sac and fertilize the eggs, which are not released but remain glued to the female's stomach for another ten or eleven months. The berried lobster guards her caviarlike eggs with her life, folding her tail up over them when marauding fish or stormy seas threaten and constantly serrating them clean by moving her swimmerets.

But when the by-then transparent eggs begin hatching, the mother wants nothing more to do with her offspring. She stands up on her toes, shakes off anywhere from 6,000 to 90,000 larvae and scoots away without giving a thought to either maternal instinct or overpopulation.

From the moment on that always cloudy day or dark night when they begin to rise to the surface of the sea, the orphan lobsterlings have every reason to develop their racial instincts of fear and caution. The odds are one in a million against any larval lobster living long enough to become any human's love potion. The ⅓-inch-long lobsterlings, whose beady Martian eyes are completely out of proportion to their bodies, are preyed upon by a number of fish, such as cod; overwhelmed by swift currents that they are not strong enough to fight; and even attacked by their slightly larger cannibal playmates, who don't hesitate to devour them when hungry enough. For two months during their free-swimming stage, lobsterling movements are limited to rising to the surface at daybreak and sinking slightly at night. Only when they finally descend all the way to the bottom, do the infants begin to resemble their parents, but their troubles are still far from finished. They are still plagued by bottom fish, more cannibal relations and a score of sicknesses, including the deadly blood disease "red-tail." It takes seven molts or change of shells before they reach the ripe old age of one year and the odds are 10,000 to 1 against them completing the journey from that point on.

Luckily, for himself and amorists everywhere, the lobster does have several things going for him which enable him to hang in there. First, his anatomy is well adapted to his environment. *Homarus* is like a knight in blue-steel armor, the sea his steed, his tread so delicate and precise that a three or four pounder can jog over a flounder without disturbing it. As noted, he or she can be many colors, including bright gold, and in fact, a recent rare "golden blonde" female find (the chances of catching same are "one in five million"), caught off Hampton, Virginia, has proved that blondes do have more fun even among lobsters. When she went on exhibit at Coney Island's New York Aquarium, resident marine biologists reported that all the male lobsters began chasing her around the tank, possibly "because she was the first blonde they'd ever seen." No such male reactions were reported concerning the powder-blue specimen, one pound in weight, exhibited by the New York State Ocean Science Laboratory at the Long Island Boat Show in 1973. Lab scientists theorized that this "freak of marine nature" may have gotten her color because of a missing enzyme in her genetic makeup. The lobster has molted several times, yet each time the shell returns in a brilliant light blue.

Whether *Homarus* is black, yellow, spotted, scarlet or powder blue usually depends on his diet and the local waters. All these colors blend in well on the ocean floor, where he spends most of his time hiding under rocks or camouflaged in patches of seaweed. The spiny lobster of tropical waters has an entirely different life style, about which relatively little is known. Sometimes these lobster tail providers even stage incredible undersea "marches." Abruptly, as if on signal, they move out in long parallel columns from their rocky hideaways toward offshore waters. Covering the ocean floor for miles, they soon disappear into the darker depths, their destination as much a mystery as their reason for leaving. The spiny lobster can also make a loud noise by rubbing his long antennae against his horny armor, perhaps communicating with prospective mates. But the less exotic *Homarus* doesn't seem to be able to "sweet-talk" anyone. His long sensitive feelers or antennae sweep back and forth to sense the presence of enemies, and when alarmed he swims rapidly backward by quick movements of his muscular tail. If cornered, though, he will snap out fiercely with pincer claws as large as two-thirds the weight of his body. These have been known to break a man's fingers and to reach up and snap a Maine sea captain's briar pipe in half. One writer even mentions, without verification, "the largest lobster ever caught...armed with pincers fifteen inches long, powerful enough to snip off a man's *arm*." So it can easily be seen how potentially dangerous a nasty live lobster can be to nude diners, especially *male* nude diners. *Homarus* will hang on for dear life once he's got the male nude diner by the finger or whatever. It's just as Charles Kingsley observed in *The Water Babies* when he wrote, "And still the lobster held on!"

Homarus is also protected by his external skeleton, which makes for an almost impenetrable suit of armor. Although he cannot taste and smell in the strict sense of the words, the 50,000 to 100,000 tiny hairs that cover his body convey the equivalent of touch, taste and smell stimulations to his nervous system through hundreds of thousands of minute passages at the roots of the hairs. Particularly sensitive are the hairs on the antennae and those on the feet. These "taste" all objects on the ocean floor as the lobster explores the bottom for food and are vital to his or her sexual functioning. However, water pollution seems to be disrupting the life functions of these antennae, according to Dr. John Todd of Cape Cod's Woods Hole Oceanographic Institution. Dr. Todd sees this as an important "early-warning system" for man himself. It appears that tiny quantities of spilled oil in seawater, even as little as a few parts per million of oil, adversely affect the minute sensing hairs on the lobster's antennae. Vital "messages" carried by chemical agents called pheromones get "scrambled," upsetting *Homarus's* feeding and sexual behavior. "We are looking at an early monitoring system," says Dr. Todd. "It is possible that certain pollutants could make it impossible for marine life to communicate. The lobster's sex pheromone, for example, might be destroyed, suppressed or mimicked by pollution."

His antennae bristles likewise account for the lobster's sense of balance. Cut his antennae off after balancing a lobster on his head and he will suffer no pain, but will remain in this awkward position for several hours. The hairs also compensate for the lobster's lack of an organ comparable to our ear. Though he is deaf, he does sense noise as vibrations. Until Revolutionary times, great lobsters were caught in New York Harbor, but the incessant cannonading scared them off and not one has been taken there since. As a result the only lobstering done today on a fairly large scale near New York Harbor is by seven boats in the Mud Hole and Seventeen Fathoms grounds southwest of Ambrose Light, but even these traditional spots are deteriorating due to the sewage sludge and industrial wastes dumped there. One lobsterman says, "I used to get loads of lobsters out there. When you'd get an easterly wind, you'd get a lot of lobsters. Now when you get a blow, it erupts all that junk, the sludge and wastes, and this smears all the pots. When you pull up the pots, the lobsters are dead."

Handicapped by the lack of almost all senses as we know them, the lobster, for all his thousand eyes, is nearly totally blind and quite myopic. But his poor eyesight matters little, as *Homarus* is a bon vivant of essentially nocturnal habits, shunning the sunlight. Whether he lives in two or two hundred fathoms of water, he explores the bottom in search of food and sex mainly after sundown. Concealing himself in rock crevices, seaweed or his burrow in the mud, he captures his prey by stealth, eating almost anything living on the bottom, from fish to other lobsters. He may even resort to scavenging should live prey be scarce. Few people would consider eating a vulture, even for sex, but that is exactly what most scientists have regarded the lobster as up to now—a vulture of the sea—though most recently one researcher has called this a canard, claiming that *Homarus* doesn't feed on carrion and refuse or at least has never been observed doing same. As for *Homarus's* cannibalistic predelictions, keep fifty unpegged lobsters together in an artificial pond too long and they will soon become one large lobster. *Homarus* also acts like a dog at times. If he finds more food than he can eat at a sitting, he buries the excess like a dog buries a bone by bracing his rear legs and using his front legs and mouth appendages to cover the food with sand. It may be, too, as recent experiments suggest, that *Homarus's* multiple eyes are sensitive to light on a scale beyond our comprehension, and that his vision can be as acute as the fabled hawk's. His eyes, which turn ruby red during a storm, do shun light, however, and *Homarus* probably depends on his sensory hairs to track prey. So responsive to food are these hairs that a lobster will react to a trail left in the water by a finger which has barely grazed a piece of meat.

The outlandish lobster also has the amazing ability to grow new legs, claws or other parts should he lose them in a fight or find the need to shuck them in order to escape an enemy. This regenerative ability, called autonomy, is shared with a number of animals, not including us mammals, who pay for our "higher organization" with an almost complete loss of the capacity. (Our bodies can only heal wounds, repair internal tissues and grow fingernails and hair.) Scuba-divers have reported instances of captured lobsters escaping by "throwing" their claws. These are always cast off at the same seam near the body, and *Homarus* can actually dismember himself without being touched. So exact is this incredible natural process that when the lobster molts, his body growth automatically slows if a new part has to be grown, letting the younger part catch up with it. Sometimes *Homarus* will even grow a double claw to replace an old one, which accounts for those strange specimens often served in restaurants and prized by the superstitious as especially phallic. A lobster with just *one* claw, however, is only a loser, and anybody served a single-clawed specimen fresh from a fight should demand that he be taken back and replaced by the winner. Lobsters are always "right-handed" or "left-handed," though, never "ambidextrous," and one claw is invariably larger than the other.

Of all the amazing aspects of the lobster, molting is probably the most fantastic. Molting is an exact process associated with growth. Only by casting off his bones (shedding his inelastic shell) can the lobster grow big enough to be eaten. In contrast to the female, which molts every two years, the young male lobster molts every summer. After feeding rapaciously, *Homarus* lies on his side and the membrane joining his body and tail splits across the back. Curling up into a V-shape, he then begins working himself out of his bone suit. Soon the brilliant colors of his new shell begin to show. He pulls his entire body through the narrow slit, including his claws, which must be drawn through openings only a tenth their size. The whole process takes from five to twenty minutes. When *Homarus* is done there is only one clean slit in the shell, which looks as if it had been made by a razor-sharp knife. Nothing else is split or cracked and *Homarus's* old shell, right-side-up, looks like it's still alive and thriving. With yet another skeleton of his old life behind him, the reincarnated creature crawls away to the security of his burrow, where he absorbs seawater and grows 50% heavier and from 7–20% in length. His shell can be pierced by a fingernail at this time and he has to watch out for predator lobsters and cod, so he stays holed up, denuded and vulnerable, for the several weeks that it takes his jellylike armor to calcify. Furthermore, *Homarus* must go through all this about ten times in his first year and with decreasing frequency after that.

Unlike the soft-shelled crab (simply a blue-claw crab that has shed its shell), the shedded nude lobster is no love-food delicacy at all after he molts. Soft-shelled lobster is rubbery, watery and unpalatable, and it is probable that *Homarus* will die if handled during molting time. Honest lobstermen carefully return all soft-shelled lobsters to the sea, just as they throw back any berried females and all lobsters measuring under 33/16 inches or over 5 inches from the eye socket to the end of the carapace. These conservation measures, enforced in one way or another since 1824, still do not prevent the 35,000 or so U.S. and Canadian lobstermen from trapping about 90% of all legal-sized lobsters each year in their over four million fish-baited pots, which *Homarus* finds easy to enter but impossible to escape from. These lobster pots are shaped like little quonset huts. Made of oak slats and hoops with nylon netting for the "throats," they can cost as much as $18 apiece. Coated with tar to protect them against sea worms, they are baited with fish remains called "curry" and set about 180 feet apart on the bottom. Three bricks inside each weigh them down and bright orange markers indicate each string's location. It's hard work lowering them 400 to 600 feet deep and they are left set for about two weeks. Lobstermen say that their prey is very cagy, walking around the pots several days before deciding whether or not to enter. One would think that lobstermen would be a rich breed as a result of their highly specialized skills, but in Maine, for instance, their gross median income is only about $4,600 for their back-breaking labor, with very few indeed earning over $10,000 a year. Recent research may, however, improve this situation by increasing the lobster crop. A computer study made at the University of Rhode Island, for example, shows that laws protecting large lobsters ultimately *reduce* the total catch without increasing the lobster population. It seems that large males cannot mate with smaller females, but that these females tend to drive away prospective small mates when sexier large lobsters are around, apparently in accord with the universal law that all us sinners want what we cannot have. Other encouraging studies have shown that egg-bearing females can be transplanted to virgin areas to start new lobster communities. Transplanted colonies in British Columbia and other parts of the Pacific appear to be doing well and one in Russia has already succeeded.

Trouble with Russian lobstermen working the rich beds of the Continental Shelf has recently been causing a lot of gray hairs among already grizzled New England lobstermen, one company suffering losses of $300,000 last year. Russian trawlers rape the bottom in pursuing migrating schools of fish and destroy the many traps (up to 100 on a string) that lobstermen connect to buoys and markers on the surface. One writer claims that as the lobsterman moves out to deeper waters in search of his dwindling prey, the scene is being set "for a conflict as natural as that between the free-ranging cowboys and the farmers who attempted to fence off water holes and cattle trails in the early west."

Trawler competition, lobster's surge in popularity and the increasingly high cost of hand labor—so essential to the industry—has, in any event, driven prices sky high, the demand for lobster far exceeding the supply. From a record catch of 130 million pounds in 1885, the total has dropped to about 80 million pounds today, two of three live "Maine" lobsters, in fact, coming from Newfoundland or Canada. Canada also exports most of our canned lobster, and Conley's Lobster Company in St. Andrews-by-the-sea boasts the world's largest live lobster distributing plant, as well as the world's largest holding tanks for *Homarus*. The prospects are not so bright as with oysters, but there is hope in sight. Conservation laws, for example, have succeeded in bringing the catch up from an all-time low of 33 million pounds in 1918, and hatcheries or "farms" have learned to grow lobsters to eating size in one-fourth the time it normally takes.

"Lobster farming" is practiced in several countries today. In France, for instance, on the isle of Houat, lobstermen raise egg-carrying lobsters in a nursery that looks something like a greenhouse. "We watch over the eggs until they hatch," one Houat "farmer" explains. "When the baby lobsters are little-finger length we set them free near bricks that we have sunk just off the shore. The bricks have holes in them that we hope the little lobsters will hide in. Of course, they will still be hunted by other fish, but perhaps, given a better start, more of them will survive. In the twenties, something like this was tried both by the Americans and by the Japanese. They didn't try to control the experiment, though. They just hatched the eggs and threw the little lobsters into the sea, where they all disappeared into a million mouths. We have our bricks that we make specially, and we have divers who will go down from time to time to check things out and make sure that everything is going well."

In America a different kind of lobster farming has been pioneered by researchers at the Massachusetts Lobster Hatchery in Vineyard Haven, where *Homarus* is raised in warm water (72 to 75°F) the year round. This results in edible one-pound, two-year-old lobsters, rather than the one-pound, seven or eight-year-olds we customarily eat. By keeping the lobsters warm all year, the various chemical reactions that are part of the metabolism of cold-blooded animals proceed more swiftly and *Homarus* grows much more quickly. Authorities say that if lobster farming becomes a reality on a large scale, it will greatly reduce the pressures on heavily fished grounds, where lobster populations are dwindling, and prices will consequently go down. Just as helpful, however, would be federally controlled conservation laws, such as antipollution measures, an increase in legal lobster size to 3½ inches and "self-destruct" lobster pots that when lost would deteriorate after a period of time, enabling trapped lobsters to go free instead of dying for no purpose at all. Meanwhile, short-sighted lobstermen, opposed to most such measures, are getting their $1.50 to $2.50 a pound this year, depending on the season. This compares to upwards of $1 a year ago and the consumer is paying about $4 retail for that same one-pounder, while restaurants charge about $7 for a lobster dinner. It's not unusual to shell out $15 for a two-pounder in a good seafood restaurant and the price of anything over that size is prohibitive. Furthermore, unless conservation measures and commercial hatcheries succeed, the situation will likely become even bleaker, for the lobsterman as well as the consumer. "Lobsters hibernate longer and grow more slowly when water temperatures go below the optimum level, and a period of sunspot inactivity has recently depressed water temperatures below that point," says Robert L. Dow, director of marine research for the Maine Department of Sea and Shore Fisheries. "Unless there is some unforeseen change, the meteorologists tell us the trend will continue until the mid-1970s or 1980." A Canadian biologist adds that by 1980 there will be a demand for some 20 million more pounds of lobster than can be landed, and many dealers feel that the dockside price per pound will rise to $4.50 or more long before then.

If one can afford the prices, though, lobsters of all sizes and weights are readily available in the United States. In fact, one now defunct New York restaurant, The Lobster, even offered its customers a choice between males and females, commissioning a designer to create "crustacean corsets for girl lobsters" so that diners could tell the difference. The largest lobster ever landed anywhere appears to be a forty-seven pounder caught off the Virginia Capes in 1935, but the official record is held by a forty-two-pound, seven-ounce monster whose mounted shell is on display at the Boston Museum of Science along with a standing offer of a $100 reward to any fisherman who can improve upon the catch. The Boston giant, caught off Massachusetts in 1934, was three feet long and about fifty years old, but there have probably been bigger ones taken. An article in an old issue of the *Maine Fisherman*, for example, reveals that downeasters once netted lobsters as heavy as fifty pounds but had trouble marketing such tremendous specimens. Some dealers have told us of huge specimens weighing over 100 pounds, and recent discoveries of large lobster colonies 100 miles off the New England coast, which U.S. lobstermen are now working, may even result in still greater, barnacle-encrusted specimens, but most gourmets will tell you that two small chicken lobsters are better than one large lobster anyway. An experienced Brooklyn lobsterman, Charlie Morreale, who operates the *Cowhide Charlie* out of Sheepshead Bay, agrees that large lobster meat can be tough. "Some lobsters can run as high as 80 pounds, real big," he adds, "but they're too big—you wouldn't want to hand an 80-pound lobster to a customer, would you? We get a 20-pounder now and then, although it's even hard for a 20-pounder to get into a trap."

It is, in fact, a traditional rule of thumb that the smaller the lobster, the better the taste, provided *Homarus* is selected wisely in the first place. Lobsters must be purchased alive and active, preferably packed on ice in a fish store, for weighed right out of a tank they contain up to three ounces of pure water each, this useless weight coming high at today's prices. Similarly, *Homarus* should be inspected live before being ordered in a restaurant, but if this isn't practical it's still possible to determine a cooked lobster's freshness. A fresh, cooked lobster is always bright red in color, has a tangy seashore odor, and its curled tail will spring back quickly after being straightened out. The tail, incidentally, is one way the sex of a lobster can be determined, females having broader tails than males, which isn't always the case among their purchasers. Care should also be taken when buying supermarket lobsters, which are often culls not worth the bargain price paid for them. Again, the test is that any uncooked lobster whose tail hangs limp, or whose legs aren't moving, is either dead or dying. Nor should one try to keep *Homarus* alive in a mixture of salt and water; store him in a cold part of the refrigerator for no more than several hours at the longest. Finally, the buyer should never accept South African lobster tail meat as lobster meat—as noted, it is simply not the same thing. Neither is the "Shlobster," nature's newest seafood–public relations product, which is in reality a giant shrimp dredged in Gulf waters off Alabama and Mississippi and is said to have the color and taste of a lobster.

King crabs and other varieties are also often passed off as lobster meat by unscrupulous restaurants, especially in Chinese dishes. But then the common crab, which Middleton calls "a promoter of lust," should be given some consideration as a love food in itself. After shrimp, it is our most popular shellfish. Alaska's gigantic king crab *(Paralithodes cam-tschatica)* has a flavor a little like lobster and the symbolic claws of the huge crustacean, which averages ten pounds in weight, have become the forty-ninth state's second most important fish product. Dungeness crabs, Jonah crabs, rock crabs, red crabs, green crabs, lady crabs, buster crabs from Mexico and Kona crabs from Hawaii are just a few of the species Americans enjoy in stimulating gumbos from the Louisiana bayous, in numerous soups and stuffings and in spicy crab cakes. The claws of many crabs, particularly the stone crab of Florida, are so delicious that fishermen often remove them and return the crabs to the water to grow more for next year. The classic favorite here, though, is the blue or hard crab of the East Coast. Blue claws go through most of the arduous life processes and hardships of the lobster, but the odds against a crab larva reaching maturity are one million to five or five times better than the lobster's.

The same rules apply for buying blue claws or lobsters, but eating them whole is much messier. For a love feast, it is suggested that the crabs be cooked and the meat picked out in advance before being prepared in any of a number of tempting recipes. Maryland is *the* place to dine out on blue claws and soft-shelled crabs (molted blue claws) today. H.L. Mencken claimed that there are more than fifty ways to prepare the crab meat of his native state and Maryland still holds an annual three-day Hard Crab Derby in late August at Crisfield, where a beauty pageant "Miss Crustacean" is chosen and many memorable recipes can be sampled. The best blue crab dish we've ever tasted is the snow-white lump crab meat served on toast points over all of which about half a pound of melted butter is poured (this is a specialty of Baltimore's Chesapeake House). As good as backfin, a luxury ($4.50 a pound) taken from the part of the crab next to the back flipper, this dish is almost as delicious and effective a love food as lobster. But not quite. Lobster still has more of an aura to its name, and lovers of both sexes are immensely more impressed by its price and reputation.

Should anyone want to impress his/her lover *before* eating lobster, as well as after downing this renowned aphrodisiac food, it's easy to learn how to "hypnotize" *Homarus* prior to cooking him. Senator Edmund Muskie of Maine once demonstrated this old trick on Dinah Shore's national T.V. show, but probably the champion *Homarus* hypnotizer is headwaiter Frank Hashorva from Downingtown, Pennsylvania. Hashorva, who "hypnotizes," or puts his lobsters to sleep by rubbing their backs where they're hardest, has even worked out an act where a lobster stands on its head, takes his business card in its claw and presents it to someone, as well as routines where the lobster waves two miniature Japanese umbrellas or does back flips into his hands. "Putting a lobster to sleep isn't too difficult," says the crustacean trainer, "but making one perform takes skill and timing. And one misstep can be dangerous. I usually show this by having a lobster grind a pen in half with its claw." Hashorva admits that his costars invariably wind up cooked each evening, but he swears he's never eaten one of them—he'd feel like a cannibal, he says.

Lobster can be eaten numerous ways, hot and cold, but it is generally agreed that *Homarus* tastes best when steamed and dipped in a butter sauce. The boiling of *Homarus* is the subject of much controversy, as Buchwald's apocryphal Society for the Prevention of Cruelty to Lobsters indicates. Though Canadian biologists have reported that the lobster feels no pain when dropped into boiling water, not having the requisite nervous equipment, the very real Massachusetts Society for the Prevention of Cruelty to Animals suggests that a lobster be "anesthetized" (so that he can be boiled without "visible signs of discomfort") by first soaking him in a mixture of two quarts of cold water and one pound of salt. Likewise, a kindly New Jersey marine biologist, after calculating that *Homarus* suffers for at least a minute before expiring in boiling water, devised a method whereby he places his lobsters in cold water, which he brings slowly to a boil. According to one report, "When the water reached a temperature of 70°C, the subjects gradually swooned and fell on their sides and at 80°C could be safely pronounced dead," the lobsters all the while "quite passive," and "showing no rebelliousness, nor making any attempt to escape."

Gordon Gunter of the Gulf Coast Research Laboratory has also suggested several ways of easing the lobster's lot for those squeamish about their violent reactions when plunged into boiling water. Gunter recommends placing the crustaceans in a pot of cool fresh water and applying a low flame that will slowly but steadily raise the temperature to 104°F. At this point, the water feels only lukewarm to the hand, but the combination of fresh water, which has some anesthetizing effect by leaching salt from the body fluids, and the temperature increase, by now above the tolerable level, will cause the lobster "to die easily." He also suggests that a small wire lattice be placed in the pot so that the animals on the bottom don't come in contact with the heated metal. As soon as the lobsters are dead, the heat can be turned up and the water boiled quickly.

Yet no matter how humane one tries to be, it remains a fact that *Homarus* is impossible to eat without first cooking him alive or guillotining him with a sharp knife. Regardless of the method used, the plugs or bands on his claws should not be removed until after he's expired—or there will likely be a war on the kitchen floor in the course of which *he* won't be humane to any part of your anatomy. To steam your lobster it is best to use an inch of seawater supplemented by a heaping teaspoon of salt (and by a half a cup of sherry to enhance the flavor if desired). When the steam builds up to a head, add the live lobsters, cooking smaller ones about fifteen minutes and larger specimens twenty to thirty minutes. As for boiling, which will definitely boil out some of a lobster's flavor, by the way, plunge *Homarus* headlong into percolating salted water or seawater and let a one and a half pounder simmer for about ten minutes. (Most swear by exactly five minutes for the first pound and one minute for each quarter pound thereafter, a little too raw for us.) Immediately after cooking, immerse the now bright-red lobster in cold water, and let drain; this will seal in the flavor and make for easier handling. Work at opening *Homarus* over a large bowl in the kitchen sink in order to catch some of the juice, which makes a delicious bisque when combined with milk, butter and seasonings.

Preparing a cooked lobster for the plate is not as complicated as it seems, either. The easiest way is to place *Homarus* on his back and with a sharp knife cut his undershell in half lengthwise. Remove the stomach, which is just back of the head, and the intestinal vein, which runs from the stomach to the tip of the tail and resembles a line of black thread. Do not discard the green tomalley (or liver) or the coral roe; they are both delicious and have often been used for hors d'oeuvres in the love cookery. The black dung in the intestine, incidentally, indicates the freshness of a lobster, showing that he has not emptied the bowel, which he will do if kept in a tank for just a few days. Eating a lobster is also a routine operation, once one gets the hang of it. Use a lobster cracker, nutcracker or hammer to break but not crush the shell of the big claws, and simply pull off the walking legs and knucklelike joints and joyously suck out the sweet morsels of meat. To remove the meat from the tail, use a small lobster or cocktail fork, which will also serve, as will a nut picker, to unloose any hidden tidbits elsewhere in the shell. The cookbook *Domestic Management* (1800) instructed the housewife never to let her servingman crack the claws of a lobster "between the hinges of a dining room door, but take it into the kitchen." That rule probably still holds true today, but the only other rule obligatory in eating *Homarus* is to never be ashamed to use your fingers.

There are literally hundreds of easily obtainable recipes for lobster. These include lobster with champagne, lobster tarts, the mayonnaise of embellished lobsters that Monselt invented and various Chinese dishes, including Chow Lung Hai (Chinese garlic lobster) and the tasty spicy Szechwan dishes to be had at restaurants like New York's four-star Shun Lee Dynasty. American recipes even include the deceptively entitled "Maine Lobster Cake," but this is merely a marble cake, so named for no known reason.

The ubiquitous Maine Lobster, considered the best of the cold-water breed, is too often broiled and dried out in sections inland. Downeasters themselves generally prefer to steam or boil it for the best effects. Yet they, too, often broil, fry, bake, stuff and hash *Homarus*, using the lobster in stews, "glops" and outdoor bakes, preparing it over a charcoal grill, steaming it in seaweed and even going so far as to cook it on a ship engine's exhaust pipe. William C. Roux's *What's Cooking Down In Maine*

(The Bond Wheelwright Co., Freeport, Maine) is a fine little cookbook on the subject recommended to all. "Even without dissertations or poems of praise," the author believes, "it is certain that the Maine lobster can stand on his own claws, his reputation sure, his place high in the culinary world. For no matter how you prepare or serve him, he is always a gustatory marvel and a joy forever."

But then the same can be said for largely unfamiliar foreign lobster dishes conducive to amour. Though its name belies the fact, *Lobster à l'Américaine* is one such European delicacy that probably originated in France. *Homard à l'Américaine*, as it's more properly called, is raw lobster meat sautéed in oil and served with a rich tomato and white wine sauce. It may have been invented by the chef M. Reculet at Noel Peter's restaurant during the seige of Paris, where the proprietor named it in honor of some customer from across the Atlantic. A second explanation holds that the provocative dish originated in Brittany's Armorique, and that its present name is simply a misspelling of *Homard à l'Armoriquaine*. On the the other hand, Escoffier believed it had been exported to America by a Nice chef as *Langouste de la Méditerranée*, where lobster was substituted for the clawless crawfish in the recipe and it went back to France as *Homard à l'Armoriquaine*. Regardless of its origin, it's a lobster libido-loosener that is served too little in the country whose name it bears.

The creamy restorative Lobster Thermidor is another highly regarded *Homarus* recipe whose origins are debatable. Some authorities say Thermidor may have been invented for Napoleon, or "devised originally by some French cook displaced by the Revolution to an English kitchen." Others contend that this classic fare was named for Victorian Sardou's play *Thermidor* and first served to the public on the evening of January 24, 1894 at the one-famous *Chez Maire* restaurant. According to this account, the controversial French drama closed after one performance, but the toothsome dish remained a long-running hit. In point of fact, there are British stuffed lobster recipes like Dr. Alexander Hunter's "Lobster Dressed in the Shell" (see Ester B. Aresty's *The Delectable Past*) that date back as early as 1804. Dr. Hunter's cookbook, which included this enticing "receipt," was aptly subtitled: "Cookery worthy of the notice of those medical practioners who ride in their chariots with a footman behind, and who receive two-guinea fees from their rich and luxurious patients."

Lobster à la Portos, valued by lovers for its champagne, and *Lobster Amandine*, whose praises are sung for its almonds, are but two more foreign contributions to the lobster love cookery, as is the gratin of tails of crayfish served in a magnificent sauce at Madame Point's Restaurant de la Pyramide in Vienne—if one can stomach the prices there. Neither should Lobster Fra Diablo and other Italian and Spanish recipes be ignored. Yet America herself has classic lobster fare that rivals anyone's. When your pocketbook can stand it, take a tip from us and try Baked Lobster Savannah at Boston's venerable Locke-Obers, for example—it costs $16 and is comprised of lobster meat amalgamated with Lobster Newburg sauce, green peppers, mushrooms and pimentos, which is all shell-baked with Parmesan cheese.

Lobster Newburg itself is more economically priced and remains probably the most popular of all lobster love recipes. The creation has an interesting history. This delectable invention should have blazoned the name of Charles Wenberg, a late-nineteenth century shipping magnate, across the pages of menus everywhere. But he was foolish enough to displease the great restaurateur Lorenzo Delmonico. Wenberg had discovered the dish in South America and on his return described it glowingly to Delmonico. Lorenzo soon instructed his chef to prepare the shelled lobster in its rich sauce of sherry, thick cream and egg yolks, serving the dish "with aplomb and all the trimmings" to his wealthy patron and naming it Lobster Wenberg in his honor. So it remained on Delmonico's menu for almost a month, until Wenberg, well in his cups, got into a drunken brawl in the estimable restaurant's main dining room and had to be bodily ejected. The very next day the dish appeared on an enraged Lorenzo's menu as Lobster Newburg, perhaps in honor of the city on the Hudson, which name it retains to this day.

Lobster Newburg, of course remains a princely dish by any name, but all the gourmet chefs in the world can't improve on the basic flavor or Priapian powers of lobster plain. One may secretly yearn to dine in the secret rooms of Laperouse in Paris visited a few pages back. There lovers can share *langoustines* in cognac and cream, or enjoy a classic dish like *Homard en Bellevue à la Parisienne*. Yet steamed lobster at home is just as effective, and far more convenient. Local lobster suppliers near the docks should be tried first in areas near the sea, but thanks to modern air express service excellent fresh lobsters can be obtained at fish markets deep inland. In fact, Edward Meyers, who started Maine's Saltwater Farm (York Harbor, Maine 03911) as a young Princeton graduate, guarantees live delivery by jet up to 1800 miles away should there be no lobsters living where you live and love. Saltwater Farm's lobsters, a relative of whom (long since eaten) once sliced a ribbon that opened a new bridge in Maine, are featured in complete rockweed Downeast clambakes ready to cook and serve from a disposable lobster steamer.

Using such fresh lobster specimens, erotic dishes can be prepared that are second to none in the aphrodisiac cookery. As Rabelais punned, anyone who plunges into *Homarus*, will almost certainly "plunge *in media res.*" Who doesn't remember that scene in *Tom Jones* in which the love-famished Mrs. Waters and Tom voluptuously sucked at lobster claws and lapped up raw oysters (a perfect combination in more ways than one), voraciously working themselves into a sexual frenzy that necessitated a mad dash for the bedchamber. Fielding didn't write about it, but the morning after, Tom and Mrs. Waters might have been found praising the powers of the sensuous shellfish, a phallic-clawed creature whose flavorsome potency can't be questioned by the palate nor parts below—a failproof provocative that may act absurd and look ridiculous, but does things for the libido sublime.

COURSE SEVEN

Stalking For Stimulants:
Being A Salmagundi
Or Kookbook Of Strange Dinners
For Strong-Stomached Sensualists

Although seafood as a group has generally been eulogized as the safest
and most foolproof of aphrodisiac foods, love hunters have by no means
forsaken stalking for stimulants—if only to be able to converse about the
legendary powerful effects of wild things from the jungle. Sex and the
hunt have always been intimately related. Wild game and other jungle
fare has been reputed through the ages to endow lovers with the strength
to dispense their charms with glorious profligacy and insensate fury. Ar-
temis, the Greek goddess of wildlife, was also a fertility goddess, and it is
interesting to note that our word venery, for indulgence of sexual desire,
or coition, derives from the French *venerie*, referring to the art of hunting.

More important, most wild animal meats are what nutritionists call analeptic, or strength-giving, particularly dark-fleshed ones, Petronius referring to this when he wrote, "To encourage my jaded body...I applied to myself strong meats...so great was my care to acquit myself honorably with my mistress."

An analeptic diet, according to John Davenport, "best promotes the secretion of seminal fluid." The eminent Victorian goes on to tell us, drawing from Brillat-Savarin and many other writers, "that those meats in which 'azezome' is found are the most nutritious." Azezome is the organic ingredient in animal fiber imparting the red and brown appearance to uncooked and cooked meats, and "constituting the much admired taste of game and venison." Wild game is particularly worthy in an amorous analeptic diet and the lover who adopts same, Davenport declares, "becomes consequently very well fitted to make the sacrifices exacted by the calls of love, to which he (or she) is then more frequently solicited." Along these same lines, the sagacious Shaykh Nefzawi included strong meats in his sexual regimen. His *Perfumed Garden* instructs that "if a man will passionately give himself up to the enjoyment of coition, without undergoing great fatigue, he must live upon strengthening foods...the quality of the sperm depends directly on the food you take."

Besides being rich in both azezome and protein, wild animals claim the advantage of having a longer-standing aphrodisiac reputation than their domesticated cousins. Our primitive progenitors ate the sexual parts of numerous species to absorb their prowess or prolificacy in lovemaking, and valued all parts of wild beasts from head to hoof, particularly the liver, which was widely believed by the ancients to be the seat of sexual desire. Many communal rites developed from these beliefs, knots of fact and fantasy that medical science still hasn't satisfactorily unraveled. Paola Mantegazza observes in his *Sexual Relations of Mankind* that the ancient Prussians brought roast testicles of mountain goat, bull or bear to the bridal bed so that the wife "might be fertile and give birth to many children," and that "with the same object in view, they refrained from serving at the nuptial table, the flesh of any castrated animals." The old Chinese names for various sexual positions illustrate this same principle, clearly showing that they had observed the wild beasts in action and desired to emulate them, wildly exaggerating their sexual skills. *The White Tiger Leaps, The Tiger Climbs The Mountain, The Crooning Monkey Embraces The Tree, The Dogs In Autumn, The Mustang Hops* and even *The Unicorn Shows Its Horn*, were all favorite Chinese techniques. The Unicorn, of course, is a legendary creature, but the one-horned unicorn of old is believed by some to have been the two-horned black bull (white or red stripe down its back) called the Great Ox or auroch, which once roamed the forests of Europe. Although the last aurochs are supposed to have died in captivity in 1627, there has been at least one newspaper ad soliciting hunters to track down the "almost extinct" aphrodisiac animals in the Caucasus mountains. The unicorn was the medieval alchemist's symbol of health and resurrection, but the only way to catch one was to somehow get it to "lay its head in a virgin's lap." These superstitions weren't strange for the times, though—the medieval Chinese, for example, believed that jade was the congealed sperm of dragons.

Such beliefs persist to this day. African hunters, for instance, still eat the raw organs of lions to assure a bridegroom's virility on his wedding night, and among the African Suk the lion's heart is held to give sexual strength to a lover. Recent interest in the lion as the King of Amorous Animals can be seen in the newspaper coverage given mangy and decrepit "Fraser, The Lion Who Could," an old rake who died in 1972, but who in his last sixteen months (at the equivalent in years to a human of 100) served a pride of eleven sensuous lionesses and sired thirty-three cubs, leaving one of his wives expecting. Not really the magnificent beasts that "Born Free" books make them, lions are worse scavengers than hyenas and will eat their young if hungry enough. But they were worshiped as symbols of virility in many ancient lands. At the temple of Amun Ra in Egypt, among other places, priests were employed solely to bathe tame lions in perfumed water and soothe them with incense and sacred music.

The more ferocious or dangerous the beast, the more it has been valued in the love cookery, and not only by primitive peoples. *Animelles*, the sexual organs of wild animals, are famous in French cooking and were specially used to create the successful *Garniture financiere* that reinvigorated financier John Law, the legendary Scotsman who fled a murder charge in England to become France's Minister of Finance and creator of her first system of paper currency. In turn of the century America potent "jungle dinners" became a craze among sophisticates. (At one such dinner given in a cage by an amateur lion tamer, four mature lions roamed about at will and a few of the less courageous diners were occasionally seen to leap two or three feet high in the air when nuzzled on the ankles.) Similarly, Norman Douglas advised in *Paneros* that tenderized tiger testicles "crushed and mingled with arack of rice are much extolled by certain Eastern races," and American folklore has it that the mattress springs will sing all night if we merely "Rub with wolf's grease the doorway through which the married couple pass on their way to the nuptial bed."

Penis of wolf was a standard ingredient of Roman love tonics, and the reputation of the wolf is evident in our modern use of the word for a cunning male Casanova. But at least one old love recipe recommends employing the creature's private parts as a charm to make a woman *faithful*. No less an old-world scholar than Albertus Magnus instructs in the *Book of the Marvels of the World* that: "If thou wilt have a woman bee not visious nor desire men, take the private members of a Woolfe, and the haires which doe grow on the cheekes or eyebrows of him, and the haires which lie under his beard and burne it all, and give it to her to drinke, when she knoweth not, and she shal desire no other man." Magnus doesn't explain how to slip the fair damsel said potion "when she knoweth not," or consider that she might choke to death on the "haires" and never desire anything again. Yet his ideas were in keeping with the times. *The Perfumed Garden*, for example, gives a recipe for rubbing the virile member with "gall from a jackel," which would "stimulate the sexual parts and increase their vigor." Another quaint teacher of yore instructed suitors to send the udder of a hyena to their prospective lovers in gift-wrapped boxes or wear said hyena udder around the wrist as a kind of magic amulet, lest they flunk his course in sex education. Hyenas couldn't have laughed much about such a state of affairs—especially about Pliny's prescription recommending hyena's eyes—but they were no worse off than many animals.

Pliny, for instance, also most specifically noted that the *right testicle* of a crocodile, or crocodile teeth worn as a bracelet on the *right arm* were conducive to love. Crocodile sperm was once regarded as another effective love medication. Grimoire's medieval *Black Book* prescribed "foure droppes of crocodile semen" in a mixture consisting of burdock seeds and a goat's *left testicle*, among other ingredients. This last preparation—and Grimoire didn't tell where a knight could purchase the crocodile semen—took about "twenty-one dayes" in the making before ye could "Rubbe said mixture on ye genitalia and await ye results." Crocodile, usually salted, is still eaten in some parts of the world, but its look-alike the alligator has a better culinary reputation. Alligator tail, once a feast food among the Mayans, is said to be indistinguishable in taste from pork. Others suggest that the musky-tasting *feet* of the American Cayman species are the part to eat and a dish called *Alligator 'a l'Indienne* remains on the menus of a few Parisian restaurants to this day.

Among the reptiles, edible species of the phallic snake have a better reputation than alligator. The early Egyptians favored serpents, and French physicians in the reign of Henri II advised their patients to partake of *anguilles des bois* (snakes and adders) at least once a week each spring. One writer tells us that the widely traveled and well-versed Robert Ripley of *Believe It Or Not* fame "attributed his renowned virility largely to a diet that regularly included such delicacies as rattlesnake ragoût."

Pies of minced snake were quite popular in Paris at *La Tour d'Argent* (the first public restaurant in the West) which opened in 1533, and in China (where there were public eating places long before that date) cooks made and still make delicious entrees from common garden variety snakes. The Arabs continue to powder lizard and drink it with sweet wine, and South Americans enjoy their traditional chickenlike iguana lizard. Today in Malaya rattlesnake *blood* is considered most-potent fare. Among Malaysian Chinese in Kuala Lumpur, says a recent news item, it is customary for a woman to catch a rattlesnake for her husband if and when he needs rejuvenation. While the rattler is still alive she must make a tiny opening in its tail, and hold the wriggly reptile down while her mate sucks its blood neat from the aperture. More and more western visitors to Hong Kong are sampling such sensuous snake dishes, and dealers were at last report exporting about $350,000 of the reptiles annually from the mainland. The best time to eat snake is recorded in the old Cantonese proverb "When the cold winds come, the snakes are fat"—snakes beginning to store up tissue for hibernation in autumn. The gall is the most favored and expensive part of the reptile and is commonly popped into a glass of wine and swallowed in one gulp as a cure for almost everything from impotency to piles. Tourists usually enjoy it in a thick soup or in a dish of wok-fried shark's fin and snake meat. This last after all, is not unknown here in America, where rattlesnake sausages were served at the 1973 Texas World's Fair. Fried rattlesnake is often eaten in the western United States. Skinned and gently sauteed in butter it is a dish fit for Priapus. Each year, on the second weekend in March, the Sweetwater Rattlesnake Roundup is held in Sweetwater, Texas, thousands of rattlers captured by hundreds of specially insured amateur hunters wearing double-thick boots and operating metal snake hooks. After being milked of venom, the snakes are skinned and the meat is sold for $2.50 per pound or deep-fried in buttermilk batter and cracker meal for 50 cents per piece.

Not everybody hankers for such "boa meets girl" recipes, but as Mark Twain observed "Tastes are made, not born," there is probably no *instinctive* aversion to any food. Really big game, from patently phallic snakes and giraffe necks to the "purse-size elephant's ballocks" cited by Rabelais, has been hunted down by the love hunter since time immemorial. The Romans cheered themselves hoarse at the Colosseum, where as many as 11,000 wild animals from giraffes to crocodiles, were slaughtered in an afternoon, and then ate the beasts during their evening orgies. In France, Napoleon once partook of a wild game dinner that featured gazelle, loin of wild boar, antelope cutlets, porcupine and roast ostrich with pomegranate jelly. For that matter, from the days of Louis

XIV to the present Frenchmen have patronized Corcellet's famous delicatessen near the Paris opera, where the rage this year is big game dishes made from animals culled from African herds to conserve vegetation. Particularly popular are giraffe neck, alligator tail, camel's hump, elephant's trunk vinaigrette and roast hippo (despite the fact that the diner must wait sixteen hours for his elephant trunk to cook and ten hours for his toothsome hippo hip). "We get the carcass in manageable pieces," owner Paul Corcellet says of the hippopotamus steaks. "It's mainly the legs which provide the best meat, of course...we prepare them in a sherry sauce." Furthermore, the problem is not that these recipes are too far out for French lovers. Not at all. "The problem," Corcellet says sadly, "is that this stuff is all deep frozen and French people are just not keen on frozen food." They apparently prefer fresh dishes like python, which one French retailer says "tastes just like hippo" (not that that comparison helps much).

The French have a long tradition of eating beasts from the jungle. Alexander Dumas, great lover that he was, gave numerous recipes for dishes like elephant feet and filets of kangaroo in his *Grand Dictionaire de la Cuisine*. During the seige of Paris, which lasted 135 days in 1870–1871, jungle animals were killed and served on a wide scale for the first time in France. A butcher named De Bros bought the two famous elephants Castor and Pollux from the *Jardin d'Acclimation* for 27,000 francs. Slaughtering them, he sold the morsels at a great profit. The zoo, like the ornamental ponds at Tuileries, sold every one of its animals—yaks, zebras, buffalos—and all were eaten. This resulted in dishes like *Crépinettes de Gros Giber* (Big Game Sausages), *Daube de Serpent* (Daube of Python), *Civet de Lion, Bear à la sauce Toussenel* and *Escalope d'éléphant with shallots sauce*. The recipe for Big Game Sausages begins: "Take 40 pounds of hippopotamus, rhinocerous, wild bear, wart hog, or aardvark meat...." *Daube de Python* instructs: "Cut four pounds of filet from a young python...." "Singe and clean a young lion" begins the *Civet de Lion* recipe. Everything but "First catch your unicorn...."

The delicacy department of any food store and a number of restaurants will reveal that epicurean American lovers don't disdain such undomesticated dishes, either. No longer are globe-trotting "gastronomades" the principle consumers of such exotic goodies; there's no want of love foods on earth for Sir Epicure Mammons and surfeit likely slays more sensualists than hunger. One New York eatery serves stuffed rattlesnake, roast muskrat and those fried ants and stuffed beetles coming up, while Chicago's Cafe Bohemia offers elk or buffalo stew, as well as strips of lion, tiger or elephant meat on its bill of fare. Strips of elephant meat are supposed to be especially tasty. Called "biltong" they are very popular in

South Africa, where the meat is dried after elephants are culled from the huge herds in Kruger National Park and sold to butchers. The meat of "an elephant facing due east" when shot is particularly valued in the love cookery there.

Anyone wanting to do some exotic aphrodisiac cooking at home will also find ample opportunity. Similar "gourmet" foods are at least a $2 billion business annually in America, the volume having more than doubled in the past six years. Over 15,000 products are available. Even conservative firms like Lever Brothers and the A&P are getting into the act. Safeway Stores, the country's second largest food chain, has opened a Washington branch, Safeway International, which offers about 4700 far-out gourmet delights, including elephant meat, kangaroo steak ($3.50 a can), frozen rattlesnake meat ($4 a pound) and tiger meat ($2.79 a can). Such foods are aimed at the affluent among us, as well as various ethnic groups, and industry spokesmen predict that next year's sales will exceed all previous records. People are so obsessed with wild beasts, in fact, that Brigitte Bardot's sister Mijanou has a profitable business making pillows shaped like snakes, octopuses and other creatures, her latest being a six-foot long crocodile sleeping bag one can crawl into—Brigitte doesn't come with it.

Throughout the world man's predilection for potent big game has driven many species to the shores of the Dead Sea of extinction. Today at least three species of rhino are becoming extinct because the Chinese value their powdered horn *(hsi chio)* as an aphrodisiac—a large horn brings $1000 in what is definitely a seller's market. Chinese males apparently want to look like the rhino up front and are not unaware of his prodigous size at the opposite lower end, but Chinese women also believe that rhino horn works wonders for them. The brilliant sixteenth century woman poet Huang O wrote of this in her poem "Soaring Clouds". She and her lover shared out one piece of "magic rhino horn," and "the whole night long ... the bee clung trembling to the flower stamen."

American chemists claim that rhino horn powder contains no magic substance that could be classed as an aphrodisiac and Britain's Prince Philip, Queen Elizabeth's consort, once denounced it as "useless," telling an audience of eastern diplomats and ambassadors that the belief that rhino horn is a potent aphrodisiac "is complete poppycock—a laughable travesty of the truth." This, however, did little to change the tactics of the millions in the Far East and Africa who believe "the magic powder" to be the most powerful sex stimulant known to man. In some places powdered rhino horn is literally worth its weight in gold, and in London alone a million dollars worth of the substance, mostly from South Africa, is auctioned off each year. Two-hundred rhinos must die to produce that much powder, but protection measures have only succeeded in forcing the price still higher. They have also prompted some strange poaching cases. Recently, for example, thieves broke into a natural history museum in Jakarta, Indonesia and sawed the horns off seven stuffed rhino heads.

Just a year or so ago, the great Indian one-horned rhinocerous had to be protected in a special sanctuary in the Assam Forests because poachers were killing the bad-tempered three-ton beast for its fifteen-inch horn, which they ground up into powder and smuggled to overseas Chinese colonies or into China itself. Unfortunately, the sanctuary hasn't succeeded and aphro hunters still abound, though their quarry is so scarce that they often palm off powdered pig or boar tusks as the real thing. Similarly, the hippo (its snout and foot were also recommended by Pliny) may become an endangered species, especially now that hippo milk is being touted as the newest potion to rouse the passions. Laws and science have a hard time changing tradition. Though scientists insist that the magical powder made from rhino horn is no different from gelatin extracted from the bones of animals and that hippo milk is no more effective than Elsie's, poachers still continue to risk their lives and the ecology to bring back a prodigious rhino horn or milk a pregnant hippopotamus.

Smaller wild game like monkey also has its strong supporters among love hunters. Roast monkey stuffed with peanuts is a great Nigerian favorite. Monkey *lips* are especially esteemed in India, and the Indian sex manual the *Kama Sutra* recommends one of the most unappetizing recipes to be found among love potions, suggesting that various ingredients be mixed with "monkey excrement" and thrown in the face of the desired one, who will immediately "succumb"—to what it does not specify. In Paris nowadays frozen marinated monkey cutlets are served at Corcellet's, and many people still value monkey testicles. These last recall the "monkey gland era" in organotherapy at the close of the nineteenth century, when the testes of apes and monkeys were transplanted under the abdominal walls of humans in the false belief that they contained large amounts of male sex hormones that would restore the recipient to a vigorous sexual life.

Lovers intent on monkeying around would do just as well with the kangaroo tail soup that many Australians relish, not to mention those kangaroo testicles that Australian aborigines swear by (with the thought in mind that they'll really make one hop around in bed). For that matter, our only American marsupial, the opposum, is eagerly eaten by some— baked it tastes like suckling pig. Native remedies also include the beaver testicles American Indians once favored—which work on the assumption that they'll make you as busy as a beaver in the boudoir. Panther penis from the American wild west is an easy prescription to understand, but we are hard pressed to explain why penis of hedgehog gave *brio* to the Romans of old. Neither can we offer any reasonable explanation for armadillo, roast Indian bat or guinea pig, which poor creature has been tested for about everything. Yet eating is believing and one man's poison is another's love meat, be it the sloth South Americans prefer, the puma enjoyed in Central America, the parrots eaten in Mexico, the "Bow-Wow Stew" listed on one early San Francisco menu along with "stews ratified" or the ants and flies eaten throughout the world.

Ants and flies can't easily be explained as love food of even the most decadent voluptuaries, but they certainly are valued as such in various parts. Woodchoppers in Kansas, it's said, sometimes uncover large quantities of white ants under rotten logs, and scooping the insects up by the handful, they serve them in stimulating sandwiches buttered or garnished with mustard. Ants are also considered a tasty treat in South America. The Jivaros swallow them raw or stew them, and Mexican Indians crush them up for a potent mead. They are now available, chocolate covered, in U.S. gourmet shops, and certain African natives dote on a pie made from banana flour, sweet white ants and bees, which they say tastes like honey nougat.

To our knowledge, no one is yet marketing aphrodisiac insect crackers in place of the traditional animal ones, though this might not be a bad idea, for bugs have a long history as aphrodisiacs in the form of salves, foods and medicines. Insects are recommended in the *Kama Sutra* for external use, it being suggested therein that if "a man wishes to enlarge his lingam (penis), he should rub it with the bristles of certain insects that live in trees, and then after rubbing it for two nights with oils, he should again rub it with bristles as before." Well, to each his own lingam, and insect bristles aren't the worst remedy we've seen in books of old. Even the black widow spider—who works up an appetite during mating and usually eats her partner (sometimes she lets him live in her web for a few days until he dies)—has been recommended for women, as have a staggering variety of what we'd consider vile victuals. About the only bug we can't find sworn by in the love cookery is silverfish, though some constant reader will surely send in a time-tested recipe for same. Flies haven't yet premiered in America, but natives near Lake Nayassa in South East Africa press them into what they consider delectable "Kunga cakes" large as a human head, while a native tribe of the Amazon is a bit more discerning, pulling off wings, legs and heads before eating their buzzing flies. The list of such comestibles is endless—man will eat anything to nourish or stimulate himself or his lover, including honey-coated bumblebees (available at your friendly neighborhood gourmet store), chameleons, stuffed South American beetles, breaded palolo worms, grubs, crickets (cages of which are offered for sale in the Bangkok market), roast caterpillar, silkworm pupae, fried Mexican agave worms, fried grasshoppers (those relatives of the lobster), locusts (Mohammed's wives used to send him trays of them as presents), cicadas (a favorite of Aristotle's) and highly nutritious sun-dried termites (prized in Rhodesia at 7¢ spoonful), in addition to sundry TV dinners. Bedbugs, for instance, are not mentioned in any *Larousse Gastronique* of love, but cockroach is enjoyed in China, Thailand and French Guinea. A Mossi love formula, as unforgettable as it is fulsome, instructs us to mix well "one cockroach, one salamander and a piece of cotton that has dried a penis after intercourse" and "conceal it in a loved one's food." One Captain Laplace, an early traveler in China, even described a feast he attended there in which the main course consisted of "maggots of an immense size." His greatest difficulty was "to seize his prey floating in the various bowls of gravy," the chopsticks in his unaccustomed hands "always eluded by the delicious morsels he coveted."

Even the Biblical manna may have been an insect, or at least an insect by-product. It's well known that John the Baptist lived on Shakespeare's "lucious locusts" in the wilderness, but not so familiar is the theory, expounded in Dr. F. S. Bodenheimer's *Insects as Human Food*, that the granular sweet manna of the Israelites may well be the sweet secretions of certain aphids, which are indeed collected and savored in various parts of the world. Many insects are, in fact, high in calories and a dietary boon to numerous tribes. So far as we know only one Westerner has ever advocated using them similarly: the Englishman V. M. Holt published a little book in 1885 called *Why Not Eat Insects?* "The insects eat up every blessed green thing that do grow and us farmers starve," Holt reasoned. "Well, eat *them* and grow fat!" He then proceeded to give a series of recipes, including "Fried soles with woodlouse sauce," "curried cockchafers," "fricasse of chicken with chrysalids," "boiled neck of mutton with wireworm sauce," "cauliflowers garnished with caterpillars" and "moths on toast."

The most notorious aphrodisiac insect potion is the deadly Cantharides or Spanish fly made from the ground-up bodies of a tiny irridescent blister beetle *(Lytta vesicatoria)*. First discovered in Spain but now found throughout southern Europe, this inch-long blister beetle was made infamous by De Sade (see Course Twenty). It has a 5000-year-old history as an aphrodisiac, acting as a painfully severe irritant to the sexual organs and in the smallest quantities causes blinding pain, depression, abortion and even death in women. Everyone knows that old macho tale about the young girl who copulated with the gearshift knob in her boyfriend's car after having had Spanish fly powder slipped into her coke, but though the substance may make a woman wild with desire, it more often has horrible effects. In South Africa several years ago the wives of six absent businessmen were seduced by six wife-chasers, who mixed large quantities of Spanish fly into their food. All six women died agonizing deaths.

No sane sexologist would recommend Spanish fly, yet the sword slays its thousands and the table knife its tens of thousands, as the old proverb goes, and all kinds of curious viands have been prepared to please all kinds of appetites. It remains a sad fact (to most of us, anyway) that lovers have sunk so low as to trap and eat the rat and his relatives in the rat race for virility. Honeyed dormice, for example, was a favorite at Roman orgies, and one latter-day French chef invented a pastry made from field mice. Some people have actually preferred the company of mice and rats to other people and taken them as token lovers. There is indeed a case on record of an eighteenth century Englishwoman who customarily slept with a rat and a nest of mice—and she claimed, what's more, that they made better lovers than any man she'd ever bedded down with. But as far as the eating majority is concerned, the rat and his relatives have to be high up there among the most loathsome of foods. Rat is still served in France, incidentally, where, for all those wanting to avoid it, it's called *steak à la Tonnelier*. During the seige of Paris, labeled rat meat was sold at the rat market in the *Place de l'Hôtel*, the rodents costing 3 francs apiece (as opposed to 10 francs for cats) and dishes like *salmis de rats à la Parisienne* could be had in restaurants for about 15 francs. "Rat," according to one gourmet "has a slightly musky taste that is not unpleasant," though it has to be submitted "to prolonged cooking to destroy the harmful germs." Rodents from the winemaking Gironde plants are used for *steak à la Tonnelier*, and should anyone want a recipe for *Grilled Rat à la Revenge* or something, it follows:

> Secure one well-fed rat. Clean, singe and boil the rodent a long time. Clean again, carefully cut off the tail, and cover with a light layer of oil, topping with coarsely chopped shallots. Brown under a broiler. Rat, they say is especially effective grilled outside on the barbecue over old vineshoots, but you couldn't tell by us.

It's but a small and logical step from rat to cat, and that step has been taken briskly in the quest for love. Today the Cantonese Chinese are known for their fondness for cat, which they believe is not only delicious but a slinky sexy animal that improves virility. A local writer attests that the "Dragon or Tiger Stew" of a leading Cantonese restaurant in Hong Kong, "is a most expensive autumn dish that in reality is the meat of cat stewed with a variety of herbs, which takes the chef at least 2-3 days to prepare."

Man's best friend has fared far worse than the cat among the Chinese, who value the dog as an aphrodisiac almost as highly as they do rhino horn. However, the Chinese aren't the only lovers who have favored Fido. The Phoenicians regularly roasted canines over their campfires, boiled puppy dog was a Roman delicacy and Captain Cook's men enjoyed the vegetarian South Sea dog now extinct but said to taste much like lamb. Such pets and hunting companions are commonly raised for food in various parts of the world, often by people who regard our consumption of pork, beef, milk and other foods as being taboo. The French ate spaniels during the Franco-Prussian war to satisfy their hunger pangs, and in Korea, as many GI's, this writer included, discovered too late, the sukiyaki was often made from dog meat, not beef. We'd been wondering why there weren't any stray mongrels around, and then one day we stumbled upon two ROKS roasting one by a hillside near the 38th parallel (the dog meat didn't taste bad at all, until we learned that it was dog meat). Likewise, during his recent extensive travels in Communist China, another author claims he saw but *two* dogs on the streets; apparently the government had demanded some years previously that all dogs be killed and eaten because they ate food that could be consumed by human beings.

As for the aphrodisiac appreciation of dog meat, Chinese in Canton, Hunan, Kwangsi, Szechuan and several other provinces believe that the black chow in a garlic sauce is exceptionally virile and sexy. The Chinese warlord Chang Chung-ch'ang, who earned the title of "the general with three long legs" from Shanghai prostitutes in the 1920s, is said to have eaten black chow meat every day of the year. "The Dog Meat General," as he came to be called, used to take on whole brothels at a time, or so the story goes. There are some who suggest that Chang also owed his third nickname, "72 Cannon Chang," to that old devil dog meat. He was dubbed "72 Cannon Chang" because his manhood supposedly equalled 72 stacked silver dollars in length and diameter.

Another amusing story about dog meat, told in a recent issue of the Taiwan government publication *Free China Review*, concerns a prize pedigreed dog given to Viceroy Lo Hung-chang, one of the most eminent Chinese officials of the nineteenth century, by General Charles George Gordon, widely known as "Chinese Gordon," or "Gordon Pasha." A few days after Gordon presented the valuable show dog to the Viceroy, he received a letter of thanks, reading in part: "As I am in advanced age, I usually take little food. Therefore, I have only been able to take a very small portion of your delicious meat, which, indeed, has given me great gratification."

Today in Hong Kong restaurants dogs (as well as cats, raccoons and other household pets) are selected live from cages wheeled to the table. The black chow is still considered to be the most excellent aphrodisiac by all concerned. Although the sale and consumption of dog meat is forbidden by law there (offenders can be jailed for six months) the butchers get around this by putting out red-lettered signs heralding the arrival of "special beef," "goat meat" or "fragrant meat," as often as not supplied by "dognapers." Large signs outside Taipei's Chin Ting Restaurant in Taiwan proclaim that the establishment maintains its own "dog ranch" complete with a licensed veterinarian to supply the ten to thirty dogs it uses each day in "smoked," "red-cooked" or "dog soup" specialties. Chin Ting's management is confident that it will eventually win permission to ship canned dog meat to other Southeast Asian countries, if not to the United States.

Dog meat is preferred by the Chinese during cold weather, for reasons that are buried in folklore, and last winter Formosa University Hospital appealed to local lovers to stop eating dogs. Their tastes had created a serious shortage of the animals for medical experiments because owners who usually supplied dogs to the hospital were selling them at higher prices to restaurants. Here in the States an untrusting few still give Chinese restaurants wide berth for fear of the use of dog in dishes that might euphemistically be called Pork-Fi-Do, but there is no hard evidence of such abuses. There may come the revolution, though, if America's pet population explosion—pets have doubled to more than 65 million in the past five years alone—doesn't soon come under control. It boils down to either cruelly barbecuing the strays threatening to overrun us or destroying them or putting the pill in Lassie's Alpo. The first doesn't seem likely, however, judging by an example of our dogmeat taboo given by Frederick J. Simoons in his *Eat Not This Flesh*.

> A good illustration [Simoons writes] is the recent case of Andrew O'Meara, a United States Army officer, who killed, skinned, and put a stray dog on a spit in Peoria, Illinois, to demonstrate means of military survival to some friends. He was prosecuted under an Illinois statute against cruelty to animals, pleaded guilty, and was fined the maximum $200 permitted by the statute. An interesting aspect of the case is that though Lt. O'Meara killed the dog with a sudden blow, and could have pleaded innocent, he felt public pressure sufficiently to plead guilty. ...The judge in the case had received crank letters and threatening phone calls, one from as far away as Washington, D.C., to make certain that he 'did his duty.'

"Man is the only animal that eats its friends," instructs an old proverb and this applies to the hunter's faithful horse or camel as well as his dog.

Camel, especially beloved by the Arabs, has been consumed since earliest times. The Persian ruler Darius, who had a staff of 10,000 devoted solely to his culinary needs, preferred smoked camel hump, and Aristophanes claimed that this dish was served to Greek royalty, who relished it. One Arab recipe used fat from the hump of the camel as a love food ingredient, in keeping with their phallic outlook, and another love potion called for burning camel bone with certain plants to obtain a black pigment which women used mixed with antimony as an eyebrow paint that would "win any man at a glance." Similarly, instructs the *Perfumed Garden,* "one of the remedies against sterility consists of the marrow from the hump of a camel, which the woman spreads on a piece of linen, and rubs her sexual parts with."

Despite the fact that *chameau!* (camel) is about the vilest thing you can call a Gaul, camel hump, stomach and feet in recipes like camel couscous, roast camel's fillet, camel pilaf, camel's paunch `a la Marocaine` and *Ragoût de Chameau* `a la Tomate` remain favorites of French gourmands today. Perhaps because it has *two* humps, the dromedary is considered a still more effective love dish. But the most satisfying, or at least the largest and most expensive camel dish extant, is the roast camel the Bedouins serve at wedding feasts. All one needs for this concoction is a gross of eggs, a gleam of fish, a coop of chickens, a large shorn sheep and one unsuspecting camel. Just fill the fish with the eggs, chock the chicken with the fish, stuff the sheep with the chickens, and then clog the camel with the sheep, roasting it for a few days over an open fire. Finally, *voila!* A prodigious bill of fare, though a low-down trick Roy Rogers would never have pulled on Trigger.

Roy Rogers and Trigger aside, however, far more low-down tricks have been played on the horse than the camel. One ideal aphrodisiac in the Middle Ages was penis of horse. This mighty organ was cut off in full erection, cooked highly spiced and sometimes served in a cream sauce. The Tartars, too, swore by penis of horse and also used horsemeat for the true steak tartare (see Course Nine), but *they* also ate books to acquire the knowledge therein—there is no evidence that they consumed any sex manuals or pornographic works. The Romans, on the other hand, put their trust in a concoction made of mare's milk. Horse meat has generally been taboo to most Europeans, but the French have valued it since long before the Revolution, despite numerous prohibitions on its sale. *Cheval,* which can be stallion, mare, filly or even gelding, has for centuries been a staple at Parisian *boucheries de cheval,* where wooden horse's heads covered with gold leaf are the traditional decoration above such butcher shops. During the Napoleonic wars, one officer actually fed his wounded troops on their dead horses, using cavalry breastplates as pots and concocting a horsemeat soup prepared with gunpowder. The French, who also invented a dish called *Donkey's Brains à la diplomat*, held a horsemeat banquet prepared by the master chef Balzac (no kin to the novelist) in 1852 at the Grand Hotel in Paris. The menu, enjoyed by Dumas, Sainte-Beuve, Flaubert and 129 other guests, read as follows:

Soup: *vermicelli in horsemeat broth*
Hors d'oeuvre: *Horsemeat sausages and roast saddle of horsemeat*
Entrees: *boiled horsemeat à la mode, ragoût of horsemeat, filet of horsemeat with mushrooms*
Vegetables: *potatoes fried in horsemeat oil*
Salad: *lettuce sprinkled with oil of horsemeat*
Dessert: *rum and horsemarrow cake*

When this official banquet ended, a sated toastmaster concluded "that horse is as good to eat as beef," and horse has ever since been a respected dish in the French cuisine, butchers asking as high as $2.30 for horse filet at last report. Some fifty horses a day were slaughtered for the Parisian market up until recently, the average Frenchman consuming about 3½ pounds of *cheval* annually, more than Americans do of lamb, using it in roasts, steaks, with beef or pork in sausages and most often in a raw "hamburger" eaten with onions and other seasonings. The situation has changed somewhat since 1965, when cases of salmonellosis food infection broke out at a Parisian girl's boarding school due to a butcher selling tainted horseflesh (he was promptly jailed), but the drastic drop in horseflesh consumption at the time seems to have taken a turn upward—for better or worse horsemeat now represents 12% of all the meat consumed in France, some 300,000 horses a year.

It's not that the French are inhumane to horses, just the most practical of people. Having long held that horseflesh is a health food that fortifies the blood and helps the anemic lover, they always lard the lean meat or add fat before cooking. Horsemeat is imported there from Poland, Czechoslovakia, Ireland, Yugoslavia, Italy and Canada. Robert Imbert, president of the French Horsemeat butcher's union, constantly reminds his countrymen how prehistoric cave paintings show hunters in pursuit of wild horses and how the ancient Persians lived on horsemeat. Imbert says that all his children and grandchildren have been reared on horseflesh, even strained and added to their baby food. The meat, he says, is high in vitamin B, is leaner than beef and has a higher protein count, and is free from tapeworm, TB or tenia. His favorite recipe calls for marinating the meat for two days in white wine, oil, vinegar, parsley, thyme, laurel, rosemary, juniper berries and salt and pepper to taste before cooking it slowly. Another equine champion, Helen Marcillac, who

works at Twentieth Century Meats in Laurelton, New York, but comes
from a long line of French horse-traders, adds that horsemeat is the
cleanest, healthiest meat that comes from any animal. Mrs. Marcillac,
who dispenses classic recipes for dishes like *equine au vin, equine à la king*
and sweet and sour equine, claims that horsemeat cures the sick and
spurs husbands to long nights of lovemaking. "You give him a nice steak
in the evening," she says, "and you have a nice 'I love you in bed.' "

Here in America horsemeat has traditionally been used for pet food,
but there are numerous instances of its human consumption on record.
None was eaten at the famous $50,000 "horse banquet" held at Sherry's
in the Gay Nineties—the millionaire guests were served while sitting as-
tride their mounts, drinking champagne from rubber truncheons and
eating pheasant from oat bags. But the Harvard Faculty Club did begin
serving horsemeat steaks during World War II and many of us ate it
unknowingly or not in those days of meat rationing. Furthermore, humans reportedly consume 25% of the pet food manufactured in the
United States.

Only recently has horsemeat become a big business in America.
Today, with what might be called "price rationing," American gourmets
and lovers are eating roast saddle of horse in unprecedented numbers. It
all began in April of 1973 when Kent Carlson, who has long owned Carlson's House of Choice Meats across Long Island Sound in Westbrook,
Connecticut, got disgusted with rising beef prices and applied for a special license allowing him to sell plainly labeled horsemeat to his customers. Mr. Carlson tells us that he sold some 3000 pounds of the horseflesh
in one form or another on his first day of horse-trading. This despite the
presence of thirty riders on horseback protesting cruelty to animals. The
riders, he says, were actually a kind of "spur to sales," a moving, living
advertisement pointing the way to the store, and he almost wishes they'd
protest again.

Not that Carlson's House of Choice Meats needs anything but its
horsemeat, though. In the first eight months after his opening, Mr. Carlson sold over 280,000 pounds of horseflesh in cuts ranging from hamburger to porterhouse. His success has inspired similar enterprises in
Buffalo, New York, New Haven, Connecticut and Lewiston, Maine,
among other places, and he and associates have just formed a national
franchise of twenty stores, which will be located primarily in the North
"because we found out by our hate mail that most Southerners are
against horsemeat eating."

Such equine emporiums are thriving mainly because of low horsemeat
prices—nothing over $1 a pound. Horsemeat hamburger, for example, is
a cheap 59¢ a pound, compared to 99¢ for the lowest grade beef hamburger; horsemeat sirloin steak is 85¢ a pound and porterhouse steak

89¢; Delmonico steak is 95¢ and tenderloin steak 99¢. Whats more prices haven't changed since the opening and there is no danger that suppliers will run out of horsemeat, there being numerous feedlots where horses are raised for meat in Virginia, Pennsylvania, Connecticut, Texas, North Carolina and other states. "There are over 15 million horses in this country," Carlson says, explaining that there's more than enough meat to meet demands.

Low prices aren't the only factor that has helped Carlson's Choice Meats "set a track record in The Horsemeat Derby." Quality is another reason; many of his regular customers are well-to-do people with supposedly refined taste buds summering in Long Island beach resorts across the Sound. "Horsemeat is cut exactly like beef," he says. "It's just as tender and tastes the same—you wouldn't be able to tell the difference." Mr. Carlson suggests several rules for the novice horsemeat cook whose purchase hasn't been pretenderized: 1) Baste all steaks; 2) Cook roasts slightly longer and at lower heat; 3) Mix a small amount of cooking oil with the ground meat; 4) Cut London broil and top round steak on the bias; 5) Tenderize the meat whenever possible. Actually, horsemeat has generally been regarded as sweeter and duller in taste than beef. Everybody's favorite cut here appears to be porterhouse and Mr. Carlson estimates that about 80% of those who try any horsemeat come back week after week for more. Everyone, it seems, is galloping down to the horsemeat market quicker than Secretariat, and Carlson's success has inspired all the inevitable puns: change grading cuts from prime, choice and good to win, place and show; "need a lift, get a horse"; "horsemeat la spur to l'amour"; and so forth.

Hippomanes, rather than horsemeat plain, is probably the most famous of all horse food aphrodisiacs and was widely used by the Romans in their love potions. Experts disagree as to just what constituted hippomanes. Virgil described it as "a bitter virus flowing from the vulva of rutting mares" in one place, but in another instance he agreed with Ovid, Juvenal and Pliny that the substance is the black or brown swelling (or caul) that appears on a colt's head at birth. In size and shape this resembles a fig. It is bitten off by the mare before she gives milk to her offspring. More likely, considering the better sexual connections, hippomanes was the discharge of a mare, but at any rate, its reputation is exceeded by no other ancient aphrodisiac. Hippomanes, however, has to be swallowed with the blood of one's beloved to insure the best results. Caligula (who once made his horse a consul of Rome) was "thrown into a phrensy" when his wife administered such a love potion to him.

One notable case of hippomanes' "wonderful effects" was cited by the ancient writer Pausanias, who describes the amazing votive offerings of a Roman named Phormis Menalius.

His two gifts in Olympia are two horses and two charioteers, one of which horses the Aelians assert to have been made by a magician, of brass, into which metal he had previously infused the hippomanes, and which, in consequence, possessed the power of exciting horses to mad desire for coition.... Horses desire connection with this image not only in spring, but every day throughout the year, for, breaking their bridles or running away from their driver, they rush into Altis [a temple] and attack the horse in a manner much more furious than if it was the most beautiful mare.... Their hoofs, indeed, slip from the side of the image but nevertheless they never cease neighing vehemently and leaping furiously on the figure until they are driven off by the whip or by some other violent means, for till such methods are applied, it is impossible to disengage them from the brass.

Though the horse has in one way or another spurred many to mount or be mounted, the rider or love hunter himself has often fared no better than his trusty steed. Mae West may not really use her "ashes of men" for perfume, but roast loin of Ms. or Mr. and similar dishes have been popular since the first rock people spied the tenderer fish-fed shell people. Anthropologists have unearthed many prehistoric human skulls split open with their brains extracted and bones split for marrow. "In ancient days," Mantegazza relates, "the most 'eaten' parts of the human, by savages, were the breasts and the male genital organs. This formed a vast ceremonial, in which males, especially young males, were castrated alive, their genitals being cooked and eaten by the High Priests, who also consumed cooked female breasts at the same time." He neglects to tell us that these same priests, at least in Mesolithic times (15,000–10,000 B.C.), were often "domineering females who led intoxicated lives," at least according to psychiatrist Mary Jane Sherfey. Dr. Sherfey believes that at the time: "Short-lived kings were torn to bits and eaten by priestesses, who also invented human sacrifice.... Wild women raged through the countryside tearing asunder any man they met. Orgiastic celebrations prevailed." The good shrink, whose sources we cannot verify, also claims that these priestesses probably invented circumcision, possibly in part to please women demanding multiple orgasms. They are reminiscent of those fair participants in the Grecian Dionysian orgies, who, clad only in their own skins, drank themselves to a pitch of excitement and then tore to pieces a live bull representing Dionysus, god of wine and revelry. These gentle creatures had to kill the bull with their teeth alone and eating its flesh raw in the raw was a necessary part of the ritual.

Men were no less avaricious in their quest for potency. The livers of young boys, for example, were considered a restorative for old men in Chaldean times, and when we toast someone with a "Skol!" we are honoring the skulls that Vikings used as cups to drink the blood of their victims. Even the Hindus, far gentler than the Norsemen, and no great meat lovers, tried to catch the spirit of a once-virile man as his corpse was being carried to the pyre by throwing flowers on the body and later using them in a love potion. The Massagetac, who lived in the Caucasus mountains in the fifth century b.c., considered it a great honor for a virile grandfather to be eaten by his heirs. All his good qualities were said to be transferred to the diners, and they were, in fact, shamefaced if he died diseased and unfit for human consumption.

There's no end to the weird stories about cannibalism and sex. Garry Hogg in *Cannibalism and Human Sacrifice* cites an early African traveler who tells the following Grand Guignol tale:

> Probably the most inhuman practice of all is to be met among the tribes who deliberately hack the victim piecemeal whilst still alive. Incredible as it may appear, captives are led from place to place in order that individuals may have the opportunity of indicating, by external marks on the body, the portion they desire to acquire. The distinguishing marks are generally made by means of colored clay or strips of grass tied in a peculiar fashion. The astonishing stoicism of the victims, who thus witness bargaining for their limbs piecemeal, is only equalled by the callousness with which they walk forward to meet their fate.

Yet the debtors who were consumed bit by bit by their creditors in Africa and the criminals among the Chinese and North American Indians who were force-fed parts of themselves hacked off piece by piece (say a finger at a time) offer examples no less inhuman than Hogg's cannibals. Nor do those South American tribes that buried their corpses a week or so before eating them or castrated young boys to make them grow plumper, or broke their victims' legs with the same thought in mind. In *Gluttons and Libertines*, Marston Bates, even relates one instance where New Guinea cannibals took "the feces of a man who had been shot" and gave them to the man's wife, "who ate them after cooking them, mixed with edible ferns and wrapped in banana leaves." Professor Bates also notes that "Food and sex were sometimes neatly combined when the men would copulate with a female corpse before cutting it up for eating. They had the story of a man who got his penis cut off because he dallied too long for the patience of his hungry friends."

Human history is replete with examples of cannibalism, and not only among so-called savages. The philosophic stoics of the third century saw no harm in the practice; Frenchmen ate each other to survive at Alesia when beseiged by Caesar, just as Spaniards did at Sagunto in Valencia when trapped by Hannibal; and the crusaders sometimes ate their victims, one of them testifying that infidels tasted "better than spiced peacock."

Legend has it that when King Richard the Lion-Hearted fell ill from ague during the Crusades he was cured by the following prescription:

> *Take a Saracen, young and fat,*
> *In haste let the thief be slayne,*
> *Opened, and his skin off flayne,*
> *And saddled full hastily,*
> *With powder and spicery*
> *And saffron of good colour.*

Another olden King, Canibas of Lydia, had an appetite "so fiercely compelling," an English writer tells us, that "one night the glutton unfortunately devoured his wife." Ditto for Thys, King of the Pophlagonians, who also gobbled up his wife—there is no mention of just what cuts either royal diner especially preferred. But cannibalism has by no means been confined to distant lands. Smollet, who told of reading in a history of the Congo of "negroe's heads sold publically in market," might well have looked to his own people. Instances of cannibalism in the British Isles themselves are rather common. King Ethelfrith was even accused of encouraging it at his court, and one woman, later hung for the crime, declared on the scaffold that "If ye had the experience of eating men and women's flesh, ye would think it so delicious that ye wold never forbear it again." Finally, there is no doubt as to the authenticity of the most infamous of British cannibals, Sawney Beane, an ogre who lived with his large family in a cave by the Galloway shore. Beane robbed, murdered and ate some one-thousand men, women and children over a twenty-five year period, even pickling some of them. King James I himself personally led the expedition that finally captured olde Sawney, who only seems to be rivaled by a Fiji Island chief (Ra Undre Undre ate 900 people all by his lonesome) in his consumption of human meat.

We all know of Rabelais' "Pilgrims Salad," which Gargantua made with six pilgrims, lettuce, salt, vinegar and oil, this fiction reflecting the fact that cannibalism was widespread in medieval times, where we find such aphrodisiac prescriptions as human testes (swallowed but chopped first) as a cure for impotence; "wormwood soaked in virgin's urine or undiluted menstrual blood"; and putrified flesh combined with hair and nail parings from corpses. Generally considered more inspiring while alive, the bodies of women were rarely devoured, although the Hungarian Countess Bathory once had eighty peasant girls strangled to death and then took a bath in their blood in an attempt to restore her fading powers. Some medieval lovers thought it logical to drink each other's blood to become closer. One widow went to the extreme of eating her dead husband's heart, "that she might remain constant," and a certain

French court lady actually wore a relic around her neck consisting of her dead husband's genitals—these being embalmed, perfumed and encased in gilded silver. But then France has always had its food eccentrics nonpariel. The kinky Prince de Conde, for instance, didn't eat corpses, but he did dine with them. Toward the end of his life he announced that he himself was dead and since dead men didn't eat, neither would be. His doctors tricked him, however, telling him that dead men *do* eat, but from then on M. le prince would only eat at table in the presence of corpses that the doctors supplied.

Cannibalism was often practiced in medieval France. Often the practice was ascribed to werewolves and vampires, but these were in reality no more than the drinking man's (or woman's) cannibal. Gilles de Retz, a companion of Joan of Arc and the prototype for Bluebeard, preferred the raw entrails of infants. Children were killed and sold in butcher shops, and at least one innkeeper slit the throats of sleeping travelers and cut up their carcasses for the marketplace. The French particularly valued *goblets d'amour* when they contained the blood of red-haired people. Yet Rabelais warned his countrymen that all cannibals should beware of whom they consume, noting that one can die of colic by eating certain prudish sour souls "fricasse for breakfast."

The word cannibalism itself derives from the name of an American Indian tribe. When Columbus encountered the Caribs upon landing in the Lesser Antilles, these natives gave him their name as *Canibalis*. This word was merely a dialectic form of *Caribes*, and these people were Caribs themselves, but the Spanish thereafter called the whole Carib tribe *Canibalis*. The very first discovery of cannibalism in the New World occurred when Dr. Chanca, the ship's physician on Columbus' second voyage, entered a Carib house in the Lesser Antilles and saw there a pile of bones and skulls. Because many of these fierce, bold warriors ate human flesh, their name was being used within a century in Europe as a synonym for man-eaters, cannibalism being substituted for the classic "anthropophagy."

The Caribs of the South American coast were far more adventurous and warlike than those of the larger islands like Cuba. In fact, at the time of Columbus, the natives in the Lesser Antilles used two separate languages, the men speaking one and the women another. This situation had developed when fierce South American Caribs invaded the islands some years before. Butchering and eating all the relatively peaceful Arawak inhabitants, the invaders claimed their women, but such aphrodisiacs didn't work very well, for in retaliation, the women devised a separate "female language" based on *Arawak*, refused to speak *Carib* and for generations thereafter maintained silence in the presence of all males. Sad to say, this did not deter the Carib warriors from fighting more wars for human flesh, or even from continuing to break their enemies' legs in order to be able to eat them later at their convenience. But then the Amazon female warriors of old were even less merciful. According to one ancient historian, they crippled the males they captured and made them sex slaves. When reproached by the Scythians about the limping gait of her male servants, their Queen Antianara is said to have replied, "The lame best perform the act of love."

We've already encountered those savage Indians who would slice off and eat the sexual parts of their slain enemies before assuming conqueror's rights to the helpless women of a conquered tribe. But in the Solomon island group select warriors themselves were fattened and prepared in various ways for love feasts. Especially choice tidbits were the eyes, cheeks, brains, rump and calves, the rest being relegated to the dogs. As for roasted white man—called "long pig" by the Polynesians, Maori and Fiji Islanders—the natives generally felt that their tobacco-smoking, meat-eating and other bad habits made whites inferior in taste to locals reared on organically grown vegetables. Whites were a little tough, they complained, and often had to be sent back to the kitchen. The Tahitian who told French novelist Pierre Loti that the "white man, when well roasted, tastes like a ripe banana" was an atypical exception to the rule. By most accounts all human flesh tastes like pig or pork, but is "more delicate" in flavor and "never produces any painful feeling of satiety or induces vomiting." Some cannibals use the flesh raw, like plugs of chewing tobacco; others smoke-dry it, while still others cremate the bodies and use the ashes to flavor soups or hot drinks. Oddly enough, the favorite cuts among the majority of tribes seem to be filet of footsole and palm of hand. Further, no anthropologist has to our knowledge ever reported a cannibal claiming that human meat doesn't taste good. In fact, the Fiji Islanders are so fond of same that the greatest compliment they can bestow on any Cordon Bleu dish is to say that it's "as tender as a dead man."

Cannibal tribes in both the Pacific and Africa often sought virility from their slain enemies, the liver and the testicles of young victims said to be best of all. A typical feast among the Maoris of New Zealand was recounted by one writer toward the end of the last century: "An English sailor who, with a number of his comrades, was taken prisoner...says that after the killing of his companions, holes were dug in the ground, in which great wood fires were made, and a number of large stones made intensely hot therein. The cut-up bodies of the sailors were placed over the hot stones, upon which had first been scattered some green leaves, the whole being covered in with a straw mat and then well damped with water. This preparation took place in the evening. Next morning found the banquet 'well cooked,' says this horrible record." The feast described was not so horrible, however, as those of the Battas of Sumatra, whose laws called for eating all criminals and prisoners of war, "the criminal, or prisoner, as the case may be...tied to a stake and eaten alive, each person cutting off a slice according to taste or fancy, until all the flesh is devoured."

In America, the Aztecs practiced cannibalism centuries before the first Europeans arrived, one chronicler even mentioning a fricassee or stew of little children in which their emperor indulged. Prescott relates the pomp and ceremony of their epicurean cannibalism in his account of the Spanish Conquest. "The most loathsome part of the story," he writes, "the manner in which the body of the sacrificed captive was disposed of—remains yet to be told. It was delivered to the warrior who had taken him in battle, and by him, after being dressed, was served up in an entertainment to his friends. This was not the coarse repast of famished cannibals, but a banquet teeming with delicious beverages and delicate viands, prepared with art, and attended by both sexes, who, as we shall see hereafter, conducted themselves with all the decorum of civilized life. Surely never were refinement and the extremes of barbarism brought so closely into contact with each other." Not so "refined," though, were those occasions when the Aztecs actually tore the hearts from their living victims on their sacrificial altars. Nor were their supermarkets very "civilized." It was, in fact, the sight of a human leg among raw dressed meat in a butcher's stall near an Aztec temple that caused the Spanish to lose all interest in local meat dishes.

Cannibalism continued in the New World with the arrival of the white man, though on a much more limited scale. Well-known is the story of the Donner Party trapped en route to California in the Sierra Nevada. These starving emigrants ate a number of their companions to survive the winter of 1846–47. Not so familiar are cases of man-eating among whalemen adrift on the sea, such as that of the survivors of the sinking of the *Essex* on which Melville in part based *Moby Dick*, nor the strong possibility that colonists may have resorted to cannibalism in early Jamestown. Yet aside from acts of cannibalism as a dietary necessity, as witnessed in the recent Uruguayan plane crash in the Andes, there seem to be none but psychopathic cases of cannibalism here, and this is indeed the case with almost all people in modern times. One African country today has a law requiring that meat be sold with a piece of the hide attached to prove that it isn't human (a law that possibly is a reaction to the human flesh markets of nineteenth century West Africa), but no one else seems to be worrying much about the problem. A Gallup Poll, however, has found that 70% of Uruguayans would resort to cannibalism under the same circumstances as those encountered by the survivors of the Andean plane crash, and a similar poll conducted by author D. Keith

Mano among 1000 Americans (200 responded) "produced 45 per cent YES, 40 per cent NO, 15 per cent unsure."*

De Sade recommends human flesh as an aphrodisiac, though the Marquis could hardly be called a sane sexologist. Some will remember that Minski, the 7'3" Jack and the Beanstalk monster in De Sade's *Juliette*, resided in a house where the chairs were made from human bones and ate human flesh from a living table made of a row of naked women, one pressed atop the other, using no tablecloth, and for napkins wiping his fingers on their flowing hair. In one scene, Juliette, after sampling a very tasty ragoût, asks if it was beef, veal, venison or bird that made such a delicious dish. "It's your chambermaid," the monster answers her. De Sade wrote elsewhere that human flesh best nourishes the lover by building rich and healthy spermatozoa and quickly replenishing it. In still another place he describes cutting off slices from the buttocks of people at orgies and tells of various women eating the genitals of their victims.

Although De Sade and other madmen prescribed human flesh as a love potion, the only apparent modern vestige of the superstition that seems to have survived in the belief among some prostitutes that swallowing human semen will cure T.B. Without recommending cannibalism, outdoorsman Bradford Angier does note that "animal proteins are desireable in direct relation with their chemical similarity to the eating organism, [therefore] for the fullest and easiest assimilation of flesh materials, human meat cannot be equalled." But this is offset by the theorizing of Stanley Garn and Walter Block, who coldly calculate in *The American Anthropologist* that "one man...serves 60, skimpily.... Considering the cost, then, the nutritive value of cannibalism may therefore be viewed as questionable, unless a group is in a position to consume its own number in a year." Besides which a recent study reported in the *Manchester Guardian* claims that humans (or Americans, at least) are "unfit for human consumption." It seems that the average American's bodily tissue contains twelve parts per million of DDT—the maximum level considered safe for consumption being seven parts per million.

---

*The most horrible example of cannibalism in recent history occurred during the Seige of Leningrad in W.W.II. Human meat patties sold for 300–400 rubles on the black market, husbands and wives consumed each other and parents even ate their children. As Harrison Salisbury writes in *The 900 Days:* "Here and there passed a man or woman with a face full, rosey and soft, and a shudder ran through the crowd. For these were the most terrible people of their day." If all the tales Salisbury documents are true, this would be the only case recorded in the history of the West where relatives were eaten wholesale. No westerner, though, has yet embraced a "waste not, want not" philosophy, or agreed with the cannibal Cocomas tribe, who believe "It is better to be inside a friend than to be swallowed up by the earth."

In any event, the great majority of people are in agreement with the great majority of animals regarding their own flesh—fortunately, most would add. As Hans Hasse puts it: "Man probably survived in Africa because he smelled and tasted so bad to lions and other predators, not because he was a tool-making animal. Anthropologist Wayne Leaky tells of many instances of lions sniffing humans in tents there and walking away disdainfully. Man-eaters are the psychopaths of the animal kingdom—weak, sick, wounded—one in 100,000."

So it is with man himself. In short, although unkosher comestibles like roast loin of Ms. or Mr. and so many others examined in these pages may make for interesting conversation among those with strong stomachs and have all definitely been valued as aphrodisiacs somewhere at one time or another in history, mankind has generally preferred less-exotic game than *Homo sap.* No matter how they might really taste, most dishes from the preceding zoo of sensual delights will cause our minds to rebel and reel when they're placed before us on a plate. Anyone wanting to prepare same (almost anything, that is, but human meat) can consult a number of sources, e.g., *The Explorer's Cookbook* by Luther and Conda Douglas, but most will prove culture-bound enough to settle for a Pepto-Bismol casserole and proceed toute suite to the more conventional (or at least easier-to-prepare) wild stimulants in the chapter following.

COURSE EIGHT

Saner Game For Love Games:
The Bare Facts
About The Well-Hung Bear,
The Horny Hare,
The Harassed Hart & Co.

"And the naked newly-erect savage hunted...side by side, the savage man and savage woman wandering free together."
—F.W. Hackwood, *The Good Old Days*

All psychological and "analeptic strength-giving powers" provided by exotic wild creatures are readily available in large and small game more commonly stalked by love hunters. Brillat-Savarin, who used to carry wild game around in his pockets until it assumed a "high" enough flavor (as a result he himself usually smelled pretty "high"), tells us that "Game is one of the luxuries of the dinner table; it is a food healthy, heating, savory, tasty, and easy of digestion." Most gourmands would agree with the master, as would many a naked couple hunting "newly-erect" like that primitive pair in our epigraph.

Of those "animals good to eat which live free in the woods and fields," Brillat-Savarin includes partridge and various birds (see Course Ten), foxes, badgers, rabbits, venison and "all other cloven-footed animals." There is space here for only the most fabled among these love stimulants, but at the onset it should be remembered that all wild game is among the most difficult of foods to cook correctly. Always Savarin's directive must be followed: "If we throw into a pot of water salt and a piece of beef, we will obtain some soup and some boiled meat. But if instead of beef we put wild boar or venison in the pot, we will have but poor fare; in this respect, butcher's meat has the advantage. Under the directions of a skillful cook, however, game undergoes a great number of scientific modifications and transformations, furnishing the majority of the highly flavoured dishes on which a transcendental gastronomic art is based."

Sexual prowess has been consciously sought from wild game at least since the first civilized man hired a cook, and the art hasn't been forgotten. Recipes like Raymond Oliver's *cascalopes d'animelles au soleil* (floured and fried sexual organs of animals) abound in the love cuisine. Surprisingly, small game such as rabbit has long been among the most popular of such foods. Aphrodite was identified with the hare, and the ancient writer Paulinus cited the testes of the rabbit as an effective stimulant. A traditional fertility symbol, the rabbit has only one psychological drawback for the thinking sensualist—although eating rabbit may convince lovers that they can perform just as frequently as their quarry, "their consummation may be reached just as rapidly." Maybe this is why those same West Indians who go into ecstasy at the sight of palm-worms fried in fat and baked snakes refuse to touch stewed rabbit with a ten-inch pole. Nevertheless, rabbit remains a staple on the list of love foods recommended by sexologists. Since ancient times it has been popularly associated with sexual strength and license; Catullus writes of "rabbit-ridden Spain" in this connection, and Pliny asserts that if a pregnant woman ate the testicles, womb or rennet of a hare, she would always bear virile boys. Eating the fetus of a hare was said to end barreness forever.

Americans kill and consume an estimated 50 million rabbits and hares every year and eat 50 million more pounds of rabbit meat raised as domestic breeds. Believe it or not, the animal is some one-hundred times more widely shot than any other American game, including deer. But this has been so wherever the prolific rabbit breeds since ages before the Romans hunted him down in the Laurentine forests. The ancient Mayans are known to have domesticated the fecund creature, raising rabbits "large and good to eat" which cost ten cacao beans each—this was two beans more than the all-night price of a Mayan prostitute. Love potions featuring the rabbit were common in the Middle Ages; Pierre Mora included one in *Zekerboni* which employed the "kidney of a hare" and guaranteed that "marvellous success will follow."

Although among the English hares were believed "to nourish melancholy," they ate plenty of them roasted or boiled to nourish potency. Thomas Dawson's *The Good Housewife's Jewel*, one of the first English cookbooks, gives a recipe "To Boile Coynes [rabbits]," and English kings such as Richard II and roguish Henry VIII, who liked "the wings of a small rabbit," often thumped their tables for more of the dish. Among the rabbit concoctions Englishmen enjoyed were "larded rabbits" and the "hash of rabbits and lamb" mentioned in Samuel Pepy's diary. However, the much quoted recipe of "Mrs. Hannah Glasse" in the English *Art of Cookery* (1746)—"First catch your hare"—is a myth, the recipe really beginning "Take your 'hair' when it is cased (skinned)." As for "Welsh Rabbit," this is simply an error for "Welsh Rarebit," which is toasted bread covered with toasted cheese, mustard and pepper, having nothing to do with rabbits whatsoever.

In America, all the rabbit Casanova could have wanted was here for the taking by the settlers. Though "Hare Pye" is featured in Mrs. E. Smith's *The Compleat Housewife*, America's first cookbook, we have generally preferred the cottontail *(Sybrillagus foridanus)*, a light-meated breed that is by far the most prevalent, easiest to prepare and tastiest species. Featured in the sensuous Creole cookery, even older cottontails were made edible by long moist cooking. As for hare (of the genus *Lepus*), one American wild game expert offers the following opinion: "The wild hares are not worth much, except when very young. The older ones are composed mostly of steel thews and are best dressed with a hacksaw, if at all. Whereas a rabbit will weigh up to three pounds, a hare gets big enough to kick a hole in you at 12 pounds or so."

Europeans do not share this native dislike. International rabbit recipes include German *Hasen Pfeffer*, French *Civit de Lievre*, Southern Italian *Coniglio Agrodolu*, Dutch *Hazenpeper*, Belgian *Konifnmet* and even a recipe where rabbit is prepared as Sauerbraten. But the most renowned of all such European dishes is the classic English jugged hare. The French, who eat almost as much rabbit as they do lamb, particularly relish this delicacy from across the Channel. "Jugged" hare is not an inebriated rabbit, but hare prepared in earthenware pots, its sauce sometimes thickened with the animal's blood. Gourmets insist on what are called "three-quarters" for this dish—hares born at the beginning of the year that have reached no more than five pounds, in contrast to the full-grown European hare's usual eight pounds or so. The Spanish also prefer the hare, once offering it in a red wine sauce "flavored with 'Chillies' and bacon." There is, in fact, a Spanish proverb *vender gato por liebre*, to sell a cat for a hare, that originated when Spanish hostels palmed off cat as hare, a practice that may continue today, at least judging by the fact that hare is often displayed in their markets paws intact to prove that it isn't some mangy Tom from the alleys.

Sensuous gourmets should beware that wild hares and rabbits often carry the disease tularemia or rabbit fever, which can be fatal to humans; rabbit must therefore be well-cooked to kill any bacteria present and carefully bled and eviscerated as soon as shot if hunted, the hunter wearing rubber gloves or the like. In addition to the many dishes mentioned, there are recipes for rabbit paprikas, barbecued rabbit, rabbit creole, wild rabbits' tongues ("For six persons allow sixty tongues...scald, cool and skin them," Alexander Dumas wrote in his recipe collection) and even rabbit spaghetti sauce available in many wild game cookbooks. There are certainly enough recipes for us to effectively utilize this abundant food for love, which we shoot and bury wastefully throughout the country wherever the rabbit massacres crops. Domesticated rabbit is a good source of protein. Moreover, one female can produce five litters a year—about 150 pounds of marketable rabbit—at a low cost to breeders and, thus, to consumers. In short, it is an ideal food in these inflationary times.

Squirrel is small game somewhat more flavorsome than rabbit, due to its nut diet, and we waste it even more indiscriminately than we do the rabbit. Brillat-Savarin, while in exile in America, relates how "we knocked over six or seven gray squirrels, which are thought well of in these parts" and tells how he enjoyed them "stewed in Madiera." Early Americans knew that squirrel is one of the best of small game animals to eat, mild in flavor and easy to cook—broiled squirrel, for example, is simply skinned, brushed with butter and cooked until crisp and brown. This relative of the rat could be put to good use by homeowners plagued by him. Young grey squirrels of less than a pound, or fox squirrels at about two pounds, are preferred for any squirrel dish. Squirrel is treated essentially like chicken; it may be fried, broiled, casseroled, whatever. Native recipes for this aphrodisiac fare ready for the taking right out of the oaks in Central Park or suburban back yards include squirrel mulligan, squirrel pie, Brunswick Stew and a concoction called Seminole or Squirrel Soup.

Other small game favored by sensualists range from the "wildcat nose" cooked by American colonists to the "pickled beaver tail" once served in San Francisco restaurants. The beaver, its name a slang expression for the female sex organ since before burlesque days, was nearly wiped out before silk hats replaced those made of beaver pelts. Beaver was served at least once at the governor's mansion in Williamsburg, capital of the Virginia colony, and one Englishman, dining in Canada, reported that its flesh tasted excellent, "like fat pork sandwiched between layers of finnan haddie." Mountain goats, sheep and wild boar were also all considered effective in America at one time or another, and still are when available. Though it is rather fatty, raccoon too was valued, and there is a recipe for Muskrat Stew (to be found in *The New England Cookbook*) that the Indians considered a succulent dish because the creature "lives lovingly only on roots, grasses and such things." Such foods may be difficult to obtain, but they are available. The Maryland Gourmet Mart in New York City, for example, offers almost every sort of frozen game bird and meat, including wild turkey, mouflon (wild sheep), boar, turtle, rabbit, hare, beaver, elk, reindeer, bear and buffalo.

Among larger native game, the three animals most extensively hunted were buffalo, bear and deer, only the last of which is popular today. Authentic buffalo is mentioned in an Arab recipe for enlarging the penis which calls for rubbing the organ with "the butter of a she buffalo." In America, the buffalo (as our bison is commonly called) is responsible for all the Bull-names (Sitting Bull, White Bull, etc.) of the great plains Indian chiefs and warriors. American buffalo herds were, of course, virtually eliminated as a major food in a planned government policy to exterminate the American Indian for the benefit of "civilization," and about the only way one can get fresh buffalo meat for home use today is to request a carcass from a national park superintendant when a large buffalo herd, like the one protected in South Dakota's Custer State Park, is being thinned out each year.

Buffalo was long a staple food for man, judging by drawings on the walls of prehistoric cave dwellings and bone deposits found close-by. Hump of buffalo was a Chinese love food, and the American Indian often dried bison meat, cutting it into wide strips that came to be called "jerky" (from the Spanish *charqui*). But of the vast herds here in America, herds that could often be seen spreading out ten miles in every direction, the *"Buffalos, buffaloes, thousands abreast,/ A scourge and amazement, they swept to the west"* of Vachel Lindsay, all that our "Buffalo Bills" took were the hides and delicate tongues; leaving the rest to rot, they sometimes later claimed the bones for fertilizer. The only remaining herds are those protected by the U.S. Government, but buffalo meat can still be had at certain restaurants and scientists are trying to cross the bison with beef cattle for future generations. Former Secretary of the Interior Stewart Udall calls buffalo steak "more succulent by far than the steak of a longhorn steer," and the chef at New York City's Explorer's Club says "Bison is better than beef. Best roast I ever cooked." Besides Chicago's Cafe Bohemia, already cited, New Orleans's Pittari's Restaurant serves buffalo steak, and San Francisco's Tommy's Joynt makes a delicious buffalo stew.

Bear is a bit more difficult to come by today, but it has a reputation exceeding buffalo's as an aphrodisiac. Bear meat bestows courage and makes you strong for love, said the ancients, enabling a man to bear hug his lover until she yields. Bear paw was and still is a Chinese favorite.

"So smooth and delicious it melts in your mouth," is the way the epicurean philosopher Mencius described it, but his favorite dish had to be elaborately baked in clay and simmered in a rich broth of herbs, chicken and wine before being edible. Today, the paw is similarly baked packed in mud; when the mud cools and hardens it is torn off, and the hair comes off with it. After being simmered a long time to lose its gamey smell, it is sliced and served with a rich sauce.

The Romans liked their bear in the form of steaks. Some claimed that those great beasts which had fought in the arena and gorged on human flesh didn't taste too good, but this was probably because of the adrenalin flowing into their tissues when the animals were killed in combat. In early America the Indians "sweetened" various stews with bear fat, and the colonists used it in place of cooking oils. New Englanders were in fact taught by the Indians to use bear grease in preparing baked beans, the pork fat now used being their own idea. Davy Crockett, it's said, in one year managed to kill 105 of the animals to provide food for his family.

"According to folklore," according to Ms. Germaine Greer, "the orgasm of a male bear lasts nine days." That might be too much to bear, but at any rate, bear was served to bares at the bedroom-restaurants in Gold Rush San Francisco. It was esteemed all along the Coast, except for the grizzly, of which one historian wrote: "Only the appetite of a famished hunter can relish the flesh of an old one." Once, in fact, the town of Monterey was saved from starvation because of bear meat, but as in most of the country, the animal was slaughtered wholesale there for "sport" or because it endangered livestock. About the only thing we've done for the bear is honor him by creating the most famous of children's toys in his image. A Brooklyn candy store owner named Morris Michtom fashioned the first teddy bear out of brown plush in 1902 and named it after President Theodore ("Teddy") Roosevelt.

Anyone who can obtain bear—an eccentric diner's club in England had one shipped whole from Canada in a coffin—should be sure to cook it well. Though bear meat tastes best rare, there is danger of trichinosis if the meat hasn't been frozen at $0°F$ for three weeks or longer. The meat varies in flavor and tenderness, depending on such factors as age, and whether the animal is a nursing sow or a male killed during rutting season. Its cooking also depends on its age and size; most any wild game cookbook will give complete directions for recipes including everything from bear hash to whole braised bear with sweet potatoes.

Venison (which includes deer, moose, elk, caribou and other species) is far more valued today as a love food than bear. The truth is that no part of the deer or its relations, from antlers to genitals, has been spared in the search for the perfect aphrodisiac (see Course Eighteen). "Perhaps the reason why the ancients attributed the property [of inducing love] to the genital members of the deer, Davenport writes, was from the supposition that it was the receptacle of the bile; that the abundance and acrid quality of this fluid caused lasciviousness and that the stag being transported by an erotic furor during the rutting season, he was the most salacious of animals." Paulinus recommended the testes, penis and semen of the stag for lovers, though he neglects again to mention the problem of collecting the last for elixirs, and the early Greeks and Romans believed that the erotic truffle sprang from the earth from the seminal fluid of mating deer. Nor was venison meat by any means neglected. The Persians dined intimately on stag venison, and Solomon fed his 700 wives and 300 concubines great quantities of harts, roebucks and fallow deer. The Romans liked their deer boiled at their orgies, and that lusty red-haired giant Charlemagne, the father of fifty, often breakfasted on a whole joint of venison.

At the time of Marco Polo, Deer Kidney Soup and Deer Head Soup were considered restoratives among the Chinese. Venison was one of the few choice meats allowed at Henry VIII's festivals, especially "haunches of venison cooked to rags and powdered with ginger" (the ginger, at least in Queen Victoria's recipe two centuries later, used "to keep the flies away..."). The meat is featured in many of the great ribald orgies in literature. Rabelais has King Grangonsier serve eighteen fallow deer at the munificent feast he makes for his son Gargantua on his return after defeating King Picrochole, and in *Don Quixote,* Cervantes writes of venison hanging off tree branches for the Rabelaisan marriage feast of Camacho the Rich. In real life, Madame DuBarry is said to have used venison to arouse Louis XV, just as venison chops were featured at fashionable dinner parties here at the turn of the century for essentially the same purpose. Today it is said that Manchurians are particularly fond of roast venison as a love food, believing that it supplies an abundance of sex hormones.

In Manchuria and other parts of the world deerkind is still being stripped of its phallic antlers by mankind striving for rejuvenation. The antlers are thought to contain ample phosphorous, that stiffener so prominent in the pharmacopia of sexual folklore. *Tanko-krin,* a drink made from ground reindeer antlers and alcoholic brine, is now popular in Russia, according to a *Newsweek* world survey of aphrodisiacs that are presently in vogue. The Chinese also put their faith in same, though not so loyally as in rhino horn, reindeer antlers selling for only one dollar a pound on today's market. In Hong Kong, powdered deer antlers (*lu kung*) can be purchased in many shops, but the Chinese and other peoples are apparently unaware that deer can often trick the love hunter—a number of antlered *does* have been bagged by sportsmen, some boasting nine racks of horns but actually being sterile females.

Deer only became the more dignified "venison" when the Normans invaded England and bestowed the name upon a dish Saxon diners had featured for centuries. The meat soon became royal cuisine. Feudal lords enjoyed it at banquets heralded by a blast of the hunting horns where juicy haunches of venison were roasted on spits in great fireplaces and downed with copious draughts of English ale or foreign wine. Shakespeare writes of "hot venison pastry" prepared for fat Falstaff, and another writer noted that "England...hath more fallow deer than all Europe that I have seen."

American Indian braves ate deer meat to become more virile and fleet of foot (perhaps to evade pursuing husbands). Roast venison was their favorite, but they didn't have to tell the English colonists much about the dish. A venison stew was, in fact, cooked in a great pot over an outdoors fire at the first Thanksgiving feast. The Indians did, however, show us how to make pemmican, another strength-giving meat preservative for travelers, made by mixing powdered dried venison with melted bone marrow from a bear, dried vegetables and dried fruits such as cranberries.

Venison itself will do just as much if not more for the libido as the genitals of deer and similar byproducts. The dishes that can be prepared from the deer and its relatives would fill several cookbooks. There is, for example, the ancient Aztec recipe consisting of chipped venison and corn meal wrapped in corn husks and steamed, and their concoction of venison served in a *mole* or chocolate sauce, which is said to have contributed a flavor similar to wine. Then there is the classic English dish of umbles, these being the heart, liver and entrails of deer. "In olden times," we're told, "umbles were the perquisite of the huntsman. When the lord and his household dined, the venison pastry was served on the dais, but the umbles were made into a pie for the huntsman and his fellows. Hence the origin of the saying about eating humble pie."

Dishes like umbles made men far from humble in matters of the bed; hence, perhaps, the sexual renown of English gamekeepers like Lady Chatterley's Mellors. As a matter of fact, almost all cuts of venison are as tasty and trusty, if properly prepared, but the buck is preferred to the doe and the young to the old animal. A young buck dressed out and hung to age about ten days in a cool dry place is venison of the first order. Especially delicious are the haunch, filet, loins and chops, but the neck, hind legs, liver and brains have also been esteemed in the aphrodisiac cookery. All that remains, then, is to bag a deer, have it butchered, and serve it with verve. Such hearty hart meat, like the horny hare and company, has been known to make lovers put Lady Chatterley and her lover to shame.

COURSE NINE

Beef In The Raw For The Bawdy:
Our Menu Including
Bull's Balls And Filet Mignon,
The Original Sir Loin,
Cow-Bull Computer Dating
And Mating,
The $1,000,000 Search For The Perfect Steak,
Tournedos, Steak Tartare, Et. Al.

"Brother, I had to fill this belly, and when I did, I put a whole cellar full of pepper on my steak, for aphrodite, what the hell you call it. And now I'm rarin', I'm like asbestos inside . . ."

—James T. Farrell, *Gashouse McGinty*

Farrell's Casey, a young man making haste toward a brothel, wasn't far from the truth in his estimate of his worthy sirloin, for prosaic beefsteak, as sexologist Havelock Ellis points out, "is probably as powerful a sexual stimulant as any food," wild or domesticated. Just 6 ounces of beef will provide 77% of one's daily protein requirements and 63% of daily iron needs, not to mention the fact that most beef cuts contain less than 250 calories for a 3½-ounce serving. This is good news indeed for the average American, who even at currently galactic prices eats far more beef than any other meat—some 114 pounds a year—in dishes ranging from extravagant Tournedos Rossini, Chateaubriand and Filet Mignon Marquis De

Sade to the lowly hamburger and still lowlier, yet far more elevating, bull's testicles.

There are several good reasons why bull's testicles (variously called bull's balls, Rocky Mountain oysters, prairie oysters and Spanish kidneys) are the most fabled of beef aphrodisiac dishes. For one, the bull himself has been recorded as a symbol of virility since primitive man began painting pornographic pictures on cave walls. Among early medical prescriptions featuring Ferdinand, his lower parts were naturally featured far more frequently than the more conventional cuts above. The Roman writer Paulinus unequivocally recommends bull urine. Bull dung was featured in Navajo Indian love recipes and France's redoubtable Dr. Venette speaks of "penis of bull killed during May and October (the mating seasons)" for men wishing to obtain powerful erections.

A more appetizing bull dish is the sixteenth-century recipe for Pie of Bull's Testicles invented by Bartolomo Scappi, chef to Pope Pius V. "Boil four bull's testicles together with salt," Scappi instructs all would-be lovers. "Cut into slices and sprinkle with salt, pepper, nutmeg and cinnamon. Then, in a pie crust, place layers of sliced testicles alternated with mince of lamb's kidneys, ham, marjoram, cloves and thyme." Long after Scappi, the famous French neurologist Brown-Sequard, who founded the much disputed "science" of organotherapy in 1889, claimed that both he and his patients had greatly enhanced their sexual prowress by eating bull's testicles. The seventy-year-old scientist went so far as to transplant these testicles under the abdominal walls of patients, apparently working on the theory that men with three testes are better in bed than those with a mere two, but it has since been established that testicles cannot store sex hormones such as testosterone and that when transplanted they wither and die anyway. Dr. Reuben is probably close to the truth when he advises in his *Everything You Wanted To Know About Sex*...that bulls' testicles contain "a fair dose of male sex hormone" and "eaten absolutely fresh and absolutely raw...might have done *some* good" for the "under par," but he too notes that "most of the hormone is destroyed by the gastric juices." Nevertheless, a patent restorative medicine called Vigosan, unavailable in the United States but highly popular in Europe, uses testosterone from bull's testicles among its ingredients.

The virile bull has long been prized by lovers throughout the world for his lower parts. The prudish among us in ages past acknowledged his sexuality by using euphemisms such as "a cow's father," "a cow creature," "a male cow," "a Jonathan" and "a gentleman cow" for "bull." Today, however, bull's balls are called just that in some restaurants in France and Spain. Always lauded by men and "interesting" to women, they are invariably served fresh and are best when accompanied by a dry Spanish wine. Sometimes the meat is cut into thin slices, dipped in batter and then fried in olive oil flavored with rosemary, the circles of meat tasting like very rich veal. In America such "Spanish kidneys" are often prepared with saffron and caraway seed. Few aphrodisiac dishes are so psychologically effective, but then, to sound a sour note, there's no telling where the particular bull's balls came from. Could be they belonged to a superstar like that bull belonging to French widow Yvonne Cordier. Farmer Marcel Huchon sued widow Cordier, 87, recently because her bull entered his pasture and made love to all of his eight cows, claiming that "they were young virgins of irreproachable virtue...too young to know about vamping or even flirting." Widow Cordier, in her defense, insisted that "the bull is not the villain in the case...*alors*, Huchon's a grown man who should know better than to tempt the devil." Then again your bull's balls might have been the property of a pedigree named Lindertis Evulse, a $176,400 champion, who nevertheless flunked all his fertility tests. He never did impregnate a single heifer even after undergoing corrective surgery, and nobody ever found out exactly what had gone wrong.

Just as popular as bull's balls, at least in the Far East, are gallstones from the common cow. Canada Packers says that these cost about a thousand dollars a pound, for they get only two pounds of the little growths from their yearly slaughter of hundreds of thousands of cattle. But as the gallstones are the basis for an aphrodisiac potion used there for centuries, oriental lovers are quite willing to pay the price.

In any case, prosaic beefsteak will probably serve man and woman as well as the best bull's balls or cow gallstones. Contemporary medical opinion substantiates Havelock Ellis' findings in most respects and history certainly vindicates him. In the Dionysian orgies mentioned a few pages back it was beef that those rapacious naked priestesses tore apart live with their bare hands and teeth. The Arabian *Perfumed Garden* prescribes "onions cooked with beef" for impotent lovers, and Rabelais believed that salted beef "helped one find love at midnight without a candle," although it's hard to say why he quoted the old proverb "It is pleasant to see black cows burned in wood at the climax of coition." Among other Frenchmen, Talleyrand often served beef at his intimate suppers, De Sade emphatically recommended same, Dr. Venette commends "marrow of beef" as a good aphrodisiac in his *Tableau de l'Amour Conjugal* and Brillat-Savarin praises "a fillet of beef underdone in the middle, larded (French beef is generally lean) and done in its own gravy." English and American slang often associates beef with sex, "beef" having been at various times slang for "the male member," "to be in a woman's beef" meaning "to have intercourse," a "beefsteak" being "a harlot in service of a pimp" and "beefcake" today being the male equivalent of "cheesecake."

Domesticated beef is probably as abundant in azezome and as strength-giving as any wild game and is widely recommended by physicians today in restorative diets in recipes ranging from beef curry to Smothered Venus (tenderloin covered with onions). Although it doesn't enjoy the same fabulous reputation as fish, it has, in the words of Dr. George Belham, "a marked stimulating effect in body metabolism in general." Dr. Belham, who prescribes a number of beef dishes in his *Virility Diet*, does however point out the limitations of beef and any high-protein food when eaten in excess, noting that "a large meat meal is more likely to make a man feel hot and sweaty than potent, especially in hot weather" and recommending that its consumption be spread out evenly over the day.

Until bull's balls become better known here Americans will have to be content with feeding their loved ones steak, which is generally as good an aphrodisiac and certainly far more popular. As Dr. Reuben points out, "Feeding your best girl a juicy steak at a classy restaurant may set the mental wheels in motion and land both of you in bed," the secret ingredient being by far "in the atmosphere, not the steak." In the many variations discussed further on, steak remains America's favorite restaurant food, though it may soon lose its title to lobster. Gourmands have gone to great lengths trying to find the ultimate steak and generally agree that a marbled specimen of one to one and a half pounds is best. We can even specify the "best way" to cook it—your steak should be trimmed of fat and broiled over charcoal four to six inches from the grill at 120°F for fifteen seconds for each ounce on each side. That, anyway, is the opinion of Maurice Drecier, the millionaire epicure who has spent over twenty-five years and $600,000 thus far searching throughout some eighty countries for the perfect steak. Drecier carries a golden knife, with him (yes, he is also the owner of that golden caviar ball noted earlier), which he insists must be able to cut through his steak without undue effort. Other Drecier equipment includes an oak platter on which the steak must be served, a pair of silk gloves for the waiter to carry the hot oak platter, a thermometer, an odd gadget that measures the raw steak's salinity and a magnifying glass to examine its texture. The monocled, leonine-maned gourmet, arrayed in his Saville Row suit and carrying a surgeon's black bag containing his arsenal, invariably asks if the steer he is to eat was contented and unfrightened before being slaughtered, for it seems that "when a steer is frightened, its muscles contract and that makes for a tough steak."

Drecier, who has awarded hundreds of golden knives to restaurants for excellent steaks has obviously never found a perfect one and has probably tasted many that were a real "sole food," tasting "like the bottom of a pair of new shoes." While in Japan, he tested the world-famous Kobe steak, supposedly so tender because Kobe's contented cows are bottle-fed beer and hand-massaged daily, but told his shocked Kobian hosts that their mignon, which then cost $5 a pound, fell just short of the mark. The steers weren't fed enough beer or massaged with vigor, he explained mock-seriously and the next morning Kobe was clogged with drunken cattle being chased down the street by repentant masseuses. Despite Dreicer's protestations, however, former New York *Times* food editor Craig Clairborne claims that Kobe beef, which is so named because it's shipped out of Kobe, "may be the tastiest and best textured beef in the world." Some authorities, though, give the golden knife to the Wadakin or Matsuzaka beef raised near Mt. Fugi. The animals raised for this meat are kept one to a dark shed at the back of small farmers' houses, fed hot beer mash and hand-massaged top and bottom at least once a day to help distribute their weight properly.

Beef in all its forms has been selected so discriminately since Agamemnon, the king of kings, thought it such a delicacy that it was served at all state functions, his guest of honor receiving an entire fillet of beef. As for the king of chefs, Apicius, that noble Roman gives the following Stuffed Womb aphrodisiac recipe in his cookbook, which we offer for your consideration without comment: "Make as follows: Pounded pepper and cumin, two short heads of leek stripped to the soft part, rue, *liquamen* [stock]. To this pounded mixture add meat well beaten and pine kernels, and press in the well-washed womb of a cow. Cook in water, oil, *liquamen*, with a bouquet of leeks and dill."

Among the English, one writer tells us, "next to Habeas Corpus and freedom of the Press there are few things Britons have a greater respect for and a livelier faith in than beef." This faith dates back to the Saxons, whose words "ox" and "calf" were largely replaced by the Norman invaders' "beef" and "veal." In *Henry V* Shakespeare wrote, "Give them great meals of iron and beef" and in *The Taming of the Shrew* he asked, "What would you say to a piece of beef and mustard?" The British have long counted roast beef as their national dish; their famed yeomen of the guard are called Beefeaters and possibly had their name bestowed upon them because they consumed so much beef at the royal castle. To cook their huge roasts and whole animals, dogs were often employed, several of them sometimes working in relays inside wheel cages turning the beef on the spits. The long-bodied, crooked-legged "turnspit dogs" (of which was written: *"With eagerness he still does forward tend, / Like Sisyphus, whose journey has no end")* were so indispensible to the cooking of olde England that one sea captain seeking to spite the inhabitants of Bristol, who had been rude to him, stole every turnspit dog in town, knowing that "the dog ruled the roost in those days."

The futurist French cook Jules Maincave, the dadaist of French chefs, once declared that "There is nothing more delicious, in my opinion, than a beef with kummel, garnished with rounds of bananas stuffed with Gruyère cheese." Fortunately, or to the delight of most, anyway, the French have regarded steak more traditionally. At the Restaurant Laperouse in Paris, that same restaurant across the Seine where lovers are locked together in secret rooms, *steak saute Laperouse* is the classic specialty of the house. Created by chef Fernand Poisson, this consists of an excellent piece of *contre-filet* seasoned with salt and pepper, then sauteed in butter in a small pan, the sauce a reduction of chopped shallots, dry white wine, veal steak and chopped parsley. But then the French have always been most particular about their beef dishes. One Gallic trencherman was recently sentenced to eight years in prison for seizing a butcher knife and stabbing his wife to death. "You cook like a Nazi!" he cried when she overcooked his roast beef. He had only been released from prison five years before for killing his first wife because she served his roast too *rare*. French juries apparently consider such gourmet murders *crimes passionel*.

Americans, especially males, have traditionally valued a thick juicy broiled steak over fancier concoctions. It was here that beef cattle were widely bred to perfection, though of course, millions throughout the world have had a hand in the evolution of the tasty breeds we now enjoy. In America today artificial insemination is used to impregnate some 45% of all cows. Dummy females are used to trick the bulls into ejaculating the necessary semen into an artificial vagina, and about ¼ of an ounce of semen is collected from each bull at a service. This can be frozen almost indefinitely in a suitable diluting medium containing egg yolk or heated milk and antibiotics before it is placed in a syringe to inseminate a cow. Usually the procedure is simple enough, but one farmer in Iowa is presently suing a breeding service for $250,000, claiming that a bottle of their frozen bull semen exploded and a small amount of semen caused blindness in his right eye. Anyway, the hefty bulls and cows cannot damage one another via this process and the best bulls can be used to artificially inseminate 30,000 cows annually instead of the twenty-odd cows they would mate with naturally. There are even what are called Kelver Training Cows ("which simulate all the movements of a live cow...even to the discharge of a lubricant") available to neophyte veterinarians so that they can easily learn how "to enter live cows with complete confidence"—with a syringe, that is. We can now also artificially inseminate pedigreed cows and transplant the embryo to a hardier animal which will give birth to a pedigreed calf totally unrelated to it, and computers are being used by outfits like the American Breeding Service to pair off "ideal mates" for artificial insemination. ABS is very selective in choosing its bulls, too. "In 1968," according to the *Wall Street Journal*," they paid $130,000 for Emperor, a promising young bull out of Canada. Shortly after his arrival, ABS threw a 'Welcome to Wisconsin' party for Emperor at a hotel dining room while Miss Wisconsin herself played 'The Emperor's Waltz' on the piano. Emperor stayed for the entire formal banquet, and during the toasts he was served fodder on a silver platter by two secretaries costumed as French maids."

Yet Emperor can't be having much fun with dummy cows and neither can the cows he'll artificially inseminate. One hopes "animal engineering" doesn't extend itself into "human engineering," but in the meantime Ferdinand's loss is humankind's gain, resulting as it does in the hearty delicious steaks to which Americans attribute their prowess. However, although young Casey's sentiments pretty well sum up the national attitude about beef—rare steak and I'm rarin' to go—this is not to say that increasingly sophisticated diners aren't enjoying the more exotic beef dishes from steak tartare to chateaubriand.

Steak tartare, like all raw meats, has especially attracted lovers searching for potency. Medically, the reasons for this appear to lie in the fact that the all-important vitamin E in beef is lost by overcooking. Quoting various writers on the subject, Van de Velde notes that "raw flesh food is generally felt to be incompatible with our civilization." But he observes that "there are many civilized persons who prefer it," and wonders if this taste does not "spring from some obscure working of the urge to preserve the race, through an extra supply of vitamin E," the all-important tocopherol discovered in 1922 and said by some to be intimately connected with both the efficient functioning of all vitamins as well as the reproductive system. The zenith or nadir of raw-flesh eating today is practiced in Ethiopia, where primitive farmers sometimes cut strips of flesh from still-living bovines tied securely to the kitchen door. Wrapping the raw beef in a pastry bread called *teff*, they gobble it down on the spot. Steak tartare offers a better choice for most of us. Bloodthirsty about their meals as well as their conquests, martial and marital, the early nomadic Tartars almost always preferred their meat raw, but sometimes they relented a bit and placed a hunk of meat under the saddle, cooking it by friction during hours of riding. At any rate, in medieval times, traveling Hamburg merchants learned about their recipe for scraped raw meat seasoned with highly regarded stimulants such as salt, pepper and onion juice, and named it Tartar steak or steak tartare in their honor. This was the first hamburger, and hamburger remained so until some anonymous Hamburger in Germany shaped *steak tartare* into round patties and cooked them. Tartar sauce, a maxonnaise containing diced pickles, onions, olives, capers and green herbs, in turn takes its name from Tartar steak, which was often seasoned with these ingredients.

Many men prefer their steak exactly like the Tartars, or close to it, but since Ulysses roasted with his own hands a sirloin of beef, the vast majority have at least warmed it. Louis XV—called the Well-Beloved by Madame Pompadour, Madame DuBarry, as well as his subjects—enjoyed *petits soupers* of filet of sirloin braised à *la royale*, which was elaborately prepared with slivers of bacon, veal and other ingredients. Today Sophia Loren (see her *In The Kitchen With Love*, Doubleday) recommends *involtino*, which also happens to be her nickname for her husband. *Involtino* is a tip of sirloin covered with *Mortadello* (baloney) rolled, speared together with toothpicks and browned in garlic, tomatoes, basil and pepper. Sounds interesting. So does her custom of calling all those she loves by food nicknames—like her *polpette*, or "little meat ball."

Sirloin, strictly speaking, is meat from the steer's hip, but today it is sold without the prized filet and often goes by the name of shell hip or rump steak. The old Sir Loin story is myth, but it does show how highly esteemed in the past was this aristocrat of all steaks. The tale is told of numerous British monarchs, including the lusty Henry VIII, James I (on whom Jonathan Swift bestowed credit) and lastly, Charles II, who ruled in England from 1660 to 1685. In each case the monarch in question was supposed to be so pleased with the succulent slice of pink meat served him that he unsheathed his sword, laid it upon the brown-crested sirloin and knighted it, solemnly declaring, "Hereafter thou shalt be dubbed 'Sir Loin.' " The only bothersome fact is that "sirloin" actually derives from an old English word "surloin," which (from *sur*, above or over) meant simply the cut over the loin; the word came to be misspelled "sirloin" in about 1600. This, however, did not prevent writers like Scott from using terms like "the knightly sirloin and the noble baron of beef." The last, practically unheard of today, was a double sirloin, a huge joint weighing up to 100 pounds and comprising both sides of the back.

Far more appealing to beef lovers and gourmands these days are the poshest of posh meats: filet mignon, Chateaubriand, tournedos and Beef Wellington. Both filet mignon and tournedos are cut from the long, tapering muscle of beef we call the tenderloin (from just where on the tenderloin depends on which expert one reads and is hardly worth arguing about here), and chateaubriand is generally agreed to be the middle part of the tenderloin, cut two or three inches thick. All are mouth-watering, depending just as much on the preparation as the prime cut of meat. Filet mignon is decidedly the most popular of the three, generally being 1½ inches to 2 inches thick and coming from the same tender cut of beef as its rivals—that is, the best cut available anywhere. Rabelais called the female pudendum *Mignon D'Amourette*, love's dainty, and this still remains a French slang expression, just as *mignonne* means a fleshy harlot in the French vocabulary of love. We've even come across one recipe called *Fillet Mignon Marquis De Sade* printed in the New York *Times* of all places, but filet mignon is generally rather simply sautéed or grilled very quickly to keep the meat on the inside a rosy pink color. There are, however, many garnishes both simple and composite (a garnish made of many elements) that great chefs always use when preparing this choice steak.

Steak Chateaubriand has a more romantic history than filet mignon. The French writer and roué the Vicomte Francois René Chateaubriand, for whom it is named, remained active between the sheets until the sheets were pulled over him, departing this world at the age of eighty with his attractive mistress holding his hand. One old story tells us that Brillat-Savarin dined in Paris with the Vicomte on the night that an anonymous restaurant proprietor invented chateaubriand in his honor. The occasion, according to this version, was the French romantic's publication of *La Genie du Christianisme* and the succulent tenderloin was encased between two flank steaks, symbolizing Christ and the thieves. The outer steaks, seared black, were thrown to the dogs, leaving the rare and juicy tenderloin. Chateaubriand is often served with a Béarnaise sauce (hollandaise sauce to which is added tarragon vinegar, fresh parsley, tarragon and chervil) and elaborately arranged on a silver platter containing artfully placed *pommes souffles*, mushrooms and other vegetables. We remember having it at Miller's in Baltimore, at near midnight in a nearly deserted dining room, our waiter royally slicing a chateaubriand so tender and juicy that it had to have been prepared according to Prosper Montagne's directions in the *Larousse Gastronomique*—that is, brushed lavishly with butter, piquantly seasoned, and then seared under a high heat to seal in the flavor before cooking it under a low heat to the perfect pinkish degree of doneness.

But if we had to recommend one meat above all others as an aphrodisiac gourmet food, from both an historical and psychological standpoint, it would have to be the palate-tempting Tournedos Rossini. This dish is made not only from the choicest cut of beef, but combines all the erotic glamour of the *foie gras* and truffles we'll sample in later chapters. A Florentine specialty that was introduced to France in a rudimentary form by Catherine de' Medici, tournedos are small round one-inch thick pieces of charcoal-broiled filet mignon. There are several celebrated recipes for them. *Tournedos Massena*, garnished with artichoke bottoms filled with Béarnaise sauce, are broiled crisp on the outside and tender pink inside, set atop rounds of fried bread, then crowned by a slice of poached bone marrow cooked with a wine or brandy sauce and brought to the table flaming with the wine. *Tournedos Henry IV* are sautéed and served on fried croutons, an artichoke bottom filled with Béarnaise sauce placed atop each steak, the garnish generally french fried potatoes of one kind or another.

Tournedos Rossini, however, is the classic tournedos dish of the French cuisine. One tale attributes the dish to the greatest chef of our time, Auguste Escoffier, who with his partner Cesar Ritz operated the Ritz hotels in Paris and London, their plush hostels contributing the word "ritzy" to the language. *Tournedos à la Rossini*, is named for the Italian composer Gioacchino Antonio Rossini (1792–1868), best known for his *Barber of Seville.* Sacheverell Sitwell tells us that it was invented for the gourmet musician at the Antico Pappagallo in Bologna, and another story has it that Rossini conceived the dish himself at the height of his popularity. According to this old tale, Rossini was dining at the Cafe-Anglais in Paris. Tired of the beef dishes on the menu, he gave instructions for his meat to be prepared in a different way. "Never would I dare to offer such a thing—it is...unpresentable!" protested the maitre d'. "Well then, arrange not to let it be seen!" the composer countered. Ever after, we are told, tournedos were to be served not before the eyes, but behind the diner's back; hence the name in French: *tourne le dos,* "turn one's back." More likely, the first tournedos was invented by nineteenth-century French chef Antoine Beauvilliers, and his directions for cooking them indicate how the name tournedos evolved: "As soon as steak is seared on one side, promptly turn it to the other side and sear. Cook for about 3 minutes on each side, turning as necessary to prevent scorching or drying." In any case, there's do doubt that the specific dish *Tournedos Rossini* was named in honor of the composer, either in Bologna or in Paris by Escoffier or Rossini himself. And what could be more delicious? Succulent slices of filet of beef carefully sautéed in butter, set on mounds of fried bread and capped with slices of *foie gras* previously tossed in butter. The *foie gras* crowned with rich slices of truffle that have been heated in the same butter in which the tournedos are sautéed and cooked with a Périgueux sauce that is poured over the whole. One of the richest, most expensive and sexually stimulating dishes in the world.

Beef Wellington and Beef Stroganoff are other posh dishes well worth dedicating to Aphrodite. Nineteenth-century Russian diplomat Count Paul Stroganoff has the honor of having the well-known Beef Stroganoff named after him. Sold in inferior packaged form today, it is beef sautéed with onions and cooked in a sauce of consomme, sour cream, mushrooms, mustard and other condiments. Beef Wellington, another popular dish, commemorates Napoleon's greatest adversary, Arthur Wellesley, first duke of Wellington. It combines a choice cut of filet, *pâté de foie gras*, bacon, brandy and various condiments, the whole wrapped baked in a golden crust of puffed pastry and served with either a truffle or mushroom sauce. The eloquent dish, once confined to posh restaurants, is now often made at home, thanks to the introduction of frozen pastry dough. Meant to top even this "dukely dish" was the princely variation invented to honor England's Prince Albert. Filet of Beef Prince Albert, also known as Prince of Wales and London House, does not bother with pastry. The filet, wrapped in larding bacon, is sliced open horizontally but not all the way through, *foie gras* and truffles being inserted, the whole soaked in port wine and cooked to perfection in the oven with vegetables. Prince Albert garnish—mushroom caps cooked in butter and truffles cooked in Madeira—is usually served with the tantalizing dish.

Various veal dishes have also been highly praised as love foods. Pliny wrote that a woman who eats veal roasted with the plant *aristolochia* at the time of conception will bear lusty male offspring. Veal probably owes its reputation as a powerful aphrodisiac to an old myth that claimed it was more nutritious than mature beef. Brillat-Savarin used the meat for a potion for those "who get easily exhausted," feeding it to a poet and a lady author. He later found that "the poet, who was merely elegiac, has become romantic," and that the lady, "who had only written a feeble novel...has written a second one...which ends with a good and happy marriage." The early Romans spoke of the wonders of calf boiled in its mother's milk, but veal is certainly no better than other beef, if indeed it is as effective. The meat comes from calves four to fourteen weeks of age that are fed almost exclusively on their mother's milk and is too lean for broiling. It is not as popular here as in Italy, where it has long been enjoyed in dishes such as veal parmigiana and scaloppine. In fact, our comparative dislike of veal may stem from the early Saxon belief that killing calves for meat was nothing short of sinful. Still, Americans consume about four pounds of calf per capita yearly, and produce the ultimate grade, *"plume de veau,"* which is raised from Holstein stock in Wisconsin and sells for double the price of ordinary veal.

Good things have been said for beef tripe, an American "soul food"; lasagne made with beef, despite the fact that the word apparently derives from the Latin *lasanum*, or "chamberpot"; and even milk products from the cow, the *Kama Sutra* advising that "The milk of a white cow who has a white calf nestling beside her possesses (stimulating) properties...." As for yogurt, the Islamic physician Avicenna declared that "This acid milk awakens the desire for coitus in warm natures and makes the mucous membranes moist." Even hamburger has its adherents, but you'd be better off quadrupling your investment and wining and dining your *polpette* on one of the posh dishes described above. Prices, of course, aren't what they used to be. When the great Delmonicos opened in Manhattan in 1825, the cost of a full course steak dinner was 40¢—less than half the price of a cup of coffee in some elegant restaurants these days. Says one New York restaurateur, "To serve good first-class prime beef at decent prices today, we have to cut down portions to twelve ounces. Places which offer you a "full" sixteen ounces of prime meat just aren't serving prime, or the steak is about five ounces bone." This seems reasonable when you consider that a 1000-pound steer yields only fifty choice steaks.

Kansas City's famed char-broiled steaks may be a thing of the past due to a new city ordinance requiring that restaurants doing any char-broiling must install a special device that prevents the melted fat from dripping onto the coals, and Kansas City chefs claim that the fatty smoke this causes is the very thing that gives their steak its famous flavor. Excellent steak houses, however, are legion throughout the country. Among the best are Peter Luger's Steak House in Brooklyn, New York, the Coachhouse and Sparks Steak House in Manhattan, numerous restaurants in Chicago, and the Chesapeake Steak House in Baltimore. There's also good steak to be had in fabulous skyscrpaer restaurants like New York's Rainbow Room and Top of the Sixes, where the romantic panoramic views alone are almost worth the price of a meal. If a restaurant offers "U.S.D.A. prime" steak (not simply "prime," which is merely the meat packer's designation), does not freeze it and follows your instructions in the preparation, it would be hard to ruin a good steak. Proper aging (six to eight weeks) is something the customer can do little about except complain; most steak houses use a process known as "forced aging" at high temperatures that results in a tender steak with an unfortunate gamey, smelly taste. Yet diners can be sure to indicate their preferences clearly enough. After selecting the cut of steak desired (porterhouse, T-bone and club steaks are all delicious, though not as glamourous as filet mignon & co.), specify whether it should be cooked extra blood-rare, blood-rare, medium blood-rare, medium-rare, medium or well-done. The first and second are preferable from an aphrodisiac point of view. From there on feel free to follow the directions of that great steak-hunter Maurice Dreicer previously given—at the risk of being asked to leave the eatery.

But perhaps the raunchy rake or randy wench would be better off having his/her beef at home, anyway, for culinary as well as amatory reasons. Restaurant steaks today are too often precut flash-frozen products, broiled weeks before being sent to the restaurant, where they are simply thawed and cooked in ovens for 15 minutes or so before being served as "rare-charcoal broiled"—which they were at the factory maybe three months ago. Good steak still can be purchased from reliable butchers ("U.S.D.A. Prime," or "U.S.D.A. Choice"), and many butchers will put regular customers on to less expensive, tasty cuts of beef that are just as enjoyable. If money is no object and one doesn't trust butchers for some reason, choice steaks can even be ordered via airmail from various firms that advertise nationally. At any rate, whether filet mignon, steak tartare, tournedos or Smothered Venus is your dish, the proper atmosphere will help to both tenderize and/or toughen your prime choice for the evening. No doubt about it. There's even a wild rumor going around (strictly a wild rumor, though) that the Beef Industry Council may change its slogan to "Beef Is A Four Letter Word." Or, worse yet: "No Bull—Eat Beef In The Raw And You'll Cut The Mustard, No Matter How You Slice It— And That's No Bum Steer."

COURSE TEN

More Meats
And Fowl For Foul Play

"At the table of a gentleman living in the Chausée d'Antin was served up
to his guest an Arles sausage of an enormous size.... 'It is really very
large,' said the lady, casting on it a rougish glance; 'what a pity it is unlike
anything I have ever seen.' "

—Brillat-Savarin, *The Physiology of Taste*

On the branches of the very real Meat Forest, at the edge of the very
real Wine Lake, hung huge succulent hunks of every kind of roast meat
and fowl conceivable. The fabulously wealthy Chinese "Playboy King"
Chou-hsin had built the artificial lake and landscaped the woods near his
summer palace, the Deer Mansions, in about 1300 B.C., and thereafter
used his playground solely for erotic pleasures. Some 3000 naked muscular warriors were assigned to swagger about this earthly paradise, free
to eat and drink at will, were required, in fact, to do nothing save entertain the naked women roaming the woods. On a typical day, after his

charges had whetted their appetites with wine from the lake and fortified themselves with the roast meats hanging from the trees, Chou-hsin perfunctorily snapped his fingers and naked concubines were released into the forest of delights, the half-drunk warriors instinctively giving chase, pulling the women to the ground and "making love to them like wild horses." Day after day, the lake would be refilled with wine and the trees replenished with the choicest cuts of meat. At almost any hour the same chase could be witnessed, the powerful, eight-foot-tall Playboy King watching from his veranda, drunk on wine and fortified by huge haunches of meats himself—until he was finally able to make love to and reach a climax with his favorite concubine, Ta Chin.

We don't suggest that anyone follow Chou-hsin's example in some local greenbelt (his exploits may be legendary in part and most of us certainly can't afford all that meat and wine, not to mention all the extras). But the yarn does show the high esteem in which the ancient Chinese, like lovers everywhere, have held all kinds of meat from the earliest times. The *Perfumed Garden* and practically every other ancient sex manual (excepting those of the vegetarian Hindus) recommend "all sorts of meat upon the table," for almost the same reasons cited in the pages on beef and game preceding these. Modern sexologists generally agree, Dr. Iwan Block stating unequivocally, for example, that "all meat without doubt exercises a stimulating effect upon the *vita sexualis*." In this regard we're glad to note that the average American consumes some 75 pounds of other meat in addition to the 114 pounds of beef he or she eats every year. Presented here, in broad general categories, are some of America's most meritorious meats and favorite fowl for foul play. If someone's favorite has been ignored, the omission is likely due to lack of space, though we cannot abjectly apologize for excluding such love meats as goat, which we've tried and find an abomination—despite the fact that some goat devotees point out how many centenarian millionaires have been kept alive and acting like old goats on a diet of goat's milk. As the French say, you can't argue with tastes, but we prefer the entrees following.

· PUNGENT PORK ·

Recently a forty-two-year-old American lady anthropologist paid a dowry of four pigs to become one of the wives of Obaharok, the chief of a native Indonesian tribe whose "sensuous customs" she'd set out to study two years before. Her native attire consisted of bark not too strategically placed, and one newscaster (it had to be Roger Grimsby) described her husband's meager attire as a *korteka*, "resembling what you throw away when you're finished with the Charmin."

No doubt Obaharok's great allure was made possible in part by the pigs he had eaten in the past, but the pigs he received from his eager bride didn't do him much good. The lady anthropologist refused to consummate their marriage and all he could do was take a cold swim and ask Indonesian authorities to deport her. We hope everyone fares better than Obaharok, but we can only guarantee the long-standing reputation of pork as an excellent love food. One of the most mouth-watering sights of the cookery is a roast pig resting on its silver tray in the center of a table, red cherries for its eyes, its mouth pried open into a lascivious smile and stuffed with an apple or even (if ye host be especially royal and rich) a huge black truffle. Thoughts of Henry VIII at table, a wench on each knee, or of Catherine the Great with *two* studs on each knee, inevitably come to mind; huge golden goblets of wine seem a necessity, and it isn't long before the most reserved are wrestling on the rug.

Pork dishes have always evoked such images. When we think of wild boar, for instance, we remember that Cleopatra always had a choice specimen roasting for Antony at every hour of the day and night. We recall the words of the Roman poet Juvenal, who wrote: "Oh what gluttony is his who has whole boars served for himself, an animal born for banquets." Of such banquets, perhaps the vividly described was a feast attended by Petronius.

> The slaves spread coverings on our couches, when, suddenly, a great noise was heard outside and Laconian hounds rushed into the room and began running around the table. They were followed with a platter on which lay the most enormous wild boar. On its head was perched a cap of a freed slave; on its tusks hung down two baskets lined with pale leaves, one was filled with Syrian dates, the other with Theban dates; little suckling pigs made of pastry and baked in the oven, surrounded the animal as if pressing on the teats, thus giving the guests enough indication to see that it was a breeding sow that was served to them.* Drawing his hunting knife, a slave gave the wild boar a great stab in the belly and suddenly, from the opening in the animal's side flew out thrushes. Vainly the birds tried to escape, flying around and around the room; birdcatchers, provided with fowler's rods, instantly caught them and, by order of the master offered one to each guest.

Boar, as royal as the lion, and in fact the emblem of Richard III, was nevertheless a favorite of early Americans, and it can still be had here,

---

*In *The Alchemist* (1610) Ben Jonson wrote of a love potion consisting of "the swelling unctuous paps of a fat pregnant sow, newly cut off, drest with an exquisite and poignant sauce."

the Channel Islands of California, for one place, abounding with wild pigs. There are many elaborate ways to prepare boar. In one recipe, its eyes are made of egg whites and its head alone is stuffed with the cooked chopped up meat of the animal, this mixed into a rich brown sauce with truffles, pistachio nuts, garlic, eggs, parsley and other ingredients. However, except at such special feasts as an authentic Hawaiian *luau*, where a wild kalua pig must be roasted, roast domesticated pig will do as well as its wild relative in most concoctions. Many gourmet stores offer whole oven-ready suckling pigs, including the Maryland Gourmet Mart in New York City.

Pork from the pig has been offered as a love food in every conceivable form; everything but the oink has been used, and even the oink of a pig has been said to stimulate one Victorian lady (a "pigamist"?), who always took live pigs to bed along with her lover of the evening. For that matter, live pigs dressed in human clothing were used to entertain the royal court under France's puffbelly extraordinary Louis XIV. Domesticated for about 5000 years, and always cheap for man to raise because it's a scavenger, the poor porker has suffered indignities that few other animals have been subjected to in the history of husbandry. In ancient Rome, for example, pork eaters sometimes trampled the abdomen and mammary glands of a sow before slaughtering it. This barbaric procedure, they maintained, noticeably increased its flavor and potency. The animal has actually been interbred so often that no one knows how many varieties there are around the world, and this has resulted in such ironies as the American Shakers, who refrained from "generative lust" themselves, creating the famous Poland China by mating the Big White China with a lusty half-wild hog. Only in China, where Charles Lamb told us pig was roasted for the first time, do people seem to have any respect for the swine. The Chinese still argue the "Two Hundred and One Separate and Ineffable Values of the Pig" and certainly never would call their policeman pigs. But then in that civilized country the best restaurants often vie with each other in coining humble self-deprecatory names for themselves, these including "The Second-Class Establishment of Mr. Hsiang," "Enter Here If You Must," and "The Restaurant Into Which You Would Not Take A Dog."

We can't possibly do justice to all the pork products advertised as aphrodisiacs through the ages, but bacon (the best quality of which is so dear because it comes from the middle section of specially raised lean hogs) is certainly one of them. Bacon has been used by great lovers in dishes far more imaginative than breakfast foods, including some delicious salads. Rabelais, we should note, announced the conception of his lusty hero Gargantua with a bacon metaphor, although he may have been using the old French word meaning pork in general. Writing of Gargantua's parents he tells us: "Together the pair often played the two-backed beast, running and grinding their respective bacons together so blithsomely and to such good purpose that she was soon big with a fair son, whom she bore for eleven months." Which might be something to write on the napkin when serving your better-half of the two-backed beast bacon and eggs in bed.

Rabelais also often mentions the phallic sausage, opining in one place that "whatever women see, they never think, imagine or conceive it save in terms of the stout, stiff-standing dieties Ithyphallos and Penis Erectus." The pork sausage was very obviously a sexual symbol long before it was featured by the Romans at their orgies. We've already quoted Brillat-Savarin's mischievious observation on the sausage as a sexual symbol, those certain lines, with infinite variations, that many a willing woman has used while dining on sausages and wanting to express her willingness. Sausages (from the Latin "Salus" meaning salted or preserved) have been a fun food since the Chinese invented them centuries ago. The Spartans for example, hung sausages from the ceiling during their more raucous parties, men and women holding their hands behind their backs and trying to bite off their tips. Spicy sausages became such a symbol of depraved feasting and wild frivolity among the ancient Romans that they were banned in the early Christian era, and undercover sausage kitchens did a booming bootlegging business providing them to an eager public. They also fell into disrepute in the Middle Ages, when they again became associated with "sinful feasting and carousing." In the United States today we have more than 200 varieties and consume more than 14 billion pounds of hot dogs and 4 billion pounds of sausage per year (these figures include those made from both pork and beef). The world's largest sausage by the way, was made by bakers in Scunthorpe, England some years ago. For the most rapacious among our readers here is the recipe for The Great Scunthorpe Sausage: "Take up 738 pounds of ground pork and work in cereal to extend the mixture to 896 pounds. Take salt, pepper and sage and season to taste. Blend into mixture and force into 3124 feet of sausage casing (pigs intestines). Will serve 6248." Should satisfy anyone.

In Japan, sliced pig ovaries and truffles served with seaweed—only 200 yen a plate if you have a yen for it—is a highly regarded love dish, while in America baked ham, pork chops, pigs feet, pigs organs and numerous cuts of pork have been favored. At least one American centenarian, with almost as long a sex life, has attributed his powers solely to a 100-year love of fat pork. Then, of course, chitlins (this word for pigs' intestines can actually be traced back to thirteenth-century Europe), ham hocks with collard greens, and fresh pig knuckles with sauerkraut are famous Southern soul foods. In short, Americans seem to fortify themselves on all the manifold products of the pig. Like lovers the world over they eat their pork with the relish of that hero in *The Golden Ass* centuries ago, who as a result could say to his paramour:

> I'm well-armed and ready for the merciless battle to which you challenged me, the sort of battle in which no herald can intervene to part the combatants. ...I have been standing to arms all day, and now my bow is strung so tight that I'm afraid something will snap if the Advance isn't sounded pretty soon.

· MARY'S LECHEROUS LAMB ·

> *Mary had a little lamb.*
> *Its fleece was white as snow.*
> *And everywhere that Mary went*
> *That lamb was sure to go.*

Who would believe that Mary's innocent little lamb of rhyme and reality (the poem was written about a very real little girl and the pet lamb that followed her to school) could be a black sheep of the boudoir? But the fact is that Mary, in her later years, anyway, would have been better off following the advice of this parody on the original jingle:

> *Mary had a little lamb*
> *Her lover shot it dead.*
> *Now Mary shares her lamb in bed*
> *Between two hunks of bread.*

The "miraculous" lamb rejuvenation injections given by the late Dr. Paul Neihans at Lausanne's internationally famed Clinique La Praire certainly illustrate the potential of lamb. Neihans, noticing that sheep possess some cancer-resistant quality, began his experiments with cells from the crushed organs of newborn lambs. Injecting the cells intramuscularly into human beings, he claimed that they took hold in the human body, revivifying afflicted organs, generating the production of new and healthy cells, and that they were especially effective in rejuvenating debilitated sexual organs. His treatments, carried on today by Dr. Walter Michel, are obviously controversial, but many rich, prominent and aspiring Beautiful People swear by his lamb cells, attesting that they have found a Fountain of Youth and/or a long extension of their sexual lives. These renowned patients have reportedly included Pope Pius XII, Pope

Paul, Somerset Maugham, Gloria Swanson, the Duchess of Windsor, Noel Coward, Konrad Adenauer, Thomas Mann, Lillian Gish, Bernard Baruch, Charles Chaplin, Winston Churchill, several members of the Japanese Royal family and even Gaylord Hauser. The treatment takes a week and costs at least $1600, though this is a bare minimum, sexual rejuvenation costing much more and "complete" rejuvenation out of the reach of all but millionaires. Supposedly, the lamb embryo cell treatment takes years off one's looks as well, although Dr. Michel conservatively warns of possible dangers in cell therapy and makes no promises.

Lamb has had a similar reputation from earliest times, though not served through a needle. We are told that our Chinese Playboy King Chou-hsin could "cope with ten healthy and strong women in a row" while holding a "huge bronze vessel brimful of wine in one hand and a roast shoulder of lamb in the other," having each "naked woman entwine her legs around his waist while his erected member...virtually carried the weight of her body." (Shades of *The Godfather!*)

In northern China, lamb still remains a popular love dish. Lamb stewed with chestnuts and garlic is a traditional "winter dish"—winter being considered the season to build up a man's reserves of sexual strength so that he can cope with the ladies during the forthcoming spring. A number of similar recipes can be found in the oriental cookery, a few of which would not be palatable to westerners. One bloody Indian concoction calls for hanging a lamb by its forelegs, slashing its throat and pouring cayenne pepper and salt into its windpipe. Next the jugular vein is cut and its end inserted into the windpipe. The blood washes the pepper and salt into the lungs and suffocates the poor animal; the lungs are finally carved out and devoured at body temperature. The process can only be equaled by those Bolivians who castrate their sheep with their teeth.

Though such barbaric practices are not common here, it is important to note that lamb's efficacy has usually been most praised when the lamb eaten was most rare indeed. It was, for example, an aphorism of the eighteenth-century French actor and gastronome Denis Desessarts that "A leg of lamb should be anticipated like the first meeting of lovers...golden as a young German girl and bloody as a Carib." Even today lamb is eaten raw in *pâtés*. One recipe calls for the smooth blending of ½ pound of lean raw lamb ground fine, a tablespoon of fresh chopped parsley, ½ teaspoon salt, ¼ cup of fresh pine nuts and ¼ teaspoon of ground fresh pepper—this mixture removed from the blender, chilled and served as an appetizer on crackers or toast points.

Lamb love recipes have been particularly appreciated by the Turks, who had one for a molded lamb croquette called "Lady's Thigh," and the esteemed Italian chef Bartolomo Scappi was known for his lamb-testes recipes. But the full-grown male of the species hasn't been ignored either. Rabelais mentions the rams of Scythia, which were raised for tails weighing more than thirty pounds. These tails had to be supported by little carts attached to them, the rams pulling the carts around until their tails grew big enough for them to be slaughtered. Then there was Madame DuBarry's chef Manconseil, who advised Louis XV to eat ram's testicles. Both Louis and his lover praised their prodigious properties.

Today Americans eat only about forty pounds of lamb per person each year. This is far below the consumption of many countries, lamb or mutton probably being the principal meat for most nations of the world. But many relish lamb chops, leg of lamb and other cuts, generally served with mint jelly. A particular gourmet delight, at $4 a pound or more, is the "hothouse lamb" of the East, which is milk-fed lamb generally slaughtered at only three to six weeks old. It is said that Alfred Hitchcock once regularly sent his private plane east from Hollywood to obtain this specialty of New Jersey and Pennsylvania.

Lamb might ideally be served at a love feast while the hostess (or even host) belly dances. There are instruction records available for the novice navel spinner, or one can go out for dinner at some local Middle Eastern torsion works and gain inspiration from the pros while eating lamb dishes. *Shish kabob* and *donner kabob* (lamb roasted on the vertical spit) are mainstays on the menu of almost all Turkish, Greek, Syrian and Armenian restaurants, and belly dancers are an added attraction at many. At New York's Port Said, for instance, the belly dancers shimmy through the house, passing by each man with the engine running until he inserts a bill (not a coin) fore or aft (wherever there's least room).

All in all, lamb has one of the most interesting sexual histories of any animal. In fact, even the first condums (named, by the way, for a British Colonel Condum, or a French Dr. Conton, either of whom "westernized" them in the seventeenth century) were made from lamb intestines in the Middle East. Lamb injections, lamb and ram tails and testicles, plus the antics of characters like Playboy King Chou-hsin should make good conversational appetizers even if the love meal is mere mutton. As for belly dancing, here is one skill where the woman who likes her food has the obvious advantage. The Turks particularly value *zaftig* women and the best belly dancing is obviously done by those who have ample bellies and the complementary equipment above and behind.

• ORGAN MEATS •

"Organ" or "variety" meats are widely popular in other lands, but they haven't made much of a hit in America. This is unfortunate because they are relatively inexpensive here, easy to prepare and high in protein, vitamin A, the B vitamins, phosphorus and iron. Organ meats can come from the cow, calf, pig or lamb and all have well-earned reputations in the aphrodisiac cookery. The seven briefly mentioned below can be used to prepare many an exciting and "exotic" meal.

HEART: Stuffed, sewed up and braised animal hearts have been featured in numerous gourmet dishes. Beef heart is the largest, but pork and lamb hearts are widely available, too.

SWEETBREADS: These are the two large glands in back of the animal's throat and breast. Those of cattle are most generally eaten, usually either braised, panfried or panbroiled.

BRAINS: Panfried in butter after being blanched in acidulated water, calves brains are considered the most tasty of all, but beef and lamb brains are delicious, too. Like sweetbreads, they can be prepared in many ways.

TONGUE: Again, beef tongue is most common, and it is delicious cooked in liquid, sliced and sauced. Lamb tongue, much smaller, is generally bought pickled in jars.

LIVER: Panfried calve's liver is the tastiest, but beef liver has the highest vitamin A content. Beef liver can be tenderized by soaking it in milk overnight.

LUNGS: The rarest of all organ meats in America, lungs are highly valued in many foreign countries, where they are usually sautéed or braised with vegetables.

KIDNEYS: These should always be served tender and thus only cooked for short periods of time. Beef, veal, pork and lamb kidneys are available and their preparation varies. Historically, kidneys have the best reputation as a love food among organ meats.

• THE CHICKEN AND THE EGG •

Which came first doesn't matter much for our purposes because from an aphrodisiac point of view eggs have been far more highly regarded than their manufacturers. This is not to say that the chicken hasn't had its adherents. Chicken soup, for example, so often called "Jewish penicillin," has been recommended for every ailment known or imagined by man. If Dr. Sol Katz, a university professor and medical doctor, could recently testify before an august Senate committee that it is doubtless the best remedy for the common cold, then why shouldn't it work similar wonders for the incapacitated lover? Still, according to Ernest Dichter, president of the Institute for Motivational Research, the chicken's image needs some improvement. "Move chickens away from the puritanical, wholesome, taken-for-granted kind of image aura that they have had for too long," Mr. Dichter pleaded before an American Poultry Industries Conference recently. "If the steak needs its sizzle, the chicken needs its song, its dressing up, its excitement—and even sin and immorality."

Well, maybe the following will help the American Poultries Industries, for the chicken has been regarded by some as a pretty dirty old bird. Chicken, after all, is recommended in a rather odd way in the *Perfumed Garden*. The author of that celebrated Arabian sex book advises that we rush out and procure an "ass's member," boil it "with onions and a large quantity of corn," feed this dish to the chickens and then eat the chickens ourselves—still another recipe unrecorded in Fanny Farmer. Amorous Romans also showed their love of chicken in a strange manner and invented a prized dish in the bargain. It seems that in trying to stem extravagances, the Emperor Didus ordered that no hens or cocks could be served at Roman orgies. One local gourmet got around this edict by rationalizing that a castrated chicken was neither hen nor cock. Castrating all the young males in his flocks, at one flick of the knife he both increased Rome's consumption of chicken and created the more tender capon for posterity.

The lascivious Letts, like many peoples today, used both the male and female chicken as a sex symbol in several of their ancient love songs, one telling about an old farmer's "poor cock hanged in the black chicken of a young maiden." Love recipes for chicken are legion, including the dish reputedly eaten every day by the fabled Sheik Abu Ben al Hashari (the same who died in bed at the age of 117 while celebrating his 254th wedding night). Said couscous contained about seven spices in addition to the chicken, lamb and wheat pellets employed. Another chicken delight worthy of mention is Sauce Caruso. Named after its inventor, the incomparable Italian tenor Enrico Caruso, the dish is a marinara sauce with chicken livers and mushrooms added that is poured over spaghetti. Apparently, his invention worked wonders for him; Rico remained something of a sexual cutup until the very end. When he pinched a girl's derrière in a Paris park, for instance, the resulting publicity gave rise to the nautical expression "a touch of Caruso," meaning the turn of a ship's engines astern.

Chicken à la King (diced pieces of chicken in a sherry-cream sauce) and Chicken Tetrazzini (diced chicken in cream sauce flavored with sherry and baked in a casserole with thin spaghetti, cheese and mushrooms) are two more eponymous chicken dishes. The first may have been invented by New York's Foxhall Keene, enabling him to become "the world's greatest amateur athlete," and the latter was the favorite of Italian-born diva Luisa Tetrazzini, the high-caloric dish enabling her to reach great high notes on stage and elsewhere. Then, of course, there is

Chicken Marengo, which was invented in the field by Napoleon's chef during the Italian campaign (1800) when there was no butter available in which to sautée the chicken and oil had to be used instead. These are classic dishes all and worthy of any love feast, though not as potent as the Japanese sour sexual organs of cock or the rooster testes once prescribed here in America.

American folklore is replete with sex tales, sayings and off-color jokes about the chicken. There is, for instance, that famous bordello called the Chicken Ranch in La Grange, Texas, recently closed by the governor. The landmark of a brothel got its name during the Depression when destitute farmers paid their tabs with poultry, and the chickens increased in number until the madam was forced to sell eggs and fryers from a chicken ranch out in the back. Then we have the rural U.S. love charm for old maids that follows: "Raise a game rooster to eleven months old. Kill, and draw before the body cools, cut the heart out and swallow it whole as fast as it can be removed, blood and all, and if you don't choke to death you will be married in eleven months."

Despite its historic reputation as both an aphrodisiac food and a charm, however, the chicken has recently fallen into disrepute as a love food. In fact, the use of diethylstilbestrol, a female sex hormone used in converting male cockerels into capons, has been found to produce cancer in some cases and one English organic chemist claims that this same chemical endangers man's virility. Diethylstilbestrol has been banned by the F.D.A., but the female sex hormone now commonly used, estrogen, has its dangers, too. One writer tells of male visitors to an Italian seaside resort who, upon leaving, found that their virility was impaired, that their breasts were enlarged and tender and that they no longer needed to shave. It was finally discovered that the local chicken breeder, who had a virtual monopoly in supplying chicken to the town's restaurants, where it was featured on every menu, had been implanting an estrogen pellet in each of his birds at birth in order to make them grow faster. The trouble was that they grew so *fast* that the tablet didn't have time to dissolve. Males eating the town's chicken dishes were often swallowing as much as half a pill, and this accounted for their loss of virility and effeminate appearance.

One way to circumvent this problem is to buy organically raised chicken, which like all "organic" meat and fowl tastes better than chickens "scientifically" reared, most of which actually never see the light of day from the time they're eggs hatched in a giant hothouse until the time a mere eight weeks later when they're plucked. Famous for many excellent *poulet* recipes (including one using "electrocuted" chickens), the French have an especially good organic variety called *poularde de Brusse,* or "Bird With The Steel-Blue Legs." These birds take three to ten months to mature. Raised in Lyon, they are first fattened by allowing them to roam the countryside eating natural foods and then locked in dark cellars for two months and force-fed a corn and skimmed milk paste. Not only do they taste vastly superior to commercially raised varieties, but they don't detract from your sex life.

Your sex life, in any case, will definitely be more enhanced by the chicken's eggs than by the chicken itself. Eggs were praised by Casanova, as his *Memoirs* reveal, and even comprise the major ingredient of what might be called his "secret love recipe." The great lover-gourmet described the scene vividly two centuries ago:

> *Casanova:* You shall feel all through the night the ardour of my devotions.
> *His Lady:* You will not find me insensible to your offerings.
> *Casanova:* ...I have taken nothing today but a cup of chocolate and a salad of eggs dressed with oil from Lucca and Marseilles vinegar...I shall be all right when I have distilled the whites of the eggs, one by one, into your amorous soul.
> *His Lady:* I did not think that you required any such stimulants.
> *Casanova:* Who could want any with you. But I have a rational fear; for if I happened to prime without being able to fire, I would blow my brains out...

To quote Casanova a little further on, "In order to paint the diversified scene which took place between me and my lovely mistress until the dawn of day, I should have to use all the colors of Aretino's palette." But then many lovers have been equally enthusiastic about the effects of eggs, including the author of *The Perfumed Garden*. Writes the Shaykh Nefzawi: "He will fry a good number of eggs in fresh fat and butter, and when they are well-cooked, he will mix them with honey. If he will eat as much as possible of this with a piece of bread, he will be able to soothe and comfort all through the night." Elsewhere the sensuous Shiek recommends chicken broth with cream, powdered almonds and yolks of eggs, in addition to a number of other egg recipes.

There are thousands of ways to cook eggs, most of them quite stimulating. These range from most-complicated concoctions to a simple glass of cognac swallowed with an egg yolk, which is said to strengthen the weakest of men for coition. Indeed, everyone seems to have blended eggs in their love potions: the Greeks and Romans including same in numerous erotic recipes, the Chinese citing them many times as an amatory aid and medieval Europeans placing their faith in hard-boiled yolks alone. Not only chicken eggs were favored, however, the *Lucayos Cookbook* (1660) in fact claimed that for aphrodisiac purposes, "Duck eggs are superior to the Hen, as are Pigeon eggs superior to the Duck. The Sparrow gives the greatest egg of them all."

In the West, various omelettes too numerous to list have been recommended as restoratives. The Egg and Eye restaurant in Los Angeles serves omelettes cooked in forty different ways. But the real champion is New York's Mme. Romaine, who in her chic little restaurant at 32 East 61st Street whips up over 500 different kinds of omelettes for her luncheon-only trade. Anthony Quinn, Warren Beatty and Paul Newman are only a few of her celebrated customers. The eighty-year-old woman's creations range from an eggs-only omelette ($2.65) to one made with caviar, truffles, olives, croutons and walnuts ($9.95). Others include a dish made with artichoke hearts, *foie gras,* chicken, cheese, croutons and sherry sauce ($5.65), and the simple potato omelette that is Marlene Dietrich's favorite.

No matter what kind of egg dish is your choice, rest assured that the egg in general has always been one of man's most revered symbols of fertility and passion. The Greek god of love, Eros, is said to have been born from an egg. Eggs have at various periods in history been believed to increase the flow of sperm in a man's body and were sucked as a tonic for the old and impotent; they are still broken against the floor by Persian brides on their wedding nights, so that, hopefully, the maidenhead will break as quickly and completely. The Arabs, who advocate the yolks of three eggs daily for virility, also have a potent love potion made of onions boiled with various spices, sautéed in oil, and strengthened with egg yolks. Then there is a tempting Moslem aphrodisiac dish calling for whole asparagus fried with egg yolks and seasoned with saffron. The only egg recipe decidedly unappealing to the western libido is a Moroccan concoction calling for powdered bugs and egg yolks.

Even our innocuous Easter egg hunts are nothing but a remnant of ancient fertility rites, and some primitive peoples didn't dare to eat eggs because they were so sacred. In certain parts of Africa a widespread fear existed that only cooked eggs were all right to eat, although the people of the Congo thought that a lady who ate any kind of egg would immediately be ready to strip and lay down in the bush. Many Americans still believe that fertilized eggs are more potent than unfertilized ones, although there's really no difference nutritionally speaking. Similarly, natives of the Cape region believed that women who ate eggs would carry on with men of other tribes, and in the Philippines women are still forbidden to eat chickens that lay in different places for fear that they'll take on similar habits. Finally, while getting out the frying pan, we should keep in mind that quaint belief of the Romans, who liked all kinds of eggs, including those of the quail and peacock. The Romans considered that any woman who merely offered to cook eggs for a man was making a definite sexual advance—an advance from which her egg-eater would become totally powerless to retreat.

• TEMPTING TURKEY •

We'll tell the tale of Brillat-Savarin's truffled turkey and its pronounced effects on the libido under truffles a few pages on, but truffled turkey has been far from the main preference of gourmets in this country.

"One of the most beautiful presents which the New World made to the Old," turkey in its wild state was an important food to the American Indian centuries before the white man usurped their lands. "It was charming to look upon, delightful to smell, and delicious to taste," said Brillat-Savarin of turkey in its wild state. Wild turkey, held to be tastier and more libido-arousing by gourmets, is making a comeback, there now being more wild turkeys (about one million) in the United States than at the time when the Pilgrims found these shores. But this is not to put down the delicious farm-bred turkey. The domestic turkey is the only race of poultry that has descended from wild stocks native to the United States, and its breeding today constitutes a highly sophisticated $500 million a year industry that supervises the bird "from womb to tomb," employing techniques of artificial insemination just as the cattle industry does. Last year we purchased some 128 million commercial birds and consumed about nine pounds of turkey per person on an average. Even considering its relatively low price among meats and fowl, Americans obviously like the bird. It is here to stay—and not only as a Thanksgiving and Christmas dinner treat. Whether one chooses a wild or a tame bird, there's no doubt that turkey is among the most nutritious, inexpensive and delicious foods available. The frankly stupid domesticated turkey hardly knows what to eat and has to be attracted to food by colorful marbles placed in its feed, it often catches cold by getting its feet wet and frequently panics and suffocates itself, the flock pressing together in fear. But it constitutes one of the best energy foods for a long day's night that money can buy. Recent research at Cornell University has shown, for example, that turkey meat is higher in protein than any common meat except veal, one four-ounce sandwich supplying over one-half the daily protein requirements for an adult man or woman. The same university also found that turkey is highest in protein and lowest in cholesterol of all other poultry and red meats except veal and that it is extremely low in calories, too. A good conversation piece when one gets around to carving the bird is its "oysters"—turkey "oysters" having at least some psychological aphrodisiac effect, are the very choice round pieces of dark meat found in the cavities on each half of the hip bone.

• OTHER FOWL FOR FOUL PLAY •

Take a large olive, stone and stuff with a paste of anchovy, capers & oil.
Put the olive inside a trussed and boned garden warbler.
Put the garden warbler inside a fat ortolan.
Put the ortolan inside a boned lark.
Put the stuffed lark inside a boned thrush.
Put the thrush inside a fat quail.
Put the quail, wrapped in vine leaves, inside a boned lapwing.
Put the lapwing inside a boned golden plover.
Put the plover inside a fat, boned red-legged partridge.
Put the partridge inside a young, boned and well-hung woodcock.
Put the woodcock, rolled in bread crumbs, inside a boned teal.
Put the teal inside a boned guinea fowl.
Put the guinea fowl, well-larded, inside a young and boned tame duck.
Put the duck inside a boned and fat fowl.
Put the fowl inside a well-hung pheasant.
Put the pheasant inside a boned and fat wild goose.
Put the goose inside a fine turkey.
Put the turkey inside a boned bustard.
Place in a saucepan with onions stuffed with cloves, carrots, small squares of ham, celery, mignonette, several strips of well-seasoned bacon, pepper, salt spice, coriander seeds and ten cloves of garlic. Close the saucepan with pastry. Cook gently and remove pastry and any grease before serving.

The old French love recipe quoted above for an erotic *roti sans pareil,* or a roast without equal, not only shows how hard some men and women will work to seduce each other, but gives a giant hint about the vast number of winged creatures thought to be aphrodisiacs. Since the dawn of time our feathered friends have been famed for their venereal virtues. Some, like pigeons, turtle doves and partridges, were valued because they were of an extremely amorous disposition (which may explain that nonsensical gift of "a partridge in a pear tree"). Then we have specimens like the male Australian bowerbird, which has been said to stimulate human females because it goes to such great lengths to stimulate female bowerbirds—the male of one species prefaces lovemaking by making a special bower decorated with flowers and colored stems, while a second species goes to the length of actually painting its love nest, applying a mixture of berries and saliva with its beak or a fragment of bark.

Other birds have been esteemed by lovers simply because they're delicious, like the tiny roasted *papabottes* that were considered aphrodisiac in early New Orleans and eaten in one bite, bones and all, or the numerous little birds which the Italians have enjoyed so indiscriminately over the years, eating their ecology into a state of near-ruin in the process. But for still others there is no easy explanation. No one knows why the Chinese believed that the arplan "maketh a man renew his youth and astonish his household." Also remaining a mystery is why one love remedy advised us to "Use the eggs and plumage foul/ Of a midnight shrieking owl," or for that matter why even the crazy coot has been considered an aphrodisiac dish, though it's said that the kooky bird, cooked properly, is as tender and savoury as duck. Even our national bird, the eagle, has been cited as an aphrodisiac, strange as that might seem to Congress. "Dry, steep, and stew in sauce the kidneys of an eagle," the Persian King Cyranus once instructed. "Then mix them with drink or meat. The person that consumes them will be drawn into confidence and great love."

The following is but a sampling of the many birds—species strange and species palate tempting—that seem to have fired the flames of sex perpetually. Of these, duck is probably the second most famous, bowing only to the goose treated later under *foie gras.* Duck has of course reigned supreme because of its royal flavor, and the Chinese today still serve a complicated dish called The Seventeen Ineffable Precious Parts of the Duck. Duck figured prominently on a list of foods the Sumerians considered worthy of the gods; the ancient Egyptians roasted it for royalty; the Romans served it crisp and crackling brown on a bed of turnips; and the Mayans raised it domestically centuries before the Conquistadores came. Duck flavored with squash blossoms was a Chinese love delicacy, but then the Chinese have so many ways to cook duck that at a dinner some years ago in Peking it was served in over 100 dishes, each completely different from the other.

Peking duck, delicious pieces of duck rolled in a delicate pastry and served with a spicy bean sauce, is a specialty of many U.S. Chinese restaurants, but the Chinese duck dish beyond compare is The Meal of the Peking Duck, which is akin to a sacred ceremony. Generally, this begins in China with wine and the feet of the duck as an appetizer. Then comes *tch-ya-kan,* the bird's liver served with a sauce of hot condiments in which to dip it and a bamboo shoot and mushroom dish. After a fish soup, the Lacquered Duck itself is presented, a ninety-day wonder more golden and crisp than anyone else has ever cooked. Says one writer who attended such a banquet: "With this duck appears a waiter with his little hatchet (Chinese cooks do not use knives, ever). With some kind of legerdemain he divides it into manageable fragments to be wrapped with a young onion inside a wafer of unleavened bread and consumed at a bite.

No one who has encountered the duck in this form can henceforth contemplate it seriously any other way."

An American gourmet favorite is pressed duck, but while there are many complicated recipes for the entree, all require a duck press. This dish was a favorite of America's greatest eater, Diamond Jim Brady, who also liked canvasback duck, a U.S. species, and often ate two whole ones for the third course of his ten-course meals. But the best aphrodisiac duck dish is probably duck's eggs, which the modern-day chef Raymond Oliver enthusiastically recommends. Oliver, noting that the egg was considered by the Chinese to be the ideal love food because it contained "both the positive and the negative, the Yin and the Yang, the sun (yolk) and the moon (white)," ranks duck's eggs third best, after those of the plover and peewit. Duck's eggs are best eaten raw, he says, or should at least be cooked as little as possible, scrambled eggs with truffles being the "most satisfactory" cooked dish. Oliver goes on to give a recipe for duck's eggs with avocados. Here the ducks' eggs are gently boiled for twelve minutes in lightly salted water, dropped into cold water and chilled. Half an avocado is then peeled and diced, the other half crushed and mixed with "a pinch of curry powder, three pinches of celery salt and a dessert-spoonful of coconut milk." The whites of the eggs are next cut lengthwise and the yolks extracted and sieved with the crushed half of the avocado. The mixture is finally blended well and the whites of the eggs decorated with the diced avocado and served in crisp lettuce leaves.

To leave the sublime for the ridiculous again, we might note that even the ubiquitous sparrow once had a great reputation as an aphrodisiac dish. "A sparrow baked and given to a woman in her drink," Cyranus wrote, "will make her dissolve and melt away for love." The brains of the sex-loving sparrow were particularly valued, but the most foul of such fowl love potions is recorded in *The Lucayos Cookbook*:

> To increase Ye Powers take a Cock-sparrow and Pluck it whilst living, then throw it to ten wasps who will sting it to death. Add the Intestines of a Black Raven and Oil of Lilac plus Chamomile. Cook all in Beef-Fat until the flesh is in shreds. Put into a bottle and hold near for use. Ye shall see Marvels.

Such "Marvels" aside, most of us would prefer fabled love dishes such as pheasant and partridge, or even peacock, swan or ostrich. Pheasant rates three stars in any love food guide. Madame DuBarry fed herself and her royal lover on her favorite pheasant in wine sauce, and that scourge of Victorian society novelist Frank Harris often gobbled up two or three plates of the game bird as a *prelude d'amour*, washing it down with a few flagons of wine. Brillat-Savarin devotes a good number of pages to pheasant in his *Physiology of Taste*, giving very explicit instructions for its cooking. Savarin vows that the bird prepared in his manner "is worthy of being served up to angels," adding that the eyes of a group of ladies served the savory dish "sparkled like stars, their lips were glossy as coral, and their countenance became ecstatic."

The cock of the pheasant family is more attractive than the female, but the hen is better to eat. As with many game birds, it must be eaten at the *bon moment* and many epicures believe that the *bon moment* comes only when the bird is practically decomposed (which is why Brillat-Savarin literally stank from the wild game he commonly carried around in his pockets). Another aphorism of the French actor-gourmet Desessarts had it that we should "Never forget that the pheasant must be awaited like the pension of a man of letters who has never indulged in epistles to Ministers nor written madrigals for their mistresses." The same can be said of woodcock; some gourmets consider this the best of winged game birds, and one chef contends that woodcock should be eaten when extremely high "even if it gives you indigestion."

Peacock is really an oily, tough and leathery bird. Knights of old mainly relied on it as an amatory aid because it looked so good when properly prepared, and it is still eaten on occasion, but it is not available anywhere we know. "The brain of a peacock, eaten with meat, fills a person with love," Cyranus vowed and much later the eccentric painter Toulouse-Lautrec favored it, once observing that "A great burgundy is like a peacock's tail in one's mouth." Bold knights of medieval days often swore on the peacock to aid a fair damsel in distress, placing their right hand on the peacock platter and intoning, "I vow to God, the Holy Virgin, Ladies and the Peacock to accomplish my missions." The dish was certainly a magnificent sight worthy of an oath. "At banquets peacocks were served whole," one writer notes. "Instead of plucking the bird, cooks cleverly skinned it so that the feathers came off with the skin.... Finally, when the peacock was cooked... skin and feathers were added, the tail spread out. At this point the mistress of the house filled the peacock's beak with cotton impregnated with camphor and set a light to it. The bird arrived on the table spitting flames."

Partridge, much smaller than the peacock at about a foot long, is second only to the pheasant as a game bird. One early sexpert assures us that fresh-killed partridge is among the best of aphrodisiac game birds and Platina makes even stronger claims for it in his *De Valentude Tuenda*. "The flesh of the partridge is of good and easy digestion, and is highly nutritious," he advises. "It strengthens the brain, facilitates conception and arouses the half-extinct desire for venereal pleasures." Similar claims were also made for snipe, which along with the partridge was an ancient Lett symbol for the penis, and the same can be said of quail, grouse, turtle doves, pigeons, the guinea fowls that Shakespeare called turkeys, the thrush, the lark whose tongues were such a great delicacy at Roman orgies and practically every bird that can fly except the vulture (though we wouldn't be so sure that this last isn't valued somewhere, too).

Not even the ostrich could hide its head in the sand long enough to escape man's attention. The lascivious Roman emperor Heliogalabus, for one, thought ostriches so stimulating that he once ordered 600 ostrich heads, long necks attached, brought to the table, where he quickly devoured all the brains—making him either a wiley or stupid lover. The legendary swan, so often depicted in mythology copulating with humans, has also seen its day as a love food, as oily and leathery as it is, though an annual Swan Dinner is still held by the Worshipful Company of Vintners, one of London's ancient guilds, whose members do little but manage to "push it around on the plate." Swan's pizzle was particularly favored in the past, but then so were the hearts of those swallows that give us bird's nest soup. We might conclude finally with crow, as unlikely as this bird seems. Some really gruesome fowl potions have staked their claims as the real "Love Potion #9," but crow appears to be as fulsome as any of them. Yet the flesh of crows was once held to be delicious if only young specimens were eaten. And even today we're told that crows make an excellent meal if properly prepared. In fact, directly following is an American recipe for crow dug out from the archives of the Remington Arms Company: *"To eat crow [honest], simply skin the bird, salt and cut into pieces, parboil till tender and then fry with butter and onions."*

Try it, you'll like it (maybe). But we'll only eat crow if someone conclusively proves that the recipe isn't authentic.

COURSE ELEVEN

A Feastiary Of Foie Gras:
Take One Goose . . .

"My dear Mardocheus," I said when he came. "Your daughter's appetite doubles mine and I shall be much obliged if you will allow her to keep me company whenever we have *foie gras*."

"... if you are willing to pay double, I have no objections."

"Very well, that arrangement will suit me fine ..."

—Casanova, *Memoirs*

So did Casanova, preeminently wise in the ways of life and love, once offer to dine with the attractive daughter of an innkeeper and pay the bill gladly—at whatever cost—whenever she indulged her enormous appetite for *foie gras*. He knew, as did Martial, Juvenal and Rabelais much earlier, that of all the byproducts of fowl for foul play, the otherwise silly goose offers the ultimate in esculence, foie gras being an unparalleled delicacy and a *prelude d'amour* that satisfies the most demanding palate and fires the coldest heart. Be your *nom d'amour* Casanova, La Pompadour, Xaviera Hollandaise, or Silky T. Virility, you'll likely find that it does much the same.

Which is all quite an advertisement for "fat liver," and that is literally what *foie gras* means. Fortunately, however, the savoury dish served in restaurants today tastes nothing like its rather unappetizing name. Almost always fattened goose livers, and goose livers fattened by a special process as well, *foie gras* has been known as a royal dish from time immemorial, though surprisingly little has been written about it. It was enjoyed by the Romans, the Greeks and the Egyptians before them. Today, its price alone reflects its status as a gourmet food. A pound of undiluted, unseasoned *foie gras* costs close to $50 at Fauchon's, the fashionable Parisian grocery in the Place de la Madeleine, and when the loaf is seasoned down the middle with the traditional truffles and port wine flavored *gelée*—this last invented in 1772 by Doyen, chef to the president of France's parliament—the price invariably rockets skyward. No relief appears in sight for *foie gras* lovers, either. The French woman's magazine *Elle* reports that *foie gras* has tripled in price over the past six years, and although this figure is probably exaggerated, there's no doubt that the eminently pleasurable delicacy becomes more expensive every day. In New York, Rougie and George Bruck, the best canned brands, are fairly reasonable, but fresh *foie gras* goes for $75 a pound.

Among all fowl for foul play, the fowl man has played foulest in his quest for love is undoubtedly the goose that gives us stimulating *foie gras*. The phallic goose is frequently coupled with Aphrodite as a Greek symbol of love, its neck and head having often been severed and eaten or cooked raw for its resemblance to the *membrum virile*. Goose pizzle was similarly valued, and external liniments made of wild goose fat were once used "to anoint the parts of generation." Perhaps most grotesquely of all, the ancient Chinese were infamous for their love affairs with live geese, "the necks of which they were in the habit of cruelly wringing off at the moment of ejaculation in order that they could get the pleasurable benefit of the anal sphincter's last spasm in the victim," a victim they invariably ate afterwards before going on to the next goose. De Sade calls this same act avisodomy and relates that some French brothels of his day offered it on their bills of fare.

In the Hindu *Ananga Ranga* even the voice of the goose is considered a stimulant. This love manual suggests that the cries of the Hansa-goose be emulated by women during intercourse: "The sound should especially be produced when the husband kisses, bites and chews his wife's upper lip: and the sweetness of the utterance greatly adds to the enjoyment, and promotes the congress of the sexual act."

Most readers won't want to hide in the reeds studying the honk of a Hansa-goose or try any of the other foul tricks history shouldn't repeat on the beleaguered bird, but a pleasant alternative is the goose tongue recipe cited by Dr. George Belham in his *Virility Diet* as having acquired a reputation as an aphrodisiac over the centuries. Certainly few would want any part of the recipe cited by one barbarous old English cookbook telling us "how to roast and eat a goose alive, so that it will shriek when being carved—very pleasant to the beholder." Better stick to *foie gras*, which, as we'll see, is cruel enough in its preparation, enough so that it cannot be recommended to anyone with both a poor stomach and good memory.

Yet *foie gras* is delicious. The Roman Pliny recommends "the exquisite taste of the fattened goose liver," as do Horace, Martial and Juvenal. In France, where the Romans exported it as soon as they conquered Gaul, it has a reputation just as exhalted. Charlemagne, the first king to invite women to sit at table with men, once flew into a violent rage and flung his physician out of the palace when the well-intentioned doctor put him on a *foie gras*–free diet, after which he promptly sat down to consume "three plump geese" he had killed the day before. Giant Charlemagne— with his four wives, multitude of mistresses and fifty children—must surely have been something of an expert on the goose, and he is heartily seconded by many writers. Rabelais mentions goose as a food to stimulate love, and that he was familiar with *foie gras* is indicated by his observation that "Indeed, Gargantua grew…as full of matter as any goose liver ever crammed." Montaigne also wrote about *foie gras* and Dr. Nicholas Venette wholeheartedly recommends "goose-fat" as a restorative. As for Talleyrand, another great lover who preferred "heavy meals and light women," he kept what one writer calls "an enormous number of *pâtés* among his reserve stores," especially goose liver from Strasbourg, where *the* world-famous *pâté de foie gras* is made.

Foie gras has always made the most desireable of the *pâtés*, which have been legion and have included such oddities as *pâté* of lark's tongue and *pâté* of eel livers. Brillat-Savarin, *bon vivant* and *bon epicure*, who once prepared an enormously complicated *pâté* (including duck livers and truffles) so delicious that a friend died at table eating too much of it, considered goose liver so éclat that he included it in his most expensive suggested meal. In *The Physiology of Taste*, Savarin recommends "an enormous Strasbourg *pâté de foie gras* "in the shape of a bastion" as a course on his menu "for a Presumed Income of 30,000 francs or more."

In times past, "goose fatteners" or "crammers" fed the geese whose livers make *foie gras*. Each goose was tied down firmly with whipcord so that it could move only its neck, and six times a day crammers used their middle fingers to push into the throats of their geese a thick paste made of buckwheat flour, chestnut flour and stewed maize. From this practice, incidentally, came the expressions "stuffed as a goose" and "to be fed up," in both its literal and broader applications. The production of fabled *foie gras* today is hardly more humane than it was when the first farmer held a goose between his knees and stuffed maize down its throat, though it is an improvement over that time a few centuries ago when the goose was baked live in an oven that was heated gradually until its liver could swell no more. Some fourteen species of geese are used (as well as the Barberry duck), the large gray goose being a favorite. The geese are still force-fed, but today their diet is more varied, including cooked po-tatoes, beetroot, Jerusalem artichokes, beans, oats and carrots. When about six months old, those birds fated for *foie gras* are crammed into small separate pens or wooden cages along with plentiful food and sulfu-rated water. There their greedy natures eventually defeat them and they would eat themselves to death by suffocation if the farmer did not slaughter them and remove their swollen livers after six weeks or so. At that time they're so fat from their three meals a day that they can barely move, having gorged themselves on over seventy pounds of food.

Traditionally, geese for *foie gras* have been raised in France, in Strasbourg, but now only a relatively small portion come from the town. Hungary, Austria, Israel, Czechoslovakia and even Bulgaria supply most of the fattened goose livers today, although this may change with the French national budget now appropriating money to farmers willing to raise geese for *foie gras*. Still, the young farm wives, who traditionally have performed this task, seem to be rebelling against force-feeding a flock of geese three times a day for six weeks. They receive more than sixty cents an ounce for the goose livers, but don't feel it's worth working mash down a bird's throat through a funnel, the bird trying to cough its food up and struggling all the while. Right now Frenchmen consume almost 2000 tons of *foie gras* a year, while France produces only one-third of that, and the situation probably won't change appreciably for many years.

It was in Strasbourg, on the Rhine in Alsace in northeastern France, that *pâté de foie gras* was invented over two centuries ago. The renowned *pâté* is actually a *foie gras* pie, specially prepared goose liver embedded in a loaf-like edible crust. In 1762 Jean Pierre Clause (or Close) head chef to the Governor of Alsace province, invented the Elysian enjoyment, at first call-ing it *Pâté à la Contades* after his employer. Who invented *foie gras* itself is not known. One legend has it that the Roman Metellus Scipio did so, yet he used a Greek recipe, and the Greeks, in turn, who served *foie gras* as a "provocative to drinking," learned of the prized dish from the Egyptians. We know from frescoes at the tomb of the royal official Ti that the Egyp-tians force-fed geese to get *foie gras*, and the Greeks undoubtedly contin-ued the cruel practice and passed it on to the Romans. Finally, Caesar's subjects—it's said that they swelled the livers in milk seasoned with herbs and spices—brought the recipe to France where it was improved upon over the centuries. The French, unlike the English, did not care for roast goose. One early Gallic recipe, the *pot-à oie* popular up until the Revolution, called for stuffing a great goose with pheasants, quail, pigeons and herbs, roasting it, and eating the stuffing while leaving the goose itself for the servants. But their incomparable chefs did know how to make the best of any food. Jean Pierre Clause discovered a way to strengthen and concentrate *foie gras*, and perfected his discovery by surrounding it with a forcemeat of veal and chopped pork fat. His employer the Marechal de Contades, military Governor of the province of Alsace, so admired Clause's invention that he sent a second pie to Versailles, where the King applauded the *pâté par excellence* by awarding the Governor a new estate and the chef a cash grant of twenty gold pieces. Soon after, Jean Pierre Clause, possibly fortified by fame and his *foie gras* creation, married the widow of another pastry cook and went into business for himself, opening a bakery and supplying Strasbourg with his *foie gras* pie in all its glory. To the French, a slice of the rich creamy *pâté* is still as essential to the Christmas feast as cranberry sauce is to our Thanksgiving dinner.

Around the world today, and in earlier times, the goose itself has tempted the libido just as often as the French product made from its liver. Goose plucked and trussed, ready for the spit, much appealed to Egyptians of antiquity and the Roman Lucullus often served "fat goose in paste" at his unbelievably expensive dinners. Raw smoked goose served and still serves as a Russian relish, and the Saxons ate what they called *seathen* or boiled goose. The English, it should be noted, always had mixed feelings about the creature. An early traveler in France describes a "silly goose" turning a spit on which a turkey roasted. "The wild goose is a foolish bird; it's too much for one and not enough for two," says one old Yorkshire proverb. As for *foie gras*, the English seem to have looked upon it disdainfully. One of Smollet's characters in *Peregrine Pickle* comments: "This here, gentlemen, is a boiled goose; served up in a sauce composed of pepper, lovage, coriander, mint, rue, anchovies, it was one of the geese of Ferrara, so much celebrated among the ancients for the magnitude of their livers, one of which weighed upwards of two pounds; with this food, exquisite as it was, did the tyrant Heliogabalus regale his hounds." But most Britishers regarded *foie gras pâtés* as "lififerous [lethal] pies." As late as the end of last century we find an English writer condemning "the cruel practice of enlarging the birds' livers at the expense of the other parts of its body."

Geese, which the early English believed to be miraculously born of barnacles encrusted on tree branches overhanging rivers and other waters, were at first enjoyed stewed in England, but this is as untempting a dish as can be imagined. Potent goose seasoned with ambergris certainly did more for their national love life and powered, or salted, "green goose," a variety eulogized by the Elizabethan playwrights Beaumont and Fletcher, was another favorite, but such dishes soon gave way to the roast bird (first a goose pie) so celebrated in the English cuisine. The tender, juicy, stubble-goose of St. Martin, fed on truffles, was traditionally eaten on Martinmas (November 11th) as well as on Michaelmas Sunday (a festival celebrated on September 29th in honor of the archangel Michael). In literature we read of Swift's eccentric dinner, where he placed a coin under each empty plate and had his guests order their meal from a nearby restaurant, the Dean choosing "a plate of roast goose." And who can forget the immortal meal Dickens made of the traditional goose, a fattier variety than its stubble-fed brother, in the pages of *A Christmas Carol*:

> Such a bustle ensued that you might have thought a goose the rarest of all birds, a feathered phenomenon, to which a black swan was a matter of course—and in truth it was something very like it in that house. Mrs. Cratchit made the gravy...hissing hot...the young Cratchits...crammed spoons into their mouths, lest they should shriek for goose before their turn came to be helped. At last the dishes were set on and grace was said. It was succeeded by a breathless pause, as Mrs. Cratchit, looking slowly all along the carving knife, prepared to plunge it into the breast; but when she did, and when the long-expected gush of stuffing issued forth, one murmur of delight arose all round the board, and even Tiny Tim, excited by the two young Cratchits, beat on the table with the handle of his knife and feebly cried Hurrah! There never was such a goose cooked. Its tenderness and flavour, size and cheapness, were the themes of universal admiration. Eked out by apple sauce and mashed potatoes, it was sufficient dinner for the whole family; indeed, as Mrs. Cratchit said with great delight (observing one small atom of a bone upon the dish) they hadn't ate it all at last. Yet every one had had enough, and the youngest Cratchits in particular, were steeped in sage and onions to the eyebrows...

Goose, of course, is American slang for "to poke or pinch between the buttocks." The word has similar sexual connotations in England, (where it has variously meant "to possess a woman," "a harlot" and "to go wenching"), as well as in French slang, where *la petite oie* means the female pudendum, and in the Hindu language, the phrase "goose flesh" does not connote fear, but is a sign of all the passions. One American recipe tells us to make a love potion by drying and crushing to a powder the web of wild gander's foot. Wild geese take only one mate, and as a result, a pinch of the powder "in your loved one's coffee will cause her to fall in love with you and remain faithful." Aside from that, there's little to be said for the use of the nonhuman goose in the States. Americans have never really relished roast goose the way the English do, and they generally substitute native turkey for the bird at feast times. Even so, the early Settlement Cookbook included a recipe for smoked goose and one history of the cookery mentions a California *pièce de résistance* of "roast goose stuffed with snipe stuffed with hummingbirds stuffed with almonds," all of which were soaked in wine for six days and then smoke-roasted over sandalwood. Another favorite is imported smoked goose breast, a German delicacy that is a tender filet lightly cured and wrapped in a sausagelike casing of its own golden fat. Sportsmen here, of course, still value wild or "honker" geese, and the United States does breed large Embden and Toulouse geese in limited quantities, but we produce no *pâté foie gras* worth mentioning and depend mainly on French suppliers for the delicacy.

Strasbourg, and Périgeaux in the Périgord, still manufacture most quality *foie gras* from the fattened geese livers. The locals can rarely afford the dish. Its preparation is an arduous one and is largely a secret of Corden Bleu cookery. After the bile and nerves are carefully removed from the one to four pound livers, they are soaked in water and seasoned. Then they are stuffed with Périgord truffles (with which, theoretically, they should be stored for two to three years, instead of the usual six months, to absorb the delicate aroma) before being cooked to perfection. Ideally, a liver should be a light pinkish color prior to cooking and how long the livers are soaked and whether they will be steamed or baked depends on a careful grading process that can be learned only through long experience. Just what to eat with the liver is also a touchy proposition among the fastidious French of the region. For example, Leon Daudet, among the most passionate of gastronomes, relates that, "One day I had...a violent argument as to whether chicory salad lightly sprayed with absinthe should or should not be served with *foie gras.* I was against it, for in my opinion the taste of oil kills the *foie gras.*" Says another writer, "Nowadays the crime of serving *foie gras* with salad is rarely committed; its delicate smoothness should never be mingled with the acidity of vinegar."

Few, if any, restaurant chefs prepare their own *foie gras* today. Almost all excellent eateries and posh stores order their supply from France. Many types are available, including *suprême de foie gras truffé* (truffled *foie gras* in aspic jelly flavored with madeira), *bloc tunnel de foie gras truffé* (foie gras shaped for easy slicing) and *foie gras au natural* (untruffled, unseasoned *foie gras* that is used for special high cuisine dishes). In New York a source for fresh, uncanned *foie gras* is Charles and Company with two stores on Madison Avenue. At Fauchon's in Paris, the world's largest retail seller of *foie gras,* almost any variety can be obtained. Fauchon's even boasts a buyer who claims that he can tell where the goose liver comes from simply by sampling a tin of the product.

Gourmet love recipes for *foie gras* are plentiful. They include plain *foie gras* with capers, *tourte de truffes à la périgourdine* (a pie filled with truffles and *foie gras* doused in cognac), *truffes en pâte à la périgourdine* (similar to the preceding dish but using no cognac, each truffle wrapped in dough and baked about twenty minutes), *oeufs en cocotte à la périgourdine* (eggs broken over a layer of *foie gras*, cooked in a casserole and served with *sauce Périgueux*), *oeufs brouilles à la périgourdine* (scrambled eggs in which chopped truffles and *foie gras* are cooked separately in sauce and added to the eggs, the whole served together with slices of butter-fried *foie gras* and truffles), *foie gras braisé* (braised goose liver), *foie gras poche* (poached goose liver) and even *foie gras en chausson* (goose turnovers). Most of these dishes are to be eaten out, prepared by an accomplished chef, but any good French cookbook contains the recipes. We'd recommend, however, that a prepared *pâté* be enjoyed at home—you can even send out for something special like the "simple goose liver with mushrooms all topped with a madeira sauce" that's featured at Boston's popular Cafe Budapest.

All the preceding dishes are noted for their aphrodisiac qualities, and the natives who raise the *foie gras* goose similarly value the whole bird, even after the liver is out. They use the rest of the meat for conserve, cooking fat, mincemeat and a sort of *pâté*, and they buy dried cakes of its blood for use in a stimulating pudding. But *foie gras* is most potent plain, if it's the real thing, and there's little chance that the prospective naked diner will get stuck with duck liver or any *pâté* other than goose liver upon ordering *foie gras* in a quality restaurant or purchasing it at a reputable grocer's. If the *foie gras* is surrounded by a layer of fat, this should be removed, as enveloping the goose liver paste in fat is only a way of preserving it. To most appreciate its taste, eat nothing else with your *pâté*; even the salad some restaurants serve is strictly interdit, as oils and seasonings kill a *pâté's* delicate flavor. Accompanied by a good white wine, such as Champagne or White Burgundy—the livers really "mate well with any wine"—*pâté de foie gras* is indeed one of the classic aphrodisiac appetizers of all time.

COURSE TWELVE

The Erotic
Black And White Truffle

Let's drink the health of truffles black
In gratitude we must not lack;
For they assure us dominance
In all erotic dalliance.
As an aid to lover's bliss
Fate pleasureably fashioned this
Rarity, divine godsend.
To use forever without end.

—Old French poem

Presently, we were aware of an odour gradually coming toward us, something musky, fiery, savoury, mysterious—a hot drousy smell, that lulls the senses, and yet inflames them, the truffles were coming! Yonder they lie, caverned under the full bosom of the red-legged bird. My hand trembled as, after a little pause, I cut the animal in two. G——said I did not give him his share of the truffles; I don't believe I did....The poor little partridge was soon a heap of bones—a very little heap. A trufflesque odour was left in the room, but only an odour.

Thus wrote William Makepeace Thackeray, who so loved good food that he died from it (of overeating), in his *Memorials of Gourmandising*. Thackeray's panegyric was naturally on truffles, the most prized of all love foods then and now. In the world of gourmet soul food, truffles remain so much more rare and costly than any other delicacy that they must still be called, in the words of Brillat-Savarin, the "diamonds of the cookery." These close relatives of the mushroom, reputed to be a potent aphrodisiac ("Those who wish to lead virtuous lives should abstain from truffles," warns one old proverb), would cost up to $100 a pound for the black varieties at this year's relatively low prices, selling as they do for over $6 *an ounce*. Indeed, the late Hyman Goldberg, or "Prudence Penny," once chided a cookbook author for including a recipe using truffles costing $112 in the present market. But then the Italian white truffle, *perle della cucina*, or "pearls of the kitchen," is dearer still, often retailing at over $100 a pound. That all are outrageously priced and seem doomed to become even more rare and expensive, however, hardly discourages the true truffle-lover.

The tasty truffle has been éclat with gourmets ever since the first pig turned one up while rooting for acorns. Always they were considered supernatural, a divine inspirational food, "Children of the Gods," as Porphyrius dubbed them. The ancient Greeks, Theophrastus among them, believed that truffles were created by thunderbolts striking the earth during preautumnal storms—a legend based on the fact that heavy August rains bring a good truffle crop—and during the Middle Ages people thought the white varieties sprouted from witches' spit or the semen of a mating deer. The orator Cicero called them daughters of the earth conceived by the sun, and the Roman historian Pliny pronounced truffles incredible because they lived without roots. "Keep your wheat and send us your truffles," the poet Juvenal urged the Libyans; and perhaps the world's first practicing gourmet, Coelius Apicius, left six recipes for preparing the esculent fungi. The pearl of banquets has been apostrophized by poets like Pope ("Thy truffles, Périgord!") and hunted passionately by Kings like France's Louis XV. It has long been used in salads, stuffings, seasonings or eaten raw, and today some $100 million a year is spent on *truffés* by discerning cooks throughout the world.

The truffle is not only reputedly the most delicious food known to man, but it has also been regarded as a love food without peer longer than any other dish. The Romans dedicated the fungus to Venus in the belief that it stimulated love. Its aphrodisiac powers were whispered centuries before an early Italian author wrote that "Sensual men of fashion consume truffles to whet their appetites for lovemaking," long before Rabelais concocted his favorite dish of oysters and sausages flavored with the delicacy. In his groundbreaking aphrodisiac study, Davenport writes that: "The erotic properties of truffles are considered as even better established than fish. The ancient Romans were well acquainted with truffles, and obtained them from Greece and Africa, especially from the province of Libya, the fungi found there being particularly esteemed for their delicacy and flavor. In modern times, also, the truffle is highly valued for its capability of exacting the genesiac sense, it being a positive aphrodisiac which disposes men to be exacting and women complying." He goes on to point out that many writers have suspected that the truffle was in reality the fabled Dudaím, or Mandrake root (more about which in Course Eighteen).

While extremely "in" with the Romans, truffles kind of went into hiding deeper underground from the reign of Emperor Augustus to the time of France's Louis XV, although even during medieval days it wasn't unknown for a lord of the manor or a monarch to receive a basket brimful of the delicacies as a tribute from his subjects. The sage Omar Haleby recommends the fungi for use in aphrodisiac dishes and Carlsbad's Dr. Arnold Lorand, like Van de Velde in more recent times, vouches that they are "a good source of phosphorous and iron" for lovers. Old reliable Casanova, the first "sexologist" to do real field work, describes truffles in several places, in one instance telling of them "served in a very fine Dresden china and silver gilt plate." Casanova also remarks on beauty and truffles, claiming that "the beauty of the women of Turin is no doubt due to the excellence of the air and dirt," the last consisting of an abundance of truffles.

It has long been proverbial in France that "If a man is rich enough to eat truffles, his loves will be plenty." Louis XIV, Madame DuBarry and the Duke of Orleans, Regent during the minority of Louis XV, were only a few Frenchmen who eulogized this "appetizer for venereal desire" and put it to work for them in such dishes as "turkeys superbly truffled." Across the channel, the English had their faithful truffle devotees, too. "That Coryhaeus of voluptuaries, George IV," Davenport tells us, "so highly appreciated the aphrodisiac quality in truffles, that his Ministers at the courts of Turin, Naples, Florence, &c., were specially instructed to forward by state messenger to the Royal Kitchen any of those fungi that might be found superior in size, delicacy or flavour."

Yet French lovers have devoted themselves even more ardently to the pursuit of what George Sand was later to call *"la pomme féerique"* (the fairylike apple). Truffles rebounded into their fullest favor in France during the eighteenth century where we find De Sade recommending them more than once as a love food in *Justine ("un dinde aux truffes, entre un pâté de Périgueux...")* and know that Napoleon was advised to eat a few once in a while as a mild aphrodisiac. As for Madame Pompadour, she consumed so many truffles that some thought her diet endangered her health. According to Nancy Mitford's *Madame Pompadour*, Louis XV's mistress "was not strong enough for continual lovemaking and it exhausted her," so she resorted to an aphrodisiac regimen. "It can't be good for her living on a diet of vanilla, truffles and celery [all supposed aphrodisiacs]," her friend the Duchesse de Brancas was told, and when the Duchess advised Louis' mistress that she quite agreed, La Pompadour burst into tears. "The fact is, my dearest," she confided, "that I'm terrified of not pleasing the King anymore, and of losing him....I thought I might warm myself up if I went on a diet to heat the blood...which does seem to be doing me some good."

No French gourmet and lover praised truffles more than Anthelme Brillat-Savarin, that well-known epicure and little-known author of pornographic books. "For fish Savarin entertains a profound respect," one nineteenth-century writer observes, "for game, a manly affection; for pastries a delicate regard; but truffles are the beloved darlings of his heart." Brillat-Savarin discusses truffles in at least a dozen places in his redoubtable *The Physiology of Taste*, devoting seven complete pages to them in one instance, which is far more space than he devotes to any other single food. He even quotes an anonymous poem entitled *Impromptu* written about the fungi:

> To the black truffle drink, for I
> Hate the ungrateful worse than hell;
> The herb which gives us victory,
> In that short fight we love so well.
> For the strange might of love's delight
> Our God himself this good weed sent,
> On making mortals blessed intent,
> That we might use it day and night.

Savarin goes on to rhapsodize about truffled dishes that "appear like beneficient stars, and make the eyes sparkle of all sorts of gourmands of every category, whilst their faces beam with delight, and they themselves dance with pleasure." He notes the delicate white or reddish truffles which the Romans sought after in Greece and Libya, avers "who would dare to say he has been at a dinner where there was not a *pièce truffée*," wonders who "has not felt his mouth water in hearing truffles *à la provencale* spoken of" and informs us that it is generally believed that "the genetic sense" is excited by the fungi. "Who says truffle," Savarin contends, "pronounces a grand word charged with toothsome and amorous memories for the skirted sex, and in the bearded sex with memories amorous and toothsome... it is not only delicious to the taste, but is also believed to foster powers the exercise whereof is eminently pleasureable." The great gastronome of Belley then recounts the story of a husband who left his wife dining on truffled fowl with an old and hitherto faithful friend. "What shall I say, Monsieur," the voluptuous lady confessed afterward. "I put it all down to the truffles: I am altogether persuaded that they had given me a dangerous predisposition; and if I have not entirely abstained from them since (which would have been too strict a penance), at least I never eat them now but the pleasure they give me is tinged with some misgivings." Brillat-Savarin concludes that truffles make "women tenderer and men more apt to love," but since his time, as we'll see, other chefs have disagreed with his method of preparing them—claiming that there are surer ways than truffled turkey. ("A turkey stuffed with truffles," the father of *Cordon Bleu* cookery wrote in another place, "was a luxury only for the tables of the great or in homes of kept women.")

Gertrude Stein, whose Alice B. Toklas invented a recipe for truffle turnovers, might well have said a truffle is a truffle is a truffle, for the truth is that no one has ever satisfactorily defined this "wonderful cryptogram" in scientific terms. Etymologically, "truffle" may derive from the Spanish *trufa*, meaning deceit, or the Italian *traffere*, to deceive, in allusion to the evasive truffle hidden underground. In this regard, it's interesting to note that the eponymous hero of Molière's famous play *Tartuffe* was named for the Italian word for truffles. Tartuffe himself appears to have been drawn from the character of a bawdy French abbot of the period, and Molière is thought to have used *tartuffe* to symbolize the sensuous satisfaction displayed by certain religious brethren when contemplating truffles. It is said that the name came in a flash to the playwright "on seeing the sudden animation that lighted up on the faces of certain monks when they heard that a seller of truffles awaited their orders."

The truffle can best be described as a mushroom that matures underground, but there are some underground mushrooms that aren't truffles at all. The genus was once called *Hydnum* from the old Greek name meaning thunder used by Theophrastus in 300 b.c. No exact general description suffices for the complex phenomena and it is best in this short space to eschew lengthy descriptions and refer interested readers to mycologists like Malencon, whose *European Truffles, History, Morphogensis, Organography, Classification, Culture* (1938) is the scholarly monograph nonpareil on the subject. Truffles are technically the underground fruiting bodies or spore-producing bodies of a sac fungi called *Ascomycetes* (mainly in the order *Tuberales*). In nature they live in association with the roots of various trees, such as the oak, beech, chestnut or hazel. The mycelium of the fungus forms mycorrhizas on the roots of trees. These mycorrhizas contribute growth-promoting substances to the tree and the tree in turn contributes to the symbiotic relationship by providing chlorophyl and other substances necessary for the truffle's growth. This felicitous partnership between Lilliputians and Brobdingnagians (mycorrhizal fungi and truffle trees) also depends on various forest animals, from insects to wild boars. A raw truffle is essentially a warty, rindlike surface covering a series of elaborate folds which contain their plentiful spores. But because truffles live underground these spores cannot be disseminated by the wind. Therefore, nature has made the truffle's odor appealing and its taste delicious to a variety of animals besides man. These forest animals burrow or root out a truffle and devour it, but the spores pass through their digestive systems unharmed and are voided in their excrement. Miraculously alive, the spores form new truffles in different places, thus insuring the survival of the species. So exact is this scheme of things that nature even supplies a certain species of truffle beetles that can smell the underground fungi from a half mile away and find their way to them unerringly.

Cro-Magnon man probably enjoyed truffles as much as gourmets and lovers do today, at least they are abundantly found in those places in Europe where he once thrived. There are over thirty European species of truffles, and many Asian and African types, but the three most important in commerce are the Italian *tartuffi bianchi*, the white truffle, and the two species *Tuber melanospernum* and *Tuber brumali*, black truffles which grow in both France and Italy and are marketed as *truffes de Périgord* and *tartuffi neri di Norcia*. To complicate matters further, limited quantities of the Périgord-type truffles are also found in Spain, Germany, Czechoslovakia and Switzerland. No one even agrees on what a typical truffle looks, smells or tastes like. Some are as small as peas and others as large as melons; a few taste like mushrooms, others like an excellent cheese combined with filberts. Their taste definitely is not "high," and a fondness for them does not have to be cultivated as with numerous gourmet foods. Many find their odor offensive, while some swear they smell "as fragrant as wild strawberries." Perhaps a French truffle farmer, whose truffle storeroom exudes a strong licoricelike odor, best sums it up. "I love the smell," he says, "but some find it positively sickening. And did you know, there are as many truffle odors as there are cognac bouquets?" Your own nose must ultimately be the judge, yet the controversy rages on. "A faintly revolting odor," declares one gourmet. "Lily-of-the-valley," says another. "Decayed leaves"—a third. "The slightest soupcon of musk"—a fourth. "By no means appetizing," writes a fifth expert, and *he* goes on to venture that the man who first ate a black truffle must have been almost as bold as the proverbial man who first ate an oyster. One author, writing in *Holiday*, has called Italian white truffles "syzygy," which means "a couple or pair of opposites," a word as rare as the truffle and which he feels expresses the "mixture of the exotic and ordinary" that best describes them. Another gourmet opines simply that the whites smell like "pimento peppered with garlic and soaked in olive oil."

Most valued black truffles, including the French Périgords, which have been famous since the fifteenth century and are known as "Queen truffles," are a brownish black to a jet-black, roundish, and covered with polygonal warts with a depression at their tips, their flesh a violet black with brown-marginal veins. The white Italian truffles look like wizened unpeeled potatoes and do have a garlic-tinged odor that some find decidedly unpleasant. A few gourmets have even claimed that truffles are indigestible and therefore ineffective as a prelude to amour. Brillat-Savarin denies this emphatically, basing his decision on two carefully considered points: that "the truffle is easy to chew, light in weight, and is neither hard nor leathery"; and that Parisian doctors, practicing in a city famed for its truffle lovers, certified them as eminently digestible, these selfsame doctors consuming "more truffles than any other class of persons," and one in particular swallowing "enough to give an indigestion to an elephant," yet nevertheless living till the age of eighty-six.

Truffles are not yet "cultivated" in the United States, although about sixty species are found wild here, but imports can be purchased canned and sometimes fresh in most gourmet grocery and delicacy shops. The early Spanish explorers mistook our potato for the underground fungi and even named the tuber *tartuffo*, but commercial truffles are confined to a few European countries. The most renowned black species is still grown in the Périgord region of southwestern France, where up to 500 tons are produced each year. From the Quercy-Périgord, Vauclause-Gard, Drôme and Ardèche regions come two-thirds of French truffles, but they occur in many places, including Burgundy and Dauphine, where Brillat-Savarin found them "hard, deficient in flavor," and "of inferior quality." There are truffles and then there are *truffles*, as the gastronome observes, and to find good ones is not as easy as it seems. The French truffle industry actually more resembles primitive gathering than modern farming and depends more on luck than on technology; the black mushroomlike delicacies remain a mystery to the *trufficulteurs* as well as the scientists. Truffles are generally found in the sloping, stony, layered limestone soil of open woodlands—the kind of soil where grapevines and juniper bushes do well—and the climate most suitable for their growth can best be described as moderate, neither too cold nor hot, too dry or rainy. About all that man has learned to increase their production over the centuries is to plant the acorns of diseased oaks in calcerous earth, spread soil containing truffle spawn around them and wait five years or so hoping for the fungi to grow—which it does perhaps one out of ten times. As harvesting cannot begin for six years and the yield is at its maximum in from thirteen to twenty years, such truffle-farming is obviously not generally very profitable or popular.

Gathering remains the only practical way to obtain truffles, but this is complicated by the facts that the delicacy often occurs as deep as three feet below the earth and that truffle beds have been known to shift over eight miles within two or three generations. In Greece, as recently as early in this century, divining rods were used to find beds, but now more reliable methods exist. Some men are sufficiently susceptible to the scent of truffles to be able to smell them out in the air or a handful of earth, and experienced gatherers can easily spot them when they crack the ground near the surface, which is called hunting *à Poscarto*, or by the mark. Still others poke with a thin iron rod where the grass may have died because a truffle stole all the earth's nourishment, a method which might be recommended for homeowners with lawns that are a series of brown patches, but which would probably turn up nothing more than grubs or rocks. Another aid is the many species of truffle flies that live on the mysterious filaments and can be observed hovering over or boring their eggs in the ground where beds are located three inches to three feet down. Gatherers sometimes sprawl on the ground for hours watching for these swarms of insects. Men, however, aren't as accurate as "dumb beasts" in digging up the diamonds of gastronomy and they often damage the truffle beyond repair.

Despite Horatio Alger tales like that of the sickly child who kept himself and his poor family alive with his amazing gift for smelling out truffles, various animals are generally relied upon to locate the elusive fungi, which have no power to push themselves above the surface and most of which would simply rot away if it were not for man's persistence. Several domesticated animals have the ability to recognize the truffle scent with no difficulty and can be trained to track truffles. For centuries, poodles were used to find the fungi and dachshunds to dig them up. In England, the summer truffle *(Tuber aestivum)* was tracked in the beechwoods of Sussex and Wiltshire by mongrel terriers. Even ducks were once used to hunt truffles. In Sardinia today, the goat is used for this purpose; in Russia, bear cubs were used; while in France, at least traditionally the world capital of truffledom, pigs and sometimes trufflehounds, a small breed halfway between a poodle and working terrier, are so employed. A pig that appreciates the taste of truffles is bought by a typical gatherer, who has secured permission to "hunt" on one of the large estates in the French Périgord (due east of Bordeaux) for a portion of his find, and it does not take much training before the porker becomes a proficient detective. These pampered pigs tire easily and must be trundled in a wheelbarrow or carried underarm to the truffle grounds. "You walk your pig on a rope and he instinctively smells the truffle," a Périgord gatherer has explained. "Soon he develops a trick. He shoves his snout down on this side, then that side, then he opens his mouth. You pull him back quickly and give him some corn or a potato." When the pig actually goes on a hunt, he is allowed to roam free, a leather thong fastened around his mouth preventing him from swallowing the succulent finds for which he is rewarded with a handful of acorns. Sometimes the gatherer, or *caveur*, carries an iron bar to stuff in the mouth of an unmuzzled pig and a *piochon*, a wooden-handled metal claw, to finish digging up the *truffe*. It is said that some of the truffle pigs, which often weigh up to 300 pounds, even "twitch their hairy ears and execute a little hog version of a dance in anticipation of hunting truffles."

There is still controversy over which makes the better truffle-hunter, pig or dog. Truffle pigs were first used in France and can trace their pedigree to at least the Middle Ages. These long-legged sows (the females have a better sense of smell than males) were first observed hunting the "earthnut" on their own; they actually "point" at a truffle and are often called "racing" or "greyhound" pigs. Dogs, on the other hand, were introduced to France and other European countries from Italy during the truffle mania in the mid-eighteenth century, although they had been employed by poachers before this and still are. Nowadays more and more mongrels, Breton spaniels, cockers, poodles and dachshunds, are being used by the French. "Some dogs around here," says a Périgord truffle hunter, "are so enthusiastic that they'll go out poaching on other people's plantations. I know one whose owner turned down $1000 for him. A good dog, even though he smelled bad. Unfortunately, somebody poisoned him." The truffle dog, generally called a *griffon*, doesn't tire as easily as a pig and it has been pointed out that he is no glutton, that he would no sooner gobble down his find than a retriever would chew up a woodcock. Pig partisans, however, claim that the porker has a rarer sense of smell, never gets sore feet and doesn't stray after game. At least one diplomatic Provence *caveur* has resolved the controversy by permitting his pig to begin the digging but letting his dog finish the delicate operation and lay the truffle at his master's feet.

One folk belief has it that truffles should ideally be hunted by a virgin woman with a virgin sow, a good combination for a lucky male companion. In any event, a truffle pig looses its keen sense of smell at five years or so of age and younger porkers have to be used by French *caveurs*. The pigs are trained when about two years old and soon can easily scent a truffle at fifty yards. Often the gatherer's take is tremendous. Some time ago, a truffle tree near Meyssac, in the Correze, produced $1200 worth of truffles over a four-year period in a truffigenous area of only 120 square feet, which appears to be the record, but the pubescent oaks are usually not so productive. They never have been. The French, unfortunately, have been unable to establish plantations anywhere near as productive as those that flourished in the vineyards killed by the *Phylloxera* accidentally imported from California toward the beginning of the century. M. Leygonie, a wizened gnarled truffle farmer of the Périgord, partially blamed this situation on World War I in a recent interview. "So many of our farmers went to war and were killed," he said, "that their wives who had to till the land and take care of the livestock to feed their families, had no time to devote to truffles. Then, after the war, the farmers didn't go back to it. There was no prestige in truffle hunting." That has all changed today, however, and there is now even a breed of wealthy sportsmen called "weekend truffle people," who raise oaks on plantations of otherwise useless land, hiring a farmer to till the soil when needed and to flood the place a few times during very dry summers. The prestige of the truffle has so increased that prosecutions for poaching have become common in recent years.

The competition in gathering truffles is therefore, intense, to say the least. In the small lazy town of Périgueux, the center of the Périgord, many hunt the love-food delicacies and few make a living from them. Périgourdians, like all *caveurs*, are close-mouthed about their work, protecting themselves against the competition and tax collector, but some have been known to earn a million francs a year from their part-time work. Accompanied by his porker *chercheuse* (literally, "pursuer") the gatherer generally seeks out an area under the oaks where "the truffle burns the ground," such a scorched circle called *lou cramadi* in the local dialect. Usually, nothing else can grow where the truffle reigns and the barren earth is scorched and cracked. The *caveur* either recognizes the *truffiere* (truffle ground) by signs such as "fairy rings" of wilted vegetation above the earth, the strong truffle odor and the truffle flies hovering over the ground, or he puts his trust entirely in his pig. Either the *chercheuse* digs out the truffle, or the gatherer gropes obliquely with his knife in the earth until he feels a truffle, then lifting the prize by a quick lever-action and carefully covering the small hole with soil. The peasants themselves feast on the strong piquant-scented delicacies only on special occasions. They are simply too expensive. Most are traded clandestinely in town, to be marketed later fresh or canned in salt water, cognac or Madeira. Buyers must beware especially in the Provencal towns where the black truffle is sold Saturday afternoons during the mid-November through

March seasons. Here in Villon country, the land of the troubadours, there are as many charlatans as there are hagglers. Truffles in paper bags with nothing on the bottom, summer truffles *(caison)* smelling like rotten cheese, broken truffles held together by toothpicks and pepper truffles with a faint odor of petroleum—all are palmed off on the hapless buyer. The wily peasants know all the tricks, including how to fill worm-eaten truffles with black earth and how to make sham truffles from bits of bad potato wrapped in a layer of truffle earth to impart exactly the right odor. One Provence commercial buyer has complained that 40% of his purchases are just plain dirt.

When the truffle gatherers can afford the fruits of their labor, their favorite dish is *truffles sous les cendres* (truffles under the ashes): seasoned truffles sprinkled with cognac, wrapped in salt pork and fire-resistant paper and cooked under the ashes in an open hearth. Truffles are featured at regional inns in many dishes, however, especially in casseroles and omelets. Some cognescenti follow a recipe described by Apicius over 1600 years ago. Sliced and sprinkled with salt, the truffles are barely brought to a boil and then speared on twigs and partly roasted. The gourmet's delight are next placed in a saucepan with oil, wine, honey and pepper; fine flour is beaten into this mixture as it bubbles over, and the tangy delicate truffles are eaten off the twigs. But the essence of most local recipes is simplicity. There is little of the ostentation identified with dishes like the truffle ice-cream popular with *bon vivants* toward the end of last century. Truffled ice-cream originated when August Belmont, William Travers and Leonard Jerome (Winston Churchill's grandfather) wagered $10,000 that would go to the man between them who could arrange the best complete dinner. The resulting feasts, prepared by the same Delmonico's chef, were all so good that the contest was declared a draw, truffled vanilla ice-cream having been invented as a dessert for one of them. The dessert does seem an unlikely combination, but was *de rigeur* for a good number of years among the really recherché members of the international *beau monde*. Such ostentation puts one in mind of an observation Juvenal made in his *Satires*: "Nor will that youth allow any relative to hope better of him who has learnt to peel truffles." It is also reminiscent of a scene in the nineteenth-century French play *La Poudre aux Yeux*, in which two "upstart" families on seeing that expensive truffles were used in the *pâté de foie gras* ordered them added to every course of the banquet they were planning.

Such upstarts are no problem in the region around Alba, Italy, where 80% of the world's even more rare and tasty *white* truffles are found. Here a large white truffle that sold for $150 was recently found and the town's mayor says that "truffles are classified in our laws with diamonds, furs and other symbols of rich living." In Alba, as in the Périgord, the locals are usually too poor to be able to eat the delicacies they uncover. Dogs instead of pigs are used almost exclusively to track the truffles in Alba, and there is actually a "truffle-snuffler school" to teach the art to qualified canines. The school was founded in 1870 by the grandfather of its present headmaster, Battista Monchiero, who felt in his romantic Latin way that pigs were "too awkward, impersonal, and un-affectionate, taking all the fun out of discovering a truffle." It might be added that pigs, though they have a keen sense of smell for truffles, are not as single-minded or obedient as dogs, although on the other hand, a pig can be served up with the truffles he uncovers. Anyway, for about $200 Monchiero offers a three-month dog-training course, utilizing secrets passed down from father to son for over two centuries. Known locally as Professor Barot, he holds classes in the ruins of a fourteenth-century castle overlooking the village of Roddie. He begins by first starving his dogs and teaching them to retrieve toys, rewarding them with a slice of bread (the French, evermore epicurean, use cheese or meat). Then a bit of truffle is substituted for the toy and, again, the reward is food. Others train their dogs by chopping truffles into their food while they are puppies, starving the dogs for a day or two and then letting them forage in the woods where truffles have been buried in a wire box, burying the box deeper on each occasion until the dogs can scent the truffles at the depths at which they normally grow. The dogs generally quarter an area, leaving no ground uncovered, pointing at full stop and whining when they scent the fungi. Although these hounds, unlike pigs, dislike truffles, they do ultimately learn to dig them from the ground in exchange for food. For the most part, mongrels are trained, Monchiero having found that they are more intelligent than purebreds. The dogs eventually learn to deliver the potato-like white truffles without leaving a toothmark on them and have been known to smell a truffle underground from a distance of 123 yards.

A canine graduate of Professor Barot's school can be worth from $200 to $1000, and at last report Barot himself made $15,000 a year training his dogs, but the white truffle business in Alba, six miles away down the mountain from Roddie, is depressed today. The increased use of chemical fertilizer on farmland in the area seems to have hurt truffle growth and Giorgio Morra, the white truffle king, who sells them to some U.S. restaurants and gourmet stores, has fewer to export every year. Morra, addressed everywhere in Alba as "King of the Truffles," also owns the century-old Albergo di Savona Hotel, where truffle-hunters gather during the season from October through December. White truffles, unlike black, only grow wild, attached to the roots of certain plants near truffle trees, no one ever having been able to cultivate them in any manner whatsoever. Just three years ago the largest white specimen ever found was unearthed in Alba. Weighing about six ounces, it was the size of a large potato, much smaller than the largest black finds. It has been alleged that white truffles king Morra buys most of the local truffles at clandestine meetings designed to fool the tax collectors, and preserves about 90% of his purchases, most of the truffles sold in a now affluent Italy, although they can be purchased fresh at Manganaro Foods in Manhattan.

The *world* "truffle king" is now undoubtly the Urbani family of Spoleto, Italy, who deal in both white and black truffles and would not agree with those cognescenti claiming that the white gem of the vegetable world deserves more distinction than its black brother. "The Morras and the Urbanis," says one observer, "get along no better than the Montagues and Capulets, their greatest joy being to spread rumors that the other is going out of business." The Urbani estates, eighty miles northeast of Rome in Umbria, at the calf of Italy's boot, cover twenty-five miles of their own or leased land and yield millions in truffles every year. Headed by seventy-four-year-old Carlo Urbani, the dynasty has been in the truffle business since 1750 when great-great-grandfather Paul Urbani first began collecting the fungi. Umbria, in the heart of Italy, is a fertile well-watered region with a mild, sunny climate. Here, near the village of Scheggino, the 2000 workers and dog teams the Urbanis employ or buy from dig up 20,000 tons of truffles a year, 75% of which are graded, peeled and vacuum packed for export. Under Carlo Urbani alone some 20,000 "truffle seedlings" have been planted, so a supply for the future seems assured. Urbani black truffles have won more prizes than any other variety and they cannot be distinguished from Périgords even under microscopic examination, which is attested to by the fact that, despite Gallic denials, French buyers purchase fully half of the crop annually, some $5 million worth. Urbani also sells to the Strasbourg producers of *pâté de foie gras*, who made truffles a big business when they began to garnish their product with flakes of black truffles in 1782. Carlo's major trouble today appears to be that he has no willing heir for his truffle kingdom. "My children," he has recently been quoted as saying, "no longer want to live in these lonely misty hills where the truffle hides."

In America and Canada, the Urbani operation is headed by Paul A. Urbani, the fifth in the line of Pauls, a nephew of Carlo who has been described as the truffle industry's Henry Ford. We were referred to Mr. Urbani by "21," who advised us that he knew more about truffles than anyone in the world. Mr. Urbani's expertise is certainly reflected in his salesmanship. Single-handedly, he is "truffleizing" America, as he puts it; he has tried to sell capitalist truffles to the Russians and has sold a supply of truffles to the operator of a hamburger stand as well as to restaurants like The Colony and The Four Seasons. Urbani and his wife drive more than 30,000 miles a year publicizing his product and he has been known to journey 100 miles to sell a single four ounce can of truffles.

The high price of truffles "is an optical illusion," Urbani claims, the truffle really being economical considering the flavor a few slices can add to a dish. The master salesman expects to see the day when canned truffles are as common on supermarket shelves as canned mushrooms. His dream may come true if experiments begun by the U.S. Agriculture Department about thirty years ago are ever resumed. At that time, the U.S.D.A. imported French oak seedlings and began cultivating truffles. Before any results could be obtained, however, World War II broke out and the fifty or so trees were neglected and cut down too soon, none surviving. Since then, one joint project launched by the government and the New York Botanic gardens in 1950 apparently came to naught. Some botanists believe that the United States is rich in species, not in abundance, and point out that only the white truffle has been found in the twenty-one states where truffles have been unearthed; others are convinced that a serious attempt to establish the fungi commercially would be successful, but plant physiologists of the U.S.D.A. advise us that no government research has been done on truffles in the last twenty years and that none is contemplated.

Actually, truffles have even been found in New York City. In 1949 an enterprising gentleman named Lorenzo Robba and his dog Musken, a truffle hound imported from Italy, discovered the fungi in Van Cortland Park in the Bronx, among other unlikely places. Robba, a gardener by trade, and in his own words, "the only truffle hunter in the East," claimed that millions of dollars worth of truffles lay buried in the New York City area. Truffles do occur throughout New York and have been unearthed by keen-nosed dogs in Central Park, but by all accounts they do not compare with French or Italian varieties; they are mostly a yellowish brown species called *Tuber unicolor* which does not have the piquant taste of its black or white cousins. Robba, incidentally, who sometimes stalked Central Park with Urbani and linquistics expert Mario Pei, has the distinction of being the first recorded truffle hunter in America. In 1909 the old *Scientific American* reported that he and a partner named Giavelli were hunting the fungi in New York and New Jersey.

Until we can get the aristocratic truffle to grow right in the democratic soil of our own backyard, the Urbani family will continue to flourish here supplying our needs. The Urbanis have a quarter of a million dollar business annually in the United States alone. Even at $100 a pound one posh restaurant orders thirty pounds of fresh truffles at a clip from them; a certain anonymous millionaire buys fresh specimens large enough to roast like mickeys in his fireplace; and Mrs. Hess of the oil-rich Hess family buys six pounds of truffles periodically for her chef to freeze for use in case of shortages.

With truffle prices so high, it was inevitable that someone would invent a synthetic or discover a substitute fungi. Johannes J. Geldof, a Washington chef of some forty years experience did this by combining egg yolks, cornstarch, confectioner's black coloring, salt and water in the right proportions. He priced his Trufflettes at $4 for a four-ounce jar, less than one-sixth the price for the real thing, and claimed that Trufflettes have 80% of the flavor of true truffles and can be used in the same ways. The Netherlands-born chef reported brisk sales when he patented his invention six years ago, and since then the Swedes have also marketed an artificial truffle. Paul Urbani has told restaurant owners that he'd rather see them use the traditional black olives instead of these synthetic products to deceive customers ("at least they're healthier"), and all diners would agree with him in his contention that a customer who orders truffles should get truffles—not an imitation at the same astronomical prices. Some unscrupulous restaurateurs do resort to such practices, however, as the trade in truffles is relatively small (most posh restaurants, for instance, need only about $300 in truffles a year for haute cuisine) and government regulations regarding the fungi aren't strongly enforced.

Until the truffle comes down in price it will have to remain primarily a food for gourmets and lovers. That it works small miracles is attested to by the black Périgord variety, which is noted even by its gatherers for fantastic properties, being considered not only a gastronomic gem but the ultimate aphrodisiac and an excellent salve for wounds. (It is said that when workers cut themselves peeling truffles, their wounds never become infected.) French chefs agree with Brillat-Savarin about the esculent fungi's aphrodisiac properties and point out that the Greeks dedicated the ambrosia to their love goddess, Aphrodite. The French truffles and sex tradition is strong indeed. Louis XVIII ate partridges stuffed with ortolan, which in turn were stuffed with truffles—a recipe of his own invention specifically meant to please the court ladies. His ancestor Louis VIII also invented an erotic truffle dish. Unfortunately, the Duc d'Escars was called upon to help prepare and partake of *truffés à la puree d'ortolans*. The Duc ate so much that he died of a surfeit during the night, but all good King Louis had to say when informed was, "Ah! I told him I had the better digestion of the two." On the other hand, Madame Pompadour, who invented several truffle dishes, including a celery soup flavored with the fungi, encountered no such digestive problems. La Pompadour often employed truffles in her diet "to heat the blood," especially in her *Filets De Sole Pompadour*, when she had her *petit soupers* with Louis XV. (They dined alone in a special room where after each serving the table would descend through an opening in the floor to the level below and be set for the next course; in this way, reported a contemporary writer, "they were freed of all embarrassment and needed not blush on being caught unawares.") Later, La Pompadour's successor, Madame DuBarry, followed her example and used truffled sweetbreads to arouse lecherous old Louis.

Alexander Dumas père, one of the most devoted of French gourmets and rakes, called the tasty truffle the "sanctum sanctorum of the gastronomes." When the great novelist dined evenings with his favorite mistress, *Salade de Truffes* was inevitably served. Mademoiselle George, after changing into something comfortable "without any false modesty," would lead Dumas to the dining room, where at the center of a large table a huge gold and silver bowl was filled to overflowing with five or six pounds of truffles "whose priceless scent assailed the air." She would then begin to peel the truffles with a special silver knife, finally seasoning them "with milk of almonds, wine, champagne or liquor as the mood seized her." Dumas left behind five recipes for truffles in his *Dictionary of Cuisine*, claiming that "To write the History of the truffle would be to undertake a history of civilization, in which they have played a more important role than the laws of Minos or the statutes of Solon." That his son Alexander Dumas the younger emphatically agreed with him can be seen in his play *Francillion*, written years later, wherein can be found the famous Salad Francillion recipe employing truffles.

The distinctive aroma of truffles permeates almost all foods, giving especial flavor to the *charcuterie* (meats prepared and preserved at the same time) and *foie gras* of France. The flavorsome fungi have been used in salads, omelets, fondues, chocolates, inlaid in goose livers, turkey breasts, pigs feet, broiled like potatoes, served in countless sauces and shred over stylish cuisine like Cold Oysters Venice, Eggs Benedict or *supremes de volaille*. Sometimes they are simply served in a white napkin and eaten with shavings of butter or a pinch of Rosy Salt. Other famous erotic truffle dishes include such prandial delights as pheasant stuffed with truffles; the "truffled partridge in aspic" placed on an epicurean pinnacle by Elinor Glyn in her *Reflections of Ambrosia* (1902), two famous garnishes named after Brillat-Savarin, Jockey Club Salad (asparagus, raw truffles and mayonnaise), *tournedos Rossini, truffes au champagne, Terrine De Foie Gras* and many sauces. For such concoctions there are many special wines, like the *Mar-*

gaux some gourmets recommend for truffled fowl dishes, the *St. Emilion Chateau Cheval Blanc* suggested for truffles used in pastry, and the *Musigny* generally appreciated because it "smells of violets and truffles."

In all truffles recipes, say the cognescenti, fresh truffles should be used. "You haven't lived until you've tasted fresh truffle," a Parisian gourmet insists. "You must tell your American readers that they're no doubt getting pretty good ones preserved, but to taste a truffle, the *real* thing, they'd have to come to France and eat one fresh. At a very good restaurant like the Pot au Feu outside of Paris in Asnieres (where you have to reserve about two weeks in advance), they serve the highest quality truffles, because they can afford to buy them." Even if this is true, fresh truffles can be purchased in the United States if you search hard enough, some fancy grocers carrying them in season. The knowledgeable Paul Urbani, however, claims that tinned or frozen ones will do just as well in most dishes. Urbani and Morra are the best canned Italian brands, while Rougie and F. Guillot offer the best French tinned truffles.

Truffles should be prepared carefully or their delicate flavor can be ruined. Thackeray, for instance, has his Mr. Titmarsh relate how truffles were "cast into a dish a minute before it was brought to table," and as a result were "windy, and pretentious, like those scraps of philosophy with which a certain eminent novelist serves out his meat." Served in the proper way, however, truffles are quite syzyrgial indeed, surpassing all Elysian enjoyments that tempt both the taste buds and libido. One can understand why the Romans entrusted gold and silver but never the preparation of truffles to servants, peeled them with a special amber knife and served them on their best silver. Perhaps, as Savarin says, the truffle's price is "not a great misfortune, for...they would be less thought of if they were to be got in quantities and at a cheaper rate." In making an analogy between truffles and lace, one of Brillat's women friends asks him, "If lace were so cheap, do you think anyone would wear such ragged looking things?" Yet as we've seen, these gastronomic gems can be counted relatively inexpensive, too, when it is considered how a few small pieces, with their ineffable flavor and odor, can amuse the mouth and amorous sense by transforming a workmanlike dish such as an omelette or stuffed fowl into a work of art. An omelette, incidentally, can be had even more cheaply by leaving your costly fresh truffle with your eggs overnight: the eggs will absorb the truffle flavor, enabling you to make a truffle omelette the next morning and yet have your truffle for still more lovemaking during the day.

The way a truffle is cooked is also said to have a direct relation to its efficacy as an aphrodisiac. Chef Raymond Oliver believes that all combinations of truffles with lobster, eggs and fish are potent but that the best way to employ the fungi "is to scrape them, clean them, soak them in Cognac and eat them raw with a little salt." The next best *prelude d'amour* is a salad made only of truffles, lettuce, oil, wine vinegar and a little black pepper and salt. "Once truffles are cooked," Oliver says, "particularly in heavy wines or spirits, they will only retain part of their powers, and in this case, they should be considered in terms of a steady, long-term diet; not as an immediate stimulant."

There is some argument as to whether the truffle is an erotic stimulant at all, but not from the vast majority of lovers. Tradition or "thinking makes it so" is obviously very much on the side of truffles; they were the most vaunted of foods served the amorous in the French dining room–boudoir *cabinets particuliers* featured in nineteenth-century restaurants. Further, they are a source of phosphorus and iron, both of which have a good effect on sexual activity, and they are an exception to Alexander Woollcott's famous dictum that everything enjoyable is either illegal, immoral or fattening— containing less calories than most diet foods. Like oysters, which they resemble in being mostly water and rich in protein, truffles are probably primarily a psychophysiological aphrodisiac, their reputation preceding them wherever they go. That their efficacy as an incentive to venery has been praised for over 2000 years cannot harm them, nevertheless. "Whatever you do," says a native Périgourdin, "treat the erotic truffle with respect. You should use it for its savor, its fragrance and not for reasons of decoration or snobbery. Watch out, too, for those terrible restaurateurs who charge exorbitant prices just because a few slices of truffle have been thrown into some dishes." Another chef suggests two cardinal rules to follow when purchasing the fungi: "Buy fresh truffles from a trusted dealer only, as cheap mushrooms or dyed white summer varieties are sometimes sold as the real thing; and enjoy them with a companion just as savory and promising, for, at the very least, spending so much money on something to eat has always inspired a certain *joie de vivre.*"

COURSE THIRTEEN

The Amazing Topless Hot Xtomatl...
Or Love Apple...
Or Wolf Peach—
America's Favorite Aphrodisiac Fruit...
Or Vegetable

"Truly, these Apples of Love...yeeld very little nourishment to the body
and the same naught and corrupt."

—John Gerard, *Herball,* 1597

The infamous scarlet "love apple" or wolf-apple of antiquity was considered a forbidden fruit by our Puritan ancestors; it is strictly speaking a poisonous plant, a soldier in the deadly nightshade family, yet is eaten daily with no harmful effects by millions; it is botanically a fruit, but legally, by Supreme Court decision, must be regarded as a vegetable; it was once the most reviled fruit of the vegetable world and is now decidedly the most popular. The amazing berry is used in more spicy sauces, canned in more soups, drunk in more juices, indispensable to more salads, slopped on more pizzas, grown in more home gardens and pinched, poked and haggled about in more supermarkets than any ten of its closest romantic competitors. No other fruit or vegetable has its mass appeal.

Only the egg has been so favored by disappointed audiences, rampant mobs and mischievous children. Only the apple has afforded a better-known simile in poem, love song and slang. Truly, *Lycopersicum esculentum*, the common garden-variety tomato, is among the most interesting, eye-widening, mouth-watering, taste bud–tingling aphrodisiac vegetables of all time.

But while the delectable tomato makes us wish we had double our 5500 taste buds, it did not always do so. *L. esculentum* (even its scientific patronym sounds delicious) is distinctly a new world plant native to South America, where it first grew in the Andes and is still found in its wild, wrinkled and wizened state throughout Peru, Bolivia and Ecuador. Like corn it was cultivated and carried by man through Central America into Mexico, but was probably never grown by North American Indians because of its sensitivity to cold. The Mayans, whose seafaring traders brought its seed to Yucatán, called the then tiny fruit *tomatl*, or *xtomatl*, and so prized *L. esculentum* that they traced its form along with more erotic scenes on their pottery. When Cortez and his band escaped the first Aztec uprising in Mexico, they managed to buy *tomatl* seeds in the great market of Chichén Itza to bring back with their plunder to Europe, where the plant was initially called both *pomi del peru* and *mala peruviane*.

At first *L. esculentum* met no resistance in Europe, generally living up to its name and enjoying a reputation as an esculent dish indeed. The Spanish, along with other Mediterranean peoples, widely adopted the tomato and when an ingenious Spanish chef combined the fruit with olive oil, spices and onions, he created the world's first tomato sauce, which was hailed by the Spanish court. Soon, as was inevitable with every new and rare food, *L. esculentum* even acquired a reputation as an aphrodisiac.

Why tomatoes were dubbed "love apples" is a matter of some dispute. That they hailed from exotic climes and were a shapely scarlet fruit undoubtedly helped, but the designation owes just as much to semantics as sexuality. All Spaniards at the time were called Moors and one story has it that an Italian gentleman told a visiting Frenchman that the tomatoes he had been served were "Pomi dei Moro" (Moor's apples), which to his guest sounded like "pommes d'amour," or "apples of love." However, another version claims that "apples of love" derives in a similar roundabout way from the Italian *pomo d'oro*, golden apple, and still another tale has it that courtly Sir Walter Raleigh presented a tomato to Queen Elizabeth, coyly advising her that it was an "apple of love." At any rate, the tomato quickly gained a reputation as a wicked aphrodisiac, and justly or not, it has held this distinction ever since. In Germany its common name is still *Liebesapfel* or "love apple," and the expression "hot tomato" for a willing woman is common to many languages. As for the word's pronunciation, those who, like the English, pronounce it the "toe-mah-toe" are probably historically correct. The plant was first called *tomate* in Spain and Portugal and pronounced in three syllables. The "o," incidentally, has no place at all in "tomato," apparently being there because mid-eighteenth century Englishmen erroneously believed that it should have this common Spanish ending.

The tomato's scarlet past probably contributed in part to its notoriety as a poisonous plant: *L. esculentum* was reputedly a *deadly* aphrodisiac. As noted, the English traveler Gerard wrote in his sixteenth-century gardening guide that "these Apples of Love...yeeld very little nourishment to the body and the same naught and corrupt." Similarly, the horticulturist Philip Miller, a colleague of the great Linnaeus, observed that there were those who thought that "the nourishment they afford must be bad." More likely, the tomato acquired this stigma because it belongs to the deadly nightshade family. As early as 1544, the Italian herbalish Pierandrea in his *Commentaries on the Six Books of Dioscorides*, linked the "golden apple" with mandrake, henbane and belladonna, all extremely poisonous plants. In fact, all parts of the tomato plant except the fruits *are* toxic, containing dangerous alkaloids, and to this day people are caused severe digestive upset from eating them. The tomato probably suffered on a smaller scale the fate of the potato, which was introduced to Europe at about the same time. The first potato plants from America were presented to Queen Elizabeth by Sir Walter Raleigh, and her chamberlain soon planted them along the Thames. He then invited the local gentry to a banquet featuring potatoes at every course. But instead of cooking the tubers, the unsuspecting chamberlain cooked the poisonous stems and leaves. A mass stomachache resulted that set back the acceptance of potatoes in England some 200 years. Likewise, tomatoes were for centuries mostly cultivated in English greenhouses as a floral ornament, ketchup, however, being made from the juice of tomatoes, mushrooms, walnuts and other ingredients in Old Blighty all along, the *OED* source for the sauce dated 1711.

Empress Eugénie, Napoleon III's wife, introduced Spanish tomato dishes into France in the mid-nineteenth century, just as she introduced a number of fashions that held sway at the time. This beautiful, elegant and charming woman, the undisputed leader of French fashion, which led the world then as now, was especially celebrated for her smart hats. She sometimes wore five different specimens in a day. One of her favorites, a small model with the brim turned up on the side and often decorated with ostrich plumes, was consequently named the Empress Eugénie in her honor. Born Eugénie Marie de Montijo de Guzmán, the empress was the daughter of a Spanish grandee and a Scottish noblewoman. Prince Louis Napoleon at first offered to make her his mistress, but she intrigued to become his wife and prevailed—though no one knows if her spicy tomato dishes helped. Their marriage was celebrated in 1853 at Notre Dame. "The Spanish Woman" was never popular with the French people, but she strongly influenced her husband in matters of state. When the Second Empire fell in 1871, she fled to England with her husband, where she died almost a half century later in 1920, ninety-four years old and a legend in her time.

Tomatoes may have made Eugénie love and live longer, but she cannot claim the distinction of being the *first* to introduce them to the French cuisine. This honor must go to Napoleon's chef, who invented Chicken Marengo at the Battle of Marengo in Lombardy during the Italian campaign, the quite exact date being two o'clock in the afternoon, June 14, 1800. Having no butter on hand, the resourceful cook sautéed the chicken in the local olive oil, adding the sauce consisting of tomatoes, herbs, mushrooms and Marsalla wine that is still called Chicken Marengo. Later, Antonin Carême—the starving child of a family of twenty-five who became "the chef of Kings and the King of chefs"—featured stuffed tomatoes as his favorite accompaniment for a filet of beef. Carême would stuff tomatoes à la *Sicilienne*, with ham, chopped onions, etc.; à la *Florentine*, using chicken and other ingredients; and à la *Provencale*, employing chopped mushrooms, garlic and bread crumbs in his stuffing. It wasn't long before all of France was influenced by "Carême of Paris," as Louis XVIII granted him the right to call himself, and by the time Empress Eugénie came along, the tomato was already on its way to becoming almost as indispensable to the French cookery as it is to the Italian, all *provencale* or à la *portugaise* dishes still being made with them today. Actually, about the only thing unsavory the French have to say about the tomato is found in their slang expression *escraser des tomates*, "to have one's menses." In fact, an erotic tomato surprise dish called Stuffed Tipped Tomatoes probably made its debut in France. To prepare it, just peel two large tomatoes and hollow them slightly, placing in a baking dish. Take two stalks of firm cooked asparagus and brush with a sauce of basil and butter. Insert one asparagus stalk in each slightly hollowed tomato, sprinkle with Parmesan cheese, pouring melted butter over this and bake in a hot oven for about twenty minutes.

Unfortunately, America went along with England and while France and southern Europe were enjoying their hot tomato sauces, *L. esculentum* was grown here only as a curiosity or as an attractive ornamental trained on trellises. The fruit was condemned from the pulpit and marked with skull and crossbones by the doctors. Thomas Jefferson, who once wrote that he would rather be a common dirt gardener than President, grew tomatoes at Monticello in 1781; the New Orleans market offered them to more-knowing housewives of French descent; and foreign visitors and Yankee sea captains introduced tomatoes to New England and Philadelphia toward the end of the eighteenth century (housewives using them to make "catchup," "kechup" or "ketchup")—but these were barely noteworthy exceptions. The tomato was for the most part still guilty by association, and far too scarlet and shapely for the Puritan palate.

If any one man liberated *L. esculentum* it was Colonel Robert Gibbon Johnson, an eccentric gentleman of Salem, New Jersey. In 1808, after a trip abroad, Johnson introduced the tomato to the farmers of Salem, and each year thereafter offered a prize for the largest locally grown fruit. But the Colonel was a forceful individualist and wanted his introduction to be regarded as more than an ornamental bush. On September 26, 1820 (some say 1830), he announced that he would appear on the Salem Court House steps and eat *not one but a whole basket of "wolf peaches"*!

Public reaction in Salem was immediate. Declared Johnson's physician, Dr. James Van Meeter:

> The foolish colonel will foam and froth at the mouth and double over with appendicitis. All that oxalic acid! One dose and you're dead. Johnson suffers from high blood pressure, too. That deadly juice will aggravate the condition. If the Wolf Peach is too ripe and warmed by the sun, he'll be exposing himself to brain fever. Should he survive, by some unlikely chance, I must remind that the skin of the *Solanum Lycopersicum* [as it was then called] will stick to the lining of his stomach and cause cancer.

Van Meeter was there, black bag in hand, along with 2000 other curious people from miles around, to watch Colonel Johnson commit certain suicide. Johnson, an imposing figure dressed in his usual black suit and tricornered hat, ascended the court house steps at high noon as the local fireman's band played a dirgelike tune. Selecting a tomato from his basket, he held it aloft and launched into his spiel:

> The time will come when this lucious, golden apple, rich in nutritive value, a delight to the eye, a joy to the palate, whether fried, baked, broiled or eaten raw, will form the foundation of a great garden industry, and will be recognized, eaten and enjoyed as an edible food.... And to help speed that enlightened day, to help dispel the tall tales, the fantastic fables that you have been hearing about the thing, to show you that it is not poisonous, that it will not strike you dead, I am going to eat one right now!

Colonel Johnson bit and his juicy bite could be heard through the silence, until he bit again, and again, and again—at least one female spectator screaming and fainting with each succeeding chomp. The crowd was amazed to see the courageous Colonel still on his feet as he devoured tomato after tomato. He soon converted most onlookers, but not until the entire basket was empty did Dr. Van Meeter slink away and the band strike up a victory march and the crowd begin to chant a cheer that eventually led to Johnson's election as mayor when Salem was first incorporated as a township.

We should note that Colonel Johnson's words, as well as those of Dr. Van Meeter, may be apocryphal in part, but this is the way they come down to us in history through secondary accounts. An effort to get at primary sources was thwarted when we learned that a fire in the local newspaper office had destroyed all records of the period; however, several scholarly books on the Garden State endorse the Johnson yarn in essence and the prestigious Massachusetts Horticultural Society magazine *Horticulture* (August 1966), among others, firmly supports the Salem, New Jersey saga. It seems almost certain then that Colonel Johnson's bite was heard around the country, if not the world. His efforts at least turned the tide for the tomato (though he was not, of course, the first American to eat the fruit), and it was appearing regularly in markets by 1835. But prejudices still lingered. As late as 1860 the popular *Godey's Lady's Book* warned its readers that tomatoes "should always be cooked for three hours before eating," and word detective Dr. Charles Funk noted in his *Horsefeathers* that at the turn of the century in rural Ohio his mother was averse to eating what was then known "only as the love apple and believed to possess aphrodisiac properties, and was therefore feared by virtuous maidens." The myth still persists that tomatoes make the blood acid; and a "health food" brochure printed as recently as 1970 warns that: "Many vegetables are actually toxic and consuming them will pollute the body and taint the brain. Tomatoes are a bigger threat to the health of this country than any other vegetable because they are related to such poisonous plants like [sic] nightshade, belladona and tobacco." Considering that we've been so ignorant and prejudiced about an innocuous fruit for almost 400 years, we're fortunate that we've advanced as far as we have in other areas.

Actually, there isn't much meaningful controversy about whether the tomato is poisonous anymore, and not many people argue about its status as a fruit or a vegetable. Legally, *L. esculentum* is generally a vegetable, and botanically it is a fruit or berry belonging to the potato family, which includes deadly nightshade. This matter was settled in 1893 when an importer contended that the tomato was a fruit and therefore not subject to vegetable import duties. The United States Supreme Court held that it had to be considered a vegetable because it was served in soup or with the main course of a meal, although it could be considered a fruit when eaten out of hand or as an appetizer. The scientists, of course, did not consider this legal reasoning very scientific, and so we are stuck with the inconsistency today.

Tomatoes are presently a big business in the United States, with some 431,000 acres allotted to them throughout the country. Domestic production is well over 967,000 tons of fresh tomatoes annually, and another 3½ million bushels are imported into the country each year. Additionally, some 45 million pounds of canned whole tomatoes and 33 million cases of tomato juice are sold each year. We enjoy tomatoes in salads, on pizza, in spaghetti sauce, in chili sauce, topping everything but ice-cream with them. Readily available are American recipes for tomato conserves, marmalade, mincemeat, scalloped tomatoes, panfried tomatoes, one for tomatoburgers and even one for candied tomatoes. What with Pop Art posters, Campbell's Tomato Soup can has become as traditional as The Old Man In The Mountain, Andy Warhol's painting of it having last sold for $60,000—quite an advance from that day in 1897 when a young $7.59-a-week chemist named John Dorrance worked out the formula for condensing it and Campbell's Tomato Soup was born.

If there is controversy about the tomato in modern times—aside from minor disputes such as whether clam chowder should be made with milk or tomatoes, which can become violent among gourmets—that controversy concerns their taste. There are those who argue that most Americans never know the indescribable taste of a sun-ripened tomato, and judging by store-bought varieties, they are absolutely right. Most fresh tomatoes today are picked green or light pink for market because the fruit is perishable when ripe and ripens even under refrigeration. Tomatoes are therefore ripened by ethylene gas after being shipped, and although ethylene is harmless—the gas is naturally given off by bananas and McIntosh apples—this artificial process deprives the tomato of the Vitamin C it would normally gain from sunlight and substantially subtracts from its flavor. Commercial tomatoes have the texture of the apples they were first named for and quite often taste like the cellophane they are wrapped in, the term "firm slicing tomatoes" really a euphemism for "firm packing tomatoes." Sometimes growers even conspire to force this insipid product on consumers. In 1968, for example, smaller Mexican tomatoes, which are mostly imported through Arizona and are 90% vine-ripened, were outselling Florida winter varieties in the Western United States. Eighty-five percent of Florida tomatoes are picked green, but in 1969 the Florida Tomato Committee, authorized to make grade requirements for the U.S. Department of Agriculture, decided that green tomatoes could be sold at $2\frac{9}{32}$ inches in diameter, whereas vine-ripened ones had to be at least $2\frac{17}{32}$ inches in diameter. This barred 30–50% of the Mexican imports, caused tomato prices to rise, infuriated Mexican growers and Arizona merchants and worst of all inflicted more tasteless tomatoes on the American consumer. There may be a little hope in sight, however, for scientist John T. Worthington has found a method enabling growers to read green tomato density with a four-filter photometer, which enables them to know when their crops will ripen simultaneoulsly for uniform packing. At least all the tasteless green tomatoes in cellophane will ripen on their way to the market at the same time and buyers won't have to poke at them to determine their softness.

We prefer the old salt-shaker method cited by Joan Faust, Garden Editor of the New York *Times.* "This is the one made around mid-July when the patient gardener can't wait any longer," Miss Faust writes. "He ventures out to the vegetable patch, salt shaker in hand, to pluck just one rosy tomato to see how things are coming along. Who can describe his ecstasy when biting into that first tomato, lightly dusted with a dash of salt. Let's hope that this heritage is never lost to the next generations and that children will not grow up thinking tomatoes come from plastic-roofed cardboard trays..."

But millions of Americans do still know what a sunripened tomato tastes like. Summer crops from local areas are often ripened on the vine and no other vegetable is so widely grown by America's 65 million home vegetable gardeners. Tomatoes have always been the first choice for the backyard patch and those who grow no other vegetables at all often manage to raise a few staked plants. (Commercial varieties are usually not staked, but are allowed to sprawl, yielding more fruit that way.) New varieties that resist verticillium wilt, a fungus disease that attacks tomato roots, are making the vegetable even more popular in the home garden, and it is not a plant that requires a very rich soil; actually, poorer soil often aids a tomato plant, because too-fertile ground causes large leaf growth that shades the fruit and lowers the Vitamin C content that would be taken in from sunlight. Hundreds of varieties are available today. There is even a striped British variety called Tiger Tom, a hollow tomato developed especially for stuffing, and a "perennial" tree tomato (*Cyhomandra betacea*), related to the common variety, that was once cultivated by the Indians of ancient Peru. Tomatoes are grown in mini-gardens, in pots on patios, in apartment house windows, on terraces and even on houseboats. Artificially colored ones may be eaten of necessity, if there comes no open rebellion, but the scarlet, garden-ripened tomato with the unsavory past and savory taste will not without battle be forsaken. Whether they are served in way-out dishes like the "whipped cream *à la tomate* sprinkled with brandy" invented by futurist chef Jules Maincave, or brought to table stacked atop the stacked cook's bare bosom—a genuine tomato surprise—they'll remain a favorite of lovers and a symbol of love. Perhaps you'll even be lucky enough to find one so succulent and seductively shaped that you'll echo the words of Chef Louis Szathmary, Ph.D., of The Bakery, a fine Chicago restaurant. Szathmary recently picked a tomato that was definitely a doppelgänger for the gluteus maximus. "It was so sensuous," he says, "that I ate it in bed."

COURSE FOURTEEN

Green Power,
Or The Shapes Of Things To Come:
More Virile Vegetables
From A To Z

"Aware that her youth was passing and wishing to oust the rest of her decrepit lover's women, she took pains to enthrall him by the use of magic plants. At the same time she re-awakened his juvenile ardor by the judicious use of garlic, onions and other virile adjuvants."

—Kshemendra, *Samayamtrika*

In ancient Rome courtesans and housewives would line up patiently waiting their turn to drape flowers around the idol of Priapus, which was in reality nothing more nor less than a prodigious penis rudely connected with a human face. Called *olisboklius*, these stone phalli were erected almost everywhere one turned those days. Each lusty maiden or matron offered as many wreaths as she had lovers, one woman alone often hiding the giant member from sight with the number of garlands she bestowed upon it. For in addition to being a garden god, the phallic symbol of the eternal procreative power of nature, Priapus also reigned

193

as a guardian of fertility, the patron of human fecundity who helped impotent men as well as frigid and barren women and was trusted to cure the whole spectrum of sexual difficulties and insure a happy sex life.

Like most peoples, the Romans saw the connection between their agriculture-sex god and the value of fruits and vegetables in their amatory diet. Our word vegetable, for example, comes from the Latin *vegetus*, "active or lively," and both slave and patrician thought all food from the fertile earth was a spur to love. In later cultures vegetables would be spurned by the nobility, our word garbage, interestingly enough, coming from the Latin *gerbe*, meaning "green stuff," but not so among the Romans. The Roman Fabii, who took their name from the *faba*, or bean; the Piso clan, who derived their's from the *pisa*, or pea; the Lentuli, who named themselves after the *lente*, or lentil; and the great house of Cicero, which took its name from the *cicer*, or chickpea—these are only a few noble families whose patronyms honored widely hailed aphrodisiac vegetables.

Among the Hindus, who are as a rule a race of vegetarians who rarely drink stimulants, vegetables were infinitely more venerated as love foods than in Rome; many fruits, herbs and vegetables are mentioned in recipes throughout their sex manual the *Ananga Ranga*. The same holds true for most Chinese sex books, which particularly extolled garlic, leeks, onions, celery, yams, carrots and chives. Those Chinese who lived on the water even went to the trouble of growing vegetables in their boats, and the people believed so strongly in "green power" that they concocted a pill called the "sweet medicine" composed chiefly of vegetable matter and extracts (unfortunately the formula has been lost to history) which was dissolved in water and applied to the penis so that "manly vigor would flourish evermore."

Elizabethan vegetable gardens in England "sprouted all the instruments of debauchery," according to one writer. Asparagus and carrots were especially appreciated as much for their enticing shapes as for their vitamins and taste. As for France, that incomparable land of logic and culture, Rabelais writes about salads "wholly made up of venerous herbs and fruits, such as rocket, tarragon, cresses, parsley, rampions, poppy, celery...etc." Then we have Madame Pompadour, who kept an extensive vegetable garden for her royal lover, arranging it as beautifully as she arranged herself, and, but of course, Madame DuBarry, who frequently used herbs, spices and vegetables to arouse Louis XV.

Vegetables were and still are used extensively as foods for love throughout France. Casanova once described a garden in a famous Parisian bordello "so arranged that it could serve all the joys of love." It was the same in early American gardens grown "for meate or medicine," from which the leaf of periwinkle was eaten to inspire love between husband and wife; parsley to draw down the menses; dandelion for incontinence; herbs to make life merry; lettuce and camphire to restrain lust of an immediate nature; and giant asparagus, carrots and parsnips (much larger than those ever grown in England), as well as artichokes, chervil, dill and spearmint, to provoke bodily lust. None of these frontier gardens was meant for ornament but for the necessities of life, which naturally included the begetting of same.

Even common garden dirt has been sought in the quest for potency. True, some do not eat, but merely swallow, the loam, yet many a lover has thoroughly enjoyed his or her soufléed soil. Humbolt first described the geophagists or dirt-eaters called the Ottomaques of the Orinoco, who fed "on a fat, unctuous earth...tinged with a little oxide of iron." The Ottomaques, we're told, "collect this clay very carefully...and knead it into balls four or five inches in diameter, which they bake slightly before a slow fire. Whole stacks of such provisions are seen piled up in their huts...soaked in water when about to be used, and each individual eats about a pound of this material a day." Similar practices have flourished among the natives of various climes: the Aleppo fed a kind of fuller's earth called "Byloon" to pregnant women and sickly girls, the Javanese ate or still eat little balls of reddish clay called Ampo if they wish "to become thin and graceful," the Swedes enjoyed a hearty "mountain meal" called *bergmehl*, sometimes mixed with flour, and workmen in the European Kiffhausen stone quarries spread a very fine clay called "steinbutter" on their bread. But even if "men often eat dirt to become dirty old men" as one wag put it (they don't, generally, geophagists usually suffer from mineral deficiencies which the soil helps remedy), is this any worse than the American historian Prescott, an uncomprisingly foolish moralist who "ate soap under the theory that men should be clean inside as well as out?"

Among the famous vegetarians of history, who include such immortals as Plato, Milton, Voltaire, Tolstoy, Gandhi and George Bernard Shaw, a number were spirited lovers—even Gandhi was quite a dandy as a young man. This alone offers some evidence that vegetables and plants have more erotic significance than their suggestive resemblances to the genitals. Medically, in fact, raw or properly cooked vegetables are held in high esteem for increasing amatory ability because they contain ingredients that keep us in prime condition generally, which is why the vegetables that have *not* been considered aphrodisiacs over the ages are few indeed. Some have been far more favored than others, however, often for good reason, and these seventy or so are covered from A to Z in the pages following. We hope that our praise of organic peas and parsley may encourage some to start aphrodisiac gardens of their own, even, if need be, on the roof of a Volkswagen, as at least one enthusiast has done. Garlic certainly doesn't "purify the blood and clean the bowels"; eating green vegetables won't bring pregnant women boy babies, just as yellow vegetables won't guarantee girl children; and the consumption of hot peppers will not produce offspring with high spirits and artistic talent. But most superstitions about vegetables are definitely based on the fact that they're good for the health and, hence, the libido.

· ARTICHOKES ·

Three centuries ago Dr. Nicolas Venette wrote that the globe artichoke "produces...much semen and vigor...which according to the reports of sailors, is why Swedish women today give it to their husbands when they find them negligent in the indulgence of love." Many agreed with him, including Catherine de Medici (who fed her men kidneys and artichoke hearts), which explains the old French saying that artichokes, like wine, are good for ladies when gentlemen partake of them. Paris street vendors no longer hawk them with the cry *Artichokes! Artichokes! Heats the body and the spirit! Heats the genitals!"* And debauched dissolute women aren't called artichokes in England anymore. But some medical authorities still believe that the vegetable does cause urogenital stimulation. The Dutch gynecologist Van de Velde, for one, recommended artichokes (as well as celery and asparagus) because their acids are separately eliminated by the kidneys, thus exciting the urinary passages.

The globe artichoke, as it's better called, is actually the flower bud of a thistle picked before it flowers and bears no relation to the Jerusalem artichoke, a North American tuber that neither comes from Jerusalem nor is a true artichoke. Small tender globes are much tastier stuffed and steamed as an appetizer than large, woody specimens. Follow any reliable stuffed artichoke recipe for your Stuffed Artichokes Aphrodite, a sensuous dish to begin any love feast, pulling off a petal at a time and scraping off the stuffing and tender flesh with your teeth until coming to the tenderest petals, which can be eaten whole. Then remove the needles covering the base or heart and mash it in a little olive oil and vinegar. You'll find that this is the one vegetable that you'll have more of when you finish, so compact are its petals. Incidentally, scientists have only this year discovered that artichoke hearts make some beverages taste sweet after eating them, the sweetening ability of one-quarter of an artichoke heart said to be comparable to adding two teaspoons of sugar to six ounces of water. This effect lasts only about five minutes, but it has caused controversy over whether really fine wines should be served with artichokes, lest they be made to taste too sweet. A pill called "Mirlin" using cynarin and chlorogenic acid, the two chemicals largely responsible for the artichoke's sweetening effect, will probably be available as a "natural artificial sweetener" by the end of this year (see also Cardoon).

• ASPARAGUS •

"A decoction of asparagus roots boiled in wine and being taken fasting several mornings together," *Culpepper's Complete Herbal* (1652) advises, "stirreth up bodily lust in man or woman, whatever some have written to the contrary." But although its root is still used in medicines and has traditionally been a cure for every ailment from toothache to heart disease, it is the asparagus *stalk* that has generally been more highly regarded as an aphrodisiac. Being blatantly phallic has helped, of course (asparagus is still French slang for the penis), but medically speaking, the "grass," as the shoots are sometimes called, has just as much going for it. The phallic-shaped stalks are not only a definitely visual psychological aphrodisiac, figuring in a number of suggestive love dishes like creamed asparagus, but are highly nutritious and contain the chemical asparagine, a diuretic that increases the amount of urine excreted and excites the urinary passages. Asparagus also contains substantial amounts of aspartic acid, an amino acid that neutralizes the excess amounts of ammonia which linger in our bodies and make us tired and sexually disinterested. "Experiments with potassium and magnesium salts of aspartic acid," one writer observes, "have overcome cases of chronic exhaustion and increased sexual responsiveness.... Asparagus is rich, too, in potassium, phosphorus and calcium, all necessary for maintenance of a high energy level."

Van de Velde included asparagus as one of the best all-around love foods. But the sexologist merely confirmed what lovers had known for centuries. The Phoenicians probably first introduced this member of the lily family to the Greeks, who gathered it from the wild, and excluding Pliny, who believed that "one who wore asparagus as an amulet became barren," there have been nothing but raves about it as a love food ever since. Apicius spoke highly of asparagus and his fellow Romans cultivated it as early as 200 B.C., growing some stalks at Ravenna that weighed a full three pounds and gathering stems in the Getulia plains of Africa that were actually *twelve feet tall*. The most flavorful "grass," however, is thin and tender and should be cooked in as little water and as rapidly as possible—never more than ten minutes. Even the Romans knew this, their Emperor Augustus originating the old saying, "Quicker than you can cook asparagus."

Probably no other food figures in such explicitly sexual and/or obscene love poetry as the asparagus, from the poems of the early Greeks to those of the Roman Catullus. Similar sentiments are expressed in the literature of China, where asparagus was a favorite sex food, and in that of India, whose *Kama Sutra* advises that "The drinking of a paste composed of the asparagus racemous [and other ingredients]...is provocative of sexual vigor." In England the plant is mentioned from earliest times and cited again and again in medicinal recipes, as it was throughout Europe. Which led Rabelais to have Panurge declare: "My better end is my uniterminal, intercrural asparagus stalk. I hereby vow and promise to keep it succulent, with good measure pressed down and running over."

The most famous recipe for asparagus is doubtless that used by Madame Pompadour for her *petit soupers*. Surprisingly, she didn't take full advantage of the stalk's prodigious size and shape, but this French dish is certainly delectable. Instructs La Pompadour:

> Dress and cook the asparagus sticks in the normal way by plunging them into boiling water. Slice them obliquely towards the tips into pieces no bigger than the little finger. Take only the choicest sections, and keeping them hot, allow them to drain while the sauce is being prepared in the manner following—Work ten grammes of flour and a lump of butter together, a good pinch of powdered nutmeg and the yolks of two eggs diluted with four spoonfuls of water acidulated with lemon juice. After cooking this sauce, drop in the asparagus tips and serve in a covered casserole.

Asparagus came to America with the first settlers in the New World and has been a favorite ever since, home-grown in many appropriately named perennial "beds." Brillat-Savarin, who praised the symbolic stalks in several places, enjoyed them while exiled here and his *Physiology of Taste* recounts two long risque anecdotes about the vegetable. One relates the tale of two Englishmen who bought a bundle from a Parisian vendor and walked off whistling "God Save The King," the vendor observing that their asparagus might do just that, if the king ate them. The other tells of a giant asparagus tip growing in an Episcopal bishop's garden, the head so great, round and shiny that it became the talk of the town as it rose from the ground. Only when the bishop went out to cut the tempting stalk did he learn that it wasn't real, but a perfect imitation made by a local Canon, "who had carved a wooden asparagus...had stuck it by stealth into the bed, and lifted it a little every day to imitate the nocturnal growth." Since then the phallic asparagus has been the prop for many jokes sexual and otherwise, perhaps most notably in a scene from the early American movie *Young Ironsides*. In this classic, silent film star Charlie Chase attempts to eat an asparagus and it bends away. Then his girlfriend tries to eat the asparagus with him, grasping it at the stalk, but neither does that work, the asparagus even popping free when Charlie ties it into a bow. At the film's end, Charlie trips over a serving cart and grabs a stalk, but his asparagus falls over limp, all seemingly a symbol of his impotence in everything.

Before World War I, asparagus was the phallic banana joke of its day in Paris. The magazine *La Vie Parisienne* featured a full-page color drawing of a woman clad in nylons, shoes and nothing else hugging a huge shapely spear. The magazine's rival *Le Rire* went further, running a cartoon showing four different women eating asparagus four different ways: *Avec dedain!* (with disdain), *Avec hesitation*, *Avec amour* and *Avec rage* (with passion, using *both* hands).

Today white asparagus is all the rage in Europe, especially the German *spargel*, which farmers grow in mounds, picking the very tender stalks before they have a chance to push above the ground and turn green. Reports one writer on a recent Bonn dinner party: "A certain guest complimented the elegant German hostess and said, 'This white asparagus, is as beautiful as an undressed woman,' thereby probably becoming the first asparagus eater to have noted a resemblance between asparagus and the attributes of the *female* sex."

• BAMBOO SHOOTS •

Succulent bamboo shoots are still a favorite food for love among the Chinese, who prefer them with pork. The Japanese, on the other hand, use bamboo shoots, along with other vegetables, in their pan fried beef or chicken (or dog meat) *sukiyaki*. From earliest times, all over the orient, the small green sprouts plucked from bamboo stalks have been highly praised, often eaten like asparagus. The Hindu love manual the *Ananga Ranga* gives two love charms utilizing the tall, woody hollow-stemmed grasses, the first guaranteeing that "the wearer's eyes will attract all," and the second assuring that "its effect will be greatly to increase the mutual love of husband and wife." In the United States bamboo shoots naturally haven't much of a reputation, although several sexologists have included them in their regimens. Be extra careful in preparing fresh bamboo shoots. The shoots are covered with fine sharp hairs that can perforate the intestines if not removed before eating.

· BEANS ·

My love hung limp beneath the leaf
  (O bitter, bitter shame!)
My heavy heart was full of grief
  Until my lady came.
She brought a tasty dish to me,
  (O swollen pod and springing seed!)
My love sprang out right eagerly
  To serve me in my need.

This old English ballad, *The Love Bean*, reminds us that beans of all kinds were regarded as incitants to lust since earliest times. Long before it was known that they are rich in iron, copper and phosphorus, flatulent foods like baked beans, peas, lentils and radishes were believed to be effective because they enabled men to attain prodigious erections by means of their eructations, or accumulated gas.

The Roman author Petronius prescribed beans for lovers and there is an Italian saying about the effects of broad bean soup that translates as "It rises more gloriously than ever!" Chinese men also used beans to rise to the occasion, and still do, considering lobster with pickled bean-curd sauce to be particularly potent. It is said that along the Yellow River in China, in Honan Province, carp and red bean soup is regarded as an indispensable dish for newlyweds, the recipe for the soup dating back to the Tang Dynasty, when the renowned gourmet physician Meng Hsien prescribed it for people "intent on having a happy married life."

St. Jerome knew as early as the fourth century that beans "excited genital titillation" and refused to share his supply with the nuns in the convent he governed in Jerusalem. Since then Queen Elizabeth, Flaubert and Sir Richard Burton have sung the legume's praises, the latter beginning his account of a strict aphrodisiac diet with the words: "First and foremost, strong wine, vegetables, beans...." Burton spoke of haricot beans, not the common string bean or lima bean native to the Americas, which along with corn supplied many Indian tribes with their food requirements. The Mayans, in fact, planted climbing beans beside their corn hills so that the stalks would serve as natural poles, and they were of course a staple of both the early colonist diet and the chuck wagons of the west, where many fiery Mexican dishes featuring them were adopted. American folklore, incidentally, says that "if you make a string of beans and throw it up into the air, the initials made by the beans when they fall will be that of the person you are going to marry."

Probably the most important new news for lovers about the common bean is the recent announcement that the U.S.D.A. is developing a "gas-less" variety. Researchers, it seems, have discovered that an organic sugar group called oligosaccharides causes the formation of gas in the intestinal tract and have come up with a "clean bean" seed guaranteed not to cause any social distress at the dinner table or elsewhere."

• BEETS •

Often called beetroot by the English, beets and their leaves have a high nutritional value; their greens are especially rich in vitamin A, copper and iron. Like asparagus, they're also rich in aspartic acid.

Beets were not eaten except for their leaves (our chard) until Roman times. Neither sugar beets, chard nor garden beets, all members of the same family, make the blood richer, though the old myth persists, but they have long been used for medicinal purposes. The Greeks valued them so highly that they created tiny replicas of beets in silver.

White beets are mentioned by Pliny as an aphrodisiac food and we find numerous use of them in the love cookery, perhaps because they bore some resemblance to the testicles. The French word for the beet, *bettereve*, also serves as their slang for "the manroot or penis." Of the many references to this vegetable in erotic literature perhaps the most famous is Catullus' poem about a Roman matron who left her husband, because his "equipment dangled like a limp-leaved beet." Not exactly a kind comparison, but then Catullus isn't referring to healthy red-blooded beets.

• CABBAGE •

Corned beef and cabbage has been ridiculed as a pedestrian dish at least since Jiggs of *Maggie and Jiggs* comic strip fame. Nothing could be farther from the truth, in the case of cabbage, at any rate. A member of the mustard family, cabbage has been cultivated for more than 4000 years, is the most ancient of all vegetables, having an aristocratic history that makes the saying "Of cabbages and kings" mean something else than was originally intended. The pharaohs counted *brassica erica* as an aid to drinking and ate large quantities of cooked cabbage before their drinking bouts on the premise that this would enable them to guzzle more beer and wine without getting drunk. The Egyptians actually went so far as to worship the vegetable as a god, building altars for it, and the Greeks after them claimed that the heads "sprang from the sweat of

Jupiter," recommending them as a cure for baldness and many ailments. It was the Romans who gave the cabbage its present name, from the Latin *caput*, meaning head, and they too regarded the vegetable as an aid to drinking. But the Romans also saw cabbage as an aphrodisiac; Apicius vouched for it in his *De Re Coquinaria*, and Roman priests dedicated young cabbage to Priapus, the phallic guardian of fertility.

China's Great Wall was built by coolies fed on strength-giving cabbage preserved in rice wine. Thus originated sauerkraut, although the Tartars were the first to use salt instead of wine as a preservative in the recipe, and they introduced it to Germany, where cabbage itself is still called *kraut* or *kohl*. Today the most famous cabbage dish in the Far East is probably Korean *kimchi*, a highly spiced dish which is prepared in mid-November and buried in the ground in large earthern jars to preserve it throughout the cold months. South Korean troops fighting in Vietnam had to be supplied with *kimchi* to bolster their morale, for a Korean meal without it is virtually unthinkable—there is even a Korean saying that "we can live a whole year without meat, but without *kimchi* we can hardly live a week." Hot and high in vitamins B and C, *kimchi* is said to be most stimulating, but many foreigners find it burns their palates and complain that it has an unpleasant odor.

Cauliflower, kale, Brussels sprouts and broccoli are all forms of cabbage that have been esteemed as aphrodisiacs by Europeans. The vegetable's sexual associations can be found in the French slang expression *chounette*, "the little darling," for the female pudendum and *chouserie*, which was used by Rabelais and others for "copulation"; both these expressions stem from *chou*, the French word for cabbage. Similarly, the word cabbage also once served in English slang as a synonym for the female sex organ.

Brought to the Americas by the French navigator Jacques Cartier in 1536, cabbage has been cultivated here ever since in many varieties. Although a rich source of many important nutrients and recognized as such, the aristocratic vegetable does not enjoy the same prestige as it did in days gone by.

· CARDOON ·

The cardoon is probably the artichoke that ancient Greeks and Romans favored as a love food. A primitive form of the artichoke, it commanded premium prices in the Roman market and shared the same qualities as its relative, generally being grown in the dark to keep its young leaves white and tender (see Artichoke).

• CARROT •

A good source of vitamins A and E, the so-called "sexuality vitamins," carrots have been recorded as a aphrodisiac food since the Greeks extolled them as "love medicine" and called them *philtron*. In his *Book Of Good Love*, the Spaniard Juan Ruiz theorizes that the Arabs introduced the vegetable into Europe along with other sexual stimulants. Carrots did not become really popular as a food until about the thirteenth century, but they were used by the Arabs, spiced and stewed in milk, long before then, such recipes being recommended in several oriental love manuals as amatory aids. The long slender root is called *carotte* in French and is obvious slang for the penis in many languages. Grecians of old hailed the carrot as a stomach tonic as well as a love medicine, and its feathery foliage was used to decorate the hair of fashionable ladies when it was introduced into England. Brought to America by the first settlers, even the Indians enthusiastically adopted the vegetable. While we cultivate some long varieties here, our well-hung roots do not compare in size to those grown in the Far East, where the "Japanese carrot" grows to three feet and more. As for carrot seeds, they have been thought in the past to relax uterine muscles during pregnancy.

• CELERY, CELERIAC, SMALLAGE (WILD CELERY) •

Another "phallic" vegetable that has a long aphrodisiac history, celery has been prescribed as a remedy for impotence, extolled for its medicinal values by the Chinese and proclaimed by the Spanish to be a love food par excellence. The Greeks held it in such great esteem that they awarded a stalk to the winners of their nude athletic events, and in eighteenth-century France celery was known as a passion-inducer that wives prepared for their husbands in order to keep them home. Madame Pompadour vowed that her celery soup "heated up the body." She often served it to her royal lover, using the following recipe.

• MADAME POMPADOUR'S CELERY SOUP •

1 stalk of celery	1 tablespoon butter
celery stock	1 teaspoon flour
2 egg yolks	½ cup cream
1 small truffle	nutmeg

Chop celery, scald and drain. Heat in a saucepan with a tablespoon of butter. Add flour, thickened stock and the egg yolks mixed with cream. Flavor with nutmeg and garnish with sliced truffles.

Van de Velde, the author of *Ideal Marriage*, recommended raw celery as one of those foods that excite the urinary passages and the vegetable is a good source of vitamin E, many modern people believing in its efficacy, according to the sexologist Scheuer. Celery seeds have also been long known as a stimulant for sexual health. Concerning the psychology of resemblances, Dr. David Reuben, in his *Everything...sex* book, notes that "A strict diet of celery might conceivably make the penis resemble a celery stalk—wet and soggy."

• CHICKPEA •

Garbanzo, or the chickpea, is grown extensively in southern Europe, and dates back to earliest times. The Romans particularly favored it as a love food, and its history as an aphrodisiac is similar to that of the pea. Canned chickpeas mixed with a little olive oil and vinegar and a lot of grated Parmesan cheese makes a simple, unusual and delicious hors d'ouerve.

• CHICORY •

Chicory leaves are used for salads and its roots as a flavoring in or even as a substitute for coffee. Although chicory is the secret ingredient that made Creole New Orleans' coffee "black as sin and sweet as love," remember that the Turks called coffee "the black enemy of sleep and copulation." It's said that the French novelist Balzac consumed 50,000 cups of black coffee at night over a twenty-year period in order to keep himself awake to produce his numerous masterpieces. However, the coffee rotted his stomach out in the process and contributed to his early death at the age of fifty-one.

• CHIVES (See Garlic) •

• COLEWORT •

The Romans held *eruca*, a form of colewort, sacred to the phallic god Priapus, believing it to be a "salacious herb" and deriving its name from their word *uro*, to burn. Childless couples in medieval times were advised to eat colewort to become fecund. Actually, "coleworts" is simply from the Anglo-Saxon for "cabbage plants" and the vegetable shares most of the virtues of cabbage.

• COLLARDS •

Called "soul food" by blacks and whites in the southern United States, collards are also a member of the cabbage family, the vitamin A–rich vegetable sharing the same characteristics. Collards did not originate among U.S. blacks, having been known to the Greeks in ancient times.

• CORN •

Corn has a fascinating history as a food and its more than 600 uses (it may even have been used as a sizing for this book) tempt one to devote a chapter to it. But, though rich in vitamin E, its aphrodisiac reputation is hardly worth mentioning. Only Rabelais, of all the great Rabelaisian writers has written a hymn to it. "Panurge went on to praise unripe corn as a marvellous base for greensauce, which was easy to cook and to digest," he says in *Pantagruel*. "And what results that sauce produced! It... exhilerated the animal spirits...cleaned out the urethra, dilated the spermatic vessels, and jacked up the cremasters or testicle-strings...it purged the bladder, swelled the genitals, righted the foreskin, hardened the gland and rectified the penis.... In a word it possessed a thousand advantages."

Quite an endorsement, but there are few others, from an aphrodisiac standpoint. Corn on the cob is, however, one of the most delicious foods that can be served at a love banquet. It is probably the most underrated vegetable of modern times as a gourmet food, chiefly because we are used to frozen or supermarket specimens that have been laying around for weeks and taste like something less than cardboard. This is due to the fact that corn's sugar content changes to starch soon after being picked, the ears losing up to 90% of their sugar content an hour after harvesting. Corn never became a gourmet vegetable in Europe simply because it couldn't survive the trans-Atlantic voyage without losing practically all its taste. For a taste treat you'll hardly believe—indeed, an entirely different vegetable—try to obtain some just-picked corn. Ideally, the ears should be picked while the water's boiling on the stove.

• COTTONSEED OIL •

A rich source of vitamin E, the oil processed from cotton seeds is recommended by several sexologists as a cooking agent in place of butter or fat.

• COUSCOUS (See Wheat) •

• COWPEAS •

Botanically, this favorite of George Washington is closer to the bean than the pea family, but cowpeas are the source of that stimulating southern "soul food" black-eyed peas. Not much known in Europe, they probably originated in Africa, being brought to the Americas by slave-traders. Generally, they're cooked "southern style" with ham or pork back, and they're well worth trying (see also Peas).

• CRESS (See Lettuce) •

• CUCUMBERS •

Although they were thought to be an aphrodisiac among the Spanish because of their shape, cucumbers seem to have been specifically recommended by no one else. Introduced to the world through India, they are one of the few vegetables mentioned in the Bible. Such great lechers as the Roman emperor Tiberius and Charlemagne relished them, the former demanding that they be cultivated in greenhouses and served to him every day of the year. But to our knowledge they grace the marketing lists of no sexologists. Perhaps it all has something to do with the saying "cool as a cucumber," which contains some truth; on a hot day the inside of a cucumber is some twenty degrees cooler than the air outside, making it not exactly a vegetable to "heat up the body." Perhaps the "cool, unemotional" quality of the cucumber led the French to use their word for it, *concombre,* as slang for "a ponce or procurer," though its fat phallic appearance could have something to do with that, too.

• DANDELION GREENS •

Free for the picking most anywhere, dandelion greens make an excellent salad and are rich in vitamin A, iron and copper, which is why several nutritionists have prescribed them. The leaves resemble the jagged teeth of lions (hence the French *dents de lion* and our derivative word) and should be picked when young, but as with any wild food, don't gather them along highways where they may have been contaminated by automobile exhaust fumes. They can also be boiled and served as a tasty spinach substitute. The dandelion has traditionally been used to make dandelion wine, once a great American favorite (see Course Sixteen).

• EGGPLANT •

"If the lingam (penis) is rubbed with the fruit (juices) of the eggplant [among other ingredients]...a swelling lasting for one month will be produced," the *Kama Sutra* instructs. Although this is doubtless a gross exaggeration, and would be something of a Midas curse if true, the eggplant did originate in India and the prescription shows how highly it was touted as an aphrodisiac there, as it has been all over the world. Cardinal de Richelieu, who had quite a reputation as a rake, was the first to serve eggplant in France. Known as the *aubergine* to the French, Germans and some Englishmen, as *berenfina* to the Spanish and as *melanzana* to the Italians, the vegetable aroused much controversy when introduced to the old world. Various botanists called it "the mad apple" and claimed that it caused insanity. Spaniards dubbed eggplant (like tomatoes) "the apple of love" and John Gerard warned in his *Herball* (1597) that: "I rather wish English men to content themselves with the meate and sauce of our owne country than with fruit and sauce eaten with such perill; for doubtlesse these apples have a mischievous quality; the use whereof is utterle to be forsaken." Similarly, in Jamaica the "garden apple," cooked in a flour paste and seasoned with peppercorns, chives, vanilla beans and pimentos, is held to be a wicked "genital excitant."

At about the same time that Gerard was lamenting the eggplant's aphrodisiac effect in England, the concubine Rada-Hera was concocting the most famous of aphrodisiac eggplant dishes. She invented the dish for her husband, the legendary Turkish bey Mustaph Mehere—the same who weighed 400 pounds and took 170 wives and innumerable concubines over his 123-year life span (1488–1611). Rada-Hera (his second wife) made the dish so well that she was the only wife he never discarded, mainly because she kept the recipe secret and Mustaph believed that the puree was the key to his potency and longevity. So while all Mustaph's other wives were discarded when they turned twenty, Rada-Hera had free run of the palace until she died a natural death in 1571. Her secret recipe, which we haven't tried, is supposed to be as follows:

2 medium-sized eggplants	½ cup cheese
4 tablespoons butter	juice of ½ a lemon
2 tablespoons white flour	white pepper
1 teaspoon milk	cayenne pepper
1 cup milk	saffron

Broil the eggplants until tender, then peel and mash until smooth. Melt the butter in a saucepan and blend in the flour, adding salt, peppers and saffron until highly seasoned. Next add the milk and stir until the mixture comes to a rapid boil, then lower the heat and cook for ten minutes, stirring frequently. Mix in the cheese and lemon juice, then slowly add in the eggplant puree. Cook for about five minutes and serve.

Another famous eggplant recipe, its exact ingredients lost to posterity, was named in honor of a Moslem holy man, or Iman. Seems that while he was enjoying the tasty dish, a zaftig maiden passed by, letting her veil slip a trifle. The holy man fainted with pleasure and the dish was thereafter called *Iman Bayildi,* "swooning Iman."

• ERYNGOES AND OTHER SEA VEGETABLES •

Most sea vegetables, as noted in Course Two, are rich in iodine and other nutrients, and have been favored by lovers for centuries. Eryngoes, or sea holly, or "Kissing comfits," as they have variously been called, were especially collected for their fleshy roots. The roots were said to both excite and strengthen the genitalia in both sexes, and the Elizabethans even served them candied.

The sea cucumber, which the Chinese call *Tripang* and is shaped something like a black pudding, is also said to be stimulating to the genitals. It is hunted at low tide among the rocks, stored in barrels after drying and served highly seasoned, often with pepper and garlic.

• FENNEL •

We remember interviewing an old Italian gentleman who most assuredly waved a hand side to side as he explained that nothing but fennel and spaghetti were responsible for his longevity and virility. Anyway, both fennel and fennel seed are still popular aphrodisiacs in Italy and other Mediterranean countries, as they have been throughout history. The Egyptians, Greeks and Romans all vouched for fennel, using it in salads, fish sauces and fennel soup, while the Hindus had a potent recipe that mixed the juice of the fennel plant with milk, honey, butter, licorice and sugar. Actually an herb, fennel has been used like a vegetable through the ages. "To eat conger and fennel" (two hot things together) was to the Elizabethans provocative of sexual license. Thus Shakespeare has Falstaff say of another character: "He plays at quoits well, and eats conger and fennel...and rides the wild mare with the boys."

Florence fennel, or finnochio, a sweet Italian variety, is appropriately used to aromatize wines.

• HORSERADISH •

No one, to our knowledge, eats these roots whole, but their long gnarled shape and fiery taste has won them mention in the annals of aphrodisia as a seasoning.

• GARLIC, CHIVES, ONION, LEEK, SHALLOT •

The above vegetables constitute one of the three or four most famous aphrodisiac vegetable groups. Their histories as love foods parallel one another, although garlic and onions are cited far more often than the milder shallots and leeks. All four, however, appear over and over in both oriental and European recipes.

As for leeks, the dissolute Roman Emperor Nero believed that they both improved his singing voice (he alone believed he was a great artist) and his sexual prowess, eating such great quantities of them that he was nicknamed Porrophagus. The leek has the honor of being one of the few vegetables, if not the only one, that is the national emblem of a country; Wales adopted it after their warriors (wearing manly leeks around their necks) won a battle over the Saxons in the sixth century. The vegetable has only recently been identified as the fabled storgehenge that the Greeks swore by as a love potion.

Chives are also a form of onion, but the chive hasn't much of a shady past. Not, at least, compared to shallots and its other relatives. "*Eat the white shallots sent from Megara, or garden herbs that aphrodisiac are...*" Ovid wrote in *The Art of Love,* and Apicius gave several stimulating recipes employing shallots in the most famous cookbook of all time. But it was the Roman poet Martial who did most for the shallot when he wrote: "*If envious age relax the nuptial knot, / Thy food be scallion and thy feast shallot.*"

Garlic, which "makes men wink and drink and stink," according to the old proverb, has meant more to lovers than any of its pungent relatives. The Greek poet Homer sang its praises, Aristotle mentioned its medicinal qualities, and Pliny claimed it cured sixty-one different ailments. The Romans believed garlic contained magical powers and hung garlic over their doors to ward off witches, just as some people wear the cloves around their necks today to protect themselves against colds and diseases.

Oriental lovers claimed they became towers of strength through garlic; their physicians prescribed it to beautify the complexion, and Indian men still rub a mixture of lard and garlic on the penis and back to secure strong erections. Among the Japanese Ainu, garlic was held to be the most precious food of the gods, for it helped create life. The Chinese, who do not always find garlic particularly tasty, feel the same about its powers. Observes one native expert: "Usually the southerners in China do not really like garlic, spring onions and chives; therefore, the use of garlic and chives (in Shanghai dishes like stir-fried eels with dried garlic, and stir-fried river shrimp with fresh chives) is self-explanatory."

Rabelais describes a "fragrant tripe stew with garlic," served at Anarchus' wedding to an aged harlot, one of the many mentions of the bulb in erotic literature. Similarly, Ben Jonson probably referred to garlic as a love philtre in *Volpone* when he wrote:

> *Would you live free from all diseases?*
> *Do the act your mistress pleases?*
> *Yet fight all the aches from your bones?*
> *Here's a med'cine for the nones.*

There's no doubt that the English herbalist Culpepper wrote that "garlic's heat is vehement," or that the English believed that the bulb "reawakened spent desire." And William J. Robinson the noted American gynecologist, has recommended garlic over any other aphrodisiac food. "There is one spice or condiment of which I hesitate to speak," he writes, "because it is held in such contempt, and disdain in this country. I refer to garlic. There can, however, be no question as to its *pronounced aphrodisiac effect*. In fact, it stands at the head of the list. But many Anglo-Saxons would perhaps prefer their impotence to the alternative of having to eat garlic. The nations, however, who have no such loathing of the bulb of *allium sativium* ... often make use of garlic as an aphrodisiac; some do it without deliberation, instinctively so to say." Robinson goes on to tell of his experiments administering artificial oil of garlic (allyl sulfide), but found the effects not so beneficial.

Garlic, due to its strong odor, can certainly be an antiaphrodisiac, or an effective sex repellant, as well as a love food. Even the Romans, who so highly valued garlic, had a law forbidding anyone to enter into the sacred Temple of Sibyl after eating it. Common sense dictates that both partners must definitely eat the bulb for it to be effective. The same holds true of the onion, but the onion has had more supporters than detractors and has frequently been mentioned in erotic works. Believing it represented eternity, the ancient Egyptians swore oaths on the onion. Fed to the laborers who worked twenty years on the great Cheops Pyramid (2 million dollars worth of onions, garlic and radishes provided to fortify them), dispensed by Alexander the Great to his troops to promote valor, and later praised by General Grant, who once wired the War Department that he would not move his army farther without onions, the onion bulb was long believed to increase the production of sperm as well as strength. It was praised by the Greek comic writers Alexis and Diphilus in the third century B.C., the latter vouching that it stimulated sexual desire, and was recommended by both the Romans Ovid, in *Remedia Amoris,* and Petronius, who suggested "onions and snails' heads without sauce."

The poet Martial wrote that "if your wife is old and your member is exhausted, eat onions, in plenty," but he did not confine himself to this prescription. "He who is unable to show himself a man in the Cyprian's joustings," Martial advised in another place, "let him eat of onions, and he will be doughty enough. In the same way, should your anus languish, do not cease eating of bulbs and charming Venus will once more smile on your forays." The philosopher Celsus agreed with the poet, and in the first century B.C. Marcus Teriutuis Varro wrote: "Asked about bulbs, I answered: they can be eaten boiled in water for those who seek the door of love...but also with pine-kernels or flavored with rocket and pepper." We can add that onions are fine baked, too, as in a recipe called Baked Onions Supreme. First peel the skin off six large onions and parboil for fifteen minutes in salted water, draining well and placing in a casserole. Melt one-quarter pound of butter and add to this one-half cup of confectioners sugar, one teaspoon of parsley flakes, pepper and a pinch of nutmeg. Spoon this over the onions and bake in a slow oven for one hour.

In *The Perfumed Garden* of the Shaykh Nefzawi we're told of "The member of Abou el Heiloukh that remained erect for thirty days without a break, because he did eat onions," and can only conclude that anyone with important business engagements should forsake the aphrodisiac recipe consisting of honey, onions and chickpeas given in that Arabian love manual. The same might hold true for onion recipes given in many other languages, even though Dr. Robinson found that the bulbs "are not quite so powerful as garlic." Onions do share the same drawback as garlic, however, and we leave all onion eaters, men or women, with the following advice from Ovid's *Art of Love:* "She whose breath is strong smelling, should never talk with an empty stomach; and she should always stand at a distance from her lover's face." Or, as Shakespeare wrote, "Eat no onions or garlic, for we are to utter sweet breath."

Garlic cloves, by the way, are also supposed to offer the very best protection against vampires. They can backfire in this way, too, though. Recently a man in England, who so feared vampires that he went to sleep with a clove of garlic in his mouth, was found dead in his bed one morning. The cause? No, he hadn't been bitten by vampires—he'd choked to death on the garlic clove.

• LEEK (See Garlic) •

• LENTILS •

When an old man in Aristophane's comedy *Anphiareus* has his much longed for youthful vigor restored, it is only after he eats a stimulating dish of lentils. This member of the pea family, rich in iron, copper and phosphorus, has been a lover's favorite for centuries. Lentils were used in the biblical Mess of Pottage for which Esau sold his birthright to Jacob (*Genesis* 35:34). The dish is far from a "mess," as we know the word today, being a delectable treat still prepared by Arabian lovers which consists of blended lentils, onions and rice simmered in olive oil "until sweet and nutlike," and has led one writer to observe that "a hungry and nostalgic gourmet would be willing to sell his soul for a taste."

• LETTUCE, CRESS •

Although undoubtedly the most popular of salad greens, lettuce has been rated from as high as first to as low as tenth by our aphrodisiac food tasters. Lettuce takes its name from the Latin *lactuca*, for its milky juice, and it is no doubt a nutritious plant. On the positive side Martial and Columella both recommend it, and the Roman epicure and author Apicius watered the lettuce in his garden with mead every evening so that it would taste like "green cheese cakes" when he picked it mornings. Apicius also seems to have favored a combination of cress juice and pepper, while Ovid, the author of many love prescriptions, called cress *impudia*, or shameless. The Chinese, too, used both lettuce and cress as an aphrodisiac food and the fact that Rabelais is said to have brought lettuce to France with him in 1537 also speaks highly of it.

On the other hand, one old belief held that men should avoid lettuce because it hindered procreation and the Spanish believed that the leaves were an anaphrodisiac. In the brothels of Germany, Norman Douglas points out, "lettuce is devoured for ensuring a contrary effect," and he goes on to explain that "an extract of lettuce was long employed as a sedative under the name of thridau."

Perhaps the only "authority" who can settle the lettuce controversy is that lady from South Africa who has eaten 17,000 heads of it over the last seven years. A newspaper clipping in our hands claims that thirty-one-year-old Mrs. Mary Buys eats six heads of the green stuff every *day*—surely the world record. Mrs. Buy's craving or addiction is probably psychological, says Dr. Fred Stau of the Harvard Medical School, a well-known nutritional expert. Dr. Stau advises that since lettuce contains only water and some minerals which are present in other foods, it is probably helpful in maintaining the lady's trim youthful figure.

• MANIOC •

A starch food similar to the potato, Latin American manioc is the nutritious root of the cassava plant that is usually prepared boiled, but is also used in bread and tapioca. It has something of a reputation as an aphrodisiac in Brazil, but isn't common in U.S. markets.

• MUSHROOM •

Surpassed only by the truffle as a renowned "underground" love food, the mushroom was likewise dedicated to the Greek god of love, and used in hundreds of love recipes past and present. Books have been written explaining and extolling the fungi, but none, not even Robert Grave's scholarly and poetic accounts of the phenomenon, has quite succeeded. Since so much space has been devoted to the truffle (see Course Twelve), we can justify in part the relatively short space given here to the love food, but wish there was more room for its fascinating story.

Mushrooms have been confused with the truffle so often that their aphrodisiac histories are in many cases almost identical. Containing high percentages of essential glycogen and albumen, they combine all the benefits of meat without its indigestibility. Mushrooms have also been noted for the phallic shapes of their glans and erect stems. The morel, shaped like an upside-down ice-cream cone, has particularly been extolled by gourmets and lovers, but almost all varieties were at one time or another royal foods. The Egyptians for example, permitted only the Pharaohs to eat the fungi because they were considered too good for any commoner. Suetonius wrote that "mushrooms are the food of the gods," the ancient Chinese called them "the divine fruit of immortality," and the Aztecs thought they were "God's flesh." It is said that Buddha ate a bowl or two before being transported to Nirvana; Russian peasants still talk to the fungi; and the pre-Christian Guatemalans not only talked to them, but believed that their mushrooms talked back.

The Greek city Mycenae possibly takes its name from *mykes* or mushrooms, the legend being that Perseus, hot and thirsty, picked a mushroom and drank the water flowing from it, expressing his gratitude by naming the city in its honor. Most famous of all Greek mushrooms is the poisonous hallucinogenic species called *Amanita muscaria*, or fly-agaric, also symbolic of the erect penis, which was used as a sacrament in fertility rites and is still sacred to certain Indian tribes. Robert Graves has suggested that the Greeks held this species sacred because they had a taboo against eating any red food whatsoever. He further contends that Soma, the mysterious legendary drink celebrated in Vedic poems by the Aryans who invaded India in the second millenium B.C., was not mead, wine or hemp, as has been suggested, but *Amanita muscaria*. In articles in the *Atlantic*, based heavily on the works of ethnomycologist Gordon Wasson, Graves makes a strong case for the species being Soma. He points out that *Amanita muscaria* is the hallucinatory mushroom nibbled by Alice in Wonderland, Lewis Carroll having read about it previous to writing his classic. Not all of the hallucinogenic agents in the fly-agaric are absorbed into the bloodstream; some lodge in the kidneys and there mix with the urine. Thus, certain Lapps and Finns get high on the filtered urine of reindeer that have eaten the mushroom. Various Siberian tribes and a small Mongol enclave in Afghanistan go one step further: eating *Amanita*, urinating in a pot and using the sheepskin-filtered urine as a drink (mixed with milk or curds) at weddings and other festive occasions. Poachers in Scotland don't go quite so far, but are reported to mix *Amanita muscaria* and whiskey together in an intoxicating drink called the "Cathie," in honor of that insatiable lover Catherine the Great of Russia, who supposedly favored it.

The Romans served mushrooms at wedding feasts to loosen the libido and they were a favorite of the Emperor Nero, who called them a divine food—perhaps because he used them to poison his predecessor the Emperor Claudius, as Rabelais suggests. More likely, however, Agrippina, the wife of Claudius, poisoned the monarch, lacing his favorite *Amanita Caesara* dish with the juice of the poisonous *Amanita phalloides* species. Later, when Nero was told at an orgy that mushrooms were reputed to be the food of the gods, he is said to have replied, "Yes, they led to the deification of my father."

Mushrooms are mentioned in the erotic cookery of almost every country, oriental and occidental, and the word is a favorite slang synonym for things sexual. Interestingly, English slang uses the word mushroom as a synonym for the female sex organ, while in French *le champignon* is slang for the penis. Perhaps this last is not due anymore to the mushroom's suggestive stem than to the fact that it breaks through the ground with such force that it has been known to crack concrete.

Mushrooms have become increasingly popular in America. In the last thirty years, consumption has increased from 44 million pounds in 1940 to over 231 million pounds. Most of these are cultivated white varieties and descend from a clump of white mushrooms Lewis Downing of Downingtown, Pennsylvania found among his cream-colored plants in 1926. The majority of U.S. production (60%) is centered within a thirty-mile radius of Kennett Square, Pennsylvania, which became our mushroom capital during the Civil War when a greenhouse grower in the region discovered that he could raise the fungi under benches of commercial flower crops. The French, however, were the first to grow mushrooms, that man of all women Louis XV raising them in miles and miles of caves and tunnels outside Paris. Today there are those who believe that even the most legendary of aphrodisiac mushrooms, the small, pitted, spongy-capped morel, can be "factory produced," most spores for commercial mushrooms, in fact, being spawned in laboratories.

One-hundred-pound mushroom specimens have been recorded, and others are so small that they can't be seen by the naked eye. Some 50,000 varieties exist throughout the world, about 1000 being found in the United States. Many of these are delicious, but few people are expert enough to hunt them; each summer brings a rash of deaths and illness from mushroom poisoning, which has plagued man through the ages. Among the deaths attributed to eating poisonous mushrooms are Alexander the Great, the wife and daughter of the Greek dramatist Euripides, the Roman emperors Tiberius and Claudius, Czar Alexander I, Pope Clement VII and France's Charles V. *There is no way to tell a poisonous wild mushroom from a safe one except by knowing the species.* You can't tell a morbid fungi by dropping a silver coin or spoon into a saucepan where your wild mushrooms are cooking—it *will not turn black*—and onions that come in contact with poisonous fungi *will not turn brown.* Neither is it true that a mushroom is edible because animals or insects eat it with impunity. Slugs, for example, frequently feed on *Amanita phalloides,* which is so deadly that even smelling it can bring on a violent attack in humans.

Yet, despite the fact that doctors beginning with Hippocrates have warned against collecting wild mushrooms, gourmets and lovers persist in hunting down such delicious species as the morel, puffball, chicken mushroom, shaggmane, (the so-called "fool-proof four") and the rare honey mushroom *(Armillaria mellea)*. It is best to join a mycological society and hunt with the experts, but then someone has pointed out that the "experts" are usually the ones who die from poisoning. Mushroom guides abound and the hobby is so prestigious that Hollanders Workshop has recently issued a limited edition of a lavish work called the *Mushroom Book*—each of the seventy-five copies sells for $1500.

To leave a lasting impression on anyone still wanting to collect wild mushrooms in the nude, we offer the following from Lucy Kavaler's *Mushrooms, Molds and Miracles:*

> Several years ago workmen were moving a group of early 15th century mummies from a medieval cemetery in France to a new resting place. The men crossed themselves and muttered to one another with horror about the expression of unendurable pain on the faces of one family of seven. Doctors came to look and diagnosed the cause of death: the dread Death Cap had done its work all those hundreds of years ago and left its record of suffering.

Wild mushrooms, then, can either stiffen people in the proper places or inspire rigor mortis; it's best, in our opinion, to stick to the domesticated ones. Never peel or even wash these, wiping them with a damp cloth instead, unless very dirty indeed, when a quick rinse in cold water is advisable. They can be packed loosely, unwashed, in uncovered containers and stored in the refrigerator for a week without losing much in flavor. When keeping mushrooms any longer, it is advisable to dry them, soaking them in water later when they are to be used. The famed Italian dried mushrooms *funghi porcini* are sometimes available at gourmet food stores—for about $30 a one-pound bag.

· OATMEAL ·

It's quite a switch from "foods for the gods" like mushrooms and truffles to a prosaic breakfast food like oatmeal, but several sexologists prescribe the cereal in their daily regimens to build up sexual vigor. "Eat your oatmeal" is apparently an admonition better given to aging men than growing boys. Containing vitamins B and E and phosphorus, the cereal might help a methuselah to sow his wild oats. It was brose, an oatmeal porridge, that Bobbie Burns had a young girl sing about in his *Merry Muses:*

Put butter in my Donald's porridge,
For well does Donald deserve that;
I love my Donald's tartans well,
His naked arse and all that . . .

• OKRA •

The English call okra pods "lady fingers," which indicates their phallic shape. Okra is the basis for gumbo, famous as a love food since African slaves developed it when they were brought to Louisiana, though some gumbos today contain no okra at all. Blacks brought the plant, called *uehka* by the Arabs, to New Orleans and there concocted their gumbo stews, using its young pods and gumbo file, a thickening agent made from sassafras leaves. Crabs, oysters, ham, chicken and many other tempting foods are combined with gumbos. It is said that the "Casket Girls"—brides sent to the French settlers in Louisiana, so-called because their trunks were all shaped like caskets—staged a hunger strike in 1728, adamantly refusing to eat any native food until they tried some stimulating gumbo. Southern-fried okra dipped in cornmeal meal is another true "soul food," although the Egyptians were eating it similarly as far back as the early thirteenth century.

• ONION (See Garlic) •

• PARSLEY •

"Parsley grows for the wicked, but not for the just," says an old English proverb. This member of the celery family began earning its shady reputation even before the Romans, who wore curly leafed parsley garlands in their hair not only because they were attractive but because they believed that nibbling on parsley sprigs enabled one to drink more wine without becoming drunk. The Greeks crowned winning athletes with parsley at their Nemean and Isthmian games and used the herb as a flavoring, and the Romans fed it to their horses on the theory that it made them swift. The plant is described by Seneca, who tells how the tempting sorceress Medea gathered parsley and other forbidden herbs by moonlight, while the *Satyricon* of Petronius connects parsley with aphrodisiac foods and mentions that "sacred" parsley was used to cleanse "profane fingers." Both Apicius in his pioneer cookbook and Rabelais in the best of bawdy books assure us of parsley's prowess; their opinion is confirmed in part today by the discovery that parsley is rich in sexually potent vitamin E. "Parsley," due to its curly leafs, once served as English slang for "pubic hair," "the parsley-bed" meaning "the female pudendum."

• PARSNIPS •

The sweet nutlike flavor of parsnips boiled or baked is a taste treat too few people are familiar with today, this root vegetable having slipped in popularity since it was grown in colonial gardens and regarded as an incentive to venery. Parsnips were a favorite of the Roman emperor Tiberius, who imported them from Germany. The often prodigious roots share the same phallic associations as carrots. Some of the wild species, it should be noted, are extremely poisonous to both clad and unclad gatherers.

• PEAS •

Abou el Heidja has deflowered in one night
Once eighty virgins, and he did not eat or drink between,
Because he surfeited himself first with chick-peas,
And had drunk camel's milk with honey mixed.

So does the *Perfumed Garden* extoll chickpeas as a source of sexual strength, but the Arabian love manual also gives credit where it's due to green peas, noting in another place that "Green peas, boiled carefully with onions and powdered with cinnamon, ginger and cardamons, well powdered, create for the consumer considerable amorous passion and strength in coition."

All kinds of peas have been favored by all kinds of lovers since aphrodisiac foods were first mentioned in the cookery. In parts of Europe peas are still thrown in the lap of a bride on her wedding day to insure fertility. Rich in vitamin B, iron, copper and phosphorus, the little pea is certainly far more potent than its size would indicate, in everything from pea soup to "pease porridge hot, pease porridge cold, pease porridge nine days old." Said Culpepper in his *Complete Herbal:* "They [chickpeas] are under the dominion of Venus. They are thought to increase sperm." Rabelais, on the other hand, tells us that the Friar Demisemiquaver's twenty trollups had to be fed peas in order to be productive, so they have been highly regarded for both sexes.

The green pea, which takes its name from the Latin *pisum,* had the honor of being taken as the patronym of the famous Roman Piso clan, just as the *cicer* or chickpea gave its name to the clan of Cicero. Quite a mania existed for green peas in seventeenth-century France. Wrote Madame de Maintenon, Louis XIV's mistress and secret wife, from Marly in 1696: "...impatience to eat [peas], the pleasure of having eaten them, and the anticipation of eating them again are three subjects I have heard very thoroughly dealt with....Some ladies, even after having supped at the Royal Table, and well supped too, returning to their own homes, at the risk of suffering from indigestion, will eat peas again before going to bed. It is both a fashion and a madness." One authority points out that it was socially correct at this time to lick green peas from their shells after dipping the whole in a sauce. Celebrated *petit pois à la Francaise,* the directions for which can be found in any good French cookbook, was probably created at this time. It could even have originated from the following incredible recipe. The peas were "shelled just before cooking, kept wrapped in a wet napkin until ready to place in the pot. A head of lettuce, with a fresh sprig of savory inserted in its center leaves, was placed in the pot, the peas laid on the lettuce, then a pinch of salt, half a glass of water, and half a pound of butter were added. After fifteen minutes of cooking the lettuce was removed, and at the moment of serving, three three tablespoons of heavy cream, the yolk of 'a fresh-laid egg,' a pinch of pepper, and a tablespoon of powdered sugar were stirred in."

As an old American "Recipse for Cukin Pees" tells us, however, green garden peas are just as good cooked plain. Just "Gether your pees 'bout sun-down. The folin day, 'bout leven o'clock, gouge out your pees with your thum nale....Then rense your pees, parbile them and fry 'em... incouragin the gravy to seep out and intermary with your pees. When modritly brown, but not scorcht, empty intoo a dish. Mash 'em gently with spune, mix with raw tamarters sprinkled with a little brown shugar and the immortal dish ar quite ready. Eat a hepe. Eat. Eat mo and mo. It is good for your genral helth uv mind and body. It fattens you up, make you sassy, goes throo and throo your very soul. But why don't you eat? By Jings. Eat. Stop! Never, while thar is a pee in the dish." [see also Lentils]

· PEPPERS, PIMENTOS ·

Red hot peppers have been far more valued in the love cookery than sweet green or garden peppers. In Chinese provinces such as Hunan and Szechuan, for example, many natives believe that chili peppers are a sex stimulant, which is why the Szechuan school of cooking, for one, uses chili peppers lavishly in almost every dish. Hot peppers, including the chili pepper *(Capsicum frutescens)* named after Chile, are featured in many fiery aphrodisiac dishes, especially chili con carne. Native to tropical America, both hot and garden peppers are extensively planted today. A mild red variety *(Capsicum tetragonum)* is grown in Hungary to be ground into paprika, and another red variety *(Capsicum annum)* is dried and ground into cayenne pepper. Peru's government has recently decreed that hot chili sauce has aphrodisiac qualities and ordered it not to be used in prison food, advising that the sauce isn't "appropriate for men forced to live a limited life style" because it tends to "arouse their sexual desires."

The pimento, often erroneously called the pimiento (which is allspice), also comes from a *Capsicum* that originated in the New World and has been highly regarded by sensuous gourmets. The same can be said of tabasco sauce, which like chili and cayenne is made from a Guinea pepper. Most aphrodisiac lore about pepper, however, is based on spices like pimiento, or black or white pepper from the Indian *Piper nigrum*, which is examined in Course Seventeen.

· POTATOES ·

> The next in order you shall have
> A large potato, and a brave:
> It must be roasted in the fire
> That cupid kindled with desire.
> The roasting it will much cost;
> It will best itself when it is roast.
> It needs no sugar, nor no spice
> 'Twill please a Stomach n'er so nice.
>
> —*A New Year Gift*, 1661

Though it has a fascinating history (see *The Potato Book*, Bridgehampton, New York: Hamptom Day School Press, 1972), the starchy potato isn't much valued by nutritionists anymore as an amatory aid. This wasn't always so. In the seventeenth century all kinds of claims were made for this novel introduction from the Americas. "Will your ladyship have a potato pie? 'Tis a stirring good dish for an old lady after a long lent," Beaumont and Fletcher wrote in one of their plays. Later John Fletcher wrote in his play *The Loyal Subject* (1618): "Will your lordship please to taste a fine potato. 'Twill advance your withered state, fill your honor with noble itches." Thomas Heywood in *The Dumb Knight* (1633) counted roasted potatoes as a "lusty dish" and even Shakespeare credited the lowly spud with aphrodisiac virtues, mentioning the "potato-finger of the devil luxury" in *Troilus and Cresseda* ("potato-finger" then slang for the penis or a dildo) and having Falstaff implore the sky to "rain potatoes...and snow eryngoes" in *The Merry Wives of Windsor*. Today in Australia "a potato" is slang for a pretty young country girl.

All this potato propaganda led a skeptical Havelock Ellis to remark that "the Irish peasantry, whose diet very largely consists of potatoes, are even regarded as possessing an unusually small measure of sexual feeling." But then the Irish peasants might have said a thing or two about Havelock Ellis that hasn't or couldn't be recorded.

One can only say that the potato does contain a good amount of phosphorus and can be prepared in many appetizing ways. A good variety of very appealing purple, polka-dotted and striped potatoes are sold in South American markets. Potatoes survived their reputation as a poisonous plant (see Course Thirteen) to become probably the most important vegetable in the world. Its questionable aphrodisiac reputation helped the vegetable a little, as did the botanist Parmentier, whose name is still associated with the potato on French menus, and Louis XVI, who planted potato fields near his palace—not to mention Marie Antoinette, who didn't care for the spuds but did wear sprigs of potato blossoms in her hair. The versatile vegetable, on whom the fate of millions depends, has been used in everything from a recipe for Chocolate Potato Torte to a formula for eyelid-wrinkle remover. But it's "small potatoes" as an aphrodisiac, despite all those sturdy "meat-and-potatoes" men.

• PUMPKIN •

This member of the squash family originated in the Americas, where pumpkins were so ubiquitous among the pilgrims that some wit wrote the following: *"We have pumpkins at morning and pumpkins at noon,/ If it were not for pumpkin we would soon be undoon."*

"Pumpkins" has been used to describe the female breasts, but the vegetable has little more to offer in the way of sexual associations. Concerning pumpkin seeds, we might add that better things have been said of them than their offspring. "Throughout Eastern Europe the Gypsies use large portions of pumpkin seeds as a food and recognize that this prevents prostate gland and preserves male potency," one writer notes. "The raw seeds also contain hormones that are good for the genitourinary passages and promote male hormone production." We can find no solid medical testimony supporting this theory, which isn't to say that it might not be true. Pumpkin *is* rich in vitamin A and phosphorus and there is a brand new California variety called Lady Godiva, which got its name because it has "naked" seeds, that is, the seeds don't have the hard outer coat that people who like toasted pumpkin seeds find hard to crack.

• RADISH •

The radish played a dual role in early Rome; it was employed both as an aphrodisiac and as one of the cruelest of antiaphrodisiacs. On the one hand, Apicius borrowed his fellow Romans' ears in his *De Re Coquinaria* to tell them that radishes had a beneficial effect on sexually sluggish natures, while on the other, the traditional punishment for sexual offenses such as adultery in ancient Rome was the insertion of a rather large radish into the offender's anus.

Radishes mixed with honey were extolled as a love food by the Egyptians as early as 500 B.C., but their shape (*radis nois* has served as French slang for the penis of a Negro) and hot taste doubtless made them a fabled love food before this. Coupled with the facts that they are the easiest of all vegetables to grow (their name in Greek is *raphanos*, meaning easily reared), the quickest to yield, and among the least expensive of vegetables, this would give them the historical *Oscar* or *Peter* as the poor man's aphrodisiac. No wonder the Greek artisans made small replicas of them in gold, while creating images of their other vegetables in lead or silver.

Shakespeare once referred to a man's naked body looking like a "forked radish," and even before the Bard of Avon, the French writer Claude Bigothier was so fascinated by radishes as a love stimulant that he wrote a poem in 1540 to the fiery vegetable called *Raphorum Encomium* (*Eulogy of Radishes*). Radishes can range from the hot little red and white ones we prefer in America to the variously colored Asian giants like the daikon, which is a staple of the Japanese diet. The radish, in fact, originated in China and the Chinese still use it in a therapeutic tea, often growing giants that weigh over 100 pounds.

The French call the radish by the poetic name *roses d'hiver*, roses of winter, and they are used in a thousand ways all over France and Europe, carved into exquisite forms for garnishes and often served stuffed with cheese and port wine mixtures or blanched and bathed in cream. Ludwig Bemelmans described the Bavarian treatment of them lovingly in his novella *The Blue Danube*: "After the wet, scratchy leaves are cut away along with the top of the radish, it is sliced paper thin, but so that the radish remains intact, opened like a fan. It is then salted and left alone until water comes oozing out between the slices. When it has wept its last tear, then the radish is ready to be eaten."

The most taste bud–tingling photographs ever taken of the far too neglected radish were made by the S.D. Warren Company of Boston, a paper-maker seeking to display their paper's worth, which they surely did. Warren even suggests a "Radini," a 12-1 martini served with a radish instead of an olive or onion reposing in its stimulating spirits.

Crisp radishes make delicious simple appetizers when anchovy fillets are wrapped around them, and, indeed, the French often serve them on their hors d'oeuvre lists in spring. The English prefer them for breakfast with toast and butter, and some peoples relish the leafy tops in salads and soups. Finally, there is Souffle Briochin, the ultimate recipe for radishes, a dish as attractive to look at as it is to eat. The instructions for making this dish are printed below courtesy of S.D. Warren, for whom it was just created by Chef Alain M. Lenoir of Boston's Maitre Jacques restaurant.

SOUFFLÉ BRIOCHIN

12 radishes, finely grated	1 cup whole milk
3 tablespoons butter	3 egg yolks well beaten
3 tablespoons flour	5 egg whites beaten stiff
	salt, pepper

Melt butter over low heat; add flour and blend 3 to 5 minutes. Slowly stir in 1 cup of milk plus any radish juice. Cook and stir sauce with wire whisk until thick and smooth. Season with salt and pepper. Remove sauce from heat and allow to cool slightly. Add (while stirring) the well-beaten egg yolks and grated radishes. Fold egg whites carefully into mixture. Pour ingredients into 7-inch greased souffle dish. Bake 25 minutes at 375°F. or until set.

· RICE ·

Few people know that northern Minnesota produces about two-thirds of the world's wild rice crop. Though more-nutritious wild rice has a far greater reputation as an aphrodisiac than its domesticated relative, the latter is of course an immensely more important food crop to mankind. The Hindu *Kama Sutra*, for example, recommends that lovers eat "wild rice with an equal weight of honey," and another wild rice recipe from the *Ananga Ranga*, its classic companion volume, assures the reader that "the effect will be enormous vigor and the enjoyment of a hundred women." We find little mention of domesticated rice in the love cookery. Celsus, however, believed rice "stimulated the senses" and the ancient fertility rite of showering newlyweds with rice still survives in America and other lands. In China rice is almost always a separate course and is regarded as a signal for a toast.

· SHALLOTS (See Garlic) ·

· SKIRRET ·

Skirret is another (ancient) name for chervil, a member of the parsley family, its aromatic leaves often used to flavor soups and salads. We include the herb separately here as a vegetable because Dr. Nicolas Venette had such good things to say about it in his *Tableau de l' Amour Conjugal*. "The plant we call skireet, and which today is well enough known in France by that name," Venette wrote, "had such a power for exciting a man to love, that Tiberius, one of the most lascivious of all Emperors—if we are to believe the historians—had it sent regularly from Germany in order that he might use it to excite himself with his women." We might not believe all the historians—but we can try it. Which advice applies to most reputedly aphrodisiac foods (see also Chervil; Course Seventeen).

· SOYBEANS ·

Soybeans, nutritionists say, are an "almost perfect food" and contain high quantities of both vitamin B and the "sexuality vitamin," vitamin E. As old as civilization itself, the soybean helped China to survive over the centuries and its use as a food is prominent in the earliest Chinese medical prescriptions. Soy sauce, the same served in Chinese restaurants, has had such a reputation as a dynamite aphrodisiac that it became part of the salary of civil and military officers of the Japanese Imperial Court in the fifth century. It is also said to contain abundant amounts of aspartic acid (see Asparagus).

· SPINACH ·

Judging by Popeye alone, spinach might be considered something of a love food. Carl Rose's famous *New Yorker* cartoon of a boy refusing his broccoli with the words, "I say it's spinach, and I say the hell with it," shows the traditional dislike of children toward the vegetable, but kids with foresight shouldn't really hate it so, for this green powerhouse, native to Persia, has an aphrodisiac reputation dating back 2000 years. A rich source of minerals and vitamins, especially of vitamin E and the iron that supplies great vigor, spinach has been regarded in many cultures as an incentive to venery. One unusual but tempting Chinese love recipe calls for simply frying it in oil and salt until it becomes crisp and crunchy.

Napoleon did something for spinach's reputation by decorating the golden epaulettes of his colonels with what looked like gold spinach seeds and were thus referred to as spinach—the term lingers on to this day—but Popeye has done so much for the vegetable in the United States that growers in one Texas town have erected a large statue of the sailor man. Spinach is definitely good for you, despite all the rumors you may have heard. One cup of the greens contains merely forty-six calories and almost half of that same cup is high-quality protein.

· SQUASH ·

Although rich in nutrients, none of the many squash varieties have much aphrodisiac clout—at least there are few stories extant of erotic squashes of any shape. Some nutritionists do recommend squash in their restorative diets and the flowers of certain varieties were used in ancient Indian fertility rites, but there's not much more to say in its behalf. A pity, for there are so many varieties that the versatile squash, from the acorn to the zucchini, can be delicious baked, fried, boiled or steamed. Particularly valued for its resemblance to the female form is the Cajun cushaw squash, which is cooked up with sugar and spice (see also Pumpkin).

· SURNAG ·

Find some surnag (we haven't been able to) and you may be able to make a fortune advertising "a true aphrodisiac food." It is a Moroccan root, largely unknown today, but which according to Leo Africanus greatly increased potency.

• TOMATO (See Course Thirteen) •

• TRUFFLE (See Course Twelve) •

• TURNIP •

Dioscorides, the Greek physician who served as a doctor in the Roman army, wrote in his *Materia Medica* of the turnip that "the root of it being sod is nourishing... and being moist and loose flesh... provoking to venerie." But lecherous King Henry VIII preferred the greens to the roots, and the royal rake was probably right, for they are rich in vitamin A, iron and copper. Both roots and green have been used as a love food from Europe to the Orient.

• WHEAT AND WHEAT PRODUCTS •

Regretfully, there isn't room for a full discussion of the plant that gives us "the staff of life" and we can only touch upon several of the many aphrodisiac dishes deriving from wheat. Breads and cakes made from flours, for example, were fashioned into male and female phallic shapes by the ancient Greeks, and dedicated to Priapus. The Romans, who called these breads *coliphia*, used prostitutes to bake them and when the ovens cooled a little, these "baker's girls" proceeded to make love to their customers therein. Phallic cakes called *pennes* or penises were also baked in medieval France and carried to the church in processions during Easter; Palm Sunday was known as "The Feast of Penises" *(Fete des Pinnes)* in at least one small French town. Such practices in fact survived well into the nineteenth century, until the church's influence prevailed and the primitive erotic custom was abandoned, these same festive breads coming to be baked in a round shape with a cross on the top—the Lenten hot cross buns that we know today.

We've already encountered the indignant Bishop Burchard of Worms, who in the thirteenth century complained: "Have you done that which certain women are wont to do? They hurl themselves upon their face and with buttocks bared, put bread into their notch and grind it there. When the milling is done they drag out these odorous crumbs and feed them to their husbands in order to fan their lovers into hotter passion." More appetizing customs are to be found in the Roman *Confarreatio*, or wedding ceremony, in which the partners ate the forerunner of our wedding cake, a concoction made of flour, salt and water; the sesame cakes the Greeks served at wedding banquets to insure the fertility of bride and groom; and the wheat cakes baked for weddings in Elizabethan England.

Wheat itself has always stood for love and been regarded as a love food. Piny the Elder recommended cow wheat in particular. In ancient Rome, the bride held three wheat ears as talismans of fertility, and this custom survived into medieval times, when wheat instead of rice was thrown at the bride and groom. Lusty German girls in the Middle Ages even rolled naked in the wheat before it was milled, later baking this flour into bread for their lovers, who were supposed to be passion-struck the moment they ate same.

Among wheat products, wheat germ and whole wheat flour, both containing vitamin B_1 and E, are favored by sexologists over white flour. Also highly recommended is *couscous,* the "Arab dish made of granulated flour steamed over broth" that Rabelais mentioned as a favorite of Master Gaster and the Gastrolators.

"The health of many a man is undermined, and his usefulness curtailed, if not sacrificed, because he habitually eats bad bread," warned *The Young Housekeeper's Friend* in 1845. Bread today has become worse than bad; it is truly the "spongy, sqooshy, ghastly white, dehumanized, denutritized, flavorized, propionated, artificialized, shot-up, brought-down item more closely related to a Styrofoam cup than the staff of life" that Joan Weiner and Diana Collier call it in their new book *Bread.* But there are signs that a revolt may be underway in America. Good wholesome breads are available in some bakeries and every year more homemakers male and female are taking to sensuously kneading their own bread in the kitchen. The last decade has seen a renaissance of stone grist mills and the return of unbleached flour to supermarket shelves. In addition to the Weiner-Collier recipe collection, James Beard's *Beard on Bread* is an excellent book on the subject.

The story of aphrodisiac wheat dishes would not be complete without mention of macaroni, which is of course prepared from wheat flour. Both Turks and Italians have claimed that starches like macaroni and spaghetti make them more fecund and one writer has noted that the Italians, "inveterate starch lovers, take long siestas after eating platters of pasta— one has only to look at their progeny to know that there's more to their siestas than sleep." Sophia Loren's recent cookbook, *In the Kitchen with Love,* claims that pasta must always be cooked *al dente* (so that you can feel it between your teeth as you eat) and makes a good case for the dish as "the sustaining power of that purveyor of erotic vitality known as the

'Latin Lover.'" An Italian-American, John Lombino, must be a great Latin lover indeed by this standard, having on October 11, 1973 broken the world's pasta-eating record by consuming an incredible 2.2 pounds of spaghetti in two hours.

Tortellini (little pieces of pasta in the shape of an inverted navel filled with chicken and veal, egg, spices, cheese and nutmeg) has the most interesting history of all pasta dishes. Legend has it that a chef in Bologna spent a great deal of his time staring out his window at a beautiful girl across the courtyard who spent most of her time getting dressed and undressed. But she soon drew down the shade so that he could see only a little of her midsection. Nevertheless, the chef decided she had the most beautiful navel in the world and honored her by boiling up some pasta and creating the little tortellini that takes over an hour to make for two portions (see also Course Twenty-One).

• YAM •

The Elizabethans held the yam to be a highly aphrodisiac food. Often mistaken for the sweet potato, but no relation to it, *Dioscorea*, or the Chinese yam, is widely grown in America, candied yams being an especially valued soul-food. The yam, which includes some 250 species of climbing vines, only some of whose roots are edible, is believed to have originated in Africa. The barbasco, a wild yam native to Mexico, among other places, yields from its roots the steroid chemical diosgenin used in birth control pills. Diosgenin is also transformed in the laboratory into a synthetic sex hormone, 1/100 of an ounce of which used to require the preparation of a ton of bull's testicles.

• YARROW, OLD MAN'S PEPPER •

A plant with whitish flowers, yarrow has often been used as a medicine and love tonic. According to one old superstition, the drinking of such potions ensured "seven years love for wedded couples." Strictly speaking, *Achillea millefolium* is an herb, named for the legendary Achilles, who is supposed to have used one species to heal his wounds. If it could heal that famous heel, it might make everyone a little faster and slicker, too—anyway a lot of low-down heels have used it throughout history to heaten their conquests. We've classed it as a vegetable here because it is sometimes called Old Man's Pepper, which family it does not belong to, though it certainly can make old men peppery.

American folklore gives us the following advice concerning the plant: "Pick a sprig of yarrow, put the stem up your nose and say: *Yarrow, yarrow, if he loves me and I love he,/ A drop of blood I'd wish to see.* If blood appears, it shows that you are loved."

• ZUCCHINI (See Squash) •

COURSE FIFTEEN

Forbidden Fruits And Nuts

*...and at our gates are all manner of pleasant fruits, which I have laid up for thee,
O my beloved.*

—Song of Solomon

"I always determine the sexual capabilities of a woman by the way she
eats fruit," declared that great lover, minor poet and major male chauvinist Gabriele D'Annunzio. "When testing a potential bedmate, I offer
her an apple or pear to see how she eats it. Small mincing bites—the
ladylike kind—they are not good. But if she crunches the fruit, salivates
with pleasure, and crinkles her nose in enjoyment, this girl, my friend,
should prove to be a redoubtable love partner."

Centuries before, the Arabian author of *The Perfumed Garden* put it differently. "Woman is like a fruit, which will not yield its sweetness until
you rub it between your hands," wrote the Shaykh Nefzawi. "Look at the
basil plant; if you do not rub it warm with your fingers, it will not emit

any scent.... It is the same with woman. If you do not animate her with your toying, intermixed with kissing, nibbling and touching, you will not obtain what you are wishing..."

Forbidden fruits, needless to say, can be just as tempting and inspiring to men as they are to women. The effect is mainly psychological in both cases, for although fruit is rich in vitamin C and plays an important role in maintaining one in peak condition, its historical and present-day reputation as a love food is generally based on the physical resemblance of various fruits to the male and female genitalia, the banana, peach, vanilla sheathe and melon being obvious examples.

References abound in literature to apples, melons and other fruits as symbols for parts of the sexual anatomy, from Biblical times to the sex songs of the ancient Letts, and because they are believed to bestow virility, fruits have often been a mainstay of fertility rites and wedding ceremonies throughout the world. At Chinese love feasts many varieties of fruits were peeled and sliced into small pieces, the guests using toothpicks to pick up the pieces they liked. In other lands, they were often soaked in brandy, wine and rum to make them more potent, and numerous perfumes have been prepared from them. It is interesting to note that the insatiable Cleopatra chose a symbolic bowl of fruit in which to place the deadly asp that would kill her. She ended her life while sitting erect upon the throne set up in her marble tomb, bringing the asp to her full white breast, the fruit to her mouth and tasting the richness of the fruit just as the asp tasted of her.

Rabelais relates that "a little while after Cain slew his brother Abel, the earth, imbued with the blood of the just, was for one year extremely fertile in all fruits." He later compares Gargantua's codpiece to "some proud cornucopia," telling the tale of how the cornucopia originated when the goat whose milk nourished the divine infant Jupiter broke one of its horns against a rock. "Straightaway," he writes, "the nymphs filled it with fruit and flowers to present to Jove, who made of this horn a source of eternal abundance." Gargantua's codpiece was like that horn, he says enthusiastically: "forever lively, succulent and resinous; forever flourishing, pollinating and fruitifying; full of juice, a flower with pistels and teeming with fruit, in short (but it was never that!), a compendium of delights."

Fruits have been used as love foods in less conventional ways than most any other comestible. We need only quote here from Gershon Legman's scholarly *Oragenitalism: Oral Techniques in Genital Excitement*, which is almost comic in its sometimes parenthetical precautions: "Sophisticates often insert into the vagina fruits such as strawberries or cherries *(sweet, pitted cherries)*, or sections of an orange *(a seedless orange)*, or slices of apple deliciously dipped in honey; thereupon sucking or drawing them out of the vagina again, and eating them with relish. The classical fruit used in this way is the banana.... In any case, the practice of inserting solids into the vagina and sucking them out again *should not be attempted by persons with false teeth or a dental plate.*" Italics ours, and the case of the missing dentures possibly a case for Perry Mason, Dr. Welby or even Ralph Nader.

If fruits have had their champions, so have various vegetative nuts, though to a lesser extent. Roast nuts have been mentioned historically as highly aphrodisiac in nature and of course the modern slang "nuts" for the testicles or "coconuts" for the female breasts best illustrates the sexual doctrine of resemblances generally responsible for their fame. Rich in lecithin, which helps keep the arteries free of cholesterol deposits, nuts were blessed by the seductive Greek goddess of love herself. The Romans, in turn, originated the expression "nuts to you" when beautiful maidens served trays of them to men at harvest festivals (women were offered apples). Nuts were also presented to newlyweds as an aid to fertility in ancient Rome, and in later Roman times it became a custom for the husband's friends to throw nuts into the bridal chamber. A bowlful of worthy ones are presented here along with a cornucopia of fruits that outnumber but not necessarily outclass them.

• ACORN •

Though it will come as a surprise to some, acorns have been used in many ways as a food. But we can find only one recipe in the love cookery for this fruit of the oak. This is a Moroccan electuary called *madschun,* which is composed of "acorns, almonds, other nuts, sesame, honey, butter, flour, hashish and cantharide," the last two ingredients putting it outside the purview of this book.

• ALMONDS •

"A savant of the name of Djilinouss has said: 'He who feels that he is weak for coition should drink before going to bed a glassful of very thick honey and eat twenty almonds and one-hundred grains of the pine tree. He must follow this regime for three days.'" So advises *The Perfumed Garden* as to the use of almonds and other nuts as an aid to potency. The Chinese felt likewise and we quote below one of their ancient recipes combining almonds and other nuts with honey:

> Ingredients: 3 *chin* each of shelled almonds and walnuts; honey; and 2 chin each of peanuts and dried dates [a *chin* being equal to 576 grams].

Method: Soak the walnuts, peanuts and almonds in water until their skin can be peeled off. Stone the dried dates. Grind them together and use the honey as the binding base to make pills the size of walnuts. Steam them on a very low fire for 24 hours. Take one before breakfast and another before bedtime regularly [See also Honey; Course Twenty].

If the preceding Yin Taoist recipe seems complicated, remember that it may well make all efforts worthwhile. According to Chinese legend, Ke Hung of the Hsi Chin Dynasty kept taking these pills and thus became immortal. No one else seems to have been so fortunate, but almonds must have something going for them. They are still traditionally given as a wedding gift among Europeans and Americans and are used to make the paste for marzipan, the famous gourmet aphrodisiac dessert that Rabelais praised (see Course Twenty). The word "almond" has served as English slang for the penis, deriving from "almond-rock," "which is Cockney rhyming slang for cock."

Almonds, which came out of China, land of the sexy almond eye, are today the most popular of all nuts worldwide. They especially excite the Japanese, who often have English signs reading "almond" outside shops that would otherwise say "Bakery" or "Confectionary" in their own language. But then this ancient nut—it is mentioned seventy-three times in the Old Testament alone—has been associated with beauty and virility for centuries. Rich in protein, amino acids, magnesium, iron, calcium and phosphorus, and a good source of vitamins B and E, the romantic almond is also a harbinger of spring and the joyous expectancy of new life and love. In fact, the tree's pale pink blossoms appear about the time that the swallows return to Capistrano.

• APPLE, THE REAL ADAM'S APPLE •

You're playin' in my orchard, now don't you see,
If you don't like my apples, stop climbin' my tree...
—Hesitation Blues

No fruit, not even the tomato, can compare with the apple as a love symbol or a simile in love and sex poetry. Although the peach, cherry and banana offer strong competition, the apple is the only forbidden fruit to which an entire volume could justifiably be devoted.

Apples were *not* the forbidden fruit in the Garden of Eden, however. Adam never ate an apple, at least not in the Biblical account of his transgressions, which refers only to an unspecified forbidden fruit on the tree in the Garden of Eden. The Forbidden fruit of which the Lord said, "Ye shall not eat of the fruit which is in the midst of the garden, neither shall ye touch it, lest ye die" (*Genesis* 3:3) was probably an apricot or a pomegranate; the Moslems—intending no joke—believe it was a banana. Numerous fruits and vegetables have been called apples. Even in medieval times pomegranates were "apples of Carthage," tomatoes and eggplant "love-apples," dates "finger apples" and potatoes "apples of the earth." Similarly, many places have been called the original Garden of Eden. Claims have been made for Persia, Armenia, Chaldea, Basra and El Mezy near Damascus, where the waters of the Tege and Barrady divide into four streams that are said to be the four streams of Moses mentioned in *Genesis.* One seventeenth-century Swedish professor wrote a book attempting to prove that the garden was located in the Land of The Midnight Sun.

Tradition has it that Adam succumbed to Eve's wiles and ate of an apple from which she took the first bite, that a piece stuck in his throat forming the lump we call the Adam's Apple, and that all of us, particularly males, inherited this mark of his "fall." Modern scientific physiology, as opposed to folk anatomy, explains this projection of the neck, most prominent in adolescents, as being anterior thyroid cartilage of the larynx. But pioneer anatomists honored the superstition in the mid-eighteenth century by calling it *pomum Adami* or Adam's Apple. They simply could find no other explanation for this evasive lump in the throat that seemed to move up and down.

Adam and Eve's story is almost identically recounted in *The Bundehesh,* a sacred Persian book where the "fall" comes to Mashya and Mashyana, the first man and woman. The story is complete with serpent and tree, though in their shame the two lovers covered their once innocent nakedness with animal skins instead of fig leaves.

Many respected Biblical authorities, such as William Cole, claim that the sexual act was not the original sin, Adam and Eve's sin being the defiance of God instead. As for the apple being the fruit in Paradise, St. Jerome was the first to make this claim in the fourth century A.D.; the belief then inspired the folklore that it was the innocent apple, in Milton's words, "carnal desire enflaming," which caused Adam "to cast lascivious Eyes" upon Eve.

Few are aware that there is a *real* Adam's Apple Tree, *Tabernaemontana Coronia,* which is also called Nero's Crown. Why the folkname Adam's Apple Tree? Clearly a case of another claim on Eden. We quote from the *Encyclopedia of Gardening* (1838) by J. C. Loudon:

The inhabitants of Ceylon say that Paradise was placed in their country. ...They also point out as the tree which bore the forbidden fruit, the *Devi*

Ladner or *Tabernaemontana alternifoxlia* [the species name has since been changed to *coronaria*]....In confirmation of this tradition they refer to the beauty of the fruit, and the fine scent of the flowers, both of which are most tempting. The shape of the fruit gives the idea of a piece having been bitten off; and the inhabitants say it was excellent before Eve ate of it, though it is now poisonous.

Poisonous or not, the *Kama Sutra* gives a recipe for "An ointment made of the *tabernamontana coronia* (plus other ingredients) which can be used as an unguent of adornment." Anyone wanting to try the preparation might carefully consult that love manual, for the Adam's Apple Tree, or crape jasmine, or East Indian rosebay—still other names for the same plant—thrives in subtropical gardens of the United States.

The true apple has been lauded as a love fruit with far more frequency than its unrelated namesake. Old Scandinavian legends describe the apple as the fruit on which the gods would feast when they grew old and needed rejuvenation. "Comfort me with apples," says the *Song of Solomon* and today we describe a loved one as "the apple of his (or her) eye." In Greek legend, Aphrodite wins an apple as her prize in what might be called the world's first beauty contest, when Paris selects her as the fairest of the goddesses, although this particular apple has become known as the "apple of discord"—the machinations involved in selecting the first Miss Universe being the cause of the Trojan War.

In both ancient Greece and Rome lovers exchanged apples as tokens of affection or symbols of their love. The poetess Sappho wrote

> *Art thou the topmost apple*
> *The gatherers could not reach*
> *Reddening on the bough?*

Today the French still call the *api* variety apple (our "Red Lady") after the legendary Roman gourmet Apicius, who is said to have produced it by grafting. Even the lowly crab apple was considered potent by the Romans, Ovid among them, and one charming ninth-century Arabic poem shows how aptly the fruit was used as a simile for love:

> *The apple*
> *which I received from the hand*
> *Of the most charming*
> *gazellelike maiden,*
> *Which she had plucked herself*
> *from a branch*
> *That was as supple as her own body.*
> *And sweet it was*
> *to place my hand upon it*

As though it was the breast
of the one who gave it.
Pure was the fragrance of the apple,
Like the breath of the giver
One could see
the color of her cheek on it,
And I thought I was tasting her lips
When I began to eat the apple.

Sweet it was, the apple and such evocations of same, but there were those who objected to the fruit almost from the beginning. "This apple, dear Sisters," Ancren Riwle wrote in a handbook for nuns in about the year 1200, "is a token of everything that arouses lust and sensual delights." Fortunately, most everyone but nuns ignored his advice and an apple a day still helps keep sexual lassitude away. At least people have considered the apple a love food for centuries. John Ray wrote in 1670 that "An apple, an egg and a nut/ You may eat after a slut" (apparently in order to be ready for the next encounter), and Keats later praised candied apples in his "Eve of St. Agnes." As mentioned, an old German superstition went so far as to claim that eating an apple soaked in the sweat of your loved one's armpits would "increase love." One writer, Paulus Silentiarius, a sixth century Greek poet, did, however, note a certain deficiency in comforting anybody with apples, at least he gave applephiles a good line for all time to come. "If, my pet," he wrote, "you gave me these two apples as tokens of your breasts, I bless you for your great kindness. But if your gift does not go beyond the apples, you wrong me by refusing to quench the fierce fire you lit."

Rabelais called the breasts *pommes d'amour*, apples of love, and the testicles *pommes de cas pendre*; in English slang "apple dumpling soup" has meant a woman's bosom, an "apple monger" a pimp and the "apples" the testicles. All and all, there is quite a history behind Mom's apple pie: *Everything Johnny Appleseed Wanted To Know About Apples But Was Afraid To Ask*. Dating back to prehistory and the time when the poet of the *Song of Solomon* rejoiced:

As the apple tree among the trees of the wood, so is my beloved among the sons. I sat
down under his shadow with great delight, and his fruit was sweet to my taste.

(See also Eve's Date).

• APRICOTS •

Both "ladies and gentlemen" at the Court of James I, it's said, often "passed out" on the floor from aphrodisiacs. "Apricocks" were one of their favorite aphrodisiac foods, along with fruits like peaches and strawberries, but there's no reason to believe that the "sun's eggs" of the Persians might have caused their fainting spells. Nevertheless, Shakespeare was certainly echoing the beliefs of his day when he had Titania instruct her fairies in *A Midsummer Night's Dream* to feed Bottom on "apricocks and dewberries."

One of the earliest fruits known to man, apricots were possibly the "apples" in the Garden of Eden (see Apple). The Persians relied on them mixed with spices, honey and nuts; Alexander the Great probably first brought apricots to Greece, where they were highly regarded, and later the Romans found them especially effective as a seasoning in stews of pork and wine sauce.

In Chinese poetry the apricot blossom is symbolic of a "seducing nature." There could be something to the theory that apricot kernels, containing laetrile (vitamin B_{17}), are an effective "morning-after" contraceptive, just as papaya seeds are claimed by some to be—Polynesian girls said to eat a handful of these last daily to prevent pregnancy before marriage. But, and we stress this strongly, no valid scientific tests have been made on either, and so-called "health-food" prescriptions for same should be avoided like the plague (see Warning at chapter's end).

• AVOCADO •

Europeans first tasted the avocado or alligator pear when Montezuma served it to Cortez and his conquistadores. The Aztecs graphically explained that their *ahucatl* was so named from their word meaning testicle, not only because it resembled a testicle but because it greatly excited sexual passion. From then on the exotic green fruit became a favorite in the licentious palaces of Europe, especially with France's Louis XIV, who called it *la bonne poire* because it seemed to rejuvenate his aging libido. Avocados are now grown in the southern United States, the protein-rich food being served mainly in salads and desserts. The avocado is, however, an important meat substitute in parts of the world and Mexicans especially value the *aguacate* as a love food. They particularly favor tortillas with mashed avocados flavored with a little lime juice and accompanied by black coffee. The nut-flavored avocado is extra-delicious if eaten raw after being soaked in rum for a day or two; see Course Ten for an excellent avocado and egg aphrodisiac recipe.

• BANANAS •

Both the Moslems and Romans of later times believed that the plant-ain or cooking banana was the forbidden fruit in the Garden of Eden. Due to their erotic appearance, all of the many species of bananas were likely considered love foods long before this and they certainly have been ever since. Arabian slang and a score more languages make the fruit a synonym for the male organ, as would be expected, and "I had a banana with Lady Diana" was English slang for intercourse from the beginning of the century up until about 1930.

"Where the banana grows man is sensual and cruel," Ralph Waldo Emerson tells us in *Society and Solitude,* but then Emerson had more than a little of the Puritan in his transcendental soul. One of mankind's earliest cultivated fruits, Indian legend has it that the banana was the favorite of sages, who sat under the leaves of the gigantic herb and ate its fruit—hence its scientific name, *Musa sapietum,* "fruit of the wise men." Of great nutritional value to millions, the fruit is even today included in Indian offerings to their fertility gods. It has figured as a symbol in much erotic primitive poetry, as witness the following New Ireland love chant:

> *Eat the banana;*
> *I look at him;*
> *I give him the banana.*
> *As the banana is with me now,*
> *So will the man be with me.*

There are numerous erotic recipes for *Musa paradisia,* "the fruit of paradise," as the Romans called the banana. A fabled Chinese dessert is one of the best. Simply fry the bananas and keep them warm. Then cook a syrup of sugar and water until it spins a thin thread, adding sesame seeds at this point. Pour the syrup over the bananas at the table, immediately dipping them in crushed ice so that the hot fruit has a hard crunchy covering.

• CANTALOUPE (See Muskmelon)

• CASHEW •

Before being processed, the cashew nut grows hanging under the pear-shaped cashew apple; these two erotic symbols probably account for its aphrodisiac reputation among natives of India and Africa. Long a favorite of Indian lovers, cashews are popular throughout the world. Like all nuts, they are a good source of relatively cheap protein.

• CHERRY •

Much used as a simile in love poetry, from the Chinese poet Po Chu-I's "mouth like a red cherry," to Robert Herrick's "cherry ripe" and after, the cherry surprisingly doesn't have much of a reputation as a love food. At least there aren't many erotic recipes available using it, save for standards like cherry pie and Cherries Jubilee. The word, of course, has served as both a synonym for a young girl and a young woman's or young man's virginity. The Cornelian cherry *(Cornus mas)* has exceedingly hard wood that is said to have been used for the Trojan horse, and its bark yields the red dye used for the traditional Turkish fez. Berries from a dwarf form of it were believed by the Scottish Highlanders to create appetite, and they thus named the plant "Lus-a-chracis," Gaelic for "plant of gluttony."

• CHESTNUTS •

"The odor of semen, known as *odor aphrodisiacus*, is found in chestnuts" writes Dr. Iwan Bloch in *Odoratus Sexualis* (1933). Perhaps the ancient Chinese knew this, for the nut has been widely employed throughout China in love dishes such as chicken braised with chestnuts and is still included in both the Shanghai and Peking cuisine. So did the English have an erotic recipe for the chestnut, one elaborate Elizabethan dish consisting of chestnuts soaked in wine and then cooked with cinnamon, pistachio nuts, pine-kernels, rocket seed, sugar and other ingredients. Such recipes of course came to America with the first settlers, which leads us to suspect that many more than the village smithy labored under the spreading chestnut trees. The traditional American chestnut was wiped out by blight, but we still harvest a chestnut crop from disease-resistant Chinese chestnut tree varieties.

• COCOA (See Course Twenty) •

• CURRANTS •

More common in Europe, black currants are high in vitamin C and noted for their medicinal qualities. All currants belong to the gooseberry family, and American settlers used the tart red variety in practically every dish from jellies and puddings to venison. A hint of the red currant's erotic reputation can be found in the following poem by early seventeenth-century poet Richard Hughes:

> *Puddings should be*
> *Full of currants for me:*
> *Boiled in a pail*
> *Tied in the tail*
> *Of an old bleached shirt:*
> *So hot that they hurt.*

Seedless red or white currant jelly is laboriously made by professional seeders employing a goose-feather to delicately pick out the seeds one by one without damaging the berries. This jelly used to be a gourmet delicacy made only in Bar le Duc, France on the banks of the Meuse, and ever since 1559, when England's Queen Mary Stuart was given a jar of the rare jelly, it has been presented to every visiting chief of state, but just this year its last manufacturer went out of business due to prohibitive labor costs and the gastronomical rarity is no more.

• DATES •

Golden dates steamed in a casserole with ham was a favorite European love dish in days gone by. The fruit has been even more important to the Arabs, who consider the date palm a blessed tree, used as it is for fuel, fiber, shade, food and even drink—including both a coffee substitute and a beverage called "the elixir of life." Thousands of acres of date palms are now planted in California, where the fruit dangles from the trees wrapped in a heavy paper that protects each bunch from moisture and insects. The "candy that grows on trees" contains half its weight in sugar, one of the most nutritious of libido builders.

• DURIAN •

An old Malay saying has it that "When the durians fall, the sarongs rise." A lopsided, hard-shelled green fruit that is volley-ball size and covered with spikes on its outer pod, durian is widely believed to be an aphrodisiac in Malaya, Thailand, Indonesia and the Philippines. "The emperor (or queen) fruit," one of the most expensive of tropical fruits (up to $5 apiece), is believed by the Chinese to be so rich in protein that pregnant women are advised to eat it only in moderate amounts for fear that they might deliver a child "too large to come out."

The durian is so well-regarded by oriental lovers that the ownership of just one tree (they often reach eighty feet high) can make a man as well-off as if he owned a small business. It's a rough life, though, for owners often have to sleep under their trees to guard them; the fruit sometimes "falls ripe" at night and is devoured by rats.

The only trouble with the durian is that it literally stinks. Addicts say that it is no more objectionable than Gorgonzola or Camembert, but most non-Asians consider it among the foulest-smelling foods in the world, one gourmet writing that "to say it smells like rotten garlicky cheese is generous." Airlines refuse to carry durians even in sealed containers, Asian hotel rooms literally have to be fumigated after durian feasts, and one husband is reported to have chased his wife out of bed and eat her prize specimen on their hotel room fire escape.

Durian's taste is a different matter. One sixteenth-century traveler claimed that "It surpasses in flavor all the fruits of the world." A. R. Wallace, a widely traveled naturalist, described it this way in 1872: "A rich butterlike custard highly flavored with almonds gives the best idea of it, but intermingled come wafts of flavor that recall to mind cream cheese, onion sauce, brown sherry, other incongruities; it is neither sweet nor juicy, yet one feels the want of none of these qualities, for it is perfect as it is."

At the height of its season in August, many Asians travel thousands of miles to eat the aphrodisiac durian. The best of the 100 varieties is said to be grown in Thailand, and the Thai government is planning to can the fruit for export shortly. In fact, Thailand is so famous for its durians that the late President Sukarno of Indonesia, famous both for his love of women and things aphrodisiac, kept a house near Bangkok for discreet visits during the peak of the durian season.

As an additional service, your indentured aphrodisiac author has attempted to track down a U.S. source for the durian. We finally contacted the Woodside Fruit Market in New York, which is open twenty-four hours a day and whose motto is "As long as it grows, we've got it." After we explained our problem to the proprietor, he took our number, promising to call back. We're still waiting, one year later, so we must conclude that if anyone wants this expensive fruit, which is as mysterious and even rarer than the truffle, they'll have to hop aboard an airliner and fly to Asia to get it. Who knows, it might be worth the trip.

• ELDERBERRY •

He who cultivates the elderberry, says an old proverb, will die in his own bed. Amazing properties have long been attributed to the wine and other products made from *Sambucus nigra*. Said seventeenth-century English herbalist John Evelyn: "If the medicinal properties of the [elderberry] leaves, bark, berries, etc., were thoroughly known I cannot tell what our countrymen could ail for what he would not find a remedy, from every hedge, either for sickness or wounds."

• EVE'S DATE •

Since we mentioned the Adam's Apple, it's only fair to devote a few lines to Eve's Date *(Yucca baccata)*. Found in Mexico and the southwestern United States, this little-known fruit can be eaten out of hand. The dark purple Eve's Date probably takes its name because it's shaped like a stubby banana; it's tempting and sweet in taste but leaves a slight bitterness in the mouth (see Apple).

• FIGS •

The fig tree putteth forth her green figs, and the vines with the tender grape give a good smell. Arise, my love my fair one, and come away.

—Song of Solomon

Figs, by all evidence, have been causing men and women to cast off their fig leaves from ancient to present times. Consider, for example, these lines from Aristophane's *The Peace* (421 B.C.):

> *Now live splendidly together.*
> *Free from adversity.*
> *Pick figs.*
> *May his be large and hard,*
> *May hers be sweet.*

Even that symbol of prudery the fig leaf itself has been held to be aphrodisiac in nature over the years. The fig leaf was once thought to hold the same powers as mandrake (see Course Eighteen), shaped as it is "like the pendulant penis with the two testicles." But then figs themselves were considered potent love food to primitive peoples because of their resemblance to the genitalia. The Greeks, too, associated the fruit with phallic worship and made a point to serve it at Dionysian orgies. As for the Romans, they considered the fruit a gift of the god of wine and revelry, Bacchus, and held it sacred, brewing several love potions from the fig. One grisly one, recorded by Horace in his *Epodes*, was prepared from a "wild fig growing on a grave," "bones snatched from the mouth of a hungry bitch," and "feathers of a screech owl." Pleasanter is the fertility rite still surviving in many southern European countries of (gently) throwing figs instead of rice at newlyweds for good luck.

The fig is mentioned in the Biblical story of the Garden of Eden and Buddhism was born under a fig tree, Buddha's revellations coming to him while he sat under a Nepal species called *Bo*. To the Hindus the fruit is a symbol of both the *yoni*, the female genitalia, and the *lingam*, the penis. Certainly few other foods rival figs for use as scatological slang. To the Turks "fig" means anus, and among the Arabs "to nibble a fig" is cunnilingus. English features it in various expressions from "fig you" to far worse, and in French *faire la figue* means "to give the obscene finger gesture."

Figs are more alkaline and contain more mineral matter than most fruits and have been recommended as everything from an anemia cure to a laxative. They are especially delicious cut in two and soaked in orange liqueur an hour or two before being served with whipped cream.

• GOOSEBERRY •

Gooseberries are not so-named because they promote playful "goosing," but probably because they've traditionally been served with roast goose. The delicious fruit is best grown in England, but Chinese gooseberries or "Kiwi fruit," imported today from New Zealand, are also held in high regard. English slang has used "gooseberries" as a synonym for the testicles and "gooseberry-grinder" as a synonym for "a woman's active posterior."

• GRAPES •

How fair and pleasant art thou, O love, for delights! This thy stature is like to a palm tree and thy breasts to clusters of grapes.

—Song of Solomon

Much of the grape's aphrodisiac lore is to be found further on under wines (see Course Nineteen), yet the fruit itself, the first cultivated plant mentioned in the Bible, has been lauded as a love food and employed in the language of love for ages. The Greek poet Euripides praised the grape in eloquent terms and the ancients gave clusters to newlyweds in the belief that their many seeds would bless the couple with many children. Among the Romans, the juicy fruit was considered just as worthy and there is recorded a poem by Catullus that tells of a young girl so luscious that she ought "to be hid like ripe black grapes."

The grape has a long and interesting history in North America, which was of course first called Vinland by the Norsemen because so many grapevines grew here. More recently it has been recorded that a swinging London radiologist has planted grapevines around his *bed*. It's likely his lovers will keep coming back for more grapes, anyway.

• GRAPEFRUIT (See Pomelo) •

• GUAVA •

Another tropical fruit that can sometimes be obtained at specialty stores, the guava is highly valued by orientals. Chinese lovers employ almost all of the pear-shaped fruit, which is rich in tannic acid, even using its seeds in sauces and its leaves to clean the edible parts of a pig's stomach. Various guava jellies can be purchased in gourmet food stores. The guava is an excellent source of Vitamin C, calcium and phosphorus.

• HAZEL NUTS •

Hazel nuts are mostly collected in the wild in the United States today, though one cultivated hazel species yields fair filberts. The nut's aphrodisiac reputation has been obscured with time. Perhaps this is because our native hazels are inferior to European species. The English especially put great faith in the hazel nut, as is witnessed by John Gay's eighteenth-century poem *Spell*:

> Two hazel nuts I threw into the flame,
> And to each nut I gave
>   a sweetheart's name.
> This with the loudest bounce
>   me sore amazed,
> That in a flame
>   of brightest colour blazed.

As blazed the nut
   so may thy passion grow
For 'twas thy nut
   that did so brightly glow.

• HOTTENTOT FIG •

One would have to journey to South Africa to gather *Caspobrotus edulis*, a rewarding journey if what natives there say about the fruit's aphrodisiac properties is true. Hottentot women, for example, use an infusion of the fruit to ensure an easy birth and when male children are born, smear juice from the fig-shaped fruit all over the babes so that they'll grow up strong and virile. It might be worth growing in the greenhouse.

• KOLA •

The natives of North Ashanti and Sierra Leone consider the nut of the kola tree *(Cola nitida)* a powerful aphrodisiac, either chewing it or grinding the nuts for use as a stimulating beverage. One recipe, untested here, calls for mixing a teaspoon of powdered kola and two teaspoons of honey into a paste and stirring this into a cup of hot water. Kola, however, contains as much caffeine as coffee, which is decidedly an anaphrodisiac over long periods of time, so the drink should be used sparingly if at all.

• LEMON (See Lime) •

• LICHEE NUTS •

Pregnant women have been known to crave lichee nuts in the middle of the night, but not because the lichee is a favorite Chinese aphrodisiac food. Fresh lichees, which grow on prolific trees that often produce for two centuries and live for a thousand years, are very nutritious and one of the most refreshing of fruits in hot weather. A small brown fruit covered with red spines, its seeds are surrounded by a juicy white pulp. Lichees are available dried and fresh in most Chinatowns throughout the United States. Grown in southern China, they used to be sent by relays of horsemen to the capital "to make the Emperor's concubines happy."

· LIME ·

Limes, like lemons, are too acid a fruit to have much of a reputation as an aphrodisiac, but they might be of help to anyone dining nude al fresco. Good quantities of the juice taken internally or applied to the skin externally sensitize the skin to strong sunlight, leaving a nice even tan instead of a sunburn.

· MANGO ·

Mango fruit is said to be eaten in great quantities by Indian men in order to prolong sexual performance. One of the most important of tropical fruits, its varieties number in the hundreds, some of the notable dessert ones being the Alphonse of Bombay, the Ferdandin of Goa and The Kimayuddin of South India. The delectable fruit is grown in the American South but these varieties can't be compared to tropical ones in taste. One Indian poet described mangos as "sealed jars of paradisical honey," the Buddha was given a grove of them so that he could sit in the shade and meditate, and a Hindu god, Subramanya, renounced the world because he couldn't obtain a mango he desired. The mango isn't a difficult fruit to eat once one gets the hang of cutting the pulp away from its large central seed, but it might better be eaten naked in a bathtub to avoid the explosion of juice common to novices. Mangos can be peeled and eaten out of hand, or halved, peeled and pitted before being served.

The nutritious mango tastes something like a peach, but the comparison is wholly inadequate. An attractive bright yellow and red fruit, it appears erotic to some, hanging as it does like a pendulum from its long stem. A building in Angkor, built in 961 A.D., bears the following quotation under one of its most beautiful female figures: "Drawn by the flower of its glory to the fruit of the beauty of the mango tree of her body...the eye of men could nevermore tear itself away."

· MELONS ·

There are so many different melons highly regarded as love foods that it would be impossible to treat them separately here. Because of their round shape they have obviously often been compared to women's breasts in poetry and prose, yet we can recall a bit of doggerel that makes a sexual comparison between melons and men:

Men are like melons.
Shall I tell you why?
To find a good one
You must one-hundred try.

The Chinese are especially fond of the melon as a love stimulant, even using it in melon soups. One favorite is the muskmelon, the American cantaloupe, whose Persian name comes from musk perfume—which is said to be an aphrodisiac in its own right (see Course Eighteen). All melons are nutritious foods, particularly high in vitamins A and C.

• MULBERRIES •

The Chinese put their trust in mulberries for the improvement of virility, using them in various potions and sauces and eating them raw. The fruit-bearing mulberry tree is widely grown in the Far East as food for silkworms and thus the fruit is associated with sensuous silk. In America the red mulberry is not much planted anymore, but is rather common on old properties, where its fruit is most appreciated by birds, chickens, hogs and children cramming it into purple-stained mouths with purple-stained fingers. Even a few lovers must still wander in overgrown lots partaking of and frolicking in the shade of old mulberry trees. Like many things neglected, the trees seem to hold on with a tenacity cultivated trees have lost the knack for; they spring up from seed dropped by birds in the most unlikely places—even on vacant plots of land in the largest and most polluted of cities. Mulberries, aren't grown commercially anymore, despite their ease of cultivation and the many uses for their delicious fruit in desserts, wines, pastries and jams. Some of the gnarled old trees from among the 100,000 King James I had planted in England during his reign still survive today. The mulberry is a sentimental fruit, the fruit of lost youth to many, the first food ever gathered with love and so must at least be mentioned.

• NECTARINES •

See Peaches for the love story of this smooth-skinned fruit, which is a mutation of the peach and often grows on the same tree. Sometimes, in fact, a nectarine can be half peach—fuzzy on one side and silky on the other. Cultivated for thousands of years "the queen of peaches" takes its name from the Greek *nekter*, the drink of the gods.

· OLIVES ·

"Wine within, oil without," was the Roman formula for a happy love life, and the oil with which they annointed their bodies was of course olive oil. Olives themselves were considered a provocative to drinking among the Romans. So interwoven is the fruit with history—Noah's Biblical olive branch becoming the symbol of peace; some of the ancient olive trees in the Garden of Gethsemane possibly growing there since the time of Christ's betrayal; Athens named for the goddess Athena after she gave the olive to man—that it is hard to find any specific aphrodisiac dishes made from it in the history books. The olive tree, which has been known to live well over 1000 years, was simply a staple of life, yielding both food and light and grown also for its symbolism of joy, happiness and peace. Yet the fruit has always been a sexual symbol, too. Rabelais, for one, used *olives de poissy* as synonymous for the testes and the olive stuffed with red pimento has long been a symbol for the female breast in art and poetry. Green olives are those picked early, whereas the black ones are picked ripe. Both are very bitter indeed before they are soaked in a lye and salt solution and readied for market.

· ORANGES ·

If one desires another's love, he must take an orange and prick it all over with a needle, then sleep with it under his armpit. If the loved-one then eats the orange, he or she will return love.

We alluded to the above European folklore earlier, but it is far from the only erotic superstition associated with the orange. Oranges were considered a rare delicacy during the Sung Dynasty (960–1279 A.D.), when Chinese couples like the emperor Chou Pang-yen and his favorite courtesan of the moment cut them open with a silver knife and shared the pieces before making love. Long a symbol of love, orange blossoms were used by courtesans to sprinkle over their bedsheets and throughout their rooms. Ancient lovers bathed together in orange blossom water and the fruit itself was given to newlyweds in the belief that its prolific number of seeds would ensure fertility and bless them with many offspring. Today's chemists believe the orange too acid a fruit to be much of a physiological aphrodisiac, but yesterday's alchemists thought differently. A famous eighteenth-century recipe using the orange was called Angel Water and its ingredients clearly show that it had to be made by an expert. These consisted of exactly one pint of orange blossom water, one pint of rose water and one-half a pint of myrtle water. Simply shake well and add two-thirds of distilled spirits of musk and two-thirds of spirits of ambergris—if these last can still be found at your friendly neighborhood apothecary shop.

London psychologist Dr. Edward Hernandez believes the way people eat oranges can reveal their personalities. He divides orange eaters into four distinct personality types: Plungers, Peelers, Slicers and Strippers. It seems that any of the above can have strong sex drives if they also suck oranges, and the longer they suck the juice, the stronger their sex drive.

· PAPAYA ·

At the world-famous Raffles Hotel in Singapore they feature a mouth-watering dish made by halving and scooping out some of the flesh of a papaya and filling it with ice-cream. The versatile papaya, or tree melon, grown here primarily in Florida, is a staple food in many parts of the world, and its enzyme papain (which we use in commercial tenderizers) aids in the digestion of any love feast, which is one reason why West Indians use the leaves as a meat tenderizer. West Indians also add chunks of the green fruit to meat stews and Indians of Central America gorge themselves with the "paw paw" so that they can eat large quantities of food at their feasts without becoming ill. The papaya is often a prodigious melon, ranging from one to twenty pounds, and can vary greatly in taste. So symbolically erotic is the fruit to Cubans that it is not even called the papaya there anymore—for "papaya" has come to be slang for "the female fruit" or sexual organs. Never call a papaya a papaya in Cuba. Polite Cubans call the tree melon *fruta bomba*, or bomb fruit.

· PASSION FRUIT ·

As its name implies, passion fruit or granadilla (an edible fruit of the passion flower, *Passiflora edulis*) has a deserved reputation in the tropics. Its refreshing juice is delicious and the flesh is sometimes served as a topping for ice-cream and other desserts. The purple-colored passion fruit, which is borne on vines covered with striking white and purple flowers, is widely grown in the tropics for the table, especially in Brazil. It is not cultivated commercially in the United States, although another species, *Passiflora incarnata*, or the maypop, bears an edible fruit. Granadillas are too perishable to be shipped, so it's off to Brazil for anyone hankering after one. Passion fruits are made into delicious soft drinks, sherberts and jams in tropical countries, and lovers south of the border swear by them. However, the fruit's name in reality comes from the symbol of the crucifixion that Spanish Catholic missionaries saw in the plant's flowers.

· PEACHES·

Venus owns this tree...the fruit provokes lust....If the kernals be bruised and boiled in vinegar until they become thick, it marvellously makes the hair to grow again upon the bald places or where it is too thin.

Nicholas Culpepper imparts the above advice in his *Complete Herbal* (1652) in describing what is perhaps the most versatile of fruits. The peach, says one authority, "can be eaten whole like an apple, sliced with cream, dried, stewed, pickled, spiced, canned, distilled into a fine liqueur, cooked into a pie or jam—or frozen into delicious ice-cream." Used for everything from love potions to Culpepper's hair restorer, the peach has also proved versatile as an aphrodisiac.

Peaches have an intriguing history that has been traced back to ancient China. In fact, there is a legendary Chinese peach known as the "Banto," which requires 3000 years to ripen and bestows health, virility and everlasting life on anyone lucky enough to eat it. But if you can't find the elusive Banto, any peach will provide some pleasure. The Chinese considered the fruit's sweet juices symbolic of the effluvia of the *yin* or vagina and both the Chinese and Arabs, among other peoples, regard its deep fur-edged cleft as a symbol of the female genitalia. "Sharing the peach" was an old Chinese euphemism for sodomy and the Arabs still use "peach" in many slang expressions referring to oral love. In Europe the French have used the word *pêche* in similar sexual expressions, from intercourse to sodomy, and "a peach house" was once common in English slang as a house of prostitution.

The ancient Chinese employed the peach blossom as a symbol of "easy virtue," and used the term "peach" for a pretty young bride, just as it is used around the world today for an attractive girl. The most popular American peach is probably the Elberta, though surprisingly it is not considered a superior eating fruit by those who know peaches. One note of caution. No love potion prepared from peaches should ever include the leaves. They are highly poisonous and "peach tea" brewed from them has killed many persons. The same applies to the leaves of several other fruits (see also Nectarines).

• PEANUTS •

Rich in vitamin E, "the sexuality vitamin," and vitamin B$_1$, peanuts and peanut products are recommended by at least three leading sexologists for a restorative diet. Peanut butter is particularly worthy and nutritionists claim that this easily digested high-protein food makes for an adequate survival diet when combined with a citrus fruit like oranges. It's said that a jar of peanut butter is found in four out of five American homes, and apparently more of us should dip into that jar. Those with more-exotic tastes might search out the recipe that futurist French chef Jules Maincave invented during World War I for a dish called "young monkey stuffed with peanuts." But for a simple potent peanut butter soup try the following:

Sautée ½ of a finely chopped onion in one tablespoon of vegetable oil until golden brown. Blend in ½ cup peanut butter, lowering flame. Bring to a boil and season to taste with salt and pepper. Finally, lower the heat and let simmer about ten minutes.

Peanuts are used in many languages as slang for sexual symbols. They go by numerous names, including monkey nuts, ground peas or nuts, and goobers—the last (from *nguba*) being one of the few African words still retained in English.

• PEARS •

The pear, one astute observer declares, is shaped like a Rubens' nude. Celebrated in art, song and poetry as far back as 1000 B.C., the fruit has long been prized by great lovers, and many kings and princes have passionately cultivated new varieties for their tables. Pears are one of the few fruits that ripen better off the tree and the Chinese readied theirs in rooms filled with sensuous burning incense. All varieties go especially well with cheese desserts, Rabelais telling us that: *"There is no match you could compare/ To Master Cheese and Mistress Pear."*

The soft Bartlett pear, a European type, constitutes 70% of our American commercial crop, but Asian types like the Seckel have more often been referred to in erotic literature.

• PINEAPPLE •

For a really delicious aphrodisiac dessert, splurge a little and buy a pineapple picked ripe, rather than those picked green for shipment to supermarkets. You'll be amazed at how much sweeter and flavorsome it is. And for a libido-arousing drink much acclaimed in the tropics, hollow out a pineapple, crush its meat for juice and combine it with orange juice, papaya juice, coconut milk, a dash of lime and a drop of kümmel if desired. In tropical climes, this concoction is poured back into the pineapple and sipped through a straw, into which thoughtful lovers often tuck a small orchid as a decoration.

Pineapples are possibly the best known of tropical fruits and are so-named in English for their pine-cone shape; they are called *anana* in France and many other countries, from a Guarani word meaning "excellent fruit." At one time in England the fruit was called the "King-pine."

• PISTACHIO NUTS •

Pistachio nuts have been mentioned historically as an aphrodisiac food, though we can find no recipes given for them. Several sexologists recommend the nuts for virility diets, but it might be that by the time one finishes opening a platter of them at a love feast there'll be no time left for anything else.

• PLUMS AND PRUNES •

Plums are alluded to as a love food by the poet Keats in his "Eve of St. Agnes," and it's said that prunes used to be served in Elizabethan houses of ill-repute to make the customers more receptive to the often unappealing girls. Prunes, of course, are merely dried plums of special varieties, and pregnant women apparently craved them in Elizabethan times, for Shakespeare writes of a lady "Great with child and longing for stewed prunes." Plums are widely distributed throughout the world, their cultivation dating back over 2000 years. In America we mostly consume derivatives of the Chinese plum, which is just as well, for these were featured in many ancient Chinese love potions and dishes, even though the Chinese thought the plum blossom to be symbolic of chastity. The French for plum is *prunes* and this word has served as their slang for the testes. Shakespeare used "the plum tree" as a punning expression for the female pudendum.

• POMEGRANATES •

The *Kama Sutra* instructs anxious men and disappointed women to use pomegranate seeds in a preparation to enlarge the male's penis. "The fruit of the ancients" has been lauded as an aphrodisiac in one way or another ever since early Grecian times, when it was believed that the small bushlike tree that bears it sprang from the blood of Dionysus, god of wine and revelry. Mohammed instructed the faithful to "Eat the Pomegranate—for it purges the system of envy and hatred." Pliny wrote that the pith of a branch of the pomegranate tree worked wonders, and the Turks still use their word for the fruit as a synonym for the female genitals. Only the Germans, it seems, believed the "Chinese apple," as it is commonly called, to be an antiaphrodisiac. Today, in the Orient, the seeds of the fruit are prepared with confectioners sugar and served to wedding guests. Then, when the married couple reaches their new home, pomegranates are broken at the doorway, their numerous crimson-coated seeds signifying both the loss of virginity and an omen that many offspring will come of the marriage.

• POMELO •

A delicious paradisical dessert or salad is made in China with pieces of pomelo combined with oranges, dates, nuts and mayonnaise. The pomelo (ancestor of our grapefruit, but sweeter, less acid and more flavorsome) is highly valued as an aphrodisiac fruit and is traditionally served during the Chinese Moon Festival in August. Often called the shaddock after the English sea captain who introduced it to Europe, the pomelo was once known in Europe as the "Adam's apple fruit." Our grapefruit is either a mutation of the pomelo or a cross between it and the orange. It was named the grapefruit because it often grows in clusters.

• QUINCE •

The lines I see upon thy face Surpass the bloom of youthful grace.
Thy quinces drooping in my hand
Outshine young breasts that upright stand.
Winter than summer seems more warm
And springtime yields to autumn's charm.

—Paulus Silentiarius

Why this lovely old poem, which tells so well of sexual love in later years, has not been widely anthologized remains a mystery to us. It is as beautiful as:

> *You who have seen*
> *so many shadblow bloom*
> *and learned never to look in mirrors,*
> *rub your silver*
> *wedding ring, filigreed,*
> *love wounded but hunting,*
> *lovely leopard hands.*
>
> *Earth a green gold mine,*
> *stoned on dandelion wine,*
> *you splash in a swaying*
> *sea of Star-of-Bethlehem*
>
> *Naked you drink*
> *in a drift of daffodils,*
> *winter lips on spring flowers*
> *falling phalloi*
> *rice in your ashen hair.*
>
> *Naked you kneel*
> *in a field of marigolds,*
> *quince breasts etched with blue,*
> *flowers filled with Ming vases sing.*

Yet the quince is not only a symbol for aging love. This close relative of the pear, which grows on a small gnarled shrub but has among the most beautiful of fruit blossoms, was dedicated by the Greeks and Romans to Venus or Aphrodite, being a symbol of love, happiness and fertility. Still another fruit believed to be the "forbidden fruit" of the Garden of Eden, the quince was guaranteed by some medieval physicians to help women beget sons of marked energy and ability. Mentioned by Keats, it is also the subject of many ancient legends, including one that says it wards off "the influence of the evil eye." The bitter quince is not, of course, eaten raw; it is prepared in preserves, used in sauces and cooked in blends with other fruits. Cotignac, an esteemed French preserve is made from the fruit, and it is also used for a rich, stimulating wine.

· RASPBERRIES ·

Very perishable and found only in gourmet groceries, fresh raspberries of all colors are certainly an epicurean food. One of the earliest fruits known to man, the bramble berries nevertheless aren't mentioned in many aphrodisiac recipes.

• RHUBARB •

As with the peach, the leaves of rhubarb are extremely poisonous, but erotic red rhubarb stalks have been used as a love stimulant in tonics since the Chinese first cultivated the plant in 2700 B.C. In America "pie-plant" is the basis for rhubarb pies (often combined with strawberries) and is stewed with sugar as a spring tonic said to rejuvenate men and women alike. Italian lovers mix rhubarb in wine with cinnamon, ginger and vanilla for a stimulating aphrodisiac tonic. The word rhubarb comes from the Latin *rhabarbarum*, "root of the barbarians," because the Romans believed people who ate it to be barbaric in nature. In England "rhubarb" has been used as a synonym for the penis, as in expressions like "How's your rhubarb comin' up, mate?"

• STRAWBERRIES •

Strawberries are one of the few berries that have much of an aphrodisiac reputation. The early Greeks, as mentioned, had a taboo against the eating of any red foods, including wild strawberries, and this added mystery to the fruit, leading many to believe it possessed great powers. In the Middle Ages, however, pregnant women avoided the berries because they believed their children would be born with ugly red birthmarks if they ate them.

An American favorite is strawberry shortcake—the largest of which is baked at the Lebanon, Ohio strawberry festival, where a cake towering twelve feet in the air is cut with a saw each year. But there are far better aphrodisiac dishes made from the fruit. One is *fraises à la Cussy*, the strawberries, cream and champagne dessert invented by Napoleon's chef Louis de Cussy. Another is that offered by the American sexologist Professor McCary, who claimed that strawberries and pear doused in Cointreau and drenched in a fragrant sauce of beaten egg yolk, confectioners sugar, cloves and cinnamon would accrue to the benefit of any mattress maker. Excellent also are wild strawberries, or the French *fraises de bois*, both of which can be obtained at specialty markets or grown in the home garden.

• SUGARBERRY •

The sugarberry or hackberry *(Celtus australis)* is native to the northern temperate zone and grown as an ornamental in the northern United States, but few people realize that its fruit is delicious and has quite a history as a love food. Sugarberries may have been the food of the Loto-phagi, or Lotus eaters, those legendary people who lived on the northeast African coast. It's said that any traveler who ate the sweet fruit or drank the wine the Lotus eaters made from it lost all desire to return to his own home—obviously a good way to get someone to spend the night (see also Lotus; Course Sixteen).

• TANGERINE, MANDARIN ORANGES •

See Oranges for this loose-skinned mandarin group of oranges, which take the name tangerine from Tangier, Morocco, where a variety of the species is cultivated. The mandarin group derives its name from the title of the nine ranks of high officials in the Chinese Empire. They are named mandarin by analogy either from the sense of superiority implied in the title or from the color of a Mandarin's robes. At any rate, the Chinese extolled them as a love fruit.

• VANILLA •

"Oh, you flavor everything; you are the vanilla of society."

—Sidney Smith

Vanilla was thought to be wickedly aphrodisiac in Elizabethan England because the pod of the plant resembled the vagina. In fact, the word *vanilla* comes from the Spanish for "little vagina." Queen Elizabeth I used vanilla to flavor her marzipan, making it a favorite flavoring for candy ever since, and Thomas Jefferson was the first to introduce it as a flavoring in America.

Brillat-Savarin recommended vanilla as an aphrodisiac dish in the form of a dessert called "pyramid of vanilla and rose meringues." Today, however, natural vanilla is in short supply and we generally use a synthetic; there isn't enough natural vanilla in the world to flavor even the vanilla ice-cream made in America alone. Needless to say, natural vanilla is much more flavorsome and potent than the synthetic product. Madame DuBarry is reputed to have used the pods from *Vanilla planifolia* "to keep her lovers perpetually ready," but excessive amounts of natural vanilla can have toxic effects. Possibly the smell of vanilla is its real secret. "There are certain body odors which are very attractive to men and women," says Paris perfumer Jean-Paul Guerlain. "All our successful perfumes have two notes—vanilla and an animal scent. In short, they are aphrodisiacs."

• WALNUTS •

See Almonds for a famous Chinese aphrodisiac recipe employing walnuts. "The hormone value of walnuts has been widely recognized by the Chinese throughout the country," writes one Oriental expert. "They are used as ingredients in many meat dishes, notably stir-fried chicken with walnuts."

Europeans have also valued the walnut as a love food and symbol. One frankly chauvinistic English rhyme has it that: *"A spaniel, a woman, and a walnut tree./ The more you thrash 'em, the better they be."* But the Romans customarily ate walnuts at weddings as a fertility rite because "the 'double robe' of this nut, consisting of the soft husk and the hard shell, were supposed to resemble the membrane wherein the embryo infant was enfolded."

• OTHER FRUITS •

Following is a list of mostly unusual fruits that have been mentioned historically as either aphrodisiac and/or gourmet foods. Almost all are difficult if not impossible to buy, but many of these might be worth growing in the greenhouse, if only for their value as conversation pieces.

Akekia *(Akebia trifoliata)* sausage-shaped dessert fruit
Appleberry *(Billardiera longiflora)* purplish fruit eaten raw as dessert
Barberry *(Berberis vulgaris)* used for a famous Rouen conserve
Brazilian cherry *(Eugenia uniflora)* syrups and wine said to have medicinal value
Buffalo berry *(Sheperdia argentia)* makes an excellent relish for meat
Custard banana *(Aseminia triloba)* delicious American fruit called "poor man's banana"
Goumi *(Elaeagnus multiflora)* small fruits good in pies, tarts and jellies
Jujube, Chinese Date *(Zizyphus jujube)* see Lotus; Course Sixteen
Kumquat *(Fortunella japonica)* delicious fresh, preserved or candied
Loquat *(Eriobotrya japonica)* ancient fruit with many uses

Medlar *(Mespilus germanica)* ancient fruit said to "stay women's longings"

Mombin *(Spondias purpurea)* important fruit in Mexico and Central America

Monstera *(Monstera deliciosa)* unusually tasty with a pineapple-banana odor

Persimmon *(Diospyros kaki)* delicious, but only when fully ripe

Prickly Pear *(Opuntia species)* various cacti whose fruits are eaten or used for preserves, wine, etc.

Seaberry *(Hippophae rhamnoides)* coastal plant high in vitamin C used for jelly, medicines, relish for fish

Snowberry *(Chiognes hispidulum)* according to one expert, "of all wild fruits, the most out of this world."

Umbinza *(Halleria lucida)* in Basutoland these sweet berries are believed to protect people from evil spirits and bad weather

Wineberry *(Rubus phoenicolasius)* bush produces tasty sprigs of berries

Zabalu *(Lardizabala biternata)* sausage or walnut-shaped dessert fruit

· WARNING! ·

Beware of any love potions or "health foods" made from parts of fruit that are not normally eaten. Lately, to cite just one example, a California couple sampled a health food puree made from apricot kernels and within a few moments began developing an almost text-book-perfect case of cyanide poisoning (apricot kernels contain a chemical called amygdalin, which the body can convert to cyanide). Apple, cherry and peach pits can be equally dangerous in other ways, as can be peach and other fruit leaves. Obviously, wild fruit collectors should either know what they're picking and beware of insecticides in orchards, or else stay home and play the prelude to love over a bowl of store-bought fruit.

COURSE SIXTEEN

Flower And Plant Power

*And I will make thee beds of roses
And a thousand fragrant posies.*
    —Christopher Marlowe

Once upon a water-bed, an eccentric gourmet-lover served a dinner solely for its scent. The first course consisted of a lone small carnation resplendent on a silver tray, which both our host and his lady of the evening gently picked up and sniffed. For the second course his man brought a bunch of roses on a gold platter, this followed by a large magnolia floating on water in a cut crystal bowl. The fourth course was pom-pom dahlias, the next a spray of tiger lilies and the "meal" finally ended with "the delicate intake of the scent of violets."

No record exists of our passionate epicure's progress that night, and one suspects he'd have fared better by arranging for his flowers to be eaten, much as Henry VIII had candied violets, roses, primroses and hawthorn prepared for the table. At any rate, flowers and plants have at least four things going for them as love foods: their scent, beauty, good taste and their often high nutritional content. The beauty of a bloom alone is enough to make a flower appealing; many species are so attractive, for instance, that they have been named for Aphrodite. Scent, of course, is highly important. Writes one authority: "There are many theories on this in the East. For instance the Narcissus flower is everywhere supposed to excite the woman and depress the man, whilst the Mimosa bloom gives an essence the Arabs call "Fitnah," trouble or revolt, because its action is direct and powerful upon the passions of their wives" (see Course Twenty-Two).

In many cases a flower's good reputation in the love cookery can be attributed to its resemblance to the human anatomy—as with the orchid, for example—but blooms of all kinds have often been cooked for both their delicate taste and stimulating nutriments. This is not really so unusual when we come to think of it. Cauliflower, after all, is merely an enlarged malformed flowerhead; broccoli is just green undeveloped flower clusters; the artichoke is only an unripe flowerhead; and the same holds true of many so-called vegetables.

Jules Maincave, that innovative French chef who met an untimely death in the trenches during World War I, went so far as to prefer flowers over many condiments. "As for seasonings," he wrote, "they are pitiably limited. We are still using bayleaf, thyme, parsley, scallions ...whereas the progress of modern chemistry would enable us to use roses, lilies of the valley, just as well...There is nothing more delicious in my opinion, than a chicken with lilies of the valley." And Maincave was only resurrecting an idea known for centuries, an art still practiced in our time, as witness the use of rose water, violet syrup and carnation essence to flavor cakes and pastry.

The art of cooking with flowers is enjoying a revival today, in hand with the renewed interest in nature. Since this is a specialized art, those interested are referred to books like the recently published *Cooking With Flowers* by Zack Henle (Price/Stern/Sloan), which offers many off-trail recipes such as Yucca Omelet, Marigold Rice, Mum Soup and Rose Petal Salad, among others. We'll only deal briefly here with those flowers and plants reputed to be aphrodisiacs through the ages in America and elsewhere which aren't generally used as herbs, fruits and vegetables. Only the most interesting plants can be offered from the admittedly incomplete list below, which itself contains some 100 examples:

Anemone	Frankincense	Mastic	Saw Palmetto
Artemisia	Fuchsia	Moly	Sensitive plant
Asoka	Galingale	Muirapuama Bark	Snakeroot
Belladonna	Gotu Kola	Murala	Southernwood
Boyplant	Grass	Myrrh	Spikenard
Burdock	Guaiac Bark	Myrtle	Spreading Hogweed
Burra Gokeroo	Hashish	Navelwort	Spurge
Caperberry	Henna	Nux Vomica	Strombus
Cereus	Hyssop	Olibanum	Surag
Chevri	Jasmine	Orchid	Thistle
Chinchona Bark	Jimsonweed	Palmito	Tobacco
Chrysanthemum	Juniper	Pansy	Trees, various
Crocus	Khat	Peony	Tulips
Cyclamen	Kino root	Periwinkle	Turnera
Dahlia	Koisunda	Pine seeds	Aphrodisiac
Dandelion	Laurel	Polignonia	Valerian
Darnel	Lavender	Poppies	Venus's Pride
Devil's Shoestring	Lilac	Provencia	Verbena
Dita	Lotus	Pyracanthus	Violet
Dragon's Blood	Lycopodium	Rocket	Waterlily
Dufz	Maidenhair	Roses	Willow leaves
Emblia	Male fern	Sarsparilla	Witchhazel
Feverfew	Mallows	Sassafras	Yohimbe
Fleawort	Marijuana	Sativar	

• ARTEMISIA •

This genus of bitter or aromatic herbs and low shrubs has been highly regarded since ancient times. Wormwood, the chief ingredient of the deadly aphrodisiac drink absinthe, is the common name for *Artemisia Absinthium* (see Course Nineteen); SOUTHERNWOOD, another *Artemisia* species, is treated separately herein.

• BELLADONNA •

Ulcer sufferers might be surprised to learn that belladonna, which is used medically to halt acid flow to the stomach, has been considered an aphrodisiac and once formed a part of black magic love potions. Deadly Nightshade *(Atropa belladonna)* yields its narcotic from the juice of its berry and is, of course, highly poisonous. Belladonna, or "beautiful lady," does make the eyes shine and sparkle, though today's scientists don't believe it's an aphrodisiac.

• BURDOCK •

Mix burdock seeds along with ingredients like the "lefte testicle of a goat" and "four droppes of crocodyle semen" and the effects will be "marvellous," says the *Black Book* of the Middle Ages. But Burdock or gobo is generally considered a garden weed today, one of the fifty or so worst weeds of all time. It's that little plant whose burs commonly stick to clothing and it's obviously no fun rolling around in a field of burdock.

• BURRA GOKEROO •

Indians use the seeds of *Pedalium murex*, as this plant is botanically called, as a tonic to cure impotence. Burra gokeroo has also been acclaimed as a stimulant that produces prodigious erections.

• CHEVRI •

Chevri *(Sandix ceropolium)*, Davenport tells us, "is accounted as capable of exciting amorous propensities, so much so that Tiberius, the Roman emperor, the most lascivious, perhaps of men, is said to have exacted a certain quantity of it from the Germans, by way of tribute for the purpose of rendering himself vigorous with his women and catamites, and Venette says that the Swedish ladies give it to their husbands when they find them flagging in their matrimonial duties." Tiberius and Swedish ladies are as good testimonials as any, but we frankly don't know where they're selling any chevri.

• CHRYSANTHEMUM •

The Chrysanthemum was the favorite flower of the Chinese philosopher Confucius and is so beloved in Japan that it inspired a national holiday. Mum tea, mum soup made with ham and chestnuts and a complicated dish called the Chrysanthemum Bowl—including chicken, shrimp, oysters, fish, pork, spinach, cabbage, soy sauce, sherry and other famous love foods—are all Chinese favorites. One odd Chinese love philtre is made as follows:

Cook the ground powder of the chrysanthemum stone with water until a thick paste appears. While cooking, stir in the pulverized wings of butterflies. Dry mixture. Add a few drops of honey and roll mixture into tiny pills. A pill must be secreted into the sleeve of the beloved, who is then rendered submissive to all advances.

• DEVIL'S SHOESTRING •

This wild plant is enjoying something of a mini-boom in the boudoir right now in America. For what it's worth we can report that the plant is cut up into small pieces, soaked in whiskey and rubbed vigorously into the body.

• FEVERFEW •

Feverfew, also called pyrethrum and pillitory—its botanical name is generally *Chrysanthemum parthenium*—was held in high regard by the ancient Greeks. They claimed that any old wine to which feverfew was added quickly "kindled the flame of love."

• FRANKINCENSE (See Myrrh) •

• GRASS •

It may come as a pleasant surprise to homeowners that every blade of that expensive grass out on the front lawn may be worth their labors after all. Grass has been cited in love potions many times; one grass recipe is listed in the Hindu *Ananga Ranga* and another in the *Kama Sutra*. The latter advises us to "take the root of Hungarian grass *(Panicum italicum)* and the pollen of the lotus flower, pulverize them in honey and apply the composition *to the soles of the feet.*" In this way the love embrace "will thus be prolonged." Don't attempt to apply the solution while at table unless you can walk to bed on your hands.

• HENNA •

Made from the mignonette tree and widely known as a hair dye, henna has had its uses as an aphrodisiac, too. Writes Omar Haleby: "In my own experience there are very few cases of inorganic impotence which remain unalleviated should the sufferer rub his penis night and morning with henna. Eight days, or at the most two weeks, are generally sufficient...."

· HASHISH ·

Drugs are generally outside the scope of this book, but since Indian hashish, *charas*, is made into a sweetmeat called *maajun*, and is often baked into brownies and other cakes, it must at least be mentioned. Marijuana is the lest potent and hashish the most stimulating part of *Cannabis sativa*, a plant that has been frequently cited as an aphrodisiac. Many claim that both byproducts prolong the sexual act, increase sensations and increase the number of times a man can experience erection and orgasm in one night, but there have been no reliable long-term studies on the plant's sexual effects. One recent controversial study by Dr. Robert Kolodny and Dr. William H. Masters shows that marijuana may cause temporary sterility and impotence in males.

· JIMSONWEED ·

White-thorn apple, which is better known here as jimsonweed *(Datura stramonium)*, can be a deadly poison. The *Kama Sutra*, however, is confident that "if a man, after anointing his lingam (penis) with a mixture of the white thorn apple, the long pepper, and the black pepper, and honey, engages in sexual union with a woman, he makes her subject to his will." But then this manual's companion volume, the *Ananga Ranga*, says that "the man who, after enjoying his wife, catches some of his sperm in his left hand, and applies it to her left foot, will find her entirely submissive to his will." So as not to show prejudice, a recipe is also included therein for females: "The woman who before congress will touch with her left foot the organ of her husband, and will make a practice of this, undoubtedly subdues him, and makes him her slave for life." Remember—*left* hand, *left* foot.

· KHAT ·

Khat (also known as kat, gat and quat) is the small bitter leaf of the African *Catha edulis* tree that releases a substance called norpseudophedrine and a related ingredient, both of which are amphetaminelike alkaloids. Native khat chewers say the leaf is an aphrodisiac, and it is known to stimulate the chewer to vigorous physical activity by releasing adrenalin through the body. Khat is said to have been used by the Mau Maus and other Africans to make themselves braver in their fight against white settlers, and it is handed out freely in Ethiopia today when authorities want village workmen to get a road built quickly. However, there is much controversy about the drug, and it is banned in some African states. Khat opponents contend that chewers suffer from loss of appetite, constipation, gastritis, inflammation of the mouth and cirrhosis of the liver. On the other hand, a World Health Organization report showed that khat is rich in vitamin C and contains considerable amounts of iron, niacin, protein and calcium.

• KOISUNDA •

In India an astringent paste made from Koisunda is applied to the vagina walls to contract them and "make a tighter fit to give greater pleasure to the male." Kino root or wild alum (*Geranium maculatum*) is sometimes made into a tea for the same purpose.

• LAVENDER •

"Lavender and old lace" suggests all that's old-fashioned in the "prim and proper" sense of the word, but lavender's old-fashioned uses were somewhat more erotic. In *The Winter's Tale* Shakespeare writes that hot lavender is "given to men of middle age" as a stimulant. The highly fragrant dried flower buds and calyx of *Lavandula spica* yield oil of lavender, which has been valued in love potions and charms at least since early medieval times.

• LEAVES •

Write the names of several lovers on leaves and expose them to the wind. The name of your true love will be on the leaf the wind doesn't blow away. At least so believe those who practice botanomancy, or divination by leaves.

· LILAC ·

The leaves of the Persian lilac are supposed to make hair grow in "unlikely places." Lilac leaves have also been heralded as a love tonic, and the capsules of the shrub yield an abstract that orientals have used as a medicine for reducing fever. When lilacs last in the dooryard bloomed, few Americans ate or rubbed on any of them, but this has not been the case elsewhere. Says the *Perfumed Garden,* for example: "Pound very carefully pyrether, together with ginger, mix them while pounding with an ointment of lilac, then rub this compound into your abdomen, the testicles and the verge [penis]. This will make you ardent." The ointment cited was likely made from fat and lilac leaves and may or may not have gotten men on the verge of using the verge.

· LOTUS ·

Lotus flowers and lotus eaters are the subjects of many works fact and fiction. No one has yet proven the worth of *Zizzphus,* to which genus the fabled lotus of history might belong, but it is highly regarded by the Chinese, who have a lotus seed dessert called *pinh tan lian tye* reputed to be quite tasty and stimulating (see also Sugarberry; Course Fifteen).

· MALLOWS ·

Xenocrates wrote that the sap of mallows, as well as "three of its roots bound together," excited the passion of Greek women, and the Romans were said to stew oysters with mallows for a tasty love dish. Here in America the root of the marsh mallow *(Althaea officianalis)* was once used to make marshmallows, which are now made with cheaper gelatin.

· MARIjUANA (See Hashish) ·

· MYRTLE ·

"She was standing with her locks wreathed with myrtle," Ovid wrote in *The Art of Love.* "She gave me a leaf and a few berries. Receiving them, I was sensible of the divine influence as well; the sky shone with greater brightness and all cares departed from my breast." In Roman mythology

Venus was believed to have worn a garland of myrtle when she rose from the sea, and when satyrs tried to watch her bathing in the nude, she hid behind a myrtle bush. The myrtle has been a symbol of love from earliest times; the Romans offered its branches to Priapus, as tokens of their gratitude for successful sexual affairs, and the ancient Britons dedicated same to their goddess of love, always including myrtle in bridal bouquets and often planting myrtle trees near the home of newlyweds. Mentioned in Petronius's *Satyricon*, myrtle leaves, berries and flowers were used in many potions, including this medieval one recommended for sluggish women:

> The flowers and leaves of myrtle two handfuls infuse in two quarts of spring water, and a quart of white wine for 24 hours, and then distill them in a cold still and this will be a strong scent and tincture, and by adding more or less of the myrtle you may make it stronger or weaker as you please. This beautifies and mixed with cordial syrups is a good cordial and inclines those that drink it to be very amorous.

•MYRRH, FRANKINCENSE •

A bundle of myrrh is my well-beloved unto me; he shall lie all night betwixt my breasts.''

—Song of Solomon

Unfortunately, the aromatic herb sweet cicely *(Myrrhis odorata)*, common to Europe, is not the fabled myrrh of the Bible. Myrrh comes from the Greek name for perfume, but the Biblical myrrh, which is still used to make incense and perfumes, was probably obtained from the spiny shrub *Commiphora Myrrha*. Myrrh's age-old reputation is shown in the classical myth of Myrrha, a daughter of King Cinyras, whom the gods changed into a myrrh tree for having incestuous relations with her father, their child Adonis being born from the split trunk of the tree.

Frankincense has a similar erotic reputation and is also still used in incense and perfume. This Biblical aromatic generally comes from the Asian and African species *Boswellia Carteri*.

• NUX VOMICA •

"I, D'Annunzio," the Italian poet and lover reputedly told a cowering pharmacist, "though gifted to excess with organs and glands more suitable to a stallion, have reached my sixty-second birthday with a somewhat diminished capacity for the pleasures of the flesh. Without help from this compound which I have prescribed for myself, it would be difficult—though not impossible—to sustain my reputation as a lover without peer. Though strychnine may be injurious to lesser men, it has proved a boon to me as a virtuoso in the arts of love."

Thus spake Gabriele D'Annunzio in putting his seal of approval on the use of strychnine as an aphrodisiac. He was not the first nor last to do so, but "lesser men" (or more sensible men) should stay away from this lethal poison. Both strychnine and brucine are made from the poisonous seeds of the Southeast Asian tree *Strychnos nux vomica* and no matter how great their aphrodisiac powers, if they indeed have any, they're not worth risking. Small doses of strychnine to stimulate the nervous system and alert the senses, but such tonics as *Nux vomica* (made with strychnine and brucine) can bring on convulsions and death.

• ORCHIS •

The identity of the prodigious true male orchis of the Greeks and Romans has never been established. A shroud of mystery still surrounds this magic plant whose root the ancients dissolved in goat's milk. One drink of this goat milk, wrote an incredulous historian, and a man could perform as many as seventy consecutive times. Orchis is supposed to have been the main ingredient of Satyrion, the love food of those lecherous Satyrs of Greek mythology. It is a Greek word meaning "testicle," supposedly used because of the root's resemblance to that male organ. The Turkish *Orchis morio*, the truffle, mandrake and several other plants have been credited with being the male orchis of the ancients, but the identity of true satyrion has probably been lost for all time.

• PANSY •

Pansies are for lover's thoughts, the poet George Chapman wrote. Strangely enough, the pansy, which is still used as slang to describe a homosexual or an effeminate man, has something of a virile historical reputation. Frenchmen today, in fact, rub pansy oil on the eyelids to bring about love at first sight, and in times past it was rubbed on parts less highly visible.

• ROCKET •

The Romans Horace and Virgil both cited rocket *(Brasica eruca)* as a stimulating plant, and the latter poet claimed that it "gives to jaded appetite the spur." Because it was said to restore vigor to the sexual organs, rocket was consecrated to Priapus and sown around his phallic statue. In fact, the poet Columella wrote the following couplet about the practice: *"The eruca, Priapus, near thee we sow / To raise to duty husbands who are slow."*

• ROSES •

Roses remain the real flower of love, the true flower of Venus, as they have since time unremembered. Cleopatra carpeted a room with red rose petals so that their scent would rise above Mark Antony as he walked toward her; Nero used millions of the blooms to decorate a hall for a single banquet, rose water–saturated pigeons fluttering overhead to sprinkle the guests with scent, and Dioniysus, the Tyrant of Syracuse, filled his house with roses for the frequent compulsory orgies he held with the young women of his city. In fact, roses were so popular in ancient times that they actually became a symbol of the degeneracy of later Roman emperors, and it took the Church, to which the rose became a symbol of purity, to rescue it from oblivion during the Dark Ages. According to one ancient story, a number of noble Romans were suffocated under tons of rose petals dropped on them during one of Emperor Heliogabalus's orgies. The Romans loved the flower so much that they imported bargefuls of rose petals and hips from Egypt, where the growing season was longer.

The Roman expression *sub rosa* (privately, in strict confidence) is said to evolve from the legend that Cupid gave Harpocrates, the God of silence, a rose as a bribe to hush up the love affairs of Venus. In fact, the Romans believed in the flower's powers so fervently that they used rose water in their fountains. But then the Greek physician Galen had long before used a full pound of rose oil in a facial cosmetic he invented, and attar of roses still remains a much valued cosmetic ingredient to this day.

For centuries the rose has been employed to invoke love in some rather strange ways. Persian women thought that rose water was a philtre that would bring back straying lovers; one old Chinese love recipe drunk during the "fourth month" rose festivals consisted of prunes, sugar, olives and rose petals; colonial ladies made "rose tipple" to stimulate their lovers by marinating rose petals in brandy; the Irish add black currant beans and dried rose hips when brewing a bracing tea; and the

French still use rose water as an eye wash. Then we have Napoleon's empress Josephine, who, when her teeth turned bad, habitually carried a rose in her hand with which to cover her mouth when she laughed.

Many are the love recipes and potions employing the sensuous bloom, encompassing everything from baked roses to rose mince-meat pie. A flower that is rich in vitamin C (*Rosa rugosa* hips sometimes have twenty-five times the amount of vitamin C of citrus fruits), the rose also yields a syrup that was a staple of medieval apothecaries. Wild roses, more fragrant and nutritious than cultivated varieties, are best used in the many rose recipes one can choose from even today, these including rose petal salad, rose vinegar, rose bowl punch and confections like candied roses.

• SARSPARILLA •

True sarsparilla (*Smilax officianalis*) is related to the asparagus (see Course Fourteen) but isn't widely cultivated in the United States. The same legends surround its roots and asparagus; Mexican Indians, for example, have long used the roots of the vine in a concoction they believe cures impotence. In 1939, it was discovered that the sarsparilla root contains large amounts of testosterone, and today much of the male sex hormone manufactured commercially comes from the plant. Testosterone has been used for everything from increasing the size of the male organ to restoring hair to bald heads. The tea made from one or two teaspoons of the root is simmered slowly in a pint of water for five minutes and sipped slowly, the liquid held in the mouth for a time so that it can be absorbed into the buccal mucous lining of the mouth and better assimilated.

• SATYRION (See Orchis) •

• SAW PALMETTO •

The scrub or saw palmetto, found from South Carolina to Florida and Texas, is a small stemless palm sometimes cultivated for ornament. *Serenoa repens*, named for the American botanist Sereno Watson, bears one-half-inch long egg-shaped black berries that are eaten as a tonic. The berries are supposed to increase sperm in males, among other benefits, and some women have claimed that they increase the size of their breasts.

• SENSITIVE PLANT •

Mimosa pudica, the hairy sensitive plant, which might be taken to resemble the female pudendum, has achieved some reputation as an aphrodisiac. The *Ananga Ranga* gives the following unorthodox prescription employing it:

> The holy sage Vatsyayana Muni hath declared that whosoever will take the powder of sensitive plant, the root of green lotus-flowers, the *Bassia latifolia*, and barley flower; and, after mixing it up with some of his own Kama-salila (sperm) will apply it as a sectarian mark to his forehead, such a one will subdue the world of women, and she who looks upon his brow cannot fail to feel for him the most eager desire.

The sensitive plant is so called because its leaves will fold together with sufficient irritation or cloudy weather—this representing one of the most remarkable cases of physiological response in the plant kingdom. Sometimes called "humble plant" or "touch-me-not," one enthusiastic writer tells us that "the natives of the Amazon saturate its leaves with the root juices and plaster them to the soles of their feet or over their breasts to give them extended sexual power orgasm after orgasm." Soul food from the soles again.

• SOUTHERNWOOD •

A sprig of southernwood placed under the bed was believed by our forefathers to make what went on above quite lively. *Artemisia abrotanum*, one of the wormwoods (but not the species used in making potent and dangerous absinthe), is also called "old man," possibly because it was thought to do old men some good when placed under *their* beds. In medieval France, babies were rubbed with southernwood juice so that they'd never feel cold (see also Artemisia).

• THISTLE •

The ancient Greeks regarded the common thistle as highly as they did fleawort and used it in the same ways. So we see that even the most maligned of plants (thistle a word used even more contemptuously than weed) has its uses in the scheme of things. Trouble is there are so many genera and species commonly called thistle that nobody can pinpoint to which one the Greeks referred. Rabelais does, however, allude to *panic-*

aut, a species of thistle, as a means with which a woman can irritate her
lover's penis, this urtication or stinging inflaming the organ with passion.
Nettles have also been used in this way, for better or worse.

· TREES ·

Trees in general have in the last year or so have become the rage of
Tout Paris, the designation given to France's top socialites. "Tree
strength" is a new health fad said to increase one's sexual prowess. Men
and women simply strip to the waist and hug the trunks of trees with all
their might. Hopefully, the resin "seeps into the body" and gives one
"special powers." Though this method is highly recommended by Madame Marie-Louise Raguet, France's most noted "healer," we advise no
one to try same in a public park.

· TURNERA APHRODISIACA ·

As its name implies, this Mexican and African plant, commonly
known as damiana and scientifically named by Linnaeus in honor of
William Turner, author of the *New Herbal* (1551), has been widely recommended by laymen and scientists. Distributed throughout tropical
America, the plant is believed to be effective in treating impotency and is
supposed to have a tonic effect on the genitals and nervous system. Long
ago, the Aztecs used the leaves of damiana as an aphrodisiac. One contemporary writer recommends "one or two heaping tablespoons, steeped
for five minutes" in a pint of water. "Many women find a cup of damiana
tea taken an hour or two before intercourse helps them to get really im-
mersed in the sex act," she reports. "Both men and women have reported
that a cup of the tea with a little honey...tends to encourage amorous
dreams." A commercial liqueur made from damiana, called "Liqueur for
Lovers," can be purchased in the United States.

· VIOLET ·

Gather violets during the final quarter of the moon, writes the medieval
philosopher Albertus Magnus, and all your love wishes will come true. But
then Magnus was enthusiastic about anything gathered during the final
quarter of the moon. Violets, at least, are used in many delicious recipes,
which include violet syrup, candied violets and even a violet bombe made

with candied violets, ice-cream and whipped cream. And a walk in the moonlight can work wonders for anyone, with the proper company.

• YOHIMBE •

Tea made from yohimbe bark *(Corynanthe yohimbe)* has often been recommended for its aphrodisiac qualities. Sometimes ascorbic acid (vitamin C) is added to the potion, which is supposed to heighten sexual pleasures for both male and female. Says one incredulous user: "During sex, lovers feel as though their bodies were dissolving and merging into one another. Orgasm under the influence of yohimbe is beyond belief."

COURSE SEVENTEEN

Herculean Herbs And
Spices For Various Vices

Medea gather'd the enchanted herbs
That did renew old Aeson.
—Shakespeare, *The Merchant of Venice*

Herbs and spices yield to no class of foods in the aphrodisiac cookery. "Make haste, my beloved, and be thou like to a roe, or to a young hart, upon the mountains of spices," we read in the Bible; "I have perfumed my bed with myrrh, aloes, and cinnamon. Come let us take our fill of love till morning; let us delight ourselves with love." Traditionally associated with love, herbs and spices were included throughout history, and often excessively, in everything from the preparation of stimulants to magic potions. They were used as offerings to the fertility gods, amulets to wear or bedeck the bridal bed, and in ointments said to heaten and enlarge the sex organs. One French gourmet, Renouard de Villayer, even devised a spice clock in 1600, pressing a memorized sequence of different spices into the grooves at the dial hour-marks so that when he awakened at night, he or his bedmate could reach out with a wetted finger, touch the groove nearest the hour hand and then put his finger in his mouth "to taste what time it was."

The early Egyptians probably began using herbs and spices to flavor foods, and the Romans, who thought spices so valuable that they'd gladly trade a slave for a sack of pepper, raised cooking with condiments to an art. Yet as delicious and stimulating as their love dishes were, the people of Rome never for a moment doubted that they were potent, because the herbs therein were *magic*; Romans planted herbs around the phallic statues of Priapus and sprinkled herbs by moonlight, just as Seneca has the sorceress in *Medea* do.

Eastern peoples felt no different about condiment power, but their superstitions were based on a science of sorts. The Hindus, for example, were aware that a diet based as largely as their own on spices irritated the urogenital tract, causing sexual stimulation of sorts. Largely vegetarian, the Hindu placed more faith than most in herbs and spices, as the many herb recipes cited in the *Kama Sutra* clearly indicate, and in fact, every Hindu wife was trained in the art of aphrodisiac cooking with herbs. Shaykh Nefzawi's Arabian manual of love, *The Perfumed Garden*, indicates that the Arabs, those ancient monopolizers of the spice trade, felt even more strongly about love herbs. Among the numerous recipes given therein, we find one called "A Prescription for Increasing the Dimensions of Small members and for making them Splendid." The member is "vigorously rubbed with the mixture; it will then grow large and brawny, and afford to the woman a marvellous feeling of voluptuousness." And if a woman didn't want to go to such lengths for length (and here again the rubbing is as important as the ingredients) there were other simpler herb recipes.

Ming Dynasty Chinese used aphrodisiac herbs so often that their recipes sometimes surpassed the ridiculous. Wrote Tung Hsuan Tzu in *The Art of the Bedchamber:* "Obtain 3 fen [0.36 grams] of top quality *jou ch'ung jung* [a Chinese herb] and two fen of top quality *hai tsoa* [a kind of seaweed] and grind them into powder. Find a white dog born in the First Moon of any year. Use the secretion of its liver to mix the powder into a form of paste. Apply the paste to your jade-stem [penis] three times. At dawn the following day draw some fresh water from the well and wash it off. *Your jade-stem will definitely grow three inches longer.*" One of our researchers tried this (without a dog born in the First Moon), tape measured the results and swears it doesn't work, but if anybody still has faith in such unorthodox methods, consider the Chinese sulfur ribbon treatment—which seems like it would *delete* three inches from the jade-stem. Chinese women actually made sulfur ribbons for their lovers, using a length of raw silk about a foot long and an inch wide which was sewn into a narrow tube and filled with herbs and sulfur powder. Then the fair maiden employing the ribbon would circle the root of her lover's penis with it just before lovemaking time, binding it tightly. The man's urge to discharge was supposedly lessened by the binding and the sulfur powder was believed to provide sensations equally pleasureable to both partners.

Europeans were no less eccentric when it came to using condiments for love. One fifteenth-century German emperor, for example, ordered that all his women be rubbed with different spices "so that he could choose the one whose breath smelt most of tarragon, or coriander," etc., depending on his tastes at the moment. Miraculous tales of herb power were commonplace in Europe; Rabelais repeats a yarn spun by Pliny of "that Indian, who, thanks to a certain herb, could diddle it seventy times a day," and in *A Midsummer Night's Dream* Shakespeare describes a "powerful herb, the juice of which on sleeping eyelids laid will make man or woman madly dote upon the next live creature that it sees."

By the time of Louis XIV, the French were perfuming their food with spices so madly that objections were beginning to be heard. They believed strongly that the right combination of spices and herbs produced unbelievable effects. Madame DuBarry favored ginger and other ladies took to rubbing their skin with cinnamon bark as they had heard Arabian maidens did. All the English herbals at least suggested the aphrodisiac effects of herbs, and in such works as *The Squire of Baudricourt* we learn that "aromatic herbs and aphrodisiac recipes...renew weakened organisms; they bring back to life exhausted feelings and permit man to enjoy for a long time those endowments of strength so dear."

In modern times, the feeling has been much the same. "Condiments" wrote the psuedonymous Dr. Jacobus X in his *The Genital Laws* (1900), "exert on the generic appetite a positive influence, due to the congestive action which they produce on the pelvic organs. Pepper, mentioned by Dioscorides, cinnamon, vanilla, mace, pimento (and especially the small red pimento), savory, celebrated in the Priapeiae, and rocket, which according to Columella, '*excitat ad Venerem tardis,*' together with nutmeg and mustard: these are the principal." Perhaps few scientists would agree entirely with Dr. X today, but the fact remains that the age-old belief lingers on. Indeed, French, Italian and Spanish cookery is still largely based on the ancient theory that herbs and spices act as sexual stimulants, and Americans are putting more spice in their lives every year; the American Spice Trade Association reports that our consumption of spices, herbs and vegetable seasonings totaled 386 million pounds in 1971, which is an increase of nearly 42% in less than a decade.

As noted, herbs alone are recommended in many oriental recipes to improve virility, as cures for frigidity and "to increase a man's dimensions." In the West, however, herbs and spices have mainly been regarded as flavorings for foods and most continental cookbooks will indicate their best use. Again we advise that these condiments, along with their spicy histories, be employed in conventional dishes and not in the unfamiliar ones cited, which are presented mainly to spice up conversation. Following is a partial list of herbs and spices that have been included in aphrodisiac recipes through the ages. Other herbs have been covered in preceding chapters because they've been commonly used in the love cookery as plants and flowers, rather than as seasonings. Of the list below only the most prominent can be treated in any detail:

Allspice	Chervil	Hyssop	Rosemary
Angelica	Cinnamon	Kava	Saffron
Aniseed	Clove	Kola	Sage
Basil	Coriander	Licorice	Savoury
Bay Laurel Leaf	Cotton Root	Marjoram	Sweet Flag
Benzoin (spicebush)	Cubeb Peppers	Mint	Tansy
Borage	Cumin	Mugwort	Tarragon
Cà-Cuông	Curry	Nutmeg	Thyme
Calamint	Dawamesc	Orchis	Tonika
Capers	Dill	Paprika	Tumeric
Capsicum	Fo-Ti-Tieng	Pepper	Valerian
Cardomom	Gilly Flower	Peppermint	Veronica
Caraway	Ginger	Pimento	Wormwood
Celandrine	Harital		

• ALLSPICE •

Allspice, or pimento *(Pimenta officialis)*, is the dried unripe berry of an aromatic twenty to forty foot West Indian tree generally grown in Jamaica and should not be confused with pimientos, the fruits of certain *Capsicum* garden peppers (see Course Fourteen). Allspice has long been regarded and feared as an aphrodisiac, an instance of the latter reaction being found in the order pious Peter the Venerable gave to the monks under his charge at Cluny in 1132 forbidding them to eat pimento because it was "provokative to lust." Allspice takes its name from the fact that the one berry smells and tastes something like cinnamon, nutmeg and cloves combined. It has a great many uses in the cookery. Not to be applied to the squeamish male is the external "penis plaster" once made from it in China. The Chinese mixed pimento, pepper and boiled mallow and used it to moisten poultices of rice-flour, which they troweled on the male organ. This was said to be an excellent cure for impotence.

• ANISEED •

Hailing from the Middle East, anis or aniseed, distilled, makes the pernod long heralded as an aphrodisiac drink. A versatile herb, its seeds are used in sweets, cakes, as a garnish in salads, as a flavoring in fish stews and even in certain perfumes. Says the *Kama Sutra* of aniseed: "Reduced to a fine powder and softened with honey...the applications of this paste to the lingam prior to intercourse will enable you to produce orgasm in the woman and she will submit to your will."

• BASIL •

There is an Italian superstition that basil, which symbolizes love, doubles the size of the male organ, which may partially account for the heavy use of this herb in Italy. The aromatic herb is also employed in voodoo love magic ceremonies, in which it is associated with Erzulie, the Haitian sex goddess. The dried tips and leaves of the plant are generally rubbed to a powder and used to flavor soups, salads and teas. Italian country maidens often stand a pot of basil in their windows as a signal to their lovers that the coast is clear—this superstition possibly connected with Boccaccio's story of Isabella, who placed her slain lover's head in a pot, planted basil on top and watered the herb with her tears. Basil has many such customs and superstitions associated with it. The early Greeks and Romans, for example, believed that one had to curse when sowing it to insure germination. Brahmins in India still regard the plant as sacred and their women pray to a basil plant every day. Basil takes its name from the Greek *basilikos*, royal, because it was believed to have been used in making royal perfumes.

• CHERVIL •

This parsley-type herb, fresh or dried, forms the titillating flavoring in many aphrodisiac recipes, including salads, soups and sauces. It also is an ingredient of *fines herbes*, a combination of finely chopped herbs used for flavoring many foods (see also Skirret; Course Fourteen).

• CURRY POWDER •

Contrary to popular notion, curry powder is not an herb but a blending of various ingredients used for seasoning foods and making curry—a pungent East Indian dish composed mainly of vegetables, onions, meat or fish. Both the powder and the hot dish made from it have age-old reputations as aphrodisiacs. Indian curry powder usually includes cardamom seed, coriander seeds, cumin, garlic, ginger, mustard seeds, tumeric and vinegar.

• DAWAMESC •

Another spicy recipe using several herbs, this fabled Algerian aphrodisiac dish is made from cardamom, cinnamon, cloves, hemp, musk, nutmeg, oranges, pine kernels, and pistachio nuts.

• FO-TI-TIENG •

Legend has it that the Chinese herbalist Li Chung Yun was 256 when he died in 1933, just after taking his twenty-fourth wife. Moreover, he had all of his own hair and teeth and looked about fifty. Whether the story is true or not is debatable (one writer says that "it is a matter of record with the Chinese government that Li was born in 1677"), but there is no doubt that the venerable vegetarian heartily recommended Fo-ti-tieng for those desiring a long life marked with sexual vigor. Several scientists, including the French biochemist Jules Lepine, have found an alkaloid in the leaves and seeds of this low-growing plant of the pennywort family *(Hydrocotyle Asiatica minor)* that they claim has a rejuvenating effect on the nerves, brain cells and endocrine glands. The Indian sage Nanddo Narian, then 107 himself, informed his faithful that Fo-ti-tieng (which means "the elixir of long life" in Chinese) contained "a missing ingredient in man's diet without which we can never control disease and decay." Others have observed that ½ teaspoon of the herb in a cup of hot water will remove wrinkles and increase sexual energy, larger doses acting as an aphrodisiac. So off to the jungle marshes of the Asian tropics, where the herb is found. And remember, too, Li Chung Yun's more general (and better) advice: "Keep a quiet heart, sit calmly like a tortoise, walk sprightly like a pigeon, and sleep soundly like a dog." Also, said the sage, eat only food that grows above the ground, with the exception of ginseng root (for which see Course Eighteen).

· MINT, PEPPERMINT ·

According to early writers, mint leaves left potential lovers in mint condition, "stirring up the mind and taste to a greedy desire." There are many varieties of the plant, including the pungent peppermint used in making Creme de Menthe and cordials. Fresh mint has been highly regarded as a sauce for lamb, just as mint jelly is today. The versatile mints flavor many drinks, including juleps and tea, as well as candies and chewing gum. Peppermint oil was mentioned by Aristotle as an aphrodisiac, and, in fact, he forbade the use of wild mint *(Mentha sativa)* by the soldiers of Alexander the Great because he felt it so aroused them erotically that it took away all their desire to fight ("make love, not war"). In those days mint tea was made strong: one pint of boiling water was left standing for one minute and then poured over one ounce of the leaves.

· MUSTARD ·

Frederick the Great believed mustard did so much for his masculinity that he invented a drink made with powdered mustard, champagne and coffee. The history of hot mustard as an aphrodisiac is a long one. Rabelais, for example, writes that his lusty Demisemiquaver friars: "began their meal with cheese, ending it with mustard and lettuce, as Martial tells us the ancients did. As each received a dishful of mustard after dinner, they made good the old proverb: *Mustard after dinner/ Is good for saint and sinner.*"

"The rougish mustard," as it has been called, is made by adding tumeric to the mustard plant's black and white seeds. Indispensible to the American hot dog, an erotic sight to some in its own right, mustard has been used for some unusual mustard plasters indeed. Davenport notes that "Gesner and Chappel cured an atony of the virile member of 3 or 4 years duration by repeated immersions of that organ in a strong infusion of mustard seed." Most men would no doubt dispense with such dippings for a frank with mustard and sauerkraut.

· NUTMEG ·

Nutmegs "which have passed through the digestive canal are irresistible aphrodisiacs," Reinhold Gunther wrote in *Kulturgeschichte der Liebe.* The greyish brown nut of the Indian and East Indian nutmeg tree is used grated in many recipes, and is still regarded highly as an aphrodisiac in the Orient. The Chinese favor the love spice in certain teas and the Arabian Yemenites consume large amounts to increase virility. It is said that U.S. prison inmates today use nutmeg for pepping up their potency. Toulouse-Lautrec went to the extreme of carrying his own miniature grater and nutmeg cloves in order to flavor his port in Parisian bordellos, and though he was no great beauty, the ladies all loved him for his spectacular sexual prowess.

• PEPPER •

Peter Piper picked a peck of prodigious paradisical peppers, the old tongue-twister might just as well say. The berry of *Piper nigrum,* the tropical vinelike pepper plant (not to be confused with the *Capsicum* garden peppers that Peter actually picked) has certainly made many a Peter potent over the years. The ancient Greeks, for instance, employed powdered pepper mixed with nettle-seed as a nostrum for the promotion of frequent copulation, and the *Kama Sutra* includes black and long pepper in many of its love recipes.

Among the Chinese, a certain infusion of cubeb pepper leaves *(Piper cubeba)* was said to do practically everything—produce desire, strengthen the member, rear huge erections and even act as a prophylactic against gonorrhea! Similarly, Matico leaves *(Piper angustifolium)* has long been used by the Peruvian Indians as a sex stimulant, and kava-kava *(Piper methysticum)* root is used for a stimulating drink as well as in a salve that is applied to a woman's clitoris to make it feel warm and tingly during oral love when saliva activates the resin in the kava.

Medieval Europeans wholeheartedly believed that pepper inflamed the passions. One custom book of an order of nuns proscribed its use for this reason, and Davenport reports, that both "Tourtello and Peyrible assure us that pepper is a provocative to veneral pleasures." It is interesting to note that Keats, one of the most romantic of poets, used the hot stuff to pepper his tongue and thus revive his palate—which surely needed reviving from all the wine he drank. Pepper is still the world's most important spice and is well-regarded for pepping up potency throughout the world, but it should be remembered that both black and white varieties lose much of their flavor shortly after being ground. Which is why one should have fresh pepper and a peppermill on the table when planning on using pepper for an aphrodisiac meal. Americans use more pepper annually (50 million pounds) than all other seasonings combined. Here we prefer black pepper, whereas in Europe the white variety is the best seller.

• PEPPERMINT (See Mint) •

• PIMENTO (See Allspice) •

• ROSEMARY •

This flowering shrub has contributed its dried leaves and stems to many aphrodisiac recipes, and oils from its leaves and flowers figure in numerous love potions and perfumes. Bouquets of rosemary, "emblematical of manly virtues," were once presented to bridegrooms on their wedding mornings and bridal beds are still bedecked with the flowers in certain European countries to ensure conjugal bliss. Rosemary symbolizes remembrance, and Shakespeare had Ophelia present a bunch to Hamlet, perhaps to remind him of their meeting on St. Valentine's day when the melancholy Dane: "Let in the maid, that out a maid/ Never departed more."

• SAFFRON •

Saffron costs about $400 a pound today, making it the world's most expensive aphrodisiac spice. This is primarily because it takes 4,000 blossoms of the autumn crocus (*Crocus sativa*), or 225,000 of its hand-picked stamens, to make *one ounce* of saffron. But luckily a little goes a long way, for the spice has been coveted by gourmets and lovers since the Arabs introduced it to Spain in the eighth century A.D. Even before then saffron was used by the Phoenicians to flavor the moon-shaped love cakes dedicated to Astoreth, their goddess of fertility.

• SAGE •

He that would live for aye
Must eat sage in May.
—Old English proverb

The leaves of sage, a three-foot-high herbaceous evergreen shrub, are still used as a condiment, for stuffings and for a tonic tea. Oils from the entire plant serve to perfume soaps. Sage, a favorite of Marcus Aurelius, has figured in love and youth potions since earliest times, as is illustrated by the Roman saying "Why should a man die who has sage growing in his garden?" Sage "strengthens the sinews," said the ancients and the herbalist John Gerard contended that it "taketh away shakey trembling of the members," all members included. The flavorsome leaves, incidentally, were a favorite of Charles Dickens, who loved them best with the roast goose he made so famous in "A Christmas Carol" (see Course Ten).

• THYME •

"A notable herb of Venus," one writer says of thyme, and it has indeed been much valued over the years for its ability to "stir-up courage in ye conjuction." The Egyptians praised thyme, as did the Greek physician Dioscorides, that excellent Roman cook Apicius, and the knowledgeable Celsus. Medieval Europeans believed that soup flavored with thyme provoked lustful desires and the Benedictine monks still use it as an ingredient in their famous stimulating liqueur. The pungent aromatic herb is today an ingredient of perfumes as well as a flavoring for soups, sauces and salads.

• WORMWOOD (See Course Eighteen and Artemisia, Course Sixteen) •

COURSE EIGHTEEN
Musk, Civet, Mandrake and Ginseng: Today's Big Four "100,000 Volt" Aphrodisiacs

The strength of the horse, the mule, the goat and the ram, moreover, the strength of the bull ginseng bestows on thee... This herb will make thee so full of lusty strength that thou shalt when thou art excited, exhale heat as a thing on fire!
—The Artherva Veda

No one can say with authority that they'll get anyone so excited as to "exhale heat as a thing on fire," but musk, civet, mandrake and ginseng are certainly the four aphrodisiacs with the most clout these days, according to nationwide sales, and these "100,000 volt potions" surely rate special attention from all those of "a charmingly lecherous mind."

Musk oil presently ranks next to ginseng as the most heralded and desireable of the Big Four—even at up to $6.50 an ounce. Heralded it decidedly is. YES WE HAVE MUSK OIL! proclaim signs at cosmetic counters all over the land. In thousands of newspaper and magazine ads the unsavory substance is Barnumized as BEWITCHING, INTOXICAT-

ING, HYPNOTIC, EXOTIC, HAUNTING, MYSTERIOUS, ERO-
GENOUS, MYSTICAL, ALLURING, PASSION PRODUCING. "One
thing is certain—musk oil is the most popular fragrance in this country,"
Time reports authoritatively. "A Nation Goes Wild Over A New Perfume," headlines the *Wall Street Journal*. "Can a scent be both worldly
and simple?" *Vogue* rhapsodizes. "Subtle and direct? Completely natural
and yet...steal the scene? It can and it's musk." Musk has indeed become a magic word; its very name is an àphrodisiac of sorts.

Ironically, our lust for musk might well endanger the environment,
and not because it's so passion producing that it will overpopulate the
globe, either. Of the some 300 animal species man has zonked and the
971 we've driven toward extinction down the past three centuries, only a
few have been sacrificed for sex. But Rudolph the Rednosed Reindeer
had better watch out; he has good cause to pout for just this reason. Anyway, Rudolph's relative, the Asian musk deer of the Himalayas, is in
considerable danger of extinction if the latest craze for musk oil persists.

Used as an aphrodisiac in one love philtre or another for centuries,
musk is a pungent substance found in the sex glands of the twenty-inch-
high musk deer that roams the Himalayan and Atlas ranges and is in
point of fact a kind of innocuous "Bambi with tusks." The best quality
comes from Tibet, where great yellow hunters take it from the golf-ball-
sized, hair-covered scent glands beneath the animal's stomach. Male
musk deer secrete musk to attract females, which undoubtedly led to the
belief that the substance would work similarly for both male and female
humans. Just a twenty-two-ounce container of the decidedly foul-smell-
ing stuff requires the killing of up to thirty deer (the musk sold in pod or
grain form commands $4000 a pound, five times the price of gold) so it's
easy to see why the fabled potent midget is endangered.

Real musk is used as an additive and fixitive in perfumes to bind and
modify them and make their flowery scents cling, to keep their odors
true and impede evaporation. Thought to impart an aphrodisiac quality
to perfumes, too, it is so valued because of both the musk deer's connection with sex and pleasure and musk's funky animal odor. Other animal
secretions have been prized for the same reasons, including the well-
known ambergris of the sperm whale and the civet excretion from the
civet cat of Asia, Africa, and the East Indies.

In Ethiopia today these civet cats are raised commercially in cages. According to folklore, when the excretion is wanted, they are whacked on
their noses with rods poked through the cage bars, rage making their
genital scent pouches fill up so that they can be scraped for the foul smelling natural civet that is purchased by perfume factories. Some consider
such treatment of this first cousin of the mongoose cruel, to say the least;

the 28,000 member Society of Animal Rights, Inc. recently called for a boycott of Chanel No. 5 because it uses civet obtained from the two-foot-long cat. However, a team of U.S. scientists just last year visited a village near Addis Ababa, Ethiopia to investigate the situation and found no evidence of cruelty. Dr. Kenneth Bovée associate professor of medicine in the School of Veterinary Medicine at the University of Pennsylvania, pointed out that only the male cats are captured—with a net or by hand as they dart from their burrows—and that they are kept in stick cages eighteen inches wide by four feet long. The cats are well fed and cared for, if only because each is valued at about $50 (a fifth of the average villager's annual income), and "the animals live as well as the people."

Apparently, the civet is really collected quite differently from the way the old horror tales have it—at least in Ethiopia. First, a stick is inserted into the cage. The civet grabs it with his teeth, and then the animal's rear legs are held by a worker while the oil is removed from an external sac in the genital area with a spatula carved from an ox horn. Ethiopia exports about a ton (or $1 million worth) of civet oil a year. "The oil has been used for centuries," Dr. Bovée says. "It is considered an aphrodisiac and is thought to have medicinal properties in addition to being used in perfume. The villagers sometimes put a teaspoon in their coffee if they are sick." Among many others, Shakespeare must have been thinking along the same lines when he wrote in *King Lear*, "Give me an ounce of civet, good apothecary, to sweeten my imagination."

Although today's musk fad, like that of civet, was inspired by an increasing desire among consumers for "organic" products, the "musk oil" now accounting for $12 million or more in annual U.S. sales is actually artificially made from petroleum and other substances. Nobody is angry about this—least of all the male musk deer—but it does irritate some grumpy entrepreneurs. "The product they're palming off as musk oil just isn't musk oil at all," says one bonafide scent gland dealer. The artificial boom seems to have started when an enterprising chemist at Casswell-Massey, one of New York's oldest pharmacies, came across the petroleum formula in a nineteenth-century herbal and put a few bottles on the counter in the store's apothecary division. Says Ralph Taylor, Casswell-Massey's president, "Young people, who are looking for the natural in all areas, tried it, liked it, and the news spread like wildfire." So did overall store sales, which increased more than 10,000% for Casswell-Massey, and inevitably, a score of perfume manufacturers hopped on the bandwagon.

Even though the musk oil presently worn by Mss. and Misters is made from synthetics, the real thing may well be employed shortly, just as it is already used in the manufacture of other perfumes—which is why the musk deer had better keep jogging to keep his little legs in good shape.

Real musk has a long and odd history as an aphrodisiac. In *The Art and Science of Lovemaking,* psychologist Herman K. Wolf observes that the substance "was thought to be an aphrodisiac when rubbed vigorously into the penis—although the rubbing rather than preparation with which the rubbing was done probably produced the effect in question." An Arabian sage writes that "It is good [for the penis] to be perfumed with musk just before and after coitus," and the "lotus woman" (that is, the perfect woman) described in the *Kama Sutra* is blessed with sweat "the odor of musk."

Musk has been taken internally as well as externally and was once regarded as "almost an equal to ambergris for its aphrodisiacal qualities." Many instances are recorded of impotent men supposedly sexually revived by the substance. Victorian scholar John Davenport, author of *Aphrodisiacs and Anti-Aphrodisiacs* (1869) cites many cases, including a physician who claimed he "resuscitated the genital power in a man who had nearly completed his eightieth year." Davenport even gives a formula for a musk potion "whose virtue is indispensible," and as he is generally cautious in such pronouncements, we offer it for what it's worth, albeit untested and thus unrecommended by our love lab here. Instructs the good gray erotologist:

> *Take of amber, half a drachm; musk, two scruples; aloes, one drachm, and a half. Pound them all together, pour upon the mass a sufficient quantity of spirits of wine so that the liquor may cover it to the height of about five fingers' breadth. Expose this to sand heat, filter and distil it, close it hermetically, and administer it in broth in the dose of three or five drops. This liquor is also advantageous when mixed with syrup, prepared as follows:—Take of cinnamon water, four ounces; orange and rose water, each six ounces, and sugar candy the same.*

A scruple, for the unscrupulous wishing to try these recipes, is a unit of apothecary weight equal to 20 grams; a drachm is merely an archaic spelling of dram, which is a unit of apothecary weight equal to 60 grams, or ⅛ ounce; and aloes is a bitter purgative drug made from the juices of the chiefly African *Aloes* genus. All of these ingredients can be purchased from the numerous pharmacies specializing in apothecary products, such as New York's Casswell-Massey.

If Davenport's recipes make a big splash in your water-bed, then there's a chance you'll also be interested in the musk "Prescription for Increasing the Dimensions of Small Members and Making Them Splendid" cited in *The Perfumed Garden.* The remedy, in which the rub is also most likely in the rubbing, can be found in the introduction to Course Seventeen.

Today's synthetic musk has been described variously as smelling like "dirty sweat socks," "shoe polish" and "like plain hideous," the best adjectives to be found in its defense being "neutral" and "earthy." One New York Playgirl bunny, in fact, wears artificial musk oil because it seems to *repel* men (their advances are an occupational hazard which may not be covered by workmen's compensation) and as a result of such findings perfume manufacturers are starting to come out with strawberry and floral-scented variations on the original. Both men and women, however, are mainly wearing musk *au natural*, despite its disputed odor, dabbing a few drops on the wrists, temples, inside the elbows, behind the knees, etc., so that "the scent becomes part of the body chemistry."

There seems no end in sight to the musk mania as of this writing. Both sexes continue to pay outrageous prices for a putrid fuel for heating buildings rather than bodies, simply because the artificial petroleum product has been linked with the real musk which reputedly gave hypnotic powers to Cleopatra and Helen of Troy and was used by the Queen of Sheba "to drive King Solomon mad with desire." And if there is an end...according to Casswell-Massey: "Also available from the same 19th century book where we found the musk oil recipe is civet oil and ambergris oil, which we expect will follow shortly. Our chemists are even working on another old fragrance called Holy Smoke! which is supposed to be a sizzler." All we can say is that at least the little "Bambi with tusks" isn't being killed for the artificial stuff. The next formula to be marketed might even be $CH_3C_2(CH_2)_2SH$, or butyl mercaptan, or Night and Day, which true believers will continue to buy even when they find out that it's the chemical that gives the stink, or smell, or "exotic odor" to the redoubtable skunk.

Mandrake, which even surpasses musk in historical reputation, is also enjoying a strong comeback today. Ads for the root appear everywhere and our field workers have reported graffiti sprayed on subway cars reading "MAKE IT WITH MANDRAKE," which makes us wonder if such slogans weren't scribbled on the walls of Rome. For mandrake's history as an aphrodisiac can be traced back to Biblical times, the herb having been mentioned in both *Genesis* and *The Song of Solomon*. In the former reference (*Genesis* 30:14-17) we can see how valuable women thought the plant to be:

> And Reuben went in the days of wheat harvest, and found mandrake in the field, and brought them to his mother, Leah. Then Rachel said to Leah, Give me, I pray thee, of thy son's mandrakes.
>
> And she said unto her, Is it a small matter that thou hast taken my husband? And wouldest thou take away my son's mandrake also? And Rachel said, Therefore he shall lie with thee tonight for thy son's mandrakes.

And Jacob came out of the field in the evening, and Leah went out to meet him, and said, Thou must come in unto me, for surely I have hired thee with my son's mandrakes. And he lay with her that night.

And God harkened unto Leah, and she conceived and bore Jacob the fifth son.

Rachel must have highly prized mandrakes to allow her husband to spend the night with her own sister for a few, and the *Song of Solomon* shows that the roots were in great demand among men, too. The "Phallus of the field," as the ancient Egyptians called mandrake, is in reality a member of the potato family. It is popularly believed to be shaped like both the male and female figure, and in fact one ancient writer describes how medieval con men preyed on this belief.

Imposters carve upon these plants while yet green the male and female forms, inserting millet or barley seeds in such parts as they desire the likeness of human hair to grow on; then, digging a hole in the ground, they place the said plants therein, covering them with sand till such time as the little seeds have stricken root, which, it is said, would be perfectly effected within twenty days at furthest. After that, disinterring the plants, these imposters, with a sharp cutting knife, so dexterously carve, pare, and slip the little filaments of the seeds as to make them resemble the hair which grows upon the various parts of the human body.

Dudaim, which comes from a Hebrew word meaning, "pleasures of love," has been another name applied to the mandrake, and the Greeks often called Aphrodite, their goddess of love, "she of the mandrakes" or *Mandragoritis*. The Greeks also thought that Circe possessed the plant, a passage in the *Odyssey* telling of the infamous witch adding the "love apples" to her nefarious brews. Interestingly, the famed physician Dioscorides, who served as an army surgeon under Nero, used mandrake wine as a sedative in surgical operations and noted in his *Materia Medica* that it was used in love potions. But centuries later Celsius went much further, stating that after eating a little mandrake root even female elephants "are seized with so irresistable a desire for copulation, as to run eagerly, in every direction, in quest of the male." Such beliefs were echoed by Columella, who wrote: *"Let it not vex thee if thy teeming field/ The half-man Mandrake's madd'ning seed should yield."*

In ancient sex worship, the mandrake served both as a fertility and virility symbol. A woman who wore a male specimen around her neck was guaranteed to be made pregnant by her favorite lover, and women in childbirth, after having worn the root to lure a man into bed, then wore it again to ease the pains of labor. The dark-leaved, purple-flowered plant with its little yellow fruits was also highly touted as a tonic, a number of medicinal recipes employing it. So well-known was the half-man root that St. Hildegard of Bingen wrote in the twelfth century that "In mandragora the influence of the devil is more present than in other herbs; consequently man is stimulated by it according to his desires, whether they be good or bad." Macchiavelli, however, was much more enthusiastic about the love herb three centuries later in his comedy *La Mandragora*. "You must know" he wrote, "that nothing is so sure to make women conceive, as a draught composed of Mandragora. This is a fact which I have verified upon four occasions, and had it not been for the virtues of this plant, the Queen of France, as well as many noble ladies of that kingdom, would have proved barren."

Diverse medieval superstitions about mandrake became ingrained in the public mind and reinforced its reputation as a magic plant. Shakespeare recounts one such belief in *Romeo and Juliet* (Act IV, Scene 3) when he has Juliet say, "And shrieks like mandrakes' torn out of the earth,— that living mortals hearing them run mad," because it was "common knowledge" at the time that the mandrake shrieked when pulled from the ground and anyone hearing its cry cracked up. In order to gather the love-apple plant a man had to blow on a horn to drown out the shriek while pulling, or employ an animal to do the job. "Therefore they did tye some dogge or other living beast unto the roote thereof with a corde," one herbalist explained, "and in the mean tyme stopped their own ears for fear of the terrible shriek and cry of the mandrake. In whych cry it doth not only dye itself but the feare thereof killeth the dogg."

Another superstition that enhanced the mandrake's aphrodisiac reputation was the belief that it sprang up from under the gallows where criminals, especially rapists, ejaculated sperm or urinated at the instant they died. No such beliefs linger on today, but mandrake is still widely used as a love stimulant, even in the form of a modern drug called mandragorine. The roots themselves are sold all over the world, particularly in Italy and Greece, as remedies against impotence and infertility, and U.S. mail order sales remain high. Here the mayapple *(Podophyllum pelatum)* is sometimes called mandrake, but the true species is *Mandragora officianarum* of southern Europe, also known as "the devil's apple." Both of these species can be poisonous, so collectors should beware. In any case, it's highly unlikely that you'll find a mandrake with phallus and testicles clearly shown, or a "female mandrake" showing the ovaries. More likely your specimen will simply have thick tuberous roots divided into two leglike branches. As for its effects...well, potatoes are cheaper....

Ginseng, the last and most popular of today's "in" aphrodisiacs, enjoys the same reputation as mandrake, often for identical reasons, but it is far more expensive. Ginseng, which can cost up to $32 an ounce or $512 a pound for a piece of "heaven grade root," has surpassed even the truffle throughout history as a precious aphrodisiac; it has been sold in the past at $300 an ounce or $4800 a pound, which is probably the all-time record for a love food. One Chinese emperor reputedly paid $10,000 for a perfect man-figure ginseng root, or at least so the story goes. Similarly, it's said that Chairman Mao drinks a ginseng tea—made from $100-an-ounce ginseng root—at least three times a week. At any rate, the love herb (the Chinese also consider it an excellent hangover remedy) still sells briskly in oriental markets for $200 a pound and despite the protestations of modern pharmacologists, lovers throughout the world cling to the mystique of its so-called superpowers.

We mentioned earlier that Mae West and Cary Grant, among other Hollywood sex symbols, have reportedly experimented with ginseng and that dragon lady Madame Nhu carried it on her trip to America from Saigon in 1963. But then lovers have been fascinated by the "Man Plant" for over 5000 years. Like mandrake, the most potent ginseng roots are said to be shaped like a man's body, and the Chinese believe that even better results are obtained when the root is dug up at midnight during a full moon. The Chinese call ginseng, or goo-lai-san, the "elixir of life," "the herb that fills the heart with hilarity," and "the medicine of medicines." In fact, Chinese apothecaries prescribe the plant to this day for strength, virility and longevity, citing it as the number one botanical drug in their recent medical books. Ginseng is also touted as a cure for colds, constipation and inflammation of the urinary tract, and it's said to tranquilize, soothe throat and stomach, act as a painkiller, absorb bodily poisons, make the skin glow and lure girl friends and lovers from afar. All this in addition to its great sexual powers, which is said to have enabled men to procreate children at the age of seventy and over.

Ginseng roots are forked but bear little resemblance to exaggerated mail order advertisement drawings of the plant complete with perfectly formed legs, arms and penis. Small greenish flowers indicate that the roots can be dug. Ginseng lovers claim that the fabled herb tastes like licorice and adds a delightful flavor accent to tea, coffee and other beverages and dishes. The Chinese have traditionally chewed the root, worn it as a sexual amulet, and brewed it into a tea and spring tonic, but today ginseng is available in powder, capsule, honey, liquors, liquid and natural form. Even the plant itself can be ordered through the mail, all ready to be set out in your backyard or window box, but the shade-loving plant is difficult to grow and it takes five or six years for a well-formed root to develop.

An American species of ginseng (Panax quinquefolius) is in fact grown and gathered in this country, especially in the Ozarks and Appalachia. Diggers in the wild can earn from $33 to $44 per pound of dried root and our largest domestic dealer alone exports some 70,000 pounds of the herb annually. Such profits are nothing new, however, it being a matter of record that the first American ship to reach China in 1784, Major Samuel Shaw's *Emperor of China*, carried a cargo of the ginseng so dear to Chinese lovers. Before World War I, ginseng was one of the United States' chief money-making crops; 160,949 pounds of wild 'seng was exported in 1906.

Next to Imperial Chinese ginseng, available to only the most important officials, Korean ginseng has always been valued as the most potent variety by the Chinese, and taking advantage of this, the South Korean government recently announced that it will commission two chewing gum firms to manufacture a new flavor laced with the local sexy herb. But ginseng chewing gum cannot come near comparing with ginseng wine, connoisseurs say. This most expensive of Chinese wines is actually *kaoliang* (which in itself is as strong as vodka) with the roots of ginseng soaked in its cask for at least three years. The correct dosage, it's said, is to take a small glass as a nightcap regularly, but U.S. faddists claim that ginseng liqueur "produces the *total* organic high—especially after starving yourself for three days beforehand." If you can't obtain ginseng wine, but can lay hands on some amber, mandrake or ginseng root, here is an old French recipe for a love wine to be made at home: "In two pints of Chablis, crush an ounce each of vanilla beans, cinnamon sticks, dried rhubarb, and mandrake or ginseng. Let stand for two weeks, stirring daily. Strain through cheesecloth; add amber. Bottle. Use as an aphrodisiac."

Medical opinion is divided concerning ginseng as an aphrodisiac. According to the often beseiged Dr. Reuben, "prepared according to a strict recipe, it has many who vouch for its effectiveness," but the doctor hedges later when he reminds us that "The mind has such a dominant effect on sexual performance that often if a person believes a remedy works, it does." On the other side of the bed, U.S.C.'s Dean Edward S. Brady, president of the California Pharmaceutical Association, flatly rejects the herb. "The most it will do," he says, "is help your appetite. But a sexual stimulant it is not."

Meanwhile, back on the lathed ginseng farm, ginseng adherents are saying that "in the Man Plant exists a natural method of rejuvenation, of restoring vitality to depleted glandular organs by feeding them the mysterious...elements that ginseng has proven to contain." Someday, they contend, American scientists will find a miraculous drug in the herb and they cite the efforts of the Russians along these lines. "Recently," one writer observes, "Soviet scientists have isolated from the root three major components: panaxin, panaquilon and schingenin, which in combination strengthen the heart and nervous system and increase the flow of hormones. These Russian scientists also claim that the root gives off minute amounts of a unique type of ultraviolet radiation which stimulates the healthy growth of tissue especially in the endocrine system, and has a general healing and rejuvenating influence on the body. They call this subtle radioactive quality mitogenic radiation." In fact, the Russian researchers have made the fluid extract from Siberian ginseng (eleuthero) widely available to the public. They claim it has increased work endurance and mental efficiency in test subjects, brought high and low blood pressure under control in moderate cases and helped nervous disorders, including depression and chronic fatigue, and they are enthusiastic about using it to test such ailments as arteriosclerosis, diabetes and even acne.

Ginseng is available at most health food stores for anyone wanting to be mitogenically radiated and/or sexually inspired. Good grades can be had from $3 to $5 an ounce, but take care not to purchase the low-quality Japanese variety that has flooded the marketplace. For best effects, experts say one should chew a small piece of ginseng every four hours or so, saliva helping to activate its aphrodisiac qualities. However, most people prefer to make a tea from ginseng by boiling one teaspoon of the root in a pint of water for ten minutes. Not everyone agrees on its aphrodisiac effects, but, to our knowledge, nobody contends that the exalted herb will do either sex any harm—nor will any of the Big Four, especially if one rubs long or hard or gently enough.

COURSE NINETEEN

Bottoms Up But Beware:
Drinks For Naked Lovers

"Let him kiss me with the kisses of his mouth," exults the *Song of Solomon*, "for love is better than wine," yet the author of the Biblical love song reneges a bit later when he writes "drink, yea, drink abundantly, O beloved." The ambivalance shown by the poet is echoed by writers throughout history. In brief, it can be safely said that alcoholic drinks have been highly rated as an amatory aid, but only when taken in moderation.

Alcohol does lower inhibitions psychologically, inspiring Ogden Nash to observe that *Candy is dandy/ But liquor is quicker.* Physiologically booze causes blood to gorge the genitalia, among other effects, and this has led a number of scientists to vouch for its efficiency. Havelock Ellis, for instance, claims in his *Studies in the Psychology of Sex* that alcohol in its strongest forms is "above all" a "powerful sexual stimulant," particularly recommending "liqueurs, sparkling and heavy wines and many English beers." Even more specifically, the *Commonsense Book of Drinking* by Leon D. Adams cites the importance of booze to men. "Alcohol liberates existing desires that are normally held in check" Adams writes, "usually prolonging the erection and deferring climax at .10 to .15 blood alcohol level." As for women, there is some truth in the cynical old saw that the best aphrodisiac drink for a woman is that which she can be persuaded to drink the most of. At any rate, in an effort to make their partners more willing and able, both male and female have plied each other with an endless list of libido-loosening libations since the first mead was made by mankind. The most famous would include absinthe, apricot brandy, aquavit, armagnac, arrack, beer, benedictine, burgundy, champagne, chartreuse, ciders, cinnamon liquor, claret, cognac, curacao, gentian wine, kirsch, liqueurs of many kinds, madeira, port, sauterne, sherry and vodka. But the choices and combinations thereof are dynamic and are doubtless being ingeniously added to somewhere at this very instant.

Alcohol can loosen the libido, but too much of a good thing can be ruinous. In fact, Masters and Johnson have shown that overindulgence in alcohol is one of the major causes of impotence among U.S. males. Moderation is the one all-important secret behind any so-called aphrodisiac drink. "Coitus after a heavy bout of drinking is to be avoided," lovers are warned in *The Perfumed Garden*, and the Romans knew long before the Shaykh Nefzawi that too much alcohol impedes a lover, Martial counseling moderation several times, while Petronius wrote that he would certainly "cut down on wine" for a "fortifying diet."

Even such confirmed drinkers as Rabelais, who vowed "may a hundred devils trample me down if old drunkards do not outnumber old doctors," knew that "belly thumpers" should use alcohol wisely. Rabelais makes this point clear in several passages. "Bacchus, god of drunkards, is painted beardless and clad in women's clothes, an effeminate and ballockless eunuch," he writes in making his case for moderation. "The temperate drinking of liquors acts quite otherwise: the old proverb bears this out when it tells us that Venus takes cold without Ceres and Bacchus. Such was the opinion of the ancients...that Master Priapus [the phallic god of fertility] was born of Bacchus and Venus."

The seven stages of drunkenness have been defined as verbose, grandiose, amicose, bellicose, morose, stuperose and comatose; all glasses are best turned over upon reaching the third stage. "Alcohol taken in moderation will temporarily inhibit inhibitions and reduce anxiety, therefore acting as a sexual stimulant," Dr. Albert Ellis says, but this is only true, as he observes, when one eats, drinks and is merry—not moribund. Not too long ago, in fact, the late President Allende of Chile warned his countrymen that heavy drinking reduces virility and that if they didn't cut down he'd have to ration liquor. Allende's suspicions were confirmed by a recent American study of 17,000 alcoholics, which found that about 10% of the males among the group suffered from impotence, having a strong desire for sex but being unable to perform. The doctors who made the study found that none of their female patients complained of sexual inadequacy from drinking, leading them to believe that alcoholic impotence is a neurogenic disease.

In the following quick look at the hard core lore of hard liquor, wines and even "aphrodisiac" drinks like tea and a certain gunpowder brew, temperance should always be kept in mind. The best meal in the world, as Brillat-Savarin pointed out, is meaningless without the appropriate drink to accompany it, but is pointless (especially for the male) if both lovers fall asleep in bed. Only lustily aware can we sing with Rabelais:

> *Hail, meat! Praise sauce! And long live wine withal!*
> *Septembral juices grace our bacchanal*
> *To fill the paunch and elevate the cod.*

So-called hard liquor, the Dutch sexologist Van de Velde wrote, is the chief sexual stimulant among drinks. Others recommend wine—especially champagne—as a better choice, but liquor is certainly more potent physiologically. There are literally billions of choices available. In fact, H. L. Mencken wrote somewhere that a mathematician friend of his had calculated that about *eighteen billion* different mixed drinks could be prepared from the ingredients in a well-stocked bar. All of these can do their duty or damage one, from the *aqua ardens* or "ardent spirits" of medieval times to the *tanto krin* that the Russians still make with brine of alcohol and powdered reindeer antlers. Scotch, gin, pulque, vodka, kaoliang, bourbon—all liquors, in fact—have their supporters, as do mixed drinks like the martini, the julep, the Margarita, the Manhattan, the Suffering Bastard and a thousand others invented by people who, like W. C. Fields thought water "was a damn failure as a beverage." (Water, Fields said, was that vile stuff "fishes fornicate in.") We'd like to offer a good sound warning about drinking the more exotic of these mixed drinks, without sounding like one of those proverbial characters who gives good advice because he is too old to set a bad example. As the Scottish sage once said: "If a body could just find oot the exac' proper proportion and quantity that ought to be drunk every day, and keept to that, I veerily vow that he might leeve and luve forever, without dying at A', and that doctors and kirkyards would go oot of fashion." The trouble is that the risk is high while you're trying to find oot the exac' proper proportion.

The martini, honoring either the Martini and Rossi firm, or a now forgotten Italian or Spanish bartender named Martini, is a mixed drink with a particularly lascivious reputation. There are countless variations on it, including the *martini sandwich*, a dry martini between two glasses of beer. The classic dry martini ("Let's slip out of these wet clothes and into a dry martini," said Robert Benchley) is made by drinking a little vermouth, exhaling into the bowl of a cocktail glass and filling it with gin—after drinking same, no one cares about the missing olive, lemon twist or onion. James Bond, on the other hand, preferred at least "a drop of vermouth" in his martinis and Ernest Hemingway always stuck with a ratio of 11 to 1. As for the professionals, spirits specialist Robert Misch suggests a range of from 4 to 7 parts gin to 1 part vermouth, and one mathematically minded bartender recommends exactly 5.7 gin to 1.3 vermouth for "the perfect martini." Incidentally, vermouth, as we'll see shortly, may have more to do with the martini's sexual prowess than had previously been thought. In any case, the fortified wine flavored with herbs, barks and fruit peels has quite a reputation of its own. Versatile vermouth, used to make so many drinks, is a favorite aperitif in Europe, and in South America it's so admired that Argentinians and Brazilians refer to the cocktail hour as "the vermouth."

It is amazing to note how many mixed drinks have been named after actual persons—the Martini, Bloody Mary, Harvey Wallbanger, Gibson, Gimlet, Gin Rickey, Jack Rose, Rob Roy, Alexander and the Tom Collins, to name just ten. Even the words grog, hooch, kickapoo joy juice and, possibly, booze and cocktail owe their existence to real people. But the lore of hard liquor, as fascinating as it may be, has more of the bellicose and comatose than the amicose in it. It's true that liqueurs have quite a reputation. They were, in fact, invented as tonics made with brandy, sugar and various essences to revive the aging libido of France's Louis XIV. And, of course, absinthe, which we'll examine next, has been regarded as the most potent (and deadly) of all drinks. But the best advice for lovers is to take hard liquor in small portions, in cocktails as a soothing appetizer. Even mixed drinks employing tomato juice and milk are not as foolish as they sound. High-protein foods mixed with alcohol slow down the body's alcohol absorption rate. Take an egg in your beer and you'll be able to drink far more and far better than the voluptuous *vrouw* on the next stool, or the Lothario who has invited you up to see his still. Speaking of beer, incidentally, Chicago *Daily News* columnist Mike

Royko recently claimed that most mass-marketed domestic beers tasted "as if they had been passed through a horse." A panel he headed tested twenty-two domestic and foreign beers and awarded first prize to the German Würzburger brand, second to England's Bass Ale and third place to our little-known Point Special brew.

Absinthe provides the best example of just how deadly an aphrodisiac potion can be. The drink is made from various species of wormwood, *Artemisia absinthium,* the plant so named because it was dedicated to Artemesia, Greek goddess of the hunt and moon. Long prized for its aphrodisiac powers, the oil of wormwood (see Course Seventeen) can cause blindness, insanity and even death. For this reason absinthe was banned in Switzerland in 1908, in the United States four years later and in France in 1915.

Absinthe is still bootlegged in Switzerland and other places, though its sales are nowhere near those of the $100 million industry broken up when the brew was banned. Though most experts conclude that absinthe is dangerous, all agree that it is the most powerful of aphrodisiac drinks. Wormwood, its "secret ingredient," had often been lauded in the Middle Ages as a source of potency. Nicholas Flamel wrote that it was necessary, however, "to steep it for three days in the urine of a girl of sixteen years." But absinthe itself wasn't invented until 1790, when a French royalist named Dr. Pierre Ordinaire, hardly an ordinary man at all, fled France to Switzerland and began concocting it from a secret recipe that included the ingredients dried absinthium, Spanish anise, star anise, mintlike Melissa herb, coriander, camomile, Veronica, hyssop, persil and even spinach—steeping his mixture in 136 proof alcohol. Soon after Ordinaire's death his formula passed into the hands of French Major Henri Dubied and his son-in-law Louis Pernod, who recognized the aphrodisiac effects of the drink and established the world's first absinthe factory in Switzerland.

Since Dubied noticed how his mind became erotically excited after a few absinthes and that he experienced a "thrilling and most potent agitation in his genitals," almost no one has questioned the liquor's powers. Absinthe became France's favorite drink and was praised by Dumas fils, de Maupaussant, Anatole France, Verlaine, Rimbaud, Toulouse-Lautrec, Degas, Gaughin, Picasso and Van Gogh—the last artist drinking it in a concoction composed of five parts water to one part absinthe and one part black ink! Absinthe became best-known for its classic preparation, though. A lump of sugar was placed in a long-handled spoon with small holes in the bottom and your waiter poured ice-cold water through this drop by drop, both sweetening the bitter absinthe and making the blend so gradual that there was no separation of liquor and water.

The trouble was that many daredevils took their absinthe neat or combined it with other potent liquors. Absinthe freaks like the poet Verlaine and others gave the drink a bad press, and finally a number of vicious murders committed by an absinthe addict named Jean Lanfray in 1905 led to the French abolition of "the devil's liquor" ten years later. Drinkers had failed to heed the advice of authorities, one of whom wrote: "Those who experiment with absinthe will do well to remember that it has the curious property of doubling the effect of every drink that is taken after it, so that half a bottle of wine at the meal which follows it will be equivalent to a whole bottle." They paid, in varying degrees, the price of immoderation.

Yet there is no denying the aphrodisiac effects of wormwood, the most important ingredient of absinthe. Its medicinal properties were recognized by Hippocrates, Parcelsus, the Marquis de Sévigne and many more physicians and lovers throughout history. Scientists now believe that thujone ($C_{10}H_{16}O$) is the constituent of oil of wormwood that makes it so potent. "In my opinion it is the thujone in wormwood which acts as a brain stimulator and aphrodisiac," says U.S. chemist Dr. Samuel M. Pollack. "Thujone is definitely toxic. It is classified by our Government as a poison. Before the United States approves of any liquor formula, it must be *almost* 100 per cent thujone-free. Why do I say *almost*? Because vermouth also contains thujone. But when we use wormwood in vermouth, we extract it in wine and a low proof and we get a minute percentage of thujone—almost nil. Now, when wormwood is macerated 48 hours or longer in neutral spirits and then redistilled, the result is a high percentage of thujone. Thujone isn't soluble at low proof. The higher the proof, the more thujone."

No one knows, but perhaps the minute percentage of thujone in vermouth gives the ubiquitous martini its aphrodisiac reputation. At any rate, no other drink has been so widely acclaimed as absinthe. Ernest Hemingway wrote in one place, that "If you have anything wrong, this will cure it," and in another, "There is nothing like it." Certainly not the Anisette or Pernod that bartenders often attempt to foist off as absinthe substitutes with sex-stimulating properties. The latter, a greenish-colored, licorice-flavored liqueur named for the original manufacturer of absinthe, has taken the place of absinthe on the market. Pernod does not get a person drunk as quickly as absinthe, being 40-50% alcohol, but it tastes much the same. Except for the anise used to replace the banned oil of wormwood, it contains all the same ingredients, yet the essential thujone is conspicuously absent. Though it unleashes the libido by making the eye less critical and the will less obdurate, there is no proof that it is more an aphrodisiac than any liquor.

A Brazilian brew called *cachaca*, a white rum made from fermented sugar-cane juice, is probably the most popular aphrodisiac drink in South

America. Some 2000 brands, varying between 40 and 100 proof, are available and some of these are now being exported to Europe. "The poor man's blanket" (it costs only 8¢ a shot) bears brand labels reading Super Hot, Masturbation, In-And-Out, Behind The Balls, and Ball Breaker, to name but a few of the spiciest, and one bottle has a naked woman on the bottle—visible only after the *cachaca* has been drained. Swingers in Rio blend the brew with tropical fruits and nuts to make cocktails or *batidas* with names like Couples Joy, Bare Ass, Naked Twist, etc.

Used as a tonic for slaves more than four centuries ago, *cachaca* has a legendary reputation as an aphrodisiac, but then many aphrodisiac drinks of old would unquestionably be avoided by the most reckless of us. These certainly would include the early American love potion instructing that a girl wishing a young man to fall under her spell should "offer him a glass of beer, cider, or lemonade, into which she has stirred *a teaspoonful of her fingernails, which have been ground into powder.*" However much calcium said brew contains, it is less than unappealing. But then lovers drank each other's blood in medieval times and Bishop Burchard of Worms noted the even more loathsome practice of wives adding menstrual blood to their husbands' drinks. More appealing were medieval love potions made from flowerseeds, such as elecampane and vervain, the last brewed from the mistletoe berries we still kiss under Christmastimes (though it should be noted that mistletoe berries are poisonous). A matter of personal taste are drinks such as pulque, the national drink of Mexico, which is traditionally drunk while one snacks on "nutty flavored" maguey worms, these the larvae of a butterfly which bores into the maguey or agave plant that is the source of pulque.

The *Kama Sutra* even has something to say for *milk* as a powerful stimulant, "the milk of a white cow who has a white calf nestling beside her having excellent properties." Mouse's milk might also prove potent for someone's mouse, but as far as we know it is only used for scientific research—it sells at $10,000 a quart. Neither is there any evidence that Coca Cola® is very potent (though Salvatore Dali fills his swimming pool with it) but ordinary tea does come highly recommended. In other places tea has been considered an antiaphrodisiac to be avoided, just like coffee, which the Turks called "the black enemy of sleep and copulation." But as used in China, Japan and India, it may well make any boudoir boil. The "simplest" formula (untested here) calls for simmering two ounces of tea in a gallon of water for twenty-four hours. The resulting concentrate, a thick syrup, has been popular as an aphrodisiac in the Orient for centuries. Prostitutes there serve their clients one or two drops of the syrup mixed in a glass of perfumed and sweetened water with what are said to be spectacular results.

Still more unlikely, but possibly just as effective, was the gunpowder concoction used as a sex-stimulant on the American frontier. Into a mug of hot water was poured a large shot of rum and a teaspoon of black gunpowder. The hot rum, cowboys claimed, loosened the libido, and the microscopic crystals which remained in suspension in the booze after the gunpowder dissolved irritated the urethra or urinary tract, stimulating the erotic processes until the lovers were primed and fired. In short, it gave them a charge.

Fortunately, there are more salutary love drinks than gunpowder. Wine, doubtless the best of these, is becoming more popular every year in the United States (American adults downed an average of eighty-eight glasses of wine in 1972). Wine is the most aristocratic of alcoholic beverages and oenological love lore is the richest of all, the nectar of the grape whetting our taste buds instead of deadening them as liquor does. Some say that an alluring woman first discovered how to make wine, the story being that a member of ancient Persian King Jamshid's harem sneaked a drink from a jar labeled poison because she preferred death to an incessant headache, but the jar contained grapes that had fermented accidentally. The concubine according to this myth, didn't even suffer a hangover, and polished off the remainder of the grape juice before confessing her secret to the king, who so liked the way it affected her that he promptly had more made of the same. Another old tale claims that an Arab named Jabir ibn Hazzan "invented" alcohol in about 800 A.D. when he discovered the process of distillating wine. In trying to find the intoxicating agent in wine he distilled *alkuhul*, which meant "a finely refined spirit." The word itself was adopted from the word for an antimony powder used at the time as an eyelid cosmetic. According to both stories then, wine came first and it was discovered by the more sensuous of the species (women, to let statistics tell the story, being "17.6 per cent more sexual" than men).

"There is a devil in every berry of the grape," the Koran warns, and there is often a devilsome creature, male or female behind each glass of the grape. The ancient Sybarites, for one extreme example, found wine so essential to their wanton life style (they boasted that they never saw the sun rise, banned roosters from the city and made love on rose petal–filled mattresses) that most of them owned wine cellars near the seashore into which their wines were pumped through pipes from their country vineyards. The Greeks favored wine no less than their sybaritic neighbors. From earliest times ambrosia (a mixture of oil, wine, honey, chopped cheese and meal, according to Robert Graves) was celebrated as "the wine of the gods" on Mount Olympus, and Dionysus, god of the grape, was worshipped in orgiastic ceremonies the likes of which the world has not seen since. The Romans later worshipped Dionysus under the name of Bacchus, and held Bacchanalian orgies almost as wild as their Dionysian predecessors, sensuous *bacchantes* lending their sexual charms to the occasion. Apicius left behind several recipes for aphrodisiac wines, which were a favorite of city dwellers (Roman peasants generally favored spiced beer), and it was not unusual for naked orgies to be held in whole pools of wine at the town *balnea mixtra* or mixed baths.

Everyone knows that verse from the Rubaiyat of Omar Khayyam telling how *"A loaf of bread/ A jug of wine/ And thou, beneath the bough/ Were paradise enow."* But few are familiar with the story in the Arabian *Perfumed Garden* of that man who has "no other passions than for coition and good wine," who "keeps making love night and day, and his member rests only when he is asleep." This stalwart, according to the Shaykh Nefzawi, drank "nothing but muscatel wine." Yet we needn't travel to exotic places for spicy tales of "wines that mount us to the skies," as Rabelais put it. In medieval Europe, Ducange quipped that *Three things to ruin monks combine—/ Venery, gluttony, and wine.* At the court of Charlemagne a certain "mulled wine" combining "the vigor and the aromatic savor of wine, the flavor and sweetness of honey and the perfume of pure rich aromatics" was popularly believed to have amazing aphrodisiacal proprieties. But Charlemagne, frankly, distrusted the concoction, his favorite drink being hard cider—and he must have known something, considering his four wives, innumerable mistresses and fifty offspring.

That the English placed their faith in the grape can be gathered from these lines from Chaucer's *Canterbury Tales:*

> Whenever I take wine
>   I have to think
> Of Venus, for as cold engenders hail
> A lecherous mouth
>   begets a lecherous tail.
> A woman in her cups has no defense
> As lechers know
>   from long experience.

The English had their special favorites such as the "malmsey" with which witches "excited themselves to venery," Falstaff's sack or sherry (which is no longer made with rabbit carcasses put in the cask to enrich the wine) and the port they found indispensible with venerious nuts. Then there was the invention of Mad William Windom, "King of London's Streetwalkers," a special drink made of minute traces of Spanish Fly, mixed with champagne, curacao, herbs, soda water and sugar—the punch being ladled out of a mighty four-handled gold bowl which had on its frosted sides many erotic motifs in bas-relief. Such stories are the folklore of every country in the world, but few can match the flair of Italy's Gabriele D'Annunzio, who is said to have sipped his wine during love bouts from the skull of a maiden he had deflowered in Milan—the young lady rumored to have killed herself for the love of our romantic poet. It seems that D'Annunzio believed that a drink from the skull would make any man more of a man. But the tale may not be true; after all, there was also a rumor that the maestro's pillows were stuffed with locks from the heads of all the women he had taken to bed. Then again D'Annunzio could take the famed Eleanora Duse, Italy's finest actress, on a stroll through the woods and tell her, "all other women destroy the landscape, you alone, you alone become part of it." A true peasant and romantic at heart, he believed in charms strongly enough to have used a virgin's skull for his wine. Besides, the Celts and Vikings, among many peoples, had used the human cranium as a drinking cup long before him.

Wine served in a skull today would offend the sensibilities of too many of us "Civilized" peoples, who prefer generally to do our carnage secondhand. Neither should it be served at room temperature, that is, unless the room temperature is that of the wine cellars many manor houses had centuries ago, about 40 to 50 degrees. As for the right wines for the right foods, it isn't true that "any wine will do." This is a ploy not so little old winemakers have perpetuated recently to boost sales still higher. Generally speaking, red wine is taken with meat because its tannic acid aids in digestion and white wine with fish because its acids break down unsavory oils (the same reason lemon makes seafood more digestible). Shellfish are best served with a dry Chablis, Grey Rielsing or White Pinot. Fish without shells go well with a semidry wine such as Johannisberg Riesling, Semillon or Rhine wine, while Chinese foods, which tend to be spicy, won't clash with either a dry or semidry wine (*Wan Fu* is particularly good, though the Chinese make such exotic blends as black chicken wine, tiger bone wine and lichee wine). As for fowl, it is a rule of thumb that any white wine can accompany birds like chicken or turkey, whereas red-meated fowl, such as goose, duck or pheasant, can be served with either red or white wine. Meat should always be served with a dry red wine—Cabernet Sauvignon, Charbono, Pinot Noir and Red Pinot are excellent choices—except for candied baked ham, which is best with a rose. That leaves only cheese and nuts, the former eaten with just about any red wine and the latter, especially walnuts, served with a good port.

The only other rule to follow is to break any of the above rules whenever one desires for reasons of experimentation or economic necessity. Learn to be a wine buff, like most wine "experts." Throw out the names and prices of rare French vintages like Chateau Lafite-Rothschild 1806,

which goes for $106 a bottle; spirits like Grande Fine Champagne Arbal-
lot, 1794, $136 a bottle; or those often priceless Napoleon brandies that
have sold for $2800 a bottle.* When discussing the relative merits of two
wines with your paramour, be diplomatic, begin no heated arguments.
Quote the sentiments of that French gastronome who once compared
two fine wines perfectly. "Gentlemen," he said, "this is a case in which
the evidence on both sides is so convincing and interesting that I propose
to spend the rest of my life examining it and allow my verdict to be made
public only after my death." Even if you brew your own by stomping on
grapes in the bathtub, you can save the night. Simply display your
purple feet so beautiful without shoes, clink glasses and repeat the words
of the immoral James Thurber: "It's a naive domestic Burgundy without
any breeding, but I think you'll be amused by its presumption."

The most frequently mentioned wines for love, and those most highly
recommended by medical writers, would include champagne, claret, sauterne, chablis, chianti and burgundy. Not by any means is this list exclusive, however; almost every country and county champions its own
product. Rabelais suggests "a cup of hippocras-claret spiced with cinnamon," while a modern-day French gourmet, Raymond Oliver, opts for a
similar concoction. Says Oliver, "The drinks known as flips, which consist
of raw egg-yolks, sugar, some fortified wine such as port or madeira, a
little additional spirit of liqueur and some added spice such as nutmeg—
are typical love potions and act effectively as restoratives." More often,
however, a natural fully fermented white wine (an unfortified nonacid
wine that tastes dry) has been the choice of sexologists, who tend to disfa-
vor heavy, acid drinks. But then light reds also come highly recommended,
and sauterne, which is a semisweet wine, appears on a number of lists.
Finally, there are exotic drinks like the ginseng and mandrake wines cited
in Course Eighteen. For those who simply want to take the advice of the
best advertised lover of all time, following is a list of drinks that the
redoubtable Casanova mentions most frequently: "Canary Island wine,"
"rare Cerigo muscatel," "wines of Samos and Cephalonia," "the excellent
wine of Tivoli," "white Burgundy," "gatta wine," "orgeat," "ratafia liquor," "Chambertin," "refosco" and, of course, "champagne."

Above all, Casanova's favorite wine was champagne, and most agree
that its glamour alone makes it the best choice to accompany any love
feast. From his first "disgusting" taste as a child of *"graspia,"* a bitter

*One Texas lady this year bought her husband a Jeroboam of 1929 French Medoc at
auction for $9600, $93 an ounce. "It's one-of-a-kind," she explained, "and my husband is a
one-of-a-kind person." The Jeroboam, or double magnum, contains five bottles of wine,
the largest size presently made, but in the past there have been Rehoboams (6 bottles);
Methuselahs (8 bottles); Salmanezars (12 bottles); Balthazars (16 bottles); and Nebuchad-
nezzars (20 bottles).

drink made by boiling the stems of grapes stripped of their fruit in water, Casanova mentions champagne more than any other food or drink in
his multimillion word memoirs, and he most always drank of it before
and during his love bouts. No doubt a statistical study of the world's
literature of love would reveal that champagne has figured in the prelude
to love scenes with greater frequency than anything but flowers. Today
some 35.5 million gallons of champagne, or 170 million bottles—enough
to fill sixty-four Olympic-sized swimming pools—are sold each year for a
total of about $1 billion, so it must be concluded that lovers are using the
fabled wine more than ever. Champagne seems to go well with any meal
and for a festive aperitif, a champagne cocktail can easily be made by
adding a little brandy or Grand Marnier, and an orange slice or fresh
strawberry to a glass of bone-dry bubbly.

Champagne, which the French say is "like the laugh of a pretty girl,"
and "the barometer of happiness," has been associated with love and
gaiety since it was first invented. The Rolls Royce of wines is said to have
been created in its true sparkling form by Dom Pérignon, the man who
put the bubbles in champagne and after whom *Moët et Chandon* named its
most famous vintage some years ago. Dom Pierre Pérignon (1638–1715)
was a blind man who renounced the world when only fifteen and joined
the Benedictine order. Cellarmaster of the monastery near Épernay,
France, his fantastic sense of taste and smell enabled him to experiment
in improving the wines he attended. Dom Pérignon eventually found
that corks tightly drawn in his bottles would not be forced out like rags
and yet would retain naturally expanding gasses, allowing for the so-
called second fermentation in the bottle that is essential for any true
sparkling champagne. After first tasting his creation in 1705, he is supposed to have cried, "Come quickly, I am drinking stars!" The story is
unproven, but it certainly rates a toast, if only as an excuse for another
glass.

Champagne is strictly only sparkling wine produced from grapes
grown in the ancient French province of Champagne as defined by
French law; it must be fermented in the bottle, not in high-pressure
tanks, and varies from *brut*, the driest, to *doux* champagnes with up to 4%
sugar content. People are getting away from the idea that all champagne
must be French; some American California and New York State "champagnes" (though their second fermentation is usually made by the bulk
process in 500-gallon tanks) are very good indeed and less expensive as
well. But that is a matter of individual preferences to be settled by trial
and error. We can only say that French champagne has history, tradition
and gourmands on its side, while other "champagnes" have the high
cost-of-living in their corner. In any case, buy no champagne over ten

years old; after that time the wine starts to darken and lose its taste. A first-rate French champagne is Mercier Extra Dry ($7.49), and an American bottle-fermented favorite is the Schramsberg Blanc de Blancs ($8.50) that President Nixon brought to Peking to toast Mao. Then there are what are called Super French Champagnes, special blends made by the best French houses and bottled in specially designed bottles that sell for as much as $25. Among these elegant *cuvées spéciales* Dom Ruinart Blanc de Blancs 1966 ($12.99) is one of the best. Taittinger Comte de Champagne Blanc de Blancs 1966 ($21.39), Laurent Perrier Grand Siècle 1964 ($21.95), Bollinger R. D. 1961 ($15.95) and Louis Roederer Cristal 1969 ($17.35) also rank very high.

At any rate, the "civilizing Champagne" of Talleyrand, "the wine of wines," "the wine of love," "the wine of the gods," "the devil's wine," is the most celebrated of all festive drinks. This sparkling white wine (and all wines are really white; that is, the grapes' juice turns red only if it is allowed to remain mixed with its crushed black skins for awhile) has sparked more love affairs than any beverage, legal or illegal. Great beauties have bathed in it and drunk it from golden slippers; Madame Pompadour called champagne "the only wine that leaves a woman beautiful after drinking it"; and today Marlene Dietrich has a clause in her movie contract giving her the right to unlimited bubbly at any time she so desires. One Confederate General, Pierre Gustave Toutant Beauregard, to celebrate the first Battle of Bull Run, gave a ball where champagne was piped into the fountain in his courtyard and flowed for his belles all night. As for history's champion champagne drinker, he appears to be a Monsieur Willy Jourdan, who drank over forty thousand bottles in his ninety-four years—better than a bottle a day from the time he was weaned.

Some will be surprised to learn that a little wine is always lost in the second fermentation of champagne and must be replaced with *liqueur d'expédition,* a formula varying with each bottler that generally consists of a spoonful of new and old wines, cognac and sugar, the amount of sugar determining how sweet or dry the champagne will be. As concerns the best glasses in which to serve champagne, a short-stemmed tulip-shaped affair, not the tall-stemmed glasses so often used, retains the wine's bubbles and bouquet twice as long. Tinted glasses, incidentally, are a device of the past. They were introduced in the Victorian age to mask the large amount of sediment present in wines at that time and aren't necessary today. Neither should anyone try to best the record for a popped champagne cork (73 feet, 10½ inches), for when a champagne bottle cork is popped out like a bullet, gasses and bubbles escape too quickly. The cork should be eased out gently, pointing the bottle at a 45 degree angle away from you and *twisting the bottle off the cork.* It makes no difference what size bottle your champagne comes in (claret, burgundy and port are usually fuller-bodied in large bottles), and champagne is ideally served at 43 to 46 degrees F (though the French don't hesitate to drop a few ice cubes in their glasses on a hot day). Still another rule-of-thumb instructs that a very dry or *brut* champagne shouldn't be imbibed with sweet foods, which will make the dry wine taste sour. The proper way to drink champagne? According to Talleyrand, who was seized with "nausea" at the sight of "so much water" while visiting Niagra Falls, the *only* way to drink fine champagne is as follows: "You take the glass in the hollow of your hand; you warm it; you twist it around in a circular motion so that the alcohol gives off its perfume. Next, you raise it to your nostrils, inhale it, and then you put down your glass and 'talk about it.' "

Another expert suggests that all but Cyranos stick their noses deep into the wine glass to sample the bouquet of champagne and all good vintages. Wine tasting itself is best done by whistling. "Now take a sip of wine, hold it in your mouth and whistle," our authority confides. "Whistle in, not out. Try to get a nice gurgle going. This technique also allows you to taste the wine for a longer period of time. For it extends that single instant when wine, air, tongue, gums and nose come together for the first time."

All fine wines "must be treated like a lovely woman in bed," as the old Bordeaux proverb instructs. When toasting with any wine, from chianti to champagne, try the Lover's Clink, your arms entwined and glasses tilted. For the toast itself one might say simply, as Wordsworth did, "Drink pretty creature, drink," or, to paraphrase Richard Sheridan: *"Let the toast pass./ I drink to you lass./ I warrant you'll prove an excuse for a glass."* Then again more appropriate under certain circumstances might be: "May you be in heaven a half hour before the Devil knows you've died." In any case, all the drinking and amenities properly observed will prove that old saw that women enjoy the wine of Burgundy particularly when their men have drunk of it. And vice-versa. "Good wine is a good familiar creature if it be well used," Shakespeare wrote. That is, if drunk in moderation. Just recall the advice Shakespeare's porter gave to MacDuff upon being asked what things drink provokes. "Lechery, sir, it provokes and it unprovokes," the porter answered; "it provoketh the desire, but it takes away the performance."

COURSE TWENTY

Sweets Between The Sheets:
Desserts Before The
Pièce De Résistance

"This dessert will make all women want to cast off their clothes and run naked through the streets, and cause all men to cry, 'Allah be praised!' "
—*Arab recipe for majoon*

An old Persian love-dessert recipe (one made with various spices, eggs and honey) instructed the woman preparing it to throw her lover's pants into the pot along with the other ingredients. This might not have proved very appetizing if her lover had been out fertilizing the garden organically, though it did get the couple down to basics, especially if the cook threw her own pants in the pot as well. Not a bad idea at all, but surely the end of a perfect love feast is better heralded with the arrival of a dish like the phallic-shaped cakes of the Romans; or those "stimulant pastries" recommended in the *Perfumed Garden;* or a dessert made from the vagina-shaped vanilla bean (see Course Fifteen); or perhaps something chocolate from the cacao bean that medieval clergymen thought so "provocative of immorality." The list is a long one, but assembled here in broad categories are the most renowned of sweets for the sweet.

The love desserts available are in fact so numerous that we've had to be selective to the point of neglect. Flaming desserts like Crêpes Suzettes or Cherries Jubilee, for example, are so eye-appealing and delicious that they'd be a fitting end to any love meal. When or where the former dessert was invented in France is a mystery, but the enticing post-prandial pancake must have been named for a worthy Suzy, indeed, Suzette being the French diminutive for the proper name Suzanne. The thin, rolled pancakes, or crêpes, are generally heated in an orange-flavored liqueur sauce and flambéed at the table, making the blazing dessert one of the more spectacular glories of the French cuisine.

Yet the same can be said for fruit dishes like Strawberries Liberté, fresh, giant strawberries hollowed and filled with caviar, set upon limestone pedestals and sprinkled with vodka. This appetizer is so delicious that some prefer ordering it as a dessert. Or why not glazed strawberries, or the "pears and strawberries doused in Cointreau and drenched in a fragrant sauce of beaten egg yolk, confectioner's sugar, cloves and cinnamon" that one American sexologist recommends?

The truth is that there is no end to the ways one can end an intimate supper. Many people prefer a cheese course for last, and some conclude their meals with savouries in place of sweet desserts. Among the Romans these included exotic dishes like raisin-stuffed ortolans, and today Englishmen still enjoy such stimulating savouries as "Scotch Woodcock," scrambled eggs with anchovies and capers; and "Devils on Horseback," prunes wrapped in bacon. Then there is the majoon of Morocco, a traditional dish of powdered hemp, honey, fruit, nuts and spices (to which cantharides and even powdered lizard is sometimes added). We could go on for pages. That moulded Turkish sweet, its recipe unfortunately lost, appropriately called "lady's navel." Those Russian quinces sweetened and stuffed with lamb. Even the "sculpted, glazed banana" one writer has recommended, with two scoops of ice cream artfully arranged at its base. Each guaranteed, for better reasons, to make lovers repeat the last words of Brillat-Savarin's sister Pierette, who expired at the dinner table while celebrating her 100th birthday: "Bring on the dessert! I think I'm about to die!"

• CAKES AND PASTRIES •

From the blatantly phallic shaped cakes and cookies of ancient times (see WHEAT, Course Fourteen) to the Devil's Food Cake of comparatively recent vintage, cakes and pastries have held an enviable aphrodisiac reputation. Special cakes and pastries with long histories still enjoy great popularity, though none is quite as complicated in preparation as that old Arab concoction said to be a cure for impotence, this including among its 50-odd ingredients honey, ginger, vinegar syrup, cardamoms, various cinnamons, pepper, nutmeg, pellitory and kellebore. Rum cakes, for example, remain as popular as ever, and they can be traced at least to the reign of France's Louis XIV, when newly-marrieds ate cakes dipped in alcohol to liberate their libidos for the nuptial night ahead. Today's wedding cake, in fact, is but an improvement of the salt, water and flour cake both bride and groom ate at the Roman *confarreatio*, or marriage ceremony. Later this became the famous Bride Cake of olden times, composed of many spicy aromatic ingredients and topped with an icing made of white sugar and bitter almonds said to be symbolic of the pleasure and pain that were to follow. It was also believed that if a bridesmaid deposited an amulet of the cake in the foot of her left stocking and placed it under her pillow on going to bed, she would surely dream of the man destined by fate to be her partner for life. Before this was done, though, the small portions of the cake doled out to the bridesmaids had to be scrupulously bewitched. The bride held her wedding ring between the finger and thumb of her right hand and the groom had to pass each small piece through the ring exactly nine times before giving them to the eager bridesmaids.

No longer available is that aphrodisiac spiced cake of medieval times which was baked in an oven strapped over the naked body of a girl, the cake then eaten by the maiden and her lover later. But many old favorites remain with us. Frangipane is one of these. According to most authorities, the Marquis Frangipani, a pleasure-loving major-general under Louis XIV, is said to have invented the pastry cake filled with cream, sugar and almonds called frangipane or frangipani. But the most sentimental old love story has it that frangipani was the marvelous invention of Italian Count Cesare Frangipani, who presented it as a pledge of eternal love to young Catherine de Médicis when she left her native land for France.

A second almond-based aphrodisiac dessert is *blancmange*, a white sweet pudding prepared with almond milk, gelatin and flavored with rum. In the film *La Grande Bouffe* (The Big Feed) one of the dissolute characters dies while face down in a pair of large-than-life *blancmange* breasts after participating in an orgy to end all orgies.

The madeleine, also of French origin, is another ancient pastry famous to this day. These small, rich, shell-shaped cakes are doubtless the most honored pastry in all literature. Some claim they are named for their inventor, Madeleine Paulmier, a 19th century pastry cook of Commeray,

France, though Andre Simon and other gastronomes credit their invention to "one Avice, chief pastry cook" to that rake the Prince de Talleyrand. At any rate, Madeleine Paulmier, or the anonymous Madeleine for whom Avice may have named the cakes, both take their names from Mary Magdalene, the repentant prostitute whom Christ forgave. The cake also figures prominently in modern literature. It was on a visit to his mother that Marcel Proust was served the scalloped *petite madeleine*, "so richly sensuous under its severe religious folds," whose taste brought back the flood of memories resulting in his eight-volume masterpiece *Á la Recherche du Temps Perdu*. One cynic has in fact called Proust's work "the tale of a man who fell in love with a cookie." Proust's fragile madeleine, made with flour, butter, sugar and eggs, "the same weight of each," flavored with lemon rind and baked in a small but deep scallop-shaped mold, is no relation to the English sponge bun bearing the same name.

The famed Charlotte Russe is one pastry whose invention is a matter of record, having been created by Carême, the greatest French chef of his day, in honor of England's Princess Charlotte, George IV's only daughter. While in England Carême had invented a lavish pastry which he called the Apple Charlotte after the princess. Apparently he couldn't forget her, for it was while serving Czar Alexander in Russia that he created the jellied custard set in a crown of ladyfingers that he named the Charlotte Russe in her honor. Carême's creations were so valued that it's said that they were stolen from the table at the court of George IV—not to be relished at home, but to be sold in the market at astronomical prices. The master chef also adapted the rich creamy cheesecake of the Russians called the Pasha, introducing it to France where it was re-christened *coeur à la crème*.

Other famous love pastries include the *biscuit de pêches au noyan* (a peach cake) that Madame DuBarry made for Louis XV; the rum-soaked *Ali Baba* or *Baba au Rhum* created by Poland's dethroned King Stanislaus II; an inappropriately named "Nun's Cake" that called for 35 eggs and a gill of brandy, among other ingredients; English sherry-soaked Tipsy Cake, now known as the Trifle; a Chinese love cake made of wisteria blossoms; and the famous *petit fours*, the smallest of all pastries. This last, its name taken from the "tiny ovens" in which it had to be cooked, is said to have been served for the first time to France's Louis XIV while he was being entertained at a country estate. Legend has it that just one small pastry was carried in on a silver tray. This everyone considered an insult—until Louis gobbled the pastry down in one bite and cried for more.

We could regale you with titillating tales of donuts (those holes in the center possibly "invented" by a Captain Hanson Crockett Gregory of Maine in 1847); or repeat apocryphal tales of the prowess of Devil's Food

Cake, a favorite of President Chester Arthur's; Boston cream pie; and even Mom's Aphrodisiac Apple Pie. But we'd best end with marzipan, which has an old and indisputable aphrodisiac reputation. Marzipan, made basically with almond paste and sugar, is mentioned by Rabelais, who has Panurge offer a slice to an eager friar. It was highly recommended to lovers during the Italian Renaissance, when Marie de Médicis made good use of it. Raymond Oliver gives the best recipe we've seen for aphrodisiac marzipan tarts in his *Gastronomy of France,* along with the following warning: "It must be light. I have already explained that we are dealing with the problem of restoring our forces or of preparing for exertions (of the most splendid order!) and to that end we must be careful of our timing. Any undue effort of digestion can only harm the results we hope for."

One sweet fable tells of a cook of Brandenberg, Germany, named Franz Marzip, who is said to have originated marzipan for his physician employer. Other sources say that Oriental rulers had enjoyed the almond paste confection for centuries in their harems and that the crusaders brought it back to Europe in the shape of a coin of the time called the marchpane. In any event, the sweet is widely available today at quality bakers, should you eschew Oliver's or someone else's long, complicated recipe. Marzipan is often used to make confectionary sculptures of flowers, trees, plates, bowls and even nudes. The best place to enjoy it is in Lubeck, West Germany, often called "the world's marzipan capital." Lubeck claims to have achieved its renown entirely by accident, the tale being that during an ancient siege the citizens ran out of flour and turned to making bread by grinding up almonds. This "bread" caught on to become the world's most celebrated marzipan, today available as the famed Holstentors. A Düsseldorf confectionary firm has recently conspired with a local artist to invent a less conventional marzipan dish for the ladies—marzipan male genitalia, served with hot sauce.

• CHEESES •

"A dessert course without cheese is like a beautiful woman with one eye," Brillat-Savarin once said, and more and more Americans have come to agree with him. Both domestic production and cheese imports have soared skyward here in the last ten years, consumption per person increasing over 40 per cent. Hundreds of cheeses are available on the market, with this figure likely to rise even higher in years to come.

As Clifton Fadiman observed, cheese is "milk's leap to immortality," but to write definitively of the foodstuff is virtually impossible. Even Casanova, great gourmet that he was, had to be content with using cheese to bait his pretty "mouses." In his memoirs Casanova admits that he had no choice but to abandon his lifelong *Dictionary of Cheeses*, just as Rousseau had to abandon his *Dictionary of Natural History*. It would require a lifetime of work, the fabled lover complained, to cover so vast a subject.

A vendor called Cheese of All Nations in New York City carries over 1000 kinds of cheese today, barely indicating just how many varieties and shapes of cheese are known throughout the world—though perhaps just twenty of these are basic types. The origin of cheese dates back several thousand years before Christ. One tale claims that it was discovered by an ancient traveling merchant named Kanana. When he started on one long trip, Kanana put his supply of milk in a pouch made of a sheep's stomach. The heat and shaking of the pouch on the journey, plus the rennet in the lining of the pouch, caused the curds in the milk to separate from the rest of the milk and when he sat down to eat his lunch, this Arabian traveling salesman found the delicious curds.

Still another legend tells much the same story of an Arab herdsman discovering cheese in this manner. Whatever the truth, cheese was probably discovered accidentally and the acquired knowledge that the glands in the stomachs of lambs, calves and other young suckling animals give off rennet that causes the solids of milk to set quickly into curds eventually led to the establishment of the giant cheese industry we know today.

Most cheeses are named for the regions of the world where they were born. Some important examples are Roquefort for Roquefort, France; Camembert for Camembert, France; Cheddar for Cheddar, England; Cheshire for Cheshire, England; Edam from Edam, Holland; Muenster for Muenster, Germany; Swiss for Switzerland; and Limburger for Limburg, Belgium. It would be futile to try to list them all. In fact France alone has enough varieties to fill a volume. The late President De Gaulle once remarked, "How can you govern a nation which has 246 kinds of cheese?"

Cheese has long been a symbol of love, strength and fertility. Among those fortifying provisions David carried to the army before he slew Goliath were "ten cheeses," and the ancient Greeks revered cheese as a food of the gods, presenting their offerings of cheese on Mount Olympus with impressive ceremonies and supplications. Centuries later, during the reign of the Caesars, cheesemaking spread throughout the empire. Rome became a rich market for all varieties, cheeses considered a rare and toothsome delicacy at lavish overladen Roman banquet tables. Throughout Europe many romantic customs revolved around different cheeses. In Switzerland, for example, on the day a baby daughter was born to a couple, a wheel of the original Swiss cheese (*Sbrinz*) was rolled into storage. Specially marked and preserved, this "wheel of romance" laid in waiting in a cave until the day of the daughter's wedding—perhaps eighteen years or more later. Then it was rolled forth to become the "delicacy of the day" for the bridal party and all the guests.

Hundreds of cheeses are fit for any love feast—all except strong-smelling types like Limburger, which would have to be eaten by both parties if eaten at all. Cheese, of course, can be used in appetizers, entrees, sandwiches and salads as well as desserts. Gourmets and lovers have particularly valued after-dinner cheese, especially served continental style with a bowl of fresh fruit and an attractive silver bowl containing ice-water in which to wash their grapes, pear or apple. The cheeses served would depend mainly on individual preferences (in France as many as thirty cuts adorn a tray), but good choices might be Roquefort, Gorgonzola, Gruyère, Camembert, Provolone, Gouda, and a perfectly ripe Brie. Some prefer their cheese with a red wine and crackers, or French or Italian bread, and still others like a slice of apple pie with a piece of sharp Cheddar. *Apple pie without cheese/ Is like a kiss without a squeeze*, goes the old American saying. It's all a matter of taste. Simply find your favorite cheeses by trial and error and serve them at room temperature, not ice-cold and without any flavor.

• ICE CREAM AND SHERBET •

Sherbet probably came before ice cream and, though it is not as nutritious or as popular as its creamy cousin today, it is still valued as a love food. Sherbet aids the digestion, and for this reason was served between courses at the immense banquets of days gone by. Sir Richard Burton relates in his Arabian Nights that Hindu males drink sherbet while actively engaging in coitus in order to prolong the act by avoiding "overtension of the muscles" and preoccupying the brain. In another footnote to the *Ananga Ranga* the same author emphasizes sherbet's sexual reputation by observing that "No Persian will drink sherbet in the presence of his future mother-in-law." This may still be true in Persia today, but certainly no American would forsake a sherbet for his or her mother-in-law. There have been literally hundreds of frozen sherbets available here, including, believe it or not, tomato, prune, chile con carne and sauerkraut varieties.

Ice cream has just as enviable an erotic reputation as sherbet. Perhaps the first was made when the lecherous Roman emperor Nero sent runners up into the mountains for snow on which was poured honey, cream, juices and fruit pulps. In any case, "iced cream" was introduced to France by Catherine de Médicis, and has since become one of the world's most beloved desserts. Americans alone annually consume about twenty-three quarts of ice cream and sherbets per person.

Today ice cream flavors number in the thousands, including such odd blends as potatoes and bacon, horseradish, mustard, bubble gum, jelly bean, Nudie Frutti, Sophia Lemon, and Can't Elope (as in canteloupe). But most people still prefer the old standbys vanilla, chocolate and strawberry, of which Americans eat enough each year to more than fill the Grand Canyon. As for ice cream sodas, they're as popular with sweethearts as they were a century ago, and the same can be said for the malted milk, the banana split, ice cream cones, and the ice cream sundae. This last, incidentally, was concocted at the turn of the century when blue laws banned the Sunday sales of sodas and the "Soda-less Soda" or "Sunday" took its place. The ice cream cone made its first appearance at about the same time, being invented at the St. Louis International Exposition in 1904. The inventor of the banana split remains anonymous, although we do know that the world's biggest banana split (400 feet long) was recently prepared by Farrell's Ice Cream Parlours of Los Angeles.

Baked Alaska has been one of the most posh of ice cream desserts since it was created at Delmonicos in 1876 in honor of the newly purchased Alaskan territory. Consisting of ice cream on a cake base placed briefly in a hot oven to brown its blanket of meringue, it is a fitting end to any love meal. Peach melba is another old favorite. This dessert was named for Dame Nellie Melba, stage name of Australian opera star Helen Porter Mitchell (1861–1931). The great French chef Escoffier created the peach, ice cream and raspberry sauce dessert in Dame Nellie's honor. But poshest of all ice creams is that truffled concoction invented at Delmonicos late in the last century (see Course Twelve), though few would be so pretentious as to order the dish today, despite its associations with the aphrodisiac truffle. Far more delicious, nutritious and free of chemicals is homemade ice cream which can't be bought anywhere anymore. It does take effort to make, but is more than worth the trouble.

• CANDY •

Even if "candy is dandy but liquor is quicker" (or "candy is dandy, but sex won't rot your teeth"), the sweet stuff has much to say for itself as a love food. Often we think only of chocolate when we say candy, but there are actually over 2000 varieties of candy made from eighty different agricultural products. Americans alone consume almost four billion pounds of such sweets annually, twenty pounds per person, from fruit-flavored sours to chewy caramels, making candy production the seventh largest food industry in the U.S.

Peppermint sticks, sour balls, toffees, peanut brittles, fudges, jellies, gums, marshmallows, nuggets, taffies, etc., etc., etc., have all been the latest aphrodisiac fad at one time or another among lovers. In middle nineteenth century America, for example, mint lozenges imprinted with "I love you" were all the rage among sweethearts. More recently, in Germany, according to a wire service report, sales of licorice have shot up as men have taken to giving their women licorice sticks instead of chocolate. The girls claim that the licorice makes them feel "sexy" and West German scientists, after probing reports that hundreds of German girls on holiday at coastal resorts were eating licorice instead of ice cream, confirm that licorice does contain traces of the female sex hormone estrogen. But then licorice was long a medicine before it was a sweet. The Chinese believed it to be a preserver of youth and strength, and the Brahmans of ancient India vouched for its effectiveness as a sexual tonic and beautifying agent, while the Egyptian pharaohs enjoyed a stimulating beverage made of licorice called *mai sus*. The Chinese still chew the root for endurance in coition and the Hindus make a tea with it with milk and honey to increase their sexual vigor.

Candy has been around since at least 4000 years ago, when the Egyptians enjoyed a well-established confectionary art, and each pharaoh's retinue included one cook who could turn out appetizing confections made of honey, flour, almonds, dates and figs. Similarly, fruits, nuts, sweet herbs and spices mixed with honey were the sweetmeats of the early Greeks and Romans. It was probably the Greeks who brought the word candy into the language. It seems that a favorite of the lusty troops of Alexander the Great was a Persian delicacy called *kand*—a sweet reed garnished with honey, spices and coloring. The word candy itself either came to us from this *kand* Alexander's men brought to Greece, or from the Arab word for sugar, *quand*.

Candy became more important in world commerce with the spread of sugar cane culture beginning in the 15th century, and gradually made the transition from a delight enjoyed by the wealthy few to a relatively low-cost treat available to everyone. Legends abound about almost every variety of the sweet, but chocolate probably leads the list. An article in a leading woman's magazine several years back listed chocolate as one of the top ten aphrodisiacs. No one knows how the *Cosmopolitan* Ms's conducted their research, but their conclusions about this high source of quick energy seem justified historically. Chocolate, in its many forms, has been used as a love food since long before the day of St. Valentine.

Chocolate is made from cacao, the fruit of the evergeen tree *Theobroma cacao*, which was named by the Swedish botanist Linnaeus 250 years ago and translates as "cacao, food of the gods." Cacao and kola are the only two members of the large botanic family of *Sterculiaceae* that man uses as food. Inside each cacao pod are twenty to fifty beans, 400 to a pound, beans that modern-day Ecuadorians still call *pepe de oro* or seeds of gold, so important are they to the national economy. This has always been so in South America. The Aztecs used the cacao bean as currency, the unit 8000 indicated by a sack holding 8000 cacao beans, and the Mayans did likewise. In fact, the Mayans even had trouble with "counterfeiters" of cacao beans. It seems that Mayan con men filled hollowed beans with dirt and passed them off as the real thing.

The Mayans paid in chocolate at their bawdy houses, a fact noted by Bishop de Landa, who ministered to Cortez's soldiers. "He who wants a Mayan public woman for his lustful use can have one for eight to ten cacao beans," the Bishop wrote—which is something to be remembered the next time you buy or receive a small box of bon-bons. Apparently, the chocolate sexually stimulated both men and women, for the Aztecs drank it in honor of Xochiquetzal, their version of Aphrodite, the goddess of love.

Although Columbus brought back the first dark-brown almond-shaped cacao beans from the New World, it was the Emperor Montezuma who convinced Europeans that chocolate was an ambrosia for the gods, serving *chocolatl* to Cortez and his captains in great golden goblets. Montezuma may even have been the inventor of chocolate ices, for it's said that he used to send members of his court to the heights of a nearby volcano to bring back blocks of snow, over which other minions poured whipped *chocolatl.* But he made *chocolatl* the royal drink of the Aztecs and forbade it to the women of the court, much to the dismay of the ladies, who had to go to unladylike lengths to get it.

After Cortez brought *chocolatl* back to Spain, his countrymen improved upon its bitterness by sweetening and flavoring it with cane sugar, vanilla and cinnamon, and finally serving it as a hot drink. From the very beginning chocolate was denounced by the clergy in fifteenth century Spain as "immoral and provocative of immorality," but it remained in favor with the nobility for its reputedly powerful effects. The Spanish kept the new treat a secret for nearly a century, but monks finally leaked the recipe out and hot chocolate soon became the most fashionable drink in the licentious French court. By 1657, English "chocolate houses" began to appear and about a century after that, in 1765, the first American chocolate factory opened. All the while, the clergy throughout Europe continued to condemn the sweet and there are records of monasteries prohibiting chocolate for their monks because of its firing-the-furnace power.

No doubt these clerical admonitions were partly inspired by the reckless use made of chocolates, which were coated with ambergris, cantharides and other powerful sexual stimulants. Moreau of Tours gives an exaggerated account of how the Marquis de Sade used Spanish Fly in this way. De Sade may not have been guilty at all, but the story does describe what was a not uncommon practice among the more depraved nobility. Moreau writes:

> "M. de Sade gave a ball, to which he invited a numerous company. A splendid supper was served at midnight: now the marquis had mixed with the dessert a profusion of chocolate, flavored with vanilla, which was found delicious and of which everybody freely partook. All at once the guests, both men and women, were seized with a burning sensation of lustful ardour; the cavaliers attacked the ladies without any concealment. The essence of cantharides circulating in their veins left them neither modesty nor reserve in the imperious pleasures; excess was carried to the most fatal extremity; pleasure became murderous; blood flowed upon the floor, and the women only smiled at the horrible effects of their uterine rage..."

Casanova used chocolate widely, though more wisely, in his seductions, his memoirs mentioning chocolate and chocolates more frequently than any love stimulant but champagne. Dumas also favored the sweet and Brillat-Savarin devotes a chapter to it in his *Physiology of Taste*, informing us that "The Spanish ladies of the New World are passionately fond of chocolate; and not satisfied with taking it several times a day, they even have brought it to church." But chocolate became more popular than ever with lovers after a Swiss named Daniel Peter invented milk chocolate in 1876. Since then it has become the foremost of Valentine gifts, and on St. Nicholas Eve (Dec. 5th) Dutch lovers exchange chocolate initials, or use them as place cards at the dinner table.

The delicacies made from chocolate would require volumes to record, ranging from Japanese chocolate-flavored honey bars and South American chocolate-covered ants to the hot chocolate laced with cognac often served to lovers on Majorca. Several recommended for a love feast are the famous Brazilian iced drink called *Chocolatl Gelado;* the Hungarian *Csokolade Mignon,* chocolate cake squares filled with jam and topped with mocha frosting; the Australian Lamingstons, chocolate frosted chocolate squares coated with coconut; the Israeli Chocolate Date Nut Pie, made of mashed dates, milk chocolate, angel food cake, whipped cream and chopped nuts; and the traditional Irish dish, Swans Jelly, which combines cream puff pastry, melted chocolate, and whipped cream, the "swan" resting on a bed of pale green jelly.

But then perhaps you'd be better off sticking with a plain old-fashioned box of chocolates. Literally tens of thousands of molds have been made for these (50,000 at last count), and there is even a mold in the shape of a lobster. We're sorry to report, however, that no phallic shapes could be found anywhere in this country—although that same Düsseldorf confectionary previously mentioned puts out among its "desserts with a difference" true-to-life nudes made of fine Swiss chocolate. At any rate, it's probably not necessary to melt down those Hershey bars, as the chocolate alone should be enough. One old American book by Frederick S. Cozzins called *The Sayings of Dr. Bushwacker* (1867) had its hero put it this way. " 'Tea, my learned friend,' replied Dr. Bushwacker curtly, 'inspires scandal and sentiment; coffee excites the imagination; but chocolate, sir, is an aphrodisiac.' " Who Dr. Bushwacker was, or who he bushwacked, we don't know, but he's obviously right—even if thinking alone has made it so.

• HONEY •

Honey is without doubt among the first of sweets known to man and deservedly has the most renowned aphrodisiac reputation. "Thy lips, my spouse, are as dropping honeycomb, honey and milk are under thy tongue; and the smell of thy garments, as the smell of frankincense," says the *Song of Solomon*. The best of flower-power foods affords the quickest source of human energy, which explains why it has been so highly valued as a love food since ancient times. Made throughout the world by only five varieties of *Apis mellifica*, one of the over ten thousand bee species recorded, honey's color and taste varies according to the plant the bee draws nectar from. These number in the hundreds, ranging from the common U.S. clover to wild thyme honey from Mount Hymettus, which was the fabled honey of the Greek gods on Olympus. Some wild honeys can even be poisonous, if the bee gathers nectar from a poisonous plant, but these instances are rare indeed. In any event, 160,000 bees make trips to some two million flowers to gather the four pounds of nectar it takes to make one pound of honey.

An old French superstition says that if you're stung by a bee you've been injected with a powerful aphrodisiac, but most peoples have placed their faith in the bee's highly nutritious byproduct, which is 40 per cent sugar, 34 per cent fructose (fruit sugar), and 2 per cent sucrose (cane sugar), in addition to being rich in minerals, amino acids, enzymes, and B-complex vitamins. It's easy to understand why almost every modern sexologist strongly recommends honey for restorative diets. The tasty energy giver has been used similarly for ages, long before even the Greek physician Galen recommended it for lovers. The poet Ovid, among many Romans, mentioned honey ("on Hymettus flowing") as an aphrodisiac, and the Arabs believed that eating honey prolonged the sexual act. Nature's elixir has been used in England, where it was made into a honeymoon drink called mead, and is still lauded in China, where it's used as a binder for aphrodisiac pills. Practically every country in the world has sung its praises.

Among the scores of aphrodisiac honey recipes, there is even an Indian one combining honey, camel's milk and pigeon blood. In the *Perfumed Garden* Shaykh Nefzawi recommends that "he who feels sexually weak should drink a glass of thick honey before going to bed," but his best and most powerful honey recipe is really no dessert, being the eggs and honey recipe quoted in Course Ten which enables a lover to "soothe and comfort all through the night..."

Nefzawi's best recipe can hardly equal a present-day Arabian one, though. It's said that Arabian Sheikhs still paint the bodies of harem girls with honey and have them run through flowering hashish fields, pollen from the plants sticking to their naked bodies, which the lecherous old men lick clean before making love. As of now no confectioner has yet packaged this perfect dessert, though our field-workers report that Honeyed Man or Woman will be marketed sometime in the near future—all but the main ingredients, that is, in handy recycleable kits.

COURSE TWENTY-ONE

The Sex Maniac's
Quick Weight Loss Lust Diet:
A Low Calorie,
Low-Cost Love Feast

"Th' idee iv female beauty that all gr-reat men, fr'm Julius Caesar to me-self, has held, is much more like a bar'l thin a clothespole."
—Finley Peter Dunne
Dissertations by Mr. Dooley

We've since learned that the astute Mr. Dooley quoted above isn't the only observer who's a connoisseur of fleshiness. "W'at good eesa wife eef she don'ta be fat?" Thomas Daly lamented some time ago in *Da Styleesha Wife*, but today fat is definitely back, "the new plumpness," "the round look," being reflected in all the *au courant* fashion magazines. The "ghoul look" of Parisian *haute couture* doyennes is definitely on its way out by all indications, a sour fact that has curdled some of the *crème de la crème*. According to the recently published *The Beautiful People's Diet Book:* "Scrawniness is not becoming, and certainly is not sexy. Unless you have written off sex...you might as well realize that men like something to grab." The authors go on to quote similar sentiments among numerous celebrities, male and female, including one suave French diplomat. "In the Arab world," this sophisticated traveler observes, "a woman is attractive for her flesh, not her bones. Flesh is sensuous, and how modern Western woman decided it's in to be thin is beyond me."

But nobody needs Mr. Dooley or beautiful people to realize that a size AAA zaftig can be most fetching. Did any voyeur worthy of the name ever buy a ticket to see a boney belly dancer? When did the likes of Rubens, or Titian, or Renoir ever waste oils painting an emaciated nude? Isn't it true that throughout most of Western civilization the ideal Venusian love goddess was fleshy and dimpled, plump and pink as a turkey, her lover's ample girth regarded as proof positive that he had sampled the good things in life and could afford them? Such questions have in reality been posed by plump people ranging from the newly organized (but expanding) National Association To Aid Fat Americans, representing some 90 million "overweight" citizens (in round figures, of course), to portly British actor Peter Ustinov, who is presently campaigning for corpulence under the slogan, "A gentleman of considerable weight makes by far the best mate!"

It is true that "fat can be beautiful," as the NATAFA slogan proclaims, and excessive dieting weighs as heavily on the libido as the poundage it replaces. It often isn't worth an agony that brings no ecstasy—an agony that can even be fatal when it leads to *anorexia nervosa*, a disease marked by tremendous weight loss and a refusal to eat that is becoming more common among compulsive dieters today. We also know from reliable medical studies that the heftiest among us are probably the most lusty (see Course One). As the almost apocryphal Dr. Craveit has observed, one can live to be 100 by giving up wine, rich food, love, and late hours. Anyway, he says, it'll feel like 100.

All of us can't be as lucky as France's Louis XIV. On his death the Sun King's physicians discovered that his stomach was three times larger than a normal one and that therein a tapeworm of record size also lived like a *grand seigneur*. We might emulate novelist Frank Harris ("I cannot enjoy sex on an over-full belly"), eating Brobdingnagian meals with lively ladies and carrying a pump with which to wash out our stomachs just prior to making love. But it's more practical to keep in mind the Turkish bey Mustaph Mehere. That good old bey, legend tells us, lived 123 years (1488–1611), and up until the very last had at least 170 wives and just as many concubines, all of whom he divorced before they reached age 20. Mustaph never weighed less than a lusty 400 pounds. Or take (and many did gratefully) the aforementioned Lillian Russell, who ate like a longshoreman and always weighed well over 200 pounds— which didn't prevent her from having countless lovers and snaring five husbands far richer than the spurned Diamond Jim Brady, who offered her a million in cash for her hand at one luncheon. Miss Russell never bothered to diet and even her bicycle had a custom fitted saddle molded to her "every peculiarity of pose and shape." Finally, consider Brillat-Savarin's advice, as sexist as it may be. "Leanness is no great disadvantage for men," he writes, "but it is a frightful evil for women, for with them beauty is more than life, and beauty consists above all in the roundness of limb, and in gracefully curved outlines. The choicest of toilettes, the most sublime of dressmakers, cannot disguise certain deficiencies, or conceal certain angles; and it is said commonly that a lean body however beautiful she appears, loses something of her charms whenever she takes a pin out of her dress... Women who are born to be lean... cannot be more difficult to fatten than poultry."

While being fleshy is nothing to be ashamed about, we nevertheless don't want to kill anyone with kitchen kindness. We don't want to be responsible for somebody growing so heavy that he or she capsizes the water bed, or gets wedged in the heart-shaped tub for three days, as recently happened to a three-hundred pound woman in Manhattan (four plumbers and two policemen finally rescued the poor lady). There may just be a germ of use in Sir John Suckling's couplet: *Spare diet is the cause love lasts,/ For surfeits sooner kill than fasts.* Therefore, served here is a low-calorie love-feast for those who must, for medical reasons, watch their weight. No attempt would be made if this couldn't be done with authentically aphrodisiac foods, or if a caviar and filet mignon regimen were necessary that would take off two hundred pounds (sterling) in one week. Fortunately there are also better ways than No-Cal Egg Foo Young. Many delectable foods are not only aphrodisiacs, but low in calories and price as well, enabling one to dine with Gallic flair and still remain reasonably svelte. In fact, the perfect menu for an intimate love dinner or any public orgy can be planned using foods known to be both the ultimate love foods and the best diet foods.

For the first course, a good choice would be oysters on the half-shell. A half-dozen large oysters contain only 42 calories, a raw oyster being 76-89 per cent water, and the tasty mollusks have long been renowned as aphrodisiacs, perhaps more than any other food (see Course Four). We might disregard the old theory that oysters arouse in us "a sense of our primordial past," but they definitely were among Rabelais' favorite foods; Casanova did eat 50 of them every day as "a spur to the spirit and to love;" and many a poet has sung their praises. Oysters contain some phosphorus, which is known to arouse desire, and they are among the most easily digested of foods. Traditionally, the bivalves have been served by purists with just a few slices of lemon (five calories), which adds to their appeal as a diet food. American and European oysters are equally good. For variety, Canadian Malpeques or miniature Olympias from the West Coast might be served.

If any food has a greater amatory reputation than oysters, it is truffles. Few calorie charts list these delicious "underground mushrooms," however, as their cost is generally considered prohibitive. Astronomical truffle prices should discourage no one, though, for the esculent fungi are needed only in very small quantities, which makes them relatively inexpensive—especially considering the fact that they are so high in protein and minerals and so low in carbohydrates and fat. The Truffles Salad Urbani recommended for the second course will come to no more than 50 calories a portion, for it is made by simply combining about two ounces of raw truffles with lettuce, a tablespoon of oil, wine vinegar, and a sprinkling of salt and black pepper. White or black truffles can be purchased fresh or canned at gourmet grocers and food stores, or ordered from Paul Urbani, Trenton, New Jersey. A one-ounce tin sells for from $1.50 to $2.40, and the "diamonds of the cookery," are well worth the price. Truffles contain phosphorus and iron, both reputedly aphrodisiacs, and are most effective uncooked, as in the suggested salad. Truffles salad (see Course Twelve) was in fact made famous by the great novelist Alexander Dumas père, who considered truffles to be the *"sanctum sanctorum of the gastronomes."* Dumas always prepared *Salade de Truffes* with his mistress of the moment when they dined together evenings, using his special silver knife to peel the trusty truffles into a huge bowl, where their "precious scent assailed the air" and assaulted the senses.

Lobster à la Tom Jones, totalling about 100 calories for a one-pounder, is the ideal choice for the main course of a weight-watcher's love dinner. Like most seafood, *Homarus Americanus* is rich in phosphorus and low in carbohydrates. Furthermore, gourmet cooks to the contrary, it can taste no better than when steamed and served with a little butter sauce and lemon juice mixed together. Follow the directions in Course Six and there's no problem. The entire entree, including the rich butter sauce, will total no more than 200 calories per one pound lobster. An alternate choice for the main course might be a tasty cut of filet mignon, though this would be somewhat higher in cholesterol than *Homarus*. In the future, however, steaks which have low levels of those saturated fats that have been linked to heart disease may be available to all. Australian researchers have just this year found that they may be able to lower blood cholesterol an average of ten per cent—about as much as diets do that contain almost no meat, eggs and fat—rich dairy products—simply by changing the feed of cattle. The *New England Journal of Medicine* reports that this diet change interferes with the production of saturated fats by the digestive systems of livestock. One American cattle breeder is already experimenting with the process.

For a vegetable course asparagus is best. Asparagus, with its long history as an aphrodisiac, remains among the most effective of all love-foods, the shapely stalks definitely a psychological aphrodisiac and also containing highly valued chemicals such as asparagine (see Course Fourteen). Furthermore, a six-spear serving amounts to only 21 calories. Either fresh, frozen or canned asparagus may be used.

As for the "milk of Aphrodite," choose a dry white Chablis, Moselle, or Rhine wine. These not only best complement the dinner, but are among the lowest in calories of all alcoholic beverages, each averaging about 60 calories for a 3½ ounce glass. Two glasses would constitute only 120 calories.

Dessert might be any of several non-acid fruits, including bananas, peaches, cherries, and grapes. Actually, the dieter need miss nothing in the way of desserts at an aphrodisiac dinner. A fresh fruit salad made from a cup of grapes and a fresh peach and banana is as highly recommended as any aphrodisiac dessert and contains only 95 calories per serving. A sherbet, equally favored through the ages, would constitute even less.

There are, of course, other potent low-calorie comestibles to choose from. Following is a list of relatively low-calorie love foods, which have all been suggested by at least three reliable medical sources. They are: beef (rare), celery, chicken, clams, crab, fish, garlic, kidneys, kidney beans, liver, mushrooms (which can be substituted for the truffles on this menu), spinach, tomatoes, tripe, and the new cholesterol-free "synthetic" eggs. These all come highly recommended, but it would be hard to prepare a meal from them as naturally delicious, stimulating and low in calories as the one above. In fact, it's interesting and psychologically uplifting to know that oysters, truffles and lobster alone would grace any epicure's list of the top five gourmet foods. It is hard to think of any delicacies other than Beluga caviar and *pâte de foie gras* that equal them.

The entire feast, then, made from the best of love foods at a cost of twelve dollars or so, adds up at the most to a mere 532 calories—less than the majority of diets allow for dinner. Anyone on a strict 1000-calorie-a-day regimen could easily plan a sensuous breakfast and lunch from the remaining 467 calories.

As a final touch, this diet dinner requires reaching for your mate after licking the plate, for the average act of sexual intercourse burns up 200 calories, deducting same from your erotic meal so that it constitutes an infinitesimal 332 calorie total. And with all these foods so rich in taste and stimulants, you'll probably exceed that "national average," anyway.

COURSE TWENTY-TWO

The Pièce De Résistance:
A Compleat Aphrodisiac Dinner

Full nakedness! Cast-off your linen white
and closely clinging, limb to limb untie;
Off with those filmy veils: while they are on
Between us stand the walls of Babylon.
Join breast to breast, our lips together seal
And ne'er shall wagging tongues our joy reveal.
                    —Paulus Silentiarius

Nakedness is the ultimate spice for any aphrodisiac dinner (the roses of the skin are more delightful than the gold of any dress, as Apulcius put it), but there are several alternatives for those wanting to drape the body to better advantage. It might be best, for instance, to emulate a wily lover like Cleopatra, who wet her sheer clothing so that it clung to her curves, or have your body painted by an artist like Albery, whose skin canvasses (à la Utamuro) are the rage of Paris today. Or anyone a bit modest can buy a figleaf and turn over a new leaf. Fake figleafs (equipped with polyester loops that intertwine with rings of pubic hair) are available for $2. from the Adam and Eve Figleaf Company, 1505 John Fitch Blvd., South Windsor, Conn. 06074. Now there's customer service beyond the call of muse. Just be sure you're gentle when turning over the new leaf.

In any event, sexologists from Secaucus to Sweden have assured our undercover agents that the diner is definitely the best place setting for any mini-orgy, the ultimate aphrodisiac. It doesn't really matter much if the meal ends on a Murphy bed, a folding water bed, or some modern counterpart of the nineteenth century Celestial Magnetico-Electrical bed invented by England's fantastical Dr. Graham (which he claimed rendered its male users eternally potent and its female occupants prodigiously fertile). Such intimate furnishings do, however, make good conversation pieces over a last glass of champagne.

Louis XIV, for example, owned 413 beds with erotic pictures painted on the canopies "to encourage even the most frigid to thaw out a little." Madame Pompadour slept in a bed complete with built-in bath. And a French courtesan of the last century, finding herself bored with convention, actually had a model built with an elevated foot, which could be raised or lowered depending on her man-of-the-moment's height. She would place her feet in suspended stirrups, spread apart farther up, and thus be able to watch her standing lover perform to her heart's content. Those wanting to try something along these lines today can rent (for $60 a night) the Mistinguett Room at L'Hotel in Paris. Mistinguett, celebrated flapper and lover, once owned this fanciful room, in the middle of which, on a platform surrounded by a sea of plush red carpet, is an enormous white-fur-covered bed made of thousands of tiny mirrors. A bit cheaper are motels like The Experience in downtown Los Angeles. There decadence comes at popular prices—$25 for a typical room containing a fur-covered waterbed, mirrors on the walls and ceiling, TV cassettes featuring erotic movies, and "free flavored douches."

While sipping that last glass of champagne with silken pillows propped up behind the gluteus maximuses, mention might also be made of the odd ways beds have been used for love throughout history. In the seventeenth century, for instance, entire bridal parties slipped between the sheets with the newlyweds, and young brides often invited their girlfriends abed to test the powers of the bridegroom. The Greeks frequently went to bed together naked al fresco, under the sun or stars, and Louisiana's Cajun fishermen sometimes fished while making love in bed, tying a line to their big toes and casting it out the window—no one explaining what happened if they got a bite (from the fish) at the right or wrong moment. Then there was Voltaire who wrote love poems and essays on the back of his naked mistress, using her as a desk between mutual climaxes, and the English playwrights Beaumont and Fletcher, who not only shared the writing of their plays but the same clothes, the same mattress and the same women thereon. Or how about those Abyssinian couples who sleep together in the same nightgown, or the woman in Mississippi whose husband divorced her when she insisted on two double beds—one for him and one for her lover. Or those sexist Amazon women who commanded the male to lie passively on his back in bed while the female mounted his member and rode it to satisfaction.

The best time to make love in the bed of your choice is of little importance, but anyone fanatic enough to go to the trouble should know that the finest hour to plan an aphrodisiac meal would be between 4 a.m. and 12 noon. A little inconvenient for those who don't work at home, but according to research conducted by Dr. Adel Ismail at the Endocrinology Research Unit in Edinburgh, Scotland, men, at least, experience the highest levels of sexual hormones during this time span. Noting that evening is the worst time to make love (the male hormone level lowest at 8 p.m.), Dr. Ismail contends that "Man is a daylight animal, not a night-time one," which makes a good case for the aphrodisiac breakfast.

As for other furnishings, few will have the resources to decorate the dining room with $500,000 worth of flowers, à la Nero, or be able to buy a dool of doves to chase around the room naked, as was the custom of the Emperor Dionysus and his playmates. But everyone can afford to pick some flowers for the table. This last is stressed because a recent study by German botanist Dr. Kurt Jeremias of Stuttgart has concluded that flowers are definite sexual stimulants. "The perfume of some flowers such as roses, orchids, carnations and tulips," Dr. Jeremias says, "notably increases the sexual awareness between male and female."

There it is then—flowers, soft music, good raunchy conversation about love, food and drink. To conclude this feastiary of love foods, presented without further appetizers is the suggested menu from which to choose dinner. Most of these recipes have been described previously and those that haven't can be found in any complete cookbook. They constitute the most fabled erotic foods from every standpoint, but, needless to say, substitutions should be made freely if any are found objectionable, there being at least two thousand aphrodisiac dishes mentioned in these pages. The rest is all in your hands, or arms, or whatever. Just don't neglect the main course, the banquet of the body—which one Italian lover (his paramour would have put it differently) described as "breasts like ripe melons, the flanks of a plump partridge, thighs of succulent tenderness cradling a sweet-smelling fig for an appetizer..." Again—*bon appetit!* May

St. Foutin, the fornicator's friend, guide all our readers ever, young and old, man and woman, frail and fully rounded. And after both banquets are done, when gold light shines glistening upon those satin sheets with stirrups, may you wake as from a dream of old to glimpse a rose with blue ribbon soft between the bold broad blossoms of your alabaster spheres, or to find your bedraggled manhood bedizened with a fine blue silken tassel—a *cordon bleu* for the best cook in the kitchen and bedroom.

A Feastiary of Love Foods

Menu

Appetizers

Casanova's Oysters In The Raw · Sensuous Shashimi
Petites Croutes De Caviar · Angels On Horseback
Caviar & Oysters Orgasmic · Suggestive Steamers
Stuffed Artichokes Aphrodite

Salads

Tempting Truffles Urbani · Salade Francillon

Soups

Consommé Au Nids D'Hirondelles (Bird Nest Soup)
Yerchee (Shark's Fin Soup)
Madame Pompadour's Celery Soup

- continued -

~ Menu ~
Fish Courses

Lobster A La Tom Jones
Filet de Sole Pompadour
King Topetmaka's Lusty Shrimp

Meat Courses

Mountain Oysters   Steak Tartare
Steak Chateaubriand   Tournedos Rossini
            Filet Mignon

Vegetables

Truman Capote's Caviar & Baked Potatoes
      Asparagus A La Pompadour
Baked Onions Supreme   Soufflé Briochin
      Stuffed Tipped Tomatoes
Rada-Hara's Exotic Eggplant

Desserts

Crêpes Suzettes   Strawberries Liberté
Marzipan   Sherbet
      Fruits & Cheeze Continental

Wangenstein

331

COURSE TWENTY-THREE

Love Potion #9
And Other Chants And Charms:
Rx For Aching Hearts
And Lower Parts

"Does not Solomon say in Proverbs (XIII,15): *'Innocens credit omni verbo,* the innocent believeth every word,' and does not St. Paul (I Corinthians, 13) declare: *'Charitos omnic credit,* Charity believeth all.'?"
— Rabelais

Today's the season for gurus, astrologers, witches and warlocks, and before parting we'd be amiss in not offering here a spicy cauldron of love chants and charms to accompany dinner. None is guaranteed, or even recommended, but all our nostrums, like those previously cited, have been gleaned from sources and sorcerers prominent throughout history. Many such prescriptions are remarkably similar in countries thousands of miles apart and separated by hundreds of years in time. Several, such as Ovid's, are wise indeed, and some most readers will find disgusting in one way or another. The chants among these unexpurgated R_x for aching hearts and lower parts, to give one final tip, are best whispered at night or inscribed on fruit that is eaten or swallowed in a liquid—at least so the local witches and warlocks tell us.

Repeat these words, 'Kafe, Kasita non Kapla et publia file omnibus suis.' These words said, your loved one will obey you in all you desire.

—Ancient folklore

Rub your hands in sweet fern. The first one you shake hands with afterward is your true love. (But watch out who you shake hands with.)

—American folklore

A sparrow, baked and given to a woman in her drink, will make her dissolve and melt away for love.

—Cyranus, Ancient King of Persia,
Magick of Kirani

On any Tuesday, take out the bowels of the blue jay. . . . reduce to fine powder, make pellets or pills, and dry them. If one of these be given to a woman, she will be subject to a man, and vice-versa.

—*The Ananga Ranga*

Roast hummingbird hearts, grind them into a powder, sprinkle your beloved with powder and await amorous results.

—Creole Love Recipe

To win the love of a person, swallow raw a white dove's heart, point downward, and while swallowing it place your hand on the shoulder of the one in whom love is to be inspired.

—American folklore

Dry, steep and stew in sauce the kidneys of an eagle. Then mix them with drink or meat. The person that consumes them will be drawn into confidence and great love.

—Cyranus, *Magick of Kirani*

Swallow the heart of a wild duck and you may have whom you please for a husband.

—American folklore

The brain of a peacock, eaten with meat, fills a person with love.

—Cyranus, *Magick of Kirani*

Touch the loved one's hand with yours, and say the following words, 'Bestarberto corrumpit viscera epis mulieris,' and you will sexually arouse all your lovers.

—Ancient folklore

Take a human skull from the cemetery...on the eighth day of the moonlit fortnight of the seventh month (Sept,-Oct.), expose it to fire, and collect the soot...let this be painted over the inner surface of the eye lids...and the effect will be to fascinate everyone.

—*The Ananga Ranga*

Collect dust from the local chapel and blow it over a reluctant lover who doesn't satisfy you.

—Love Charm used by Breton women

As Orpheus points out in his treatise on precious stones, Liber de Lapidibus, and Pliny in the last book of his Natural History, emeralds exert a highly erective and bracing influence upon the natural member.

—Rabelais

A girl can win the love of any sweetheart she may desire by secretly throwing on his clothing some of the powder made by rubbing together a few heart leaves [limewort] which have been dried before the fire. She may, if she wishes, have a score of lovers by simply carrying the leaves in her bosum.

—American folklore

Place the eye of a wolf and the first joint of its tail in a golden vessel. Carry it with you always and you will be powerful, honorable, rich, acceptable and much loved and embraced by all women.

—Cyranus, *Magick of Kirani*

Peel an apple without making a break in the peel and then, after twining it three times around your head, throw the whole apple paring over your shoulder onto the floor. The paring will form the initial of your lover's name.

—American folklore

Take 16 linen threads: four white, four green, four blue, and four red. Twist them together to form one band and stain it with the blood of a large bird. Then, wrap a beetle in a small piece of linen and knot the colored band around it. Tie all that to the body of your loved one, and it will work magic quickly!

—Ancient folklore

Take three pubic hairs and three from the left armpit. Burn them on a hot shovel.

Pulverize and insert into a piece of bread. Dip bread in soup and feed to a lover.
—Albertus Magnus, medieval philosopher

A love potion made of a large number of red and white rose leaves and forget-me-nots, boiled in 385 drops of water for the sixteenth part of an hour, will, if properly made, insure the love of the opposite sex, if three drops of the mixture are put into something the person is to drink.
—American folklore

If you can walk around the block with your mouth full of water, you will be married that year.
—American folklore

For the magic supper all must be in the dark, no one must speak, and everything must be turned backward: including place settings, chairs at the table and the serving of the food. The women must then sit back to the table and wait for the stroke of midnight, when as soon as the town clock strikes twelve, they will see their future husbands walking toward them or suddenly standing beside them.
—Directions for the English seventeenth
century Dumb or Silent Supper

If you want to get married, stand on your head and chew a piece of gristle out of a beef neck and swallow it, and you will get anyone you want.
—American folklore

It is good luck if the bridegroom walks from his hut over a path made for him by men lying flat on their bellies; when he arrives at the bride's house, three prostrate women must form a living seat for him.
—Polynesian wedding custom

Put salt in the groom's pocket before proceeding to the church; pennies... put into the shoes of bride and bridegroom are equally effective.
—Medieval folklore

Open a bottle of white wine from which none yet has been drawn, and pour the first of the liquor which flows through the wedding ring. The bridgegroom's left sock will also do. —Ancient love charm

The new married couple should lay naked upon the ground; the bridegroom must kiss the great toe of the bride's left foot, and the bride the great toe of the bridegroom's right foot...
—Medieval love charm

These fish are taken with a dart, those with hooks; these the encircling nets draw up. And let no one method be adopted by you for all the years.
                                          —Ovid, *The Art Of Love*

I shall show you a love philtre without medicaments, without herbs, without a witche's incantations. It is this: If you want to be loved, love.

INDEX